Thanks for
your help!

Tom Price
GAO

SHAKEDOWN

SHAKEDOWN

HOW CORPORATIONS, GOVERNMENT, AND TRIAL LAWYERS ABUSE THE JUDICIAL PROCESS

Robert A. Levy

CATO
INSTITUTE
Washington, D.C.

Library of Congress Cataloging-in-Publication Data

Levy, Robert A., 1941–
Shakedown : how corporations, government, and trial lawyers
abuse the judicial process / Robert A. Levy.
p. cm.
Includes bibliographical references and index.
ISBN 1-930865-61-9 (alk. paper)
1. Torts—United States. 2. Antitrust law—United
States. 3. Frivolous suits (Civil procedure)—United
States. 4. Law reform—United States. 5. Microsoft
Corporation—Trials, litigation, etc. I. Title.

KF1250.L48 2004
343.73'0721—dc22

2004058469

Cover design by Parker Wallman.

Printed in the United States of America.

CATO INSTITUTE
1000 Massachusetts Ave., N.W.
Washington, D.C. 20001
www.cato.org

Contents

Foreword

Shakedown is a two-part tale of government-sponsored extortion using the courts. Part One—*Tort Law as Litigation Tyranny*—began when dozens of states sued the cigarette giants to recover Medicaid outlays for tobacco-related illnesses. Later, cities, counties, and states adopted similar legal strategies to go after gun and lead paint makers. Now those strategies are being refined to fleece fast food, beer, and liquor distributors.

Tort abuse, under government auspices, has three distinguishing characteristics: First, parallel litigation in multiple jurisdictions to ratchet up the cost of a legal defense, thus forcing a settlement. Second, employment of private lawyers who receive a contingency fee based on the quantum of punishment they can mete out on behalf of their government clients. Third, misuse of the judiciary as quasi lawmakers, thereby circumventing legislatures that have been unwilling to enact a tort regime more congenial to plaintiffs.

Interestingly, Part Two of the *Shakedown* model—*Antitrust Law as Corporate Welfare for Market Losers*—does not share those three characteristics. For example, the government's antitrust case against Microsoft was consolidated before a single federal court in Washington, D.C. Some private lawyers were hired by the Justice Department, but they were paid on an hourly rather than contingency basis. And the underlying legal framework was the Sherman Antitrust Act, not judge-made law.

The distinguishing mark of antitrust abuse was quite different. High-tech companies, foiled by the marketplace in their crusade against Microsoft, enlisted government help to tilt the playing field. In effect, Microsoft's rivals used antitrust as a crutch, substituting cronyism in the political arena for the rigors of competition.

The dual goals of this book are to unmask the exploitation of our tort and antitrust systems, and to suggest how those systems can be fixed. Part One begins its examination of the tort system with an introductory chapter summarizing the themes, arguments, and recommendations that are detailed in later chapters. Chapter 2 dissects the states' Medicaid recoupment suits against the tobacco industry. Chapter 3 criticizes state and local lawsuits against gun makers. Chapter 4 is an update on the cigarette wars—including the incredible saga of the 1998 master tobacco settlement and pending litigation by the Justice Department—followed by a commentary on similar litigation against lead paint makers, fatty food companies, and distributors of alcoholic beverages. Chapter 5 sets out a program for federal and state governments to overhaul tort law without trampling on traditional tenets of federalism.

Part Two, focusing on the Microsoft antitrust case, begins like Part One with an introductory chapter summarizing the chapters that follow. Chapter 7 analyzes the battle of the browser, in which the Justice Department and 20 states accused Microsoft of illegally tying its browser to its Windows operating system. Chapter 8 expands on that case to draw broader conclusions about antitrust, especially as applied to high-tech industries. Chapter 9, originally published after the Justice Department had prevailed at the trial court level, scrutinizes the judge's opinion and assesses Microsoft's chances on appeal. Chapter 10 discusses the appellate decision, the resultant settlement, and further abuses of the antitrust system by state attorneys general and the European Union. Then Chapter 10 reinforces the conclusion reached in the three preceding chapters that our antitrust laws should be repealed.

Much of the material in this book has been published, with slight modification, in the form of monographs, magazine articles, and newspaper op-eds.* I have made no effort to excise the predictions, speculations, and conjectures that, with hindsight, have not materialized. In other words, each chapter stands as originally written—including lapses, oversights, and inaccurate forecasts. Still, I reaffirm the principles presented and the logic on which they are grounded. Even though some events have unfolded differently than I anticipated—notably in the dynamic, high-tech world of software development—the concepts are still relevant and the recommendations are no less compelling.

*Note to readers: The dates of previous publication are indicated in footnotes at the beginning of each chapter or section. Occasionally, the body of the text contains time references such as "last September" or "this year." Those references must, of course, be interpreted relative to the original publication date.

Of course, I am fully responsible for any errors, omissions, and misstatements. No doubt those problems and others would have been more widespread had it not been for the invaluable assistance of my colleagues at the Cato Institute. To four of them, in particular, I express my special gratitude: Roger Pilon, Gene Healy, and David Boaz for their review and comments on draft manuscripts, and David Lampo for shepherding the book through the publication process.

Finally, thanks and much more to Diane, my wife of 28 years, who patiently tolerated my peculiar hours, which might otherwise have been devoted to family enjoyments.

PART ONE

TORT LAW AS LITIGATION TYRANNY

1. Introduction to Part One: Tort Law as Litigation Tyranny

First It Was the Tobacco Industry

Beginning a decade ago, dozens of states faced with ballooning Medicaid costs decided that litigation against cigarette makers would be a relatively painless path to fiscal fitness. Couching their legal claims in the lofty cant of public health, the states sought to recover tax-funded Medicaid expenditures for tobacco-related injuries. The legislatures could have raised taxes on cigarettes, of course. That option would have been simpler, less expensive, and quicker; and the parties who would have paid the tax—smokers and tobacco companies—would have been the same parties that would ultimately pick up any bill for court-awarded damages. Why then were lawsuits substituted for taxation?

Here's the principled answer—although not the real answer, as we shall see: While it may have been more efficient to legislate rather than litigate, when particular parties are subject to sanctions for wrongdoing, the courtroom and not the legislature is where they have an opportunity to defend themselves. The court is the proper forum for evidence, fact finding, and verdict following a trial before a jury of peers. As a just society, we cannot allow our lawmakers to embark upon a punitive crusade against a disfavored industry without guaranteeing due process of law.

Unhappily, in the real world, the reason that the states opted for Medicaid recovery suits instead of tax hikes had everything to do with politics and nothing to do with due process. Both tax increases and tobacco companies were immensely unpopular; so the states took the politically safe course by avoiding higher taxes and attacking the industry. To effect that scheme, state attorneys general and their hired-gun trial lawyers came up with a quasi tax, camouflaged as damages, based on rules of tort law that were custom-designed for extortion. It was far easier to sue a few unloved cigarette companies than to attach yet another users' fee to a product already bloated with government exactions.

That was the beginning of government's tort law shakedown, chronicled in Chapter 2. Essentially, tobacco was under siege. No fewer than 35 states plus several cities and counties sued the industry to recoup their smoking-related Medicaid outlays. Florida led the effort. A new state law stripped tobacco companies of their traditional rights and put in their place a shockingly simple rule of law: The states needed money; the industry had money; so the industry gave and the states took.

That effort commenced after 40 years of failed litigation by private individuals. During that time, not one smoker received a dollar of damages from tobacco companies, as juries repeatedly concluded that smokers are responsible for their own behavior and their own losses. Yet under the revamped tort regime, if a smoker happened to be a Medicaid recipient, individual responsibility was out the window. The same tobacco company selling the same product to the same person resulting in the same injury was liable, magically, not to the smoker but to the state. Liability hinged on a smoker's Medicaid status, a fortuity totally unrelated to any misdeeds by the industry.

The state was not even required to show that a particular party was harmed by his use of tobacco. Instead, causation could be proven by epidemiological statistics alone. Plaintiff states—filling the dual and conflicting roles of lawmaker and litigant—needed only to show that some diseases were more prevalent among smokers than non-smokers. The outcome: lawsuits created out of whole cloth—retroactively eradicating settled legal doctrine, and denying due process to a single industry selected more for its deep pockets and public image than for its legal culpability.

Then Came the Gun Makers

The implications for other industries were clear. Once the rule of law was perverted, politically incorrect businesses could count on becoming victims. Never mind that the mark of a free society is how it treats its least popular members. That didn't immunize gun makers from the next phase of litigation tyranny—the subject of Chapter 3.

Led by New Orleans and Chicago, dozens of municipalities, counties, and states filed suit against gun manufacturers for damages incurred due to the misuse of guns by criminals. Some of the suits alleged "negligent marketing"—charging that gun manufacturers flood the suburbs with more guns than legitimate customers will buy, knowing that dealers will sell the excess supply illegally to criminals in the inner city. Other suits asserted that guns are defective and unreasonably dangerous products because manufacturers design firearms without safety features that are purportedly easy and economical to install. At bottom, both legal theories rest on the unsupportable proposition that gun makers are responsible for the misconduct of their customers.

Courts are the final bulwark in safeguarding our constitutional right to keep and bear arms. Yet the courts of late have been the scene of unprecedented attacks on that right as gun control advocates have used the judiciary to make an end-run around the legislative process. Meritless litigation brought by government plaintiffs in multiple jurisdictions is just part of a plan to force gun makers to adopt policies that legislatures have wisely rejected. Moreover, the suits are used by politicians to reward their allies—private attorneys, many of whom are major campaign contributors—with lucrative contingency fee contracts.

Meanwhile, gun controls have not worked and more controls will not help. In fact, many of the recommended regulations will make matters worse by stripping law-abiding citizens of their most effective means of self-defense. Violence in America isn't due to the availability of guns, but to social pathologies—illegitimacy, dysfunctional schools, and drug and alcohol abuse. Historically, more gun laws have gone hand-in-hand with an explosion of violent crime. Only during the past decade—with vigorous law enforcement and an older population—have we seen dramatic reductions in violence, coupled with a record number of guns in circulation.

Before we compromise constitutional rights expressly recognized in the Second Amendment, we ought to be sure of three things: First, that we've identified the real problem; second, that we've pinpointed its cause; and third, that our remedy is no more extensive than necessary to fix the problem. The spreading litigation against gun makers fails all three tests. Guns do not increase violence; they

reduce violence. Holding firearms manufacturers liable will not eliminate the underlying pathologies. And a less invasive remedy already
exists: enforce existing laws.

Redress through the tort system is not the answer. Whether the
claim is a defective product or negligent marketing, government
lawsuits against gun manufacturers are baseless. The gun industry
is not responsible for the criminal misconduct of its customers. Litigation challenging the design, manufacture, and distribution of a
lawful product is no better than a theory in search of a case.

More "Deep Pockets"

Thus far, gun makers have not yielded ripe pickings for trial
attorneys and their government clients. Many of the municipal firearms suits have been dismissed; not one has produced a final judgment in the government's favor. But those legal setbacks were more
than offset by the treasure trove that the 1998 tobacco settlement
generated. Faced with a tort system that effectively foreclosed any
defense against liability, the cigarette giants decided to negotiate
rather than litigate. That decision led to the Master Settlement Agreement, or MSA, which transformed a competitive industry into a
cartel, while foisting onto smokers the $250 billion cost.

Dozens of state attorneys general collaborated to parley a sweetheart deal for the major tobacco companies in violation of the antitrust laws and the Constitution. Along the way, billions of dollars
in legal fees flowed to the private lawyers who engineered the deal.
Predictably, part of that booty has started its round-trip back into
the political process to influence state legislators, judges, governors,
perhaps some federal officials. The result has been, and will continue
to be, an avalanche of tobacco-like litigation against other friendless industries.

But first, just 10 months after the cigarette majors and the states
settled their differences for a skimpy quarter of a trillion dollars,
the U.S. Department of Justice decided that it wanted a share of the
plunder. The department's complaint alleged that cigarette companies conspired since the 1950s to defraud the American public and
conceal information about the effects of smoking. Specifically, the
federal government contended that industry executives knowingly
made false and misleading statements about whether smoking
causes disease and whether nicotine is addictive.

Chapter 4 updates the tobacco saga, beginning with an analysis of the MSA, then a critique of the Justice Department's ongoing suit. After that, the focus shifts to three other industries that have experienced, or could soon experience, a similar assault from trial lawyers and their political allies. The new targets are lead paint, fatty foods, and alcoholic beverages.

The lessons of Chapter 4 are clear: The rule of law must not yield to ambitious government officials and politically connected lawyers stalking outcast industries. Nor may states be permitted to adopt a legal regimen that retroactively punishes a particular class of defendants for conduct that was permissible when it occurred.

How Can the System Be Fixed?

Not surprisingly, as abuses of the tort system spread and costs exploded, the demand for quick fixes escalated. Congress and the Bush administration responded with a deluge of reform proposals. But those proposals encroached upon traditional state powers and could not be harmonized with the principles of federalism. Chapter 5 examines federal tort reform from a constitutional perspective, and recommends reforms that are compatible with dual sovereignty and a limited federal government.

Critics of federal tort reform have usually come from the political left and plaintiffs' lawyers, who favor a state-based system that can be exploited to redistribute income from deep-pocketed corporations to "deserving" individuals. Chapter 5, co-authored with George Mason University law professor Michael I. Krauss, offers a totally different criticism—constitutional in origin—that embraces the need for reform but reaffirms this principle: The existence of a problem, however serious, does not justify federal remedies outside the scope of Congress's enumerated powers.

We begin with the Commerce Clause but find that interstate trade does not, by itself, justify federalizing tort law. On the basis of examples involving fast food, guns, and medical malpractice, we argue that substantive federal reforms are neither necessary nor proper. If states persist in imposing unjust rules on out-of-state defendants, federal procedural remedies are available.

Next, we consider the Due Process Clause of the Fourteenth Amendment and dissect the Supreme Court's recent *State Farm* decision covering punitive damages. We also discuss the controversies over judicial activism and substantive due process. Despite the limitations of substantive due process, we conclude that the Court was correct to rein in punitive awards.

Most important, we recommend reforms that are compatible with the tenets of federalism. Some reforms can be implemented at the state level—including solutions to excessive punitive awards, curbs on joint and several liability, payment of attorneys' fees when government is the losing party in a civil lawsuit, prohibition of contingency fee contracts between government and private lawyers, and restraints on litigation by government to recover expenditures made on behalf of private parties.

At the federal level, we endorse two procedural reforms. The first involves state "long-arm jurisdiction," which determines whether an out-of-state entity can be sued in a local court. A sensible application of the Due Process Clause would exempt businesses from local court jurisdiction unless they have sufficient dealings within the state. Currently, out-of-state businesses find it exceedingly difficult to avoid oppressive state tort laws. A second federal reform concerns "choice-of-law" rules, which determine what state's laws control a multi-state suit. Frequently, tort defendants will be disadvantaged when plaintiffs select jurisdictions that have plaintiff-friendly choice-of-law rules. By establishing a federal rule—a procedural solution that leaves underlying state substantive law in place—the federal government can prevent states from exporting discriminatory tort regimes.

Taken together, state substantive reforms and federal procedural reforms can curtail abuses while respecting time-honored notions of dual-sovereignty federalism.

2. Tobacco Medicaid Litigation: Snuffing Out the Rule of Law*

Introduction

Hardly a day goes by that the newspapers, magazines, radio stations, and television networks don't bring us the latest battlefield update in the tobacco wars. If it's not the estate of a three-pack-a-day smoker contending that cigarettes are a defective product, it's a class action suit by airline flight attendants claiming injury from secondhand smoke, a nationwide settlement exchanging legal immunity for big bucks and more regulation, a proposal by an administrative agency to restrict cigarette advertising, or a court ruling on the question of whether tobacco is a drug. With tobacco so much in the news, it's easy to conclude that the underlying issues are industry-specific. That would be a big mistake. We are dealing here with moral, political, and legal questions that transcend any single industry. What's at stake is nothing less than our principle of individual responsibility, our choice between legislation and adjudication, and our constitutional right to due process—in short, the rule of law. To illustrate, consider this short hypothetical, which today is all too close to real, as we shall see.

Imagine that Joe, an avid and experienced skier on vacation in the Colorado Rockies, steps into his skis, heads down the mountain, loses control, and suffers a badly broken leg that requires extensive medical care. Back home in Florida, Joe incurs $3,500 in doctor and hospital bills. Five years later he sues the manufacturer of the skis, alleging that they were defectively designed. More precisely, because he no longer owns the skis and cannot identify the particular manufacturer, Joe sues all the manufacturers that sell skis in Florida. Never mind that he doesn't recall whether the skis were purchased in Florida; never mind that the accident occurred in Colorado. Because

*Originally published, with minor revisions, as Cato Institute Policy Analysis no. 275, June 20, 1997.

9

his medical bills were paid in Florida, Joe insists that all ski manufacturers must be held liable in proportion to their revenues in that state. And when asked how he knows that the skis were defective, Joe points to statistics showing that there is a significantly higher probability of breaking a leg if you ski than if you don't. Indeed, observes Joe, using skis exactly as they are designed to be used often leads to injury. Joe is not persuaded by data indicating that a large majority of skiers never break their legs.

Predictably, the judge dismisses Joe's claim, then sanctions his attorney for bringing a frivolous lawsuit. Not only was Joe's litigation time-barred—five years after the event—but he also failed to produce any evidence that would link his injury to the skis that he used. Moreover, even if Joe had filed on time, proven causation, and identified the ski manufacturer, he would undoubtedly have lost the case because he knowingly and voluntarily assumed the risk of injury. He was aware that skiing was risky, yet he elected of his own free will to assume that risk.

Suppose instead that Joe has an insurance policy that covers his $3,500 medical expense. Like virtually all such policies, Joe's contains a "subrogation" clause, which allows the insurance company (the subrogee) to substitute itself for Joe and sue any party that Joe could have sued. That way, if Joe has a lawful claim against someone who injures him, the wrongdoer ultimately pays and the insurance company is reimbursed. In return for agreeing to the subrogation clause, Joe gets the benefit of a much lower premium. So in this instance, it would not be Joe but his insurer that could sue the ski manufacturers. The rules of subrogation are crystal clear, however. The insurer bears the same burden of proof that Joe would have borne, and is subject to the same defenses that the ski manufacturers could have asserted against Joe. Recognizing the frivolous nature of Joe's claim, no insurance company would file a lawsuit.

Before switching our focus to tobacco, let's change the facts of Joe's accident ever so slightly. Assume if you will that Joe qualifies for Medicaid reimbursement, that the state of Florida pays the $3,500 bill, and that the state—not Joe and not his insurance company—then attempts to recover its loss by suing the ski manufacturers. What result? "Same result," you say. After all, Medicaid is just an insurer by another name. Part of Joe's Medicaid "contract" requires that he assign any lawful claims to the state—exactly like subrogation. The rules of subrogation allow Florida, as Joe's insurer, to step into his shoes and litigate on his behalf if it thinks that someone else is liable for his injury. Joe would have lost; his private insurer would have been too embarrassed even to file suit. Thus, Florida loses. Right?

Wrong. Hard as it may be to believe, the Florida Medicaid Third-Party Liability Act,[1] a 1978 statute amended in 1990 and 1994, establishes a simple new rule: The state needs money; the manufacturers have money; so the manufacturers shall give and the state shall take. That overstates the matter only slightly. Joe would get nowhere if he sued the ski manufacturers directly; yet if he happens to be a Medicaid recipient, then the same defendants selling the same product to the same person resulting in the same injury are, magically, liable to the state. By legislative fiat, liability hinges on the injured party's Medicaid eligibility—a quirk that bears absolutely no rational relationship to the defendants' alleged wrongdoing.

Under the Act, Florida is not limited to stepping into the shoes of the injured party. The statute gives the state a totally new, direct cause of action on the theory that the injury to Joe has independently harmed the state. Florida need not be concerned about waiting too long to sue; the statute abolishes all time limits.[2] Moreover, Florida can collect from the manufacturers even when losses are caused by the injured party's own fault; the statute abrogates all of the manufacturers' affirmative defenses, including assumption of risk. The state does not even have to show a link between the harm to any particular party and his use of the manufacturers' product; the statute says that generalized causation may be proven by statistical analysis and Florida can seek reimbursement from all manufacturers that sell the product within the state—even if a Florida retiree purchased and used the product elsewhere.

But it gets worse. One would think that in preparing their defense the manufacturers would be allowed to discover—by deposition, interrogatories, physical examination, and other methods of gathering evidence—whether the claimed injuries were real or fraudulent, serious or trivial, or whether the patient ever used the manufacturers' product. Wrong again. Incredibly, the Act provides that Florida is not required to identify the individual recipients of Medicaid payments; instead, the state can seek recovery for all such recipients, anonymously, as a group. That section of the statute was too much for the Florida Supreme Court. In striking it, the Court remarked,

11

"It is illogical and unreasonable to call this a fair process. . . . [I]t is violative of the due process provisions of our constitution."[3]

The application of the Florida Act to Joe's injury may seem bizarre, but the astonishing fact is, that is the law. At present, ski manufacturers selling in Florida can rest easy, not because the Act doesn't apply to them—it does—but only because Governor Lawton Chiles has shown little interest in enforcing it against them. Instead, he has focused on two industries he holds in special contempt. In fact, in March 1995 he issued an executive order directing state officials to pursue only those industries "responsible for disease and death caused by tobacco products and those responsible for disease and death caused by the sale and consumption of illegal drugs."[4] In reality, however, unless we can envision a court compelling the Medellin cartel to reimburse Florida for crack-related Medicaid costs, the tobacco companies are the real targets. Yet in principle and in fact, Florida's other industries could be on the hook in time: the governor could add to the list; a future governor may have bigger ideas; and a court has already slapped down the executive order by holding not that the Act is overbroad but that the governor had no authority to limit its application to tobacco companies.[5]

Thus, as a matter of prosecutorial discretion, only tobacco is presently under siege in Florida. Across the nation, the theory of the Florida approach is very much alive. In fact, as of early June 1997, 35 state attorneys general had filed Medicaid recovery suits against the industry.[6] Similar litigation has been filed by New York City, San Francisco, and Los Angeles, and by private citizens in Alabama and Ohio. Only Florida has codified its legal theory by enacting legislation that strips tobacco companies of their traditional rights; the others, for the moment, are proceeding under alleged common law and equitable principles that in most respects replicate the Florida statute.

Five states—Alabama, Ohio, Georgia, Nevada, and Colorado—have expressed varying degrees of skepticism about the current brand of Medicaid suits.[7] Presumably, the major tobacco-growing states will also decline to participate. Yet even if no further states come forward, the potential liability could threaten the survival of some or all of the nation's tobacco companies—a remedy arguably more painful and protracted, and surely less certain and effective, than simply declaring the product illegal. But it is not the durability of an industry that matters most. Far more weighty is the sustenance of a legal system that maximizes freedom while demanding account-ability—no small assignment when ambitious politicians stalk an unpopular industry and when anti-smoking zealots join forces with elected state judges and plaintiffs' lawyers driven by huge contin-gency fees.

The analysis that follows covers several of the more important aspects of the Medicaid reimbursement suits, using the Florida Med-icaid Third-Party Liability Act as the primary, though not exclusive, point of reference. After a brief historical review, the study examines the principal legal mutations arising under the Florida statute: abro-gation of affirmative defenses, statistical proof of causation, and market share liability. Recoverable damages are next considered, contrasting the health care costs for which the states seek indemnity with the various tax benefits and cost savings that accrue to the state from the sale of tobacco products. Finally, the analysis focuses on contingency fees, then compares public versus private law approaches to the issue of liability.

It is important to establish at the outset that this study is *not* a defense of the tobacco industry. It is a defense of the rule of law. Litigation for Medicaid reimbursement hinges on a freshly minted cause of action, created out of whole cloth by states filling the dual and conflicting roles of lawmaker and plaintiff. The result is the retroactive abrogation of settled principles of law, thereby denying due process to a single industry selected more for its wealth and deplorable image than for its legal culpability. It should be noted, however, that the industry is also being sued under conventional doctrines like common law fraud and misrepresentation, antitrust, unjust enrichment, and public nuisance. Such suits are inventive and probably meritless, but at least they do not rely upon gutting the industry's ability to defend itself. If the plaintiffs can prove any of their claims—the March 1997 Liggett settlement suggests that fraud and misrepresentation are the most likely bets[8]—then the industry will rightly be held accountable for its transgressions, but only after a trial in which commonly accepted rules are evenhand-edly applied—the same rules that would apply to any other defen-dant and any other plaintiff.

Historical Background

In over 40 years of litigation by smokers and their families, there has not been one final adjudication of damages against a tobacco company.[9] Only after disclosure of embarrassing documents suggesting that the industry knew long ago that its products were addictive did a Florida jury in August 1996 award $750,000 to a victim of lung cancer[10]; but even that single victory may not hold up on appeal. In May 1997 the same attorney, fresh from his triumph nine months earlier, represented another lung cancer victim before a different Florida jury. Despite the highly publicized admissions arising from Liggett's March settlement, the jury refused to award either compensatory or punitive damages.[11]

Industry defendants invariably prevail, first, by disputing that tobacco was shown to be the cause of a particular person's ailment and, second, by demonstrating that the plaintiffs knowingly and voluntarily assumed the risk of smoking, in which case they are responsible for the consequences of their own behavior. Further, when Congress enacted the Federal Cigarette Labeling and Advertising Act of 1965,[12] as amended in 1969,[13] the tobacco companies were able to argue that the Act preempted some common law claims because of the obligatory warning labels on cigarette packs—a position that the Supreme Court finally affirmed in the *Cipollone* case.[14] After *Cipollone*, plaintiffs could no longer contend in state court that cigarette advertising or promotion failed to warn that smoking carries serious health risks.[15] Allegations of fraud, breach of express warranty, and design defect were still viable, but they had never convinced a jury.

That was the impetus for some legal sleight-of-hand—crafty litigation by state attorneys general, beginning in 1994, grounded in a new cause of action independent of the rights of any aggrieved cigarette smoker. By amending its Medicaid Third-Party Liability Act in 1990 and 1994, Florida not only codified the new claim but also corrupted the rules of engagement in a manner that would guarantee victory if the state had to litigate. When the legislature voted to repeal the new provisions a year later, Governor Chiles vetoed the repeal.[16]

While the Florida statute still requires that the state prove either negligence or a defective product, causation, and damages, in six essential respects the amendments tilt the playing field hopelessly against the industry. Indeed, the express language of the statute leaves little room for doubt.

14

- First, "assumption of risk and all other affirmative defenses normally available to a liable third party are to be abrogated to the extent necessary to ensure full recovery by Medicaid from third-party resources."
- Second, "causation and damages . . . may be proven by use of statistical analysis" without showing any link between a particular smoker's illness and his use of tobacco products.
- Third, the state "shall not be required to . . . identify the individual recipients for which payment has been made, but rather can proceed to seek recovery based upon payments made on behalf of an entire class of recipients."
- Fourth, in assigning liability to the individual tobacco companies, the state "shall be allowed to proceed under a market share theory, provided that the products involved are substantially interchangeable among brands."
- Fifth, "the defense of repose [i.e., statute of limitations] shall not apply to any action brought under [the Act]."
- Sixth, if the state recovers damages, it is authorized to pay "reasonable litigation costs or expenses" to an outside private attorney, plus a contingency fee not to exceed "30% of the amount actually collected."

According to Florida, those provisions merely effectuate the intent of the liability scheme under the federal Medicaid statute,[17] which directs Medicaid-eligible individuals to assign to the state all rights to payment for medical care from third parties. The state can then sue the third party and any amount thus collected reimburses the state to the extent of its Medicaid expenditures on behalf of the covered individual. A portion of the reimbursed expenditures goes to the federal government, depending upon the federal percentage participation in the state plan; and any remainder goes to the patient.

Until the new dispensation, however, the state could assert only those theories of recovery that the patient could assert. The same rules of evidence, the same standards of responsibility, and the same burden of proof applied to the state, suing under subrogation, as to the patient suing on his own behalf. If a tobacco company would not have been liable in a direct suit by a cancer victim, then it would not have been liable in a similar suit by the state of Florida standing in the victim's shoes. Those fundamental principles of law have now been cavalierly dismissed by states intent upon picking the deep pockets of the tobacco industry. The potential for abuse is manifest as self-interested legislators determine the legal regime under which a few friendless, nonvoting corporations will be fleeced.

At a minimum, one would have expected that the courts would strictly scrutinize that type of opportunistic legislation.[18] It was not to be. In a suit challenging the constitutionality of the Medicaid Third-Party Liability Act, the Florida Supreme Court voting four-to-three in June 1996 upheld the bulk of the Act, calling it "a rational response to a public need"[19]—reasoning so broad as to justify almost anything. The majority noted that legislators frequently alter common law rights, and judicial review is typically deferential. Only the dissent seemed aware of the quantum difference between altering the common law and eviscerating a company's ability to dispute the charges brought against it. And only the dissent comprehended the affront to due process when a state fattens its own coffers by applying special rules—rules that operate solely when the state is the plaintiff and, in the naked words of the statute itself, "to the extent necessary to ensure full recovery."

To its modest credit, the Florida Supreme Court refused to fore-close the possibility of later challenges to specific applications of the Act. The Court held that the statute was not invalid on its face, but reserved judgment on the question whether the statute could be enforced against an actual defendant in an actual case without violating the Constitution. Furthermore, the Court did strike or modify three provisions of the Act "to avoid offending the due process guarantees of the Florida Constitution." First, the Court modified the state's abolition of the statute of limitations so as to reduce its retroactive impact; Florida will not be permitted to resurrect a claim that was already time-barred when the Medicaid Third-Party Liability Act was enacted. Second, the Court rejected Florida's bid to use *both* market share liability (whereby damages are apportioned by tobacco sales in the state) *and* joint and several liability (whereby the state can pursue any defendant for the entire damage award), finding that the two theories of recovery are "fundamentally incompatible." Still, in any given case Florida will be able to use either theory, although not the two in combination. Third, and most important, the Court threw out the utterly fantastic section of the Act that authorized the state to sue without identifying a single Medicaid

16

patient. That such a shameless provision was ever drafted, much less passed, speaks volumes about the state's aims and its legislators' regard for the rule of law.

On March 17 the U.S. Supreme Court declined to review the Florida Supreme Court's decision.[20] To many observers, the High Court's reluctance to take the case was not surprising. Florida is the only one among the 35 states seeking recovery of Medicaid outlays that is suing under a statute that has endured judicial scrutiny. Until there is a split among the various jurisdictions, or an especially egregious application of the statute in a particular case, it is unlikely that the U.S. Supreme Court will intercede. Because the tobacco companies were unsuccessful in their attempt to have the Act invalidated, Florida's suit against the industry for Medicaid reimbursement can now move forward. Trial is scheduled to begin this August; lawyers expect the battle to last several months.[21]

The dubious honor of being the first of the reimbursement actions to go before a jury will probably belong to Mississippi. Its Medicaid recovery trial is due to begin in July, having withstood a state Supreme Court challenge by Gov. Kirk Fordice, who argued unsuccessfully that the attorney general was not authorized to file suit without the governor's approval.[22] And in Texas, where $16 billion in damages is at stake, lawyers are poring through 600 boxes of documents in preparation for a trial expected to begin in late September,[23] despite polls showing that Texans disapprove of the suit by more than a two-to-one ratio.[24]

The irony—or outrage, depending upon your perspective—is that these trials were instigated by states to recover costs that they themselves incurred by voluntarily participating in the federal Medicaid program—costs allegedly attributable to a product that the states have refused to declare illegal. As Professor Richard Epstein put it: "The government can decide that it's not going to provide . . . this kind of insurance. . . . It might even . . . decide that it's going to ban tobacco. . . . But the one alternative that is absolutely unacceptable is . . . retroactively [to] impose a system of liability which nobody dreamed of."[25] Yet that is precisely what Florida, Mississippi, Texas, 35 states in all, and assorted other governmental units have done; they have retroactively imposed a system of liability that nobody dreamed of. Here's how they did it.

Abrogation of Affirmative Defenses

In tort law, an affirmative defense is one that answers the plaintiff's allegations by stating, in effect, that even if the allegations are true, the defendant should prevail because the plaintiff has no *legal* claim.[26] To take an obvious example from the area of criminal law, if a prosecutor contends that A murdered B, B might answer by asserting self-defense. Affirmative defenses include such claims as duress, statute of limitations, contributory negligence, and, most important to tobacco litigation, assumption of risk. In a nutshell, the assumption-of-risk doctrine, which until now has immunized the industry from liability, says: "If the user or consumer . . . is aware of the danger, and nevertheless proceeds unreasonably to make use of the product and is injured by it, he is barred from recovery."[27] Thus, under a traditional tort regime if a consumer knows about the risks of smoking, yet still smokes and thereby contracts a tobacco-related illness, he has no more claim against the tobacco manufacturer than would a nonsmoker who suffers the same illness from another source. Florida may thereafter provide no assistance, some assistance, or complete assistance to the victim, but the amount of assistance has no effect on the responsibility of the tobacco manufacturer to the individual or to the state.[28]

That centuries-old rule of morality and law was revoked by the Florida Medicaid Third-Party Liability Act. Procedurally, the Act lets the state circumvent the rules of subrogation and sue the industry directly. Substantively, because the Act gives a direct claim to the state, which therefore no longer stands in the shoes of a Medicaid patient, the assumption-of-risk defense ordinarily available against the patient no longer makes sense. In justifying those changes, however, Florida officials attempted to square them with the traditional law by claiming that tobacco companies fraudulently misrepresented the risks of smoking, targeted underage customers with their ads, and concealed the addictive nature of cigarettes. Consequently, the story goes, smokers could not have made an informed judgment about the dangers inherent in smoking, so the assumption-of-risk defense is not applicable. In short, smokers cannot assume a risk they know nothing about. Let's examine whether Florida's claims support that logic.

Fraudulent Misrepresentation

If fraudulent misrepresentation deprived consumers of the opportunity to make an informed judgment, one might expect that benefits under the Act would extend to the parties supposedly deceived. Instead, the Act applies not to consumers but only to the state in its role as plaintiff. Moreover, fraudulent misrepresentation, assuming it were proven, trumps any defense based upon assumption of risk. Accordingly, a plaintiff who could demonstrate fraud would not have assumed the risk of smoking. Abrogation of the defense would thus be entirely unnecessary.

Of equal importance, by filing its Medicaid recovery suit under the new Act, Florida explicitly rejected subrogation as well as any right to the claims of individual Medicaid recipients. Consequently, a declaration by the state that tobacco companies defrauded smokers is irrelevant. Instead, because Florida is a direct claimant rather than a subrogee, the state now has to demonstrate that its officials, or its taxpayers, or perhaps the public at large—not just smokers—relied on the industry's misrepresentations as a material inducement, not to smoke, but *to participate in the federal Medicaid program.*

Not only has there been no such demonstration, but none is likely to materialize. In the first instance, the state has portrayed itself as an inanimate entity, incapable of such sentient behavior as assumption of risk[29] or reliance. Second, any suggestion that Florida would have excluded coverage for smoking-related illnesses under Medicaid were it not for the industry's deception is wholly incompatible with public pronouncements to the contrary. Consider this statement by Richard Scruggs, a private attorney hired to represent the state: "[S]tates and governments must treat their indigent sick. They have no choice but to do that . . . regardless of whether they smoke, drink, or lead other risky lifestyles."[30]

Indeed, Florida distinguishes itself from a private insurance company by characterizing its Medicaid obligation as "imposed by law or statute" and funded by payroll taxes—unlike private insurers who receive premiums designed to produce a profit in return for which they voluntarily subject themselves to anticipated risks. For that reason, the state insists that it is entitled to the equitable remedy provided under the Act—a direct cause of action instead of subrogation—sheltered from the assumption-of-risk defense and its corollary requirement that the state demonstrate fraud.[31] Yes, Florida agrees that subrogation may be appropriate for a private insurer, because the insurer has already received consideration for bearing the risk; but the state itself, unimpeded by legal niceties, should be

19

allowed to pursue indemnification without subrogation in light of its obligation to pay damages caused by the acts of another.[32]

That is nothing but sophistry, of course. First, the state has no legal obligation to participate in the federal Medicaid program; the Florida legislature elects to do so, voluntarily. Second, the distinction between profit and non-profit, between premium-funded and tax-funded, is completely extraneous to the assumption-of-risk issue. Medicaid is an insurer, whether or not it makes money. Both taxpayers and policyholders provide funding so that their "chosen" insurer can cover anticipated health costs. Both state and private insurers sometimes pay for treatment that arguably would not have been necessary but for the misconduct of a third party. Yet in determining whether such misconduct has occurred, why should the state alone be allowed to bypass the usual subrogation process and hold an outsider liable even when a victim assumes the risk of his own injury? Why should Florida's Medicaid system, but not a private insurance company, be able to impose its costs upon a tobacco company that would have been exculpated but for the happenstance that a particular smoker qualified for public assistance?

Advertising

From those unanswered questions, we turn next to advertising and inquire whether smokers—especially underage smokers—were so misled that they could not have assumed the risk of smoking. Beginning as early as 1920 numerous epidemiological and experimental studies on the health hazards of smoking were reported by the media, and by 1962 more than 7,000 publications were examining the connection between smoking and health.[33] A 1954 Gallup poll indicated that 90% of Americans had heard or read that cigarettes can cause cancer.[34] Over the past 30 years, a conspicuous health warning has appeared on every package of cigarettes lawfully sold in the United States. Even children—allegedly brainwashed by crafty ads—were aware of the risks. As early as 1960, a nationwide poll by Senior Scholastic magazine found that only 2.6% of 10,000 high school students thought smoking had no connection with cancer.[35]

Given the vast amount of health-related information available from external sources, advertising by the tobacco companies could not have undermined the assumption-of-risk defense. Studies suggest that such advertising influences the choice of brand more than the initial decision to smoke.[36] For example, according to focus groups with African-American teenagers conducted by the National Cancer Institute in five U.S. cities, black youngsters are cynical, even resentful, about cigarette advertising. Those attitudes are particularly striking because activists have long complained that the industry targets inner-city kids, despite evidence indicating that the percentage of such kids who smoke on a regular basis has plummeted over the past decade.[37] Moreover, while marijuana ads are indisputably illegal, teenage use of that drug is accelerating rapidly.[38]

Any link between advertising and aggregate consumption is further eroded by a recent analysis of 1964-to-1990 data on 22 of the 24 member countries of the Organization for Economic Cooperation and Development. By 1990, six of the 22 OECD countries had banned all forms of tobacco advertising. Examining all of the countries and controlling for variables like price, age profile, and long-term trends, the study concludes that the average effect on per capita tobacco sales of the ban in those six countries was a small *increase*—not quite statistically significant, but clearly contrary to the hypothesis that ad bans will reduce overall consumption.[39] The author suggests that the higher tobacco sales may have been due to the disappearance of health warnings that would otherwise have appeared in the ads. Because those warnings probably had a deterrent effect, their disappearance could have promoted aggregate consumption.[40]

A domestic version of that theory, holding that restrictions on U.S. tobacco advertising by the Federal Trade Commission perversely raised the level of cigarette smoking, goes like this[41]: If advertising were unregulated, newer and smaller tobacco companies would vigorously seek to carve out a bigger market share by emphasizing health claims that might bolster brand preference. But in 1950 the FTC foreclosed health claims—like "less smoker's cough"—as well as tar and nicotine comparisons for existing brands. To get around that prohibition, aggressive companies then created new brands, which they supported with an avalanche of health claims. Filter cigarettes grew from roughly 1% to 10% of domestic sales within four years. Over the same period, industry per capita sales declined for the first time since 1931, by 9%—perhaps dampened by the focus in cigarette ads on tobacco-related illnesses. The only company to post higher revenues was Brown & Williamson Tobacco Corporation, a small firm that concentrated on filter brands.

In 1954 the FTC tightened its restrictions by requiring scientific proof of health claims, even for new brands. The industry returned to advertising taste and pleasure, and aggregate sales rebounded almost immediately. By 1957 scientists had confirmed the benefit of low tar cigarettes. A new campaign of "Tar Derby" ads quickly emerged with tar and nicotine levels collapsing 40% in two years. Insistent upon shutting down the flow of health claims, the FTC next demanded that they be accompanied by epidemiological evidence, of which none existed. The Commission then negotiated a "voluntary" ban on tar and nicotine comparisons.

Not surprisingly, the steep decline in tar and nicotine ended in 1959. Seven years later, apparently alerted to the bad news, the FTC reauthorized tar and nicotine data but continued to proscribe associated health claims. Then in 1970 Congress banned all radio and television ads. Overall consumption has declined slowly since that time. In today's climate, the potential gains from health-related ads are undoubtedly greater than ever—for both aggressive companies and health-conscious consumers. Thanks in good part to ill-advised government regulation, however, those gains will not be realized. Instead of "healthy" competition for market share, we can probably look forward to more imagery and personal endorsements—the very format that anti-tobacco partisans decry.

To be sure, if it can be demonstrated that tobacco companies— however they are permitted to advertise—are aiding and abetting children to obtain cigarettes illegally, those companies should be prosecuted under current law. But an appearance by Tiger Woods on television wearing apparel emblazoned with Joe Camel—the predictable outcome of current FTC and congressional restrictions on health claims—is hardly proof of targeted advertising, much less of aiding and abetting. In fact, to whatever extent it has targeted nonsmoking children, the tobacco industry seems to have been remarkably ineffectual in persuading them to smoke, particularly if we examine the years around the debut of Joe Camel in 1987. According to the U.S. Department of Health and Human Services, cigarette usage among youngsters between the ages of 12 and 17 declined from 29.4% in 1985, to 22.4% in 1990, to 20.2% in 1995.[42] Over the longer term, the average age at which smokers first regularly use cigarettes has trended slightly *upward* from 1962 through 1994.[43]

Addictiveness

If advertising has not misinformed smokers, thereby negating the assumption-of-risk defense, neither has alleged addiction rendered the defense inapplicable. Notwithstanding the assertion that many smokers are gripped by a drug-like dependence, millions of people quit smoking cold turkey; they experience only mild discomfort and, unlike drug addicts, do not require hospitalization for the effects of withdrawal.[44] Nor do smokers commit violent crimes to sustain their cigarette habit. "I'm not a doctor [but] forty million people have quit," concedes Don Beyer, the Democratic candidate for governor of Virginia, who nonetheless embraces the Clinton administration's plan to regulate tobacco as a drug.[45] Florida itself, in court papers in an unrelated 1995 case, acknowledged that "whether nicotine is addictive or not is a gray area. You have as many in the medical field that say it is as that say it isn't."[46] According to the state, breaking the habit may produce side effects, but they "last a week at most [and] can be effectively alleviated by over-the-counter remedies, such as cough syrup and analgesics, as well as by deep breathing and drinking more fluids."[47]

Author Richard Kluger, no fan of the tobacco industry, speaks bluntly about addiction:

> While new evidence had emerged [since the *Cipollone* case] showing that Philip Morris and B&W, among others, had done research on the addictive nature of nicotine and had neither disclosed it to the public nor warned against the addicting potency, many similar findings by investigators outside the industry had long since been made and published. Public-health advocates, moreover, had for years advised that nicotine was as addicting as heroin and cocaine. . . . [W]hether one categorized smoking as a practice, a habit, an indulgence, a vice, a dependency, or an addiction, it was commonly known—and had been for decades—to be hard to stop once begun. Nor could anyone say for certain how much of a daily dose served to induce addiction; tolerances differed from person to person, and the industry had in fact made available brands with extremely low dosages. How, then, to justify a claim that the cigarette makers had massively imposed an intentionally addicting product on an innocent public that had little knowledge or choice in the matter?[48]

Kluger's point is that, given the mass of other data, concealment by or misinformation from the tobacco companies may not be sufficient either to prove fraud or to defeat an assumption-of-risk defense. In particular, to override the assumption-of-risk defense, the "addicted" smoker must show that he *relied* upon the misinformation. Thus, even though the industry withheld or fabricated data, if the smoker had access to correct information from other sources, he may not have altered his behavior notwithstanding the misconduct of the tobacco companies.

Of course the central purpose of Florida's Medicaid Third-Party Liability Act is to guarantee that the state is not susceptible to an assumption-of-risk defense. That goal is accomplished by substituting a direct, so-called equitable cause of action in place of the traditional subrogation process. Prior to amending its Act, Florida had relied upon subrogation as its means of recouping Medicaid expenditures. By law, the availability and adequacy of a common law remedy like subrogation obviates the need for equitable relief.[49] But Florida has redefined "adequate." Simply put, an adequate remedy is now one that is guaranteed to win—even if that means inventing new law, applying it retroactively, and making a mockery of due process. The upshot is a bizarre action in equity—supposedly based upon what is fair and just in a given situation, not bound by the traditional rules of common law. Thus liberated from the normal restraints, the state has replaced well-settled legal principles with a discriminatory and despotic statute tailored specifically to engorge the state's treasure chest.

Unclean Hands

Even without recourse to its usual assumption-of-risk defense, the tobacco companies thought they could rely upon an analogous defense known as "unclean hands." That doctrine, which is applicable in equitable suits, simply says that the plaintiff's own fault is relevant to what, if any, remedy he is entitled to.[50] In other words, if Florida engaged in activities that had the effect of exacerbating any harms attributable to tobacco, the state might not be able to recover for those harms. Like assumption of risk, unclean hands takes into account the extent to which alleged damages may have arisen or increased as a result of the plaintiff's behavior. Also like assumption of risk, the doctrine of unclean hands is rooted in the principle that holds parties accountable for the consequences of their own conduct.

Let's assess Florida's conduct to see if its hands are unclean. For starters, if the correctness of Florida's position was so apparent, why did it take 30 years after the Surgeon General's initial warnings for the state to press its claims? Why didn't Florida opt out of the Medicaid program, or ask the federal government to exclude smoking-related illnesses from its list of covered treatments? Why didn't the state lower the nicotine content of cigarettes, or raise their tax rate, or ban their sale outright? On the other hand, if Florida wanted to preserve the pleasures of smoking for those of its citizens who paid their own medical bills, why not simply make it illegal for Medicaid beneficiaries to purchase cigarettes? Courts generally have let states decide when to treat groups differently based upon wealth,[51] and legislatures are reasonably free to require that recipients of government largesse act or refrain from acting in certain ways.[52] That solution would have curtailed Medicaid outlays, preserved the bulk of the cigarette tax base, protected the less affluent from their own misguided health habits, retained free choice for the large majority of smokers, and maintained some semblance of due process for the industry.

Despite their protestations of innocence, state officials could not have been oblivious to the barrage of criticism heaped upon the tobacco industry, dating from nearly four hundred years ago. In his authoritative history of the industry, Richard Kluger reports that King James I, in 1604, castigated smoking as "a custom loathsome to the eye, hateful to the nose, harmful to the brain, dangerous to the lung, and the black stinking fume thereof, nearest resembling the horribly Stygian smoke of the pit that is bottomless."[53] By the early 1900s, goaded by the National Anti-Cigarette League, 14 states had prohibited the sale of cigarettes.[54] When Tennessee's ban was challenged on constitutional grounds, the state Supreme Court minced no words in upholding the statute, railing against cigarettes as:

> wholly noxious and deleterious to health. Their use is always harmful; never beneficial. They possess no virtue, but are inherently bad, and bad only. They find no true commendation for merit or usefulness in any sphere. On the contrary, they are widely condemned as pernicious altogether. Beyond question, their every tendency is toward the impairment of physical health and mental vigor. There is no proof in the

> record as to the character of cigarettes, yet their character is
> so well and so generally known to be that stated above, that
> the Courts are authorized to take judicial cognizance of the
> fact. No particular proof is required in regard to those facts
> which, by human observation and experience, have become
> well and generally known to be true.[55]

In the 1950s epidemiologists Doll and Hill published a series of articles documenting the increased risk of lung cancer among smokers. They found that death from lung cancer was ten times more likely for persons who smoked 10–20 cigarettes daily than for those who did not smoke at all.[56]

That Florida officials were mindful of the dangers of smoking is incontrovertible. Their awareness is no less damaging to the state's "equitable" case than a smoker's assumption of risk would have been under the common law. When the plaintiff is at fault, unclean hands can frustrate relief. As the state's hired gun, attorney Richard Scruggs recounted the law:

> [A]ll of the states have, as the basis of their cases against the
> tobacco industry, these equitable theories. It doesn't mean
> that the tobacco industry is defenseless. They can show that
> the state has unclean hands, that the state has participated
> in the activity somehow, licensed it, or received tax revenues
> from it.[57]

Predictably, however, Scruggs's recitation of the law is one thing, but Florida's adherence to the rules is quite another. When push came to shove, here's what occurred.

Starting in 1972, the Florida prison system manufactured unfiltered cigarettes and distributed them at no cost to the state's inmates. In order to generate income, the state also sold some of its cigarettes to local governments. Those activities continued for roughly a decade despite widespread discussion in the legislature about the health hazards of smoking and the addictive power of nicotine.[58] Unclean hands? You bet. But when Philip Morris filed a pretrial motion to assure that the evidence would be admissible, Florida successfully opposed the motion and persuaded Judge Harold Cohen that evidence of the state's shared responsibility for tobacco-related illness was just another "affirmative defense," forbidden by the Medicaid Third-Party Liability Act.[59] So much for Scruggs's pledge that the doctrine of unclean hands was still alive and well.

Florida has pulled out all the stops to deny the tobacco companies any vestige of a defense. Governor Chiles, his attorney general, and the legislature, without much resistance from the judiciary, have exploited the laws they like, repealed the ones they don't, and concocted novel theories of liability whenever necessary to stack the deck. And no wonder. The state's hands are worse than unclean; they are downright filthy. Although Florida purportedly seeks recovery for all smoking-related disease, the state didn't sue companies that use tobacco leaf to fashion high-grade cigars; perhaps that's because Florida is home to the nation's leading producer of premium cigars.[60] More damaging still to the state's moral crusade, a recent report reveals that roughly $825 million of Florida's pension assets were invested in tobacco stocks.[61] Again, while the state contends that in 1992 alone "28,350 Floridians died from tobacco-related causes, representing 77 preventable deaths every day or 20% of all deaths in the State,"[62] 10 of Florida's 23 members of Congress guaranteed that federal subsidies for the industry would survive. Their 10 votes were more than enough to defeat the Durbin amendment, which would have prohibited the use of federal funds for certain tobacco programs. On June 12, 1996, the House of Representatives rejected the amendment by a two-vote margin.[63]

Perhaps most appalling of all, in an act of unparalleled hypocrisy, Florida actually embraces assumption of risk and personal responsibility in defending against a lawsuit brought by a prisoner seeking access to nicotine patches and other treatment for an alleged addiction to smoking.[64] In its October 1995 motion to dismiss the case, the state unabashedly asserts that "any future harm which Plaintiff may potentially suffer . . . is a direct result of Plaintiff himself choosing to buy and smoke cigarettes. Defendants are not responsible for Plaintiff's decision to purchase cigarettes any more than they would be responsible for Plaintiff buying a candy bar at the canteen." Continuing in the same vein: "Plaintiff is in no way entitled to medical intervention to 'cure' a habit which Plaintiff himself continues to indulge, and over which Plaintiff has ultimate control." Florida, it seems, has absolutely no compunction summoning the principle of personal responsibility whenever its own money is at stake.

That two-faced application of the law should convince anyone that the state has no moral or equitable claim against the tobacco industry. Not only did Florida reject obvious remedies that would have reduced tobacco consumption and abated the associated Medicaid outlays, but it also nurtured cigarette manufacturers with its investment capital and its approval of federal giveaway programs. Indeed, the state was itself a cigarette manufacturer for almost a decade. For their part, few if any Florida Medicaid recipients could have missed the endless warnings and incessant sermonizing about the health risks of smoking. So whether the label is "assumption of risk" or "unclean hands," smokers who receive and states that dispense Medicaid assistance are the parties principally accountable for the public health costs linked to the use of tobacco.

Even the federal government, which under President Clinton has pursued an aggressive anti-smoking campaign, acknowledges the role of personal responsibility when the question is whether the government itself should be held liable for its role in encouraging smoking. Thus, the Clinton administration now seeks congressional support for legislation that would overturn a 1993 opinion by senior lawyers in the Department of Veterans Affairs. That opinion suggests that the federal government may be liable for tobacco-linked illnesses contracted by millions of military personnel who smoked while on active duty. Sounding much like a tobacco executive, VA Secretary Jesse Brown declared that it would be a "borderline absurdity" for the government to pay "for death or disability resulting from veterans' personal choice to engage in conduct damaging to their health."[65]

The military plainly encouraged its employees to smoke. Not only were cigarettes sold on bases at a huge discount, but soldiers in combat zones were given free cigarettes as part of their rations. That is surely more of an inducement than tobacco companies ever offered their customers. And no one has ever accused the tobacco industry of preying on youngsters under enormous stress by plying them with free cigarettes. "We know there's a dichotomy," rationalized a Pentagon spokesperson, "but you have to balance the need for a healthy fighting force and an individual's right to use tobacco."[66] Rather than blame the government, Secretary Brown—who stopped smoking 35 years ago—volunteered this controlling principle: "If you choose to smoke, you are responsible for the consequences of your act."[67] Clearly, if that principle is sufficient to render the government immune from liability, it is sufficient to do that for private companies as well.

Statistical Proof of Causation

In mass tort cases, statistical evidence combined with other corrob-orating evidence can "supply a useful link in the process of proof."[68] But statistics alone are not enough. "An essential element of the plaintiff's cause of action for negligence, or for that matter for any other tort, is that there be some reasonable connection between the act or omission of the defendant and the damage which the plaintiff has suffered."[69] Even in a class action, assuming that the class is certified and the named plaintiffs prevail on the issue of liability, the remaining members of the class generally cannot recover in the damages phase of the trial unless they demonstrate individualized harm caused by the defendant.[70]

Courts steadfastly apply those classical precepts of tort law across the nation; but in Florida, in order to minimize any uncertainty surrounding its prospect for success, the state substituted its own rendition of the law of causation.

> In any action brought under this subsection, the evidence code shall be liberally construed regarding the issues of cau-sation and of aggregate damages. The issue of causation and damages in any such action may be proven by use of statistical analysis. . . . [If] the number of recipients for which medical assistance has been provided by Medicaid is so large as to cause it to be impractical to join or identify each claim, the agency shall not be required to so identify the individual recipients for which payment has been made, but rather can proceed to seek recovery based upon payments made on behalf of an entire class of recipients.[71]

In other words, under the Medicaid Third-Party Liability Act, the state could sue the tobacco industry for health expenditures attribut-able to smoking by Medicaid recipients without disclosing (1) the names of recipients, (2) such recipients who actually smoked, or (3) such smokers who had illnesses allegedly caused by tobacco. All that had to be disclosed were aggregate statistics for Florida Medic-aid recipients as a group.

In response to a due process challenge, the Florida Supreme Court upheld the part of the Act that authorized statistical proof, but excised the provision permitting nondisclosure of Medicaid recipi-ents. The Court could "find no way in which this subsection would allow a defendant to challenge improper payments made to individual recipients [or prove] that its product was never used by the recipient. . . . It is illogical and unreasonable to call this a fair process."[72] Trial court Judge Harold J. Cohen in West Palm Beach then directed the state to disclose the names of all Medicaid recipients who were treated for tobacco-related diseases.[73]

Speculation was that the state's litigation might die under the ponderous weight of 40,000 to 60,000 individual investigations. But Florida general counsel Dexter Douglas thought otherwise; he predicted that the court would limit the tobacco companies to an investigation of just enough randomly selected cases to authenticate the statistical evidence.[74] That prediction proved to be close to the mark. In February 1997 Judge Cohen gave the industry access to the names of 400,000 Medicaid patients—including burn victims, suggesting the industry may be liable if a smoker falls asleep with a lit cigarette, and patients with other injuries rarely associated with tobacco use, like mental illness. From those 400,000 names, lawyers for the tobacco companies can select 25 persons. The state will then make available their medical records and the industry can investigate those cases, and no others, in order to confirm that the aggregate data proffered by the state are reliable.[75]

Reflecting his cynicism, or perhaps his bias, Judge Cohen cautioned that his order allows the industry "to pick 25 names. It's not to go out and hound 400,000 recipients."[76] Naturally, the court is concerned about privacy; but the 400,000 patients already relinquished their claim to complete privacy when they requested Medicaid assistance. Certainly if an insurance company were filing subrogation actions, each claimant would be required to disclose his medical record. Still unclear is how the tobacco companies, without prior access to the medical records, were to choose the 25 cases to be investigated. Moreover, even if the industry had the records in advance, they did not contain smoking histories. Aggregate statistics on smoking-related illnesses cannot possibly be confirmed if the 25-person sample consisted mostly of nonsmokers.

By wresting such absurd restrictions from the trial judge, the state has again flouted the rule of law despite unequivocal instruction from its highest court: Tobacco companies must be able to investigate the legitimacy of Medicaid claims[77] and explore such questions as whether and how much each claimant smoked. Ironically, the Florida Supreme Court apparently had more influence with federal District Judge D. Lowell Jensen in San Francisco than with its own lower court in West Palm Beach. In his February 1997, 32-page opinion dismissing most counts of San Francisco's Medicaid recovery complaint, Judge Jensen explicitly repudiated the Florida lower court opinion.

> [I]n a direct suit by a smoker to recover his or her smoking-related medical expenses, the Court could inquire into any other health problems which may have exacerbated the costs of health care for that smoker. Likewise, the Court could ascertain from an individual smoker the amount of information he had regarding the risks associated with smoking. In the present suit, on the other hand, . . . it will be difficult, if not impossible, to explore these and other relevant issues.[78]

Judge Jensen concluded, "[I]n order to recover monies spent on health care for individual smokers, plaintiffs will be required to prove that each of those smokers' injuries were actually caused by smoking."[79] Less than two weeks earlier a West Virginia trial judge had dismissed most of that state's case against the tobacco industry on similar grounds.[80] And in May 1997 Maryland Judge Roger W. Brown ruled that the state had no right "to assert claims in its own name . . . for the harms allegedly caused to third party smokers, unless such claims are made in the name of each of the individually injured third party Medicaid program recipients under the equitable doctrine of subrogation."[81] So in at least three jurisdictions, only those specific illnesses shown to have been caused by tobacco will be compensable.

That approach seems eminently reasonable. Indeed, the Florida Medicaid Third-Party Liability Act artfully mandates that the state prove causation. But the mandate is empty of meaning. Unlike any other tort action by any other plaintiff, Florida's showing of causation need not be injury-specific. Instead, the state may show generalized causation based upon no more than aggregate epidemiological data—notwithstanding authoritative and near-universal acknowledgment that "[e]pidemiology *cannot prove causation*; causation is a judgment issue."[82] More precisely, causation can only be legally "established" by a coherent underlying theory—supported, but not proven, by empirical data. Because this point is pivotal, let's look at the drawbacks when mass tort plaintiffs rely exclusively on statistical evidence.

Epidemiology is concerned with the incidence, distribution, and etiology of diseases. In a legal context, the objective is to determine whether exposure to an agent caused a harmful effect. The focus is on general causation (whether the agent is capable of causing the disease) rather than specific causation (did the agent cause the disease in this individual). Epidemiological studies may be able to pinpoint the agents that are associated with a disease, quantify the increased risk, and profile the persons prone to contract the disease. Like all statistical analyses, however, the results are sensitive to the accuracy of the data and the validity of the research methods.

Most important, epidemiology cannot demonstrate that a statistical association between agent A and disease B signifies that A caused B. It is conceivable, perhaps likely, that the apparent association between A and B arises from the fact that both are highly correlated with one or more other factors, which statisticians call confounding variables. For example, there seems to be a close association between math scores and shoe size. Yet nobody would suggest that big feet enhance mathematical ability, nor that math skills cause one's feet to grow. The obvious confounding variable is age. As people grow older, they learn more about math and they wear larger shoes. Similarly, in assessing the correlation between smoking and cancer, it is essential to control for a long list of factors—for example, weight, age, diet, other lifestyle choices, family history, intensity and duration of smoking, and exposure to other causal agents, to name a few.

Ideally, controls for confounding variables should be effectuated experimentally. That is, persons to be tested should be identical in all relevant respects except that one randomly selected group (cohort) is instructed to smoke a specified amount and a second such cohort is instructed not to smoke. Then the medical histories of the individuals in the two groups are compiled over time and compared. That process may well be impermissible on moral grounds, and it's impracticable in any event. Latency periods are lengthy and varied, matched individuals are difficult (or impossible) to identify, and smokers are self-selected, not randomly selected. So statisticians must rely upon observational data, as contrasted with the experimental data that is generated when investigators are able to choose the individuals who will be exposed to an agent and those who will not. As a result, the only effective controls for confounding variables are those that can be implemented statistically, and therein lie many problems.

Not least of the problems is that multiple explanatory variables, if they are correlated with one another, will mask the separate effect of the variable at issue in the litigation. Suppose we were to hypothesize that a particular disease might be due to smoking, consumption of fatty foods, race, and income. If the four explanatory variables were significantly interrelated and each had an effect on the incidence of the disease, then we could not reliably determine the impact of smoking alone. Even more basic, in all of the Medicaid cases, every smoker for whom recovery is now sought was a Medicaid recipient. The observational data were not limited to that subset of the population, however. Accordingly, if Medicaid recipients have different characteristics than nonrecipients—due to their financial circumstances, for example—and if the differences are associated with tobacco-related diseases, the data could be fundamentally flawed. Moreover, observational studies often suffer from "recall bias"—the proven tendency for those individuals who have contracted a disease to recall more readily their past exposure to an allegedly causal agent.

Here is another, maybe simpler, way of looking at the considerable dilemma of confounding variables. Causation is most direct and straightforward when the agent is both a necessary and sufficient antecedent of the disease (nonsmokers do not get cancer, all smokers get cancer). Somewhat more complicated is when the agent is necessary but not sufficient (nonsmokers do not get cancer, not all smokers get cancer) or when the agent is sufficient but not necessary (all smokers get cancer, nonsmokers can also get cancer). The most complex relationship, and the one most difficult to sustain with statistics, is when the agent is neither necessary nor sufficient (nonsmokers can get cancer, not all smokers get cancer). It is that fourth category that we must confront in the Medicaid recovery suits.

Furthermore, statistical tests are designed to address a question that is quite different from the question the court faces. The court needs to determine, in light of the observed disparity in disease rates between a sample of smokers and nonsmokers, what is the probability that smoking has no real effect. But a test of statistical significance reasons in the opposite direction: Assuming that smoking has no real effect, what is the probability that a disparity as large as the one observed between smokers and nonsmokers could have arisen just because we studied a sample and not the entire population? While those two questions are interrelated, they are not equivalent. By analogy, assuming a fair coin, statistics tells us that the chance of two flips in a row coming up heads is one in four. That is not the same as saying: Given two heads in a row, the odds are only one in four that the coin is fair.

Put somewhat differently: When the difference in disease rates between smokers and nonsmokers is deemed to be significant, a statistician will reject the hypothesis that the difference was due to sampling error. He has not proven, however, that the real underlying disease rates are higher for smokers. Instead, he has simply ruled out one possible explanation (sampling error); alternative explanations for the observed difference are still possible—like confounding variables, nonrandom selection, recall bias, and inaccurate data. Those complexities make it essential that individualized confirmation of causation supplement any broad-based empirical data. In short, the issues are too complicated and the statistical techniques too untrustworthy to exclude case-by-case corroborative or exculpatory evidence.

That general-purpose warning takes on still greater importance in the context of the Medicaid reimbursement suits. For those suits, it is not sufficient for the state to demonstrate that tobacco is more probably than not a cause of various diseases. Indeed, the "more probable than not" legal standard ineluctably leads to the wrong damages. To illustrate: Suppose statistics "prove" that the disease rate among nonsmokers is 10 cases per 10,000, the disease rate among smokers is 16 per 10,000, and the entire increase of 6 cases is attributable to smoking. Thus, 6 out of every 16 cases among smokers, or 37.5%, are "caused" by tobacco. Epidemiologists call this measure the "attributable portion of risk" or APR. No single smoker could show statistically that his disease was more probably than not due to tobacco. Consequently, the industry that caused 37.5% of the cases would escape without liability if the "more probable than not" standard were rigorously applied. On the other hand, if the APR were, say, 60%—that is, if tobacco caused an increase from 10 cases among nonsmokers to 25 among smokers—then every smoker could show statistically that his disease was more probably than not due to tobacco. The industry would be liable for 100% of the damages even though it caused only 60% of the cases.

Because neither outcome makes much sense, the damage awards to the states, if any, would likely be based upon the APR percentage itself. If the APR is 37.5% and the Medicaid expenditures for all tobacco-related diseases, including those not attributable to smoking, are $1 billion, then the industry will be liable for $375 million. While that procedure does seem more equitable, it raises an unsettling problem. When the APR is used directly to determine the assignable damages, it is imperative that the percentage be correct. That is, the actual magnitude of the APR replaces a dichotomous "more probable than not" standard, under which a defendant is either fully liable (if the APR is any number above 50%) or not liable at all (if the APR is any number below 50%). By making that substitution, if the value of the APR is imprecise—even if the error is only a few percentage points—the impact on damages in 35 states will be in the billions of dollars.

There is one characteristic of epidemiological evidence that we know with absolute certainty—it is inescapably imprecise. It measures association rather than causation; it must deal with latency periods, interrelated confounding variables, recall bias, selection bias, sampling error, and bad data. Yet when the state is the plaintiff and loathsome tobacco companies are the defendants, Florida courts will be relying exclusively on statistics, without a shred of corroborating evidence that cigarettes caused a particular disease in a particular case. Apparently the rule of law in Florida is sufficiently malleable to serve whatever objective the state can portray as beneficent.

Somehow the soundness of that argument eluded at least one Florida columnist.

> [N]ot one of these states knows how many of its Medicaid patients even smoke or ever have smoked. Not one is prepared to produce a sick Medicaid patient and prove, with scientific evidence, that the patient's illness is a direct result of cigarette smoking. . . . The states have no such evidence. They are like a state suing General Motors on the grounds that automobiles are involved in accidents and that victims in accidents have run up the cost of Medicaid.[83]

To be blunt, it is *impossible* to demonstrate a causal link between an individual smoker and a particular tobacco company using epidemiological data alone. In order to circumvent that problem, Florida determined to base damages upon general evidence of causation rather than on specific injury. Because the state rather than an injured party is the sole plaintiff, the court would not have to determine the amount of damages to be distributed to each Medicaid recipient. But it still faces the redoubtable task of allocating the damages among the various tobacco companies. To simplify matters, the Medicaid Third-Party Liability Act provides that the state can "proceed under a market share theory, provided that the products involved are substantially interchangeable among brands, and that substantially similar factual or legal issues would be involved in seeking recovery against each liable third party individually."[84]

Under the market share doctrine, each tobacco company defendant would be liable for a portion of the aggregate damages—based upon dividing the company's Florida tobacco revenues by the corresponding revenues for all defendants combined. The market share theory originated with the diethylstilbestrol (DES) cases, in which a drug taken by pregnant women to prevent miscarriages allegedly caused medical problems in their children decades later. Because DES was manufactured by a number of companies but sold generically, neither the mother nor the child was able to name the manufacturer at the time the problems finally arose. Some courts allowed the children to recover damages merely by proving that DES caused their injury, without identifying the specific manufacturer.

Only six states have accepted the market share doctrine; many others concluded that they could not justify holding companies liable for damages they may not have caused.[85] Even the few states that have applied the doctrine to DES litigation have not been willing to expand its coverage to nongeneric products, like cigarettes, or to products consumed closer to the time of injury.[86] By common law, Florida limited market share liability to those cases where the plaintiff is "inherently unable" to determine which company manufactured the injurious product.[87] Moreover, the plaintiff had to meet a "due diligence" requirement; that is, he had to demonstrate that he "made a genuine attempt to locate" the culpable party.[88]

The obligation to locate the culpable party no longer exists under the Florida Medicaid recovery statute, nor do the other requirements for using market share liability that had applied under Florida's now-defunct common law. The plaintiff state need not show that the Medicaid patients smoked, that smoking caused their illness, or even that a particular tobacco company produced the type of cigarettes that they consumed. Nor can the company defend itself by proving that it did not manufacture a specific type of cigarette within the relevant market during the relevant time frame. In fact, no one seems to know just what is the relevant time frame. Unlike DES, tobacco has been on the market continuously since well before the birth of Medicaid; some patients stopped smoking years before they contracted cancer; others persist in smoking despite their illness. Yet those obstacles to meeting the plaintiff's burden of proof have been expunged—to be replaced by a statistical tabulation showing only the total tobacco-related sales by each company in the state of Florida over who knows what period.

Forget about demonstrating that the supposed causal agent is a generic product; the state must only represent that cigarette brands are substantially interchangeable and that each patient's injury involves similar factual and legal issues. Are there no interbrand distinctions by price, size of cigarette, filtering mechanism, or nicotine and tar content? Are there no individualized factual questions to resolve such as the number of cigarettes smoked per day, the overall time span, the state in which the smoking occurred, whether the patient was ill before coming to Florida, or the size and type of cigarette smoked? Isn't it plausible that cigarette consumption by Medicaid recipients differs in many respects (e.g., choice of brand) from consumption by the aggregate population upon which the market share statistics are based?

Notwithstanding those obvious and formidable pitfalls, Florida authorized by statute the imposition of market share liability. No other state enacted a similar statute.[89] In effect, the Florida legislature—apparently eager to use rigged litigation as a painless substitute for fiscal discipline—imposed a quasi tax on out-of-state companies. Whatever the motivation, by permitting state courts to allocate damages based upon no more than market share statistics, the Florida legislature blithely assigns liability without causation and blame without fault. Then, flagrantly misusing those statistics, as if cigarette brands were indistinguishable and injuries were factually equivalent, the state drives a final wedge between its Medicaid recovery suits and any rational view of corrective justice.

Damages

For those politicians eager to forge new law in the service of ends that they find congenial, legislation to recover public expenditures on behalf of poor people suffering from smoking-related illnesses may at first blush seem irresistible. But before too hastily enacting a punitive statute like the Florida Medicaid Third-Party Liability Act, legislators should have confirmed that there is indeed a pot of gold at the end of the rainbow.

Two questions arise: First, if the states' coffers have already been replenished by levying excise taxes on tobacco products in order to reclaim smoking-related public health expenditures, are the courts likely to permit double recovery? Second, even if there are recoverable damages not offset by excise tax receipts, will those damages be sufficient to compensate private contingency lawyers, pay litigation expenses, and reimburse the federal government for its share of Medicaid outlays?

Taking the second, less complicated question first—assuming no offset for excise tax receipts—those states that prevail in a Medicaid recovery suit will likely have few dollars to show for their efforts after funneling most of the damages back to Washington, then paying attorneys' fees and other legal costs. The federal Medicaid statute[90] requires that any expenditures recovered by the state must be remitted to the federal government in proportion to the federal participation in the state's Medicaid program. In Florida, the feds pick up about 56% of Medicaid costs; so they must receive 56% of any damage awards. Federal participation rates range from 50% to 79%; the lower the state's median income, the higher the federal outlay.[91] Mississippi receives 79% of its Medicaid funding from Washington.

To make matters worse, the federal government pays only half of any litigation costs, regardless of the federal participation rate. The state must pay the other half. Accordingly, in a state like Florida, where private lawyers are to receive a 25% contingency fee plus reimbursement of their expenses (say, another 5%), the state will retain only 29 cents out of each dollar of damages. The 71-cent balance goes to the federal government (56 cents) and to cover half of the legal fees and expenses (15 cents). In Mississippi, the state will retain only 6 cents of each dollar. Moreover, the state must still pay its own out-of-pocket expenses associated with discovery and trial.

Justifiably concerned that the federal rake-off would diminish states' incentive to litigate, Sen. Frank Lautenberg (D-N.J.) introduced a bill in June 1996 that would allow states to keep more of their winnings. The Lautenberg proposal would have reduced the federal remittance by 33% if Medicaid damages resulted from a lawsuit against tobacco companies.[92] More important than the bill itself, which did not pass, is what it says about the lengths to which some politicians were willing to go in their anti-tobacco obsession. With state legislators redefining the law and federal legislators trying to sweeten the pot, the signs of a moral crusade are pervasive.

Ironically, however, unless they are able to extort a financial settlement from the tobacco companies, the states so fervent in their rush to punish the industry may find that the huge payoff they're awaiting is illusory. For even if tobacco companies are held liable for all smoking-related public health costs—including publicly funded medical care, group life insurance, sick leave, nursing home care, pensions, and lost tax receipts that pay for retirement programs—courts are not likely to condone damage awards if cigarette excise taxes already generate net revenues to the states in excess of Medicaid costs. We come then to the first question posed above. As we shall see, recent authoritative studies confirm that the relevant excise taxes exceed the relevant health expenditures.

In its 1985 report, the Office of Technology Assessment of the U.S. Congress estimated that the personal and social cost of smoking was $2.17 per pack of cigarettes sold.[93] However, OTA made no attempt to distinguish between "internal" costs borne directly by a smoker—for example, the wages lost due to his tobacco-related illness or premature death—and "external" costs imposed by a smoker upon other persons—for example, public health expenditures for tobacco-related illnesses. Only the latter are relevant for purposes of the Medicaid recovery suits. When appropriate adjustments are made to isolate the external component of the cost, the revised estimates range from 15 cents per pack using 1986 data[94] to 33 cents per pack using 1993 data.[95] Both estimates are far below the corresponding excise taxes collected on a pack of cigarettes.

Smokers are able to impose costs upon nonsmokers because the government has decided, first, to insure the health costs of low-income and elderly persons and, second, to fund the insurance in a manner that does not distinguish between presumably high-risk smokers and lower-risk nonsmokers. If each smoker paid for his own illness, all costs would be internalized. If smokers insured themselves against tobacco-related illness and premiums reflected the health risk implicit in their smoking habits, there would be no external costs between smokers as a group and nonsmokers as a group (although there would still be external costs imposed by those individuals who contracted diseases upon those who did not). Apart from the quite separate dispute about injury due to secondhand smoke, externalities between smokers and nonsmokers arise only when the government both compels health insurance and prevents the tailoring of premiums so that they match the risk profile of the insured. Setting aside the possibility of fraud, the conduct of the tobacco companies is simply irrelevant to the problem of externalities.

Placed in perspective, states are suing the tobacco industry to recover external costs that (a) are imposed by smokers upon non-smokers, (b) could not have been imposed without the complicity of the state itself, (c) are unaffected by the conduct of the industry, and (d) are more than offset by the excise taxes flowing into state treasuries. In that context, we can review the three key studies on the social costs of smoking.

The first comprehensive analysis of the external cost of smoking was published in the *Journal of the American Medical Association* in 1989 by a team of researchers from the Rand Corporation.[96] The Rand study established the framework for subsequent research and, for our purposes, set forth three essential principles: First, if a smoker does not die from a smoking-related illness, he will die from some-thing else. Accordingly, the relevant social cost is not the entire amount spent on his illness, but the difference between the amount spent and the amount that would otherwise have been spent if he had not smoked. Second, premature death from smoking can pro-duce long-term external *benefits* in the form of lower retirement costs[97] and reduced nursing home care. Those benefits are an offset to the near-term outlays for medical care, sick leave, and group life insurance. Third, because the near-term expenses of a smoking-related illness will necessarily be incurred before any longer-term savings in retirement and nursing home costs are realized, it is important to compare apples to apples using present values adjusted for the timing of any receipts and disbursements.

Perhaps an oversimplified illustration might be helpful. Consider the social costs attributable to one smoker, an unmarried Medicaid recipient, who contracts lung cancer and dies today at age 65. His publicly funded medical costs are $20,000, paid on the date of death.

If our hypothetical victim had not smoked, he would have retired at age 65 and lived to age 70; his publicly funded medical costs would have been $8,000, paid at the later date of death; and his Social Security benefits would have been $2,500 annually beginning on his 66th birthday and terminating at death. By smoking, the deceased Medicaid recipient imposed certain costs upon the public, but he also enabled the public to avoid other outlays. From the taxpayers' perspective, the year-by-year comparison of these costs and benefits looks like this:

	Year	Costs & (Benefits)	Present Value at 3%	Present Value at 5%
Medical costs	0	$20,000	$20,000	$20,000
Social Security	1	(2,500)	(2,427)	(2,381)
Social Security	2	(2,500)	(2,356)	(2,268)
Social Security	3	(2,500)	(2,288)	(2,160)
Social Security	4	(2,500)	(2,221)	(2,057)
Social Security	5	(2,500)	(2,157)	(1,959)
Medical costs	5	(8,000)	(6,901)	(6,268)
Totals		($500)	$1,650	$2,907

Although our smoker died prematurely and the Medicaid fund expended $20,000 as a result of his lung cancer, the government avoided $20,500 of other expenses—$8,000 in medical costs that would have been incurred if he had survived another five years, and $12,500 in Social Security benefits that would have been paid over that time. On balance, purely in dollars and cents—that's what these lawsuits are all about—the public is ahead by $500 because the victim died at age 65 rather than age 70. However, the net savings disappear if we adjust for the timing of the inflows and outflows. The public's costs ($20,000) are paid when the smoker dies. The benefits are not fully realized for five years thereafter. Because a dollar today is worth more than a dollar in the future, all of the costs and benefits should be expressed in present value terms. Using a 3% discount rate—roughly equal to the long-term real return (net of inflation) on risk-free government securities—the $500 savings is converted into a $1,650 cost. And if we raise the discount rate to

5%, the public cost escalates to $2,907. The higher the discount rate, the less weight is given to the benefits that arise in the out-years.

To be conservative, the researchers at the Rand Corporation discounted for present value at a 5% real rate. They concluded that the external cost of a pack of cigarettes in 1986 dollars was 15 cents. In a later study for the Congressional Research Service, that estimate was updated to 33 cents, expressed in 1993 dollars.[98] Yet smokers were then paying an average of 53 cents per pack in taxes—60% more than the costs they were imposing. In a separate study, also focusing on 1993 dollars, Duke University economist W. Kip Viscusi reworked the Rand data and found that the medical care, sick leave, and group life components totaled approximately 51 cents per pack[99]—still lower than the excise tax rate, even without offset for retirement and nursing home savings. With all expenditures *and* savings factored in, the total external cost per pack, according to Viscusi, was 25.3 cents—less than half of the prevailing 53-cent tax rate.[100]

Those studies conclude, then, that the total taxes from tobacco far exceed public health costs of tobacco-related illnesses. Thus, the public sector—state and federal together—has no claim for damages. In order for any given state to have a legitimate claim, it would have to receive a much smaller portion of federal-state aggregate excise taxes than it pays as a percentage of health costs. Yet the typical state collects 28.6 cents per pack versus 24 cents charged by the federal government.[101] So the state's share of revenues, on average, is over 54%. By comparison, states' contributions toward the costs of the Medicaid program range from 50% in the wealthier states to only 21% in the poorer states.[102] On balance, states clearly are receiving more than they are paying.

Another argument floated by the states is that excise tax revenues cannot be counted as an offset to Medicaid outlays because the revenues may not be earmarked for the Medicaid program; that is, states can and do use the revenues for other purposes. The argument is wholly fatuous. First, we are not concerned here with sales taxes that are assessed against virtually all products, but with added excise taxes that are directly traceable to, and would not exist but for, the purchase of cigarettes. Accordingly, those incremental revenues must necessarily enter into any cost-benefit calculus involving tobacco. Second, dollars are fungible; any appropriation of cigarette excise taxes to finance general expenditures merely releases those funds that would otherwise have been used for that purpose. The released funds are available to the Medicaid program. Third, to the extent that tobacco taxes are unrestricted as to use, they are even more valuable to the state than restricted funds. Fourth, it is the state itself that controls whether tax receipts are earmarked and which dollars are ultimately spent for what purpose. It would be utterly absurd for a state to be able to avoid an offset for cigarette tax receipts by the transparent expedient of redirecting those revenues to pay for, say, highway construction.

Naturally, the tobacco companies will want to know all about federal and state excise taxes collected from smokers, as well as any pension, retirement, and nursing home savings due to premature deaths from tobacco-related illnesses. Equally certain, the states will ask the courts not to allow either the discovery of such information or its proffer at trial. In making that argument, the states will probably invoke some version of the "collateral source rule," a common law tort doctrine by which a plaintiff's receipt of benefits from a source wholly independent of the defendant cannot be introduced as evidence in support of reduced damages. For example, if the victim of a car accident incurs medical bills that are covered by his medical insurance policy, the negligent driver who hit him cannot ask the jury to exclude those costs from the damage award on the ground that they have already been paid by a third party. The existence of the insurance policy is considered to be a separate contractual arrangement between the policyholder, who pays premiums, and an insurer who bears the financial risk of injury.

Undoubtedly, the states will insist that excise taxes are paid not by tobacco companies but by consumers—a wholly independent source. But a tax on sales of a product that is the subject of litigation, sold by companies that are the defendants, collected by states that are the plaintiffs, paid by consumers who were subjected to harm, and imposed specifically because of that harm, could hardly be regarded as independent. Moreover, economists would certainly reject the notion that consumers will be stuck with the entire tax bill. Whether a firm can pass along higher taxes to its customers depends upon the price elasticity of demand for the firm's product— a measure of the change in sales volume when the price is raised or lowered. Ordinarily, consumers will pay the full amount of a tax increase only if demand is infinitely inelastic; but economists know that tobacco sales do decline when the price is hiked.[103]

There is another objection, of course, to the invocation by the states of the collateral source rule. The rule is, after all, one of many common law tort principles that the states have rejected in litigating their Medicaid recovery suits. Now the states would like to have it both ways. They abandoned their traditional claims under tort law in favor of a novel direct cause of action. They repudiated assumption of risk and specific causation, each of which is a pillar of the conventional law. Yet whenever it seems advantageous to rely selectively upon time-tested doctrines like the collateral source rule, the states are not at all bashful. That manipulative, selective approach to the rules cannot be tolerated. Even if the excise taxes received by the states were an independent and unrelated benefit—which they are not—the collateral source rule is an integrated component of tort law; its application in these lawsuits is unprincipled and offensive.

Consequently, when it comes to reimbursing the public treasury for costs associated with tobacco-related diseases, the essential premise of these lawsuits is wrongheaded. To be sure, smokers impose burdens on publicly funded health care resources; but claims for reimbursement cannot focus exclusively on the expenditure side of the ledger. The states must also take into account, first, the excise tax receipts that already compensate for smoking-related public health outlays and, second, the costs that the public would otherwise have incurred if the smoker had not smoked. Mindful of these offsetting savings, the Rand Corporation concluded: "Although nonsmokers subsidize smokers' medical care and group life insurance, smokers subsidize nonsmokers' pensions and nursing home payments. On balance, smokers probably pay their way at the current [1986] level of excise taxes on cigarettes."[104] The Rand findings, since reinforced by both the Congressional Research Service and Professor Viscusi, are even more compelling in light of today's higher excise tax rates and mushrooming costs for geriatric care.

In short, even if the attorneys general somewhere, someday, somehow persuade a jury that the tobacco industry bears the blame for smoking-related illnesses, they will have won the battle and lost the war. Quite simply, the states have suffered no monetary damage.

Choice Between Public and Private Law

The state of Florida and 34 other states, faced with ballooning Medicaid costs, have decided that litigation against the tobacco industry could help refill depleted bank accounts. But there was one large fly in the ointment. For more than four decades, juries had consistently endorsed the twin ideals of individual liberty and personal responsibility: Smokers are free to purchase and use a product they know to be harmful but, if they do so, they and not the tobacco companies are accountable for the consequences.

Those twin ideals had to be set aside. So to lubricate the wheels of justice, the attorneys general concocted a new cause of action, abandoned the rules of subrogation, abolished the assumption-of-risk defense that had blocked damages for 40 years, and eliminated any requirement that plaintiffs had to prove they were harmed by cigarettes.

Actually, it was a handful of sharp private attorneys—later to be hired at contingency fees ranging from 10 to 30% of the recovered damages—who were responsible for the novel legal theorizing that became the Florida Medicaid Third-Party Liability Act.[105] Those members of the plaintiffs' bar are now hopelessly conflicted, serving as government subcontractors with financial incentives geared to the magnitude of their conquest. The sword of the state is brandished by private counsel with a direct pecuniary interest in the litigation. On one hand, they are driven by the contemplation of a huge payoff; on the other hand they fill a quasi-prosecutorial role in which their overriding objective is supposedly to seek justice. How could such lawyers possibly evaluate with impartiality the prospect of a settlement, say, or the tradeoff between injunctive and monetary relief?

States are not poor, unable to afford salaried attorneys. Nonetheless, state prosecutors are doling out multibillion-dollar contingency fee contracts to private trial lawyers. What is worse, those contracts are awarded without competitive bidding to attorneys who are often bankrolling state political campaigns.[106] Indeed, in states like Texas and Louisiana, where judges are elected, trial lawyers give campaign contributions to the very judges who preside over their cases.[107] In Mississippi, attorney general Mike Moore selected his number one campaign contributor, Richard Scruggs, to lead the Medicaid recovery suit that goes to trial this July. Scruggs also received a $2.4 million contingency fee from a state asbestos lawsuit in 1992, after contributing over $20,000 to Moore's reelection campaign the year before.[108] In Texas, attorney general Dan Morales chose five firms for the state's multibillion-dollar tobacco litigation scheduled for trial in September 1997; four of the five firms contributed a total of nearly $150,000 to Morales from 1990 to 1995.[109]

In West Virginia, tobacco defendants successfully challenged the state's contingency fee contract.[110] Attorney general Darrell McGraw had handpicked six lawyers, without competitive bidding, and declined to specify his selection criteria.[111] He did say, however, that "the State and her citizens stand only to benefit. The State has no exposure. There are no lawyer hourly fees. There are no costs. The taxpayers are thus fully protected."[112] He could have propounded a similar argument if the state were to hire private lawyers to prosecute criminal cases, and only pay for convictions. Fortunately, we understand—even if McGraw does not—that defendants as well as taxpayers must be protected. The Supreme Court reminds us that an attorney for the state "is the representative not of an ordinary party to a controversy, but of a sovereignty whose obligation to govern impartially is as compelling as its obligation to govern at all."[113]

Our government is the single entity that is authorized under narrowly defined circumstances to wield coercive power against private citizens. When that government functions as prosecutor or plaintiff in a legal proceeding in which it also dispenses punishment, adequate safeguards against state misbehavior are essential. That is why we need the protections of the Fourth, Fifth, Sixth, and Eighth Amendments; that is why we demand proof beyond reasonable doubt in criminal proceedings; and that is why in civil litigation we rely primarily upon private remedies with redress sought by, and for the benefit of, the injured party and not the state. Only when private remedies are deemed to be impracticable or ineffective— for example, when deterrence or punishment rather than corrective justice is the predominant goal (e.g., violent crimes), when culpable defendants are typically judgment proof (e.g., many other crimes), or when the *ex ante* risk of certain conduct is so high as to require restrictions prior to actual injury (e.g., nuclear plant safety)—do we condone public prosecution, often driven by statute rather than common law.

None of those conditions is present in the Medicaid recovery suits that the state attorneys general are now litigating. The primary goal purports to be corrective justice; the defendants are not judgment proof; and the *ex ante* risks are minimal (some would say zero), because no consumer is compelled to use tobacco products. To the extent that taxpayers are alleged to have been harmed as a result of the Medicaid insurance program, laws in every state permit the government to stand in the shoes of the Medicaid recipients and recover for any injuries that they could have claimed as private litigants. Yet we are facing 35 or more *public* prosecutions. Not only have adequate safeguards not been put in place, but the protections commonly available to private defendants have been eradicated. Instead of a more efficient set of remedies—arguably the sole justification for shifting from the private to the public forum—we have a bizarre tailor-made doctrine that tilts neutral procedural rules to ensure a politically correct substantive outcome.

What then is the alternative? Are there any circumstances under which tobacco companies might be held liable for their actions and, if so, what are the best procedures for resolving such claims? Suppose, for example, that a smoker professes to be addicted because he relied upon industry misinformation; he wants to recover for injuries that he can trace to his use of tobacco. Let's look briefly at two options: (1) a private lawsuit, filed either as an individual or class action; and (2) a nationwide settlement imposed by Congress. In the private arena, about 500 lawsuits have been filed by individual smokers or their survivors, principally in Florida where a jury recently handed the industry its only loss (now on appeal).[114] Private lawyers bankrolled by $8 million from 64 law firms are also litigating 17 class actions, mostly statewide, seeking damages on behalf of all allegedly addicted smokers within a state.[115] In the public arena, the White House, members of Congress, state attorneys general, health care groups, and tobacco representatives are pushing toward a settlement that may grant the industry some form of legal immunity in return for monetary damages and consent to more stringent regulation.[116]

The major difficulty for individual plaintiffs is straightforward: they have not succeeded in convincing juries of the legitimacy of their claims. The single success story—a $750,000 award this past August, which could still be reversed on appeal—raised the hopes of plaintiffs and their attorneys. But just nine months later, on May 5, 1997, those hopes were dampened when "Woody" Wilner, the Jacksonville attorney who had won the previous case, was unable to chalk up two victories in a row.

Wilner alleged that Reynolds Tobacco manufactured a defective product and negligently marketed it to youths under the age of 18.

He also sought punitive damages for conspiracy by the tobacco companies to hide what they knew about addiction and lung cancer. Reynolds in turn mounted its standard assumption-of-risk defense: smokers are responsible for the consequences of their own voluntary acts. That argument won the day in the face of a blizzard of company documents suggesting that Reynolds, with full knowledge that its cigarettes caused cancer, launched an aggressive campaign to promote their safety.[117]

The plaintiff started smoking at age 15, the same year her grandfather, also a smoker, died of lung cancer. She conceded that she was aware of the risks, and that she quit only after her doctor demanded that she do so as a condition for performing a tummy tuck operation. Apparently, those facts were persuasive, even to jurors who were viscerally disposed against the industry. "We couldn't stand the fact that [R. J. Reynolds Tobacco Company] was not being held responsible for anything," said the youngest of the six jurors, a former smoker. However, she went on to explain that the law dictated a verdict for the defense. "It was all we could do logically," she clarified.[118]

Tenacious attorneys like Wilner and aggrieved or opportunistic plaintiffs across the country have generated no shortage of individual lawsuits, including hundreds currently pending. Still, some tobacco watchers have touted class actions as a more efficient means of litigation, especially for claims that may be too small for case-by-case litigation. The first ever smokers' class action to go before a jury is scheduled for trial in Florida in September 1998. More than a half million class members will allege that tobacco companies knew of the carcinogenic and addictive quality of nicotine but concealed the information for decades.[119] A similar suit is targeted for New York; arguments on class certification are imminent.[120]

Most states, as well as the federal government, have these requirements for class certification: (1) members of the class are so numerous that including each as a named plaintiff would be impracticable, (2) there are questions of law or fact common to the class, (3) the claims of the representative parties are typical of the claims of the class, and (4) the representative parties will fairly and adequately protect the interests of the class.[121] Although there will undoubtedly be disagreement over the composition of a class of smokers in a particular case, at least a few state judges appear willing to certify classes comprising rather diverse claims and dissimilar factual backdrops.

Even if the requirements for certification are relaxed, there is still a major legal dispute that centers on the opt-out question. Some courts refuse to allow plaintiffs to opt out of the class in order to pursue litigation on their own.[122] Other courts have held that the conscription of plaintiffs and the denial of their right to individual relief is a violation of due process.[123] Notwithstanding this unresolved controversy—which also arises in the context of a legislated settlement—class actions remain a viable litigation option at the state level.[124]

But neither class actions nor individual lawsuits have produced what plaintiffs and their attorneys want most—money damages. Jurors with little sympathy for the tobacco industry, but with great respect for the law, have consistently held, first, that each plaintiff must prove he was injured by the defendant and, second, that smokers are accountable for their own lifestyle choices. Given a choice between established law and money damages, 35 states have decided the law must be revised. With causation reduced to a statistical abstraction and assumption of risk no longer a defense, jurors can now compel the odious tobacco industry to replenish state Medicaid coffers. In place of law, we have extortion—masquerading as law—and it is with that bludgeon that the states have driven the tobacco companies to the negotiating table.

The "secret" settlement talks—rumored to have begun in late 1996, with more details emerging in April 1997—entail partial immunity from liability for the industry in return for strict curbs on advertising, disclosure of chemical additives, acceptance of Food and Drug Administration oversight, and a $300 billion fund paid over the next 25 years to compensate the states, individual smokers, and, of course, private attorneys.[125] Buoyed by Wilner's loss in Florida, but facing implacable resistance to immunity from health groups and some government officials, the industry has counterproposed to cap compensatory damages (at something less than one million dollars per smoker), preclude punitive damages, and bar smokers from recovery unless they prove they were fraudulently misled by industry statements.[126]

Meanwhile, William Osteen, a federal trial judge in North Carolina, weakened the industry's hand by holding for the first time that the 1938 Food, Drug and Cosmetic Act empowers the FDA to regulate tobacco products as a drug delivery device.[127] He added, however, that the Act does not authorize the FDA to restrict industry advertising practices. This mixed ruling, if it holds up on appeal, suggests that restrictions on nicotine content, vending machine access, and sales to minors will likely be sustained; but proposed FDA limitations on billboard colors and content, use of characters like Joe Camel or the Marlboro Man, distribution of clothing with tobacco logos, and sponsorship of sporting events will not survive.[128]

Judge Osteen's holding on advertising was not unexpected. Indeed, even if he had determined that the FDA had statutory authorization to regulate tobacco ads, many First Amendment scholars doubt that proposed FDA restrictions would have passed constitutional muster. In the 1980 *Central Hudson* case, the Supreme Court held that non-misleading commercial speech about a lawful activity cannot be regulated unless the regulation directly advances a substantial governmental interest and is a reasonable approach, no more extensive than necessary to achieve the desired objective.[129] Although there may well be a substantial interest in preventing minors from smoking, the government could certainly prohibit sales to children, require proof of age, and prosecute retailers who break the law—all without restricting advertising.

Three years after *Central Hudson*, the Court refused to "reduce the adult population . . . to reading only what is fit for children."[130] And in *Liquormart* (1996), striking down a prohibition on off-premises price advertising of alcoholic beverages, the Court declined to confer lesser protection upon "vice" products.[131] Still, one commercial speech case does seem to have gone the other way. Despite its *Liquormart* holding, the Supreme Court refused to review a Fourth Circuit opinion upholding a Baltimore ordinance that bans cigarette and liquor ads on many billboards.[132] Technically, the denial doesn't establish official precedent; the justices didn't give their reasons, and they can change their mind the next time the issue comes before them. The Fourth Circuit had determined that the Baltimore law wasn't so restrictive that it violated commercial speech rights; the ordinance granted some exceptions for cigarette and liquor billboards in industrial zones and along highways.

More problematic for the industry is the determination by Judge Osteen that the FDA has jurisdiction over tobacco products as a drug delivery device.[133] Under the Food, Drug and Cosmetic Act, the manufacturer's "intended use" of a product determines whether the FDA can regulate it as a drug. If the tobacco industry intended that nicotine in cigarettes be sold as a pharmaceutical, for example, then the FDA would clearly have jurisdiction. But Judge Osteen went a step further, holding that the industry's public pronouncements regarding intended use do not necessarily govern the classification of tobacco under the Act. Instead, the judge examined information gleaned from internal company memoranda, and he also considered whether tobacco companies might reasonably have foreseen that nicotine has a pharmacological effect on smokers. He concluded that the FDA could permissibly characterize nicotine as a drug with the "intended use" of ingestion into the human body. The "blend, filter, and . . . ventilation system" of tobacco products is, therefore, a drug delivery device.[134]

Those unfolding events—"Woody" Wilner's loss before a Florida jury, recent court rulings on advertising, and Judge Osteen's holding that the FDA can regulate tobacco—may actually facilitate settlement negotiations by more precisely defining the limits of each party's bargaining position. But perhaps overlooked in the giddiness over prospects for a resolution are a number of more fundamental concerns. May Congress approve a settlement negotiated by a handful of state officials that effectively obliterates the constitutionally protected right of citizen access to the courts? Can respect for the law, our legislators, and the judiciary survive a back room deal that provides the requisite bounty to contingency fee lawyers while denying redress to many thousands of victims who have an absolute right to pursue what they believe to be their legitimate claims? Can our national legislature wipe out pending and prospective state lawsuits without rupturing our federal system of dual sovereignty?

Most important, will traditional common law defenses and principles of evidence, causation, and damages be abolished? Will the settlement reward those states that have subverted the Constitution in a blatant attempt to expropriate assets of out-of-state nonvoting corporations? Will the $300 billion kitty from the tobacco companies be accessible to anyone with a smoking-related illness? To any state that reimbursed a Medicaid recipient who fell asleep with a lit cigarette? Or will recovery be limited to those who can prove that they were misinformed or otherwise misled into consuming a harmful product that caused their specific injury?

We must not be deceived into thinking that a neatly wrapped pact with the tobacco industry and the FDA will resolve or even mitigate the problems associated with smoking. Indeed, the bargain being bandied about is essentially no more than an extortionate payoff to rapacious states that have already recovered considerably more in excise taxes than they have laid out for tobacco-related health costs. And by assigning quasi-legislative authority to a new Food, Drug and Tobacco Administration, we will have driven another nail into the coffin of personal responsibility. An unelected and unaccountable bureaucracy will be empowered to dictate the form and composition of those products that we may consume—even though our purpose is recreational and our knowledge of the potential harmful effects is exhaustive.

The machinery of regulation, once set in motion, will not stop with ameliorative changes. Listen closely to former FDA commissioner David A. Kessler, assuring the chairman of the anti-smoking group, Coalition on Smoking OR Health, what FDA oversight of tobacco would mean: "Only those tobacco products from which the nicotine had been removed or, possibly, tobacco products approved by FDA for nicotine-replacement therapy would then remain on the market."[135] Even more frightening: there can be no doubt that tobacco is only the first in a long list of products from which the nanny state will protect us. What comes next—coffee, soft drinks, red meat, dairy products, sugar, fast foods, automobiles, sporting goods? The list is endless and the fear of repression is not mere paranoia.

Here is what psychology professor Kelly D. Brownell, director of the Yale Center for Eating and Weight Disorders, recommends to combat high-fat foods:

> Remove bad foods and the rats stay thin. Environment is the real cause of obesity. Congress could shift the focus to the environment by taxing foods with little nutritional value. Fatty foods would be judged on their nutritive value per calorie or gram of fat. The least healthy would be given the highest tax rate. Consumption of high-fat food would drop, and the revenue could be used for public exercise facilities—bike paths and running tracks.[136]

Need any more be said? Turn these personal decisions over to the government and be prepared for an erosion of freedom never before experienced in this country. But preserve the rule of law—even for tobacco companies, manufacturers of high-fat foods, and assorted other "bad actors"—and we safeguard the liberty of all citizens, those we honor as well as those we disdain.

The rule of law is developed and explicated primarily in our courts; they are the proper forum to resolve disputes between private parties. And the common law of tort is the proper legal regimen under which litigants may ask for redress. Therefore, if a state as insurer of a private party seeks recovery of Medicaid expenditures, it must stand in the shoes of the private party according to established procedures of subrogation.

Even thus shielded from abusive state power, we must remind ourselves constantly that Medicaid reimbursement claims are the ineluctable byproduct of socialized health care. When some of us have to pay for the medical expenditures of others, we should not be surprised at the insistent clamor to monitor and control eating habits, exercise, and recreation. In withstanding such intrusions, we must reaffirm the principle of personal responsibility and resist the temptation to turn upon scapegoats like the tobacco industry to make amends for our own misguided policies. Today it is tobacco companies. Tomorrow it could be anyone.

If there is a single lesson to be learned here, it is one most powerfully recounted by Sir Thomas More, a champion of due process, as he addresses his son-in-law, William Roper:

> What would you do? Cut a great road through the law to get after the Devil? . . . And when the last law was down— and the Devil turned round on you—where would you hide, Roper, the laws all being flat? . . . [D]'you really think you could stand upright in the winds that would blow then? Yes, I'd give the Devil benefit of law, for my own safety's sake.[137]

3. Pistol Whipped: Baseless Lawsuits, Foolish Laws*

Introduction

Gun makers, engulfed by a torrent of litigation from dozens of cities, were threatened by the Clinton administration during the summer of 1999 with additional claims from more than three thousand public housing authorities coordinated by the U.S. Department of Housing and Urban Development.[1] Under President Bush, further action by HUD will almost certainly be shelved. Still, ongoing city- and state-sponsored lawsuits could destroy the firearms industry, with profound implications for the rule of law and the Constitution. The government's resorting to litigation as a tactic of intimidation and extortion will have destructive consequences extending far beyond a single industry.

Here's how the current avalanche of lawsuits against gun makers unfolded. Let's go back in time to June 1997. That's when the giant tobacco companies first caved in to the state Medicaid recovery suits. Cigarette manufacturers, besieged by claims in dozens of states and sued under perverted rules of tort law that eliminated any opportunity for self-defense,[2] decided to settle—that is, to bribe the politicians instead of going to war against a punitive money grab. That capitulation—the surrender of the industry's right to market a perfectly legal product—predictably spawned a new round of litigation. This time, gun makers were pitted against the combined resources

---

*Originally published, with minor revisions, as Cato Institute Policy Analysis No. 400, May 9, 2001. See also the following articles by the author, adapted in part for inclusion here: "The Great Tobacco Robbery," *Legal Times*, February 1, 1999, p. 27; "So Sue Them, Sue Them: Cities Look to Squeeze Gun Makers," *Weekly Standard*, May 24, 1999, p. 19 (coauthored with Michael I. Krauss); "Blackmail of Gun Makers," *National Law Journal*, January 31, 2000, p. A20; "When Theft Masquerades as Law," *Cato Policy Report*, March/April 2000, vol. XXII, no. 2, p. 1; "Clinton, Gore and a Million More," *Washington Times*, May 12, 2000, p. A20.

of billionaire trial lawyers, city mayors, county executives, a state attorney general, and the Clinton administration.

In bullying gun makers, the plaintiffs have included three corrosive ingredients, carried over from the tobacco wars, in their litigation formula: First, they have sued in multiple jurisdictions, thereby escalating the industry's legal costs. Second, they have employed contingency fee lawyers, many of whom are major political donors. Third, they have tried to use the judicial branch in order to bypass the legislature. To begin, I examine that new litigation paradigm. Then I digress briefly to explore Second Amendment concerns. Next, I analyze the suits threatened by public housing authorities, the claims by some cities that gun makers are responsible for "negligent marketing," the allegation by other cities that guns are an "unreasonably dangerous" and "defective" product, and the fallout from the Smith & Wesson settlement. That's followed by an assessment of the data that allegedly link gun injuries to gun ownership; finally, a look at the various proposals that purport to remedy gun violence.

State-Sponsored Tort Suits: The New Paradigm

When public officials prosecute lawbreakers, they are fulfilling a legitimate role of government. Most of the time, that prosecutorial role is unobjectionable, often commendable. But the latest rounds of litigation—tobacco, then guns—are different in three respects, each of which threatens the rule of law.

First, coordinated actions by multiple government entities can impose enormous legal fees on defendants. As a result, those actions have been used to extort money notwithstanding that the underlying case is without merit. Just listen to former Philadelphia Mayor Edward G. Rendell (D) calling for dozens of cities to file concurrent suits against gun makers: They "don't have the deep pockets of the tobacco industry," Rendell explained, and multiple lawsuits "could bring them to the negotiating table a lot sooner."[3] Never mind that the suits are baseless. We're not dealing with law, but with extortion masquerading as law.

One effective way to stop that thievery is by implementing a "government pays" rule for legal fees when a governmental unit is the losing plaintiff in a civil case. In the criminal sphere, defendants are already entitled to court-appointed counsel if needed; they're also protected by the requirement for proof beyond reasonable doubt and by the Fifth and Sixth Amendments to the Constitution. No corresponding safeguards against abusive public-sector litigation exist in civil cases. By limiting the rule to cases involving government plaintiffs, access to the courts is preserved for less affluent, private plaintiffs seeking redress of legitimate grievances. Also defendants in government suits will be able to resist meritless cases that are brought by the state solely to ratchet up the pressure for a large financial settlement.

"Government pays" becomes ever more urgent with the recent emergence of an insidious relationship between the plaintiffs' bar and some government officials. That relationship—common to tobacco and gun litigation—is a second major threat to the rule of law.

Second, both rounds of litigation were concocted by a handful of private attorneys who entered into contingency fee contracts with the government. In effect, members of the private bar were hired as government subcontractors, but with a huge financial share in the outcome. That's not a problem, says Rendell. He announced that cities were suing gun makers only for improved safety features and changes in distribution practices, not for monetary damages. Yet one day after Rendell's disclaimer, Miami and Bridgeport filed their suits, seeking hundreds of millions of dollars in damages.[4] New Orleans asked for damages[5] and so did Chicago (in fact, $433 million).[6] The claims include not only medical costs associated with gun violence, but also the costs of police protection, emergency services, police overtime and pensions, courts, prisons, loss of population, cleaning the streets of blood, lower property values, even lost tax revenue from reduced worker productivity[7]—plus punitive damages. And nearly all of the cities have solicited private lawyers to work for a contingency fee based on those damages.

So if money isn't the primary goal, there will be a lot of attorneys working for free. Maybe that's what they deserve. After all, the gun suits aren't intended to go to trial. In fact, HUD's threat, on top of the city and county claims, was meant to promote a settlement, not a trial. No doubt, with a piddling $1.5 billion in annual revenues, gun makers are not going to yield the same treasure trove as the tobacco behemoths whose worldwide sales are $300 billion. But that's not fatal, because the real goal of the trial lawyers is to chalk up one more victory, thus demonstrating to future fatter-cat defendants that groundless legal theories are good enough when the coercive power of multiple government entities is arrayed against an unpopular industry.

When a private lawyer subcontracts his services to the government, he bears the same responsibility as a government lawyer. He is a public servant beholden to all citizens, including the defendant, and his overriding objective is to seek justice. Imagine state attorneys paid contingency fees for each indictment that they secure, or state troopers paid for each speeding ticket they issue. The potential for corruption is enormous. Still, the states in their tobacco suits doled out multibillion-dollar contracts to private counsel—not per-hour fee agreements, which might occasionally be justified to acquire unique outside competence or experience, but contingency fees, a sure-fire catalyst for abuse of power. And those contracts were awarded, without competitive bidding, to lawyers who often bankrolled state political campaigns.[8]

Government is the single entity authorized, in narrowly defined circumstances, to wield coercive power against private citizens. When that government functions as prosecutor or plaintiff in a legal proceeding in which it also dispenses punishment, adequate safeguards against state misbehavior are essential. That is why in civil litigation we rely primarily upon private remedies with redress sought by, and for the benefit of, the injured party and not the state. As the Supreme Court cautioned more than 60 years ago, an attorney for the state "is the representative not of an ordinary party to a controversy, but of a sovereignty whose obligation to govern impartially is as compelling as its obligation to govern at all."[9]

Put bluntly, contingency fee contracts between government and a private attorney should be illegal. We cannot in a free society condone private lawyers enforcing public law with an incentive kicker to increase the penalties.

Third, and perhaps most important, laws are supposed to be enacted by legislatures, not by the executive or judicial branches. In too many instances, government-sponsored litigation has been a substitute for failed legislation. That process violates the principle of separation of powers—a centerpiece of the federal constitution and no less important at the state level. Evidently, none of that matters to many of the attorneys general, mayors, and their allies in the private bar. In an attempt to circumvent the legislative process, they intend to pursue through litigation what was rejected by the legislature.

It's interesting to contrast the legal perspective on product prohibition that prevailed in 1919 with the view that prevails now—eight decades later. In 1919, we understood that Congress did not have the power to prohibit the sale of alcohol, so prohibition was accomplished by a constitutional amendment (the 18th). Today, the drug war is entirely statutory with little thought of its constitutional implications. When it comes to tobacco, the Clinton administration argued that not only did we not need a constitutional amendment, we also didn't need a statute—just a delegation of some sort to an unelected and unaccountable administrative agency (the Food and Drug Administration) with the authority to ban nicotine.[10] And in the case of guns, it seems we don't need a constitutional amendment, or a statute, or a delegation, just multiple lawsuits by means of which the executive branch uses the judicial branch to bypass the legislature and effectuate a variety of gun prohibitions. So much for limited government and separation of powers. We're left with the executive state. Return of the king. That's the regime under which dozens of cities, aided by the Clinton administration, took the gun battle to the courts—suing gun makers for "negligently marketing" a "defective product."

But before discussing those lawsuits, a quick but important detour.

To Keep and Bear Arms

At the same time that cities are suing the gun industry, a Texas appeals court is reviewing a lower court decision that invalidated a federal statute on Second Amendment grounds. Thus, the Supreme Court, for the first time in over 60 years, may soon revisit the right to keep and bear arms. Does the Second Amendment secure that right? If so, what restrictions can governments place on its exercise? The answers to those questions could determine the outcome of litigation, and legislation as well, directed at stricter gun control. So let's look briefly at the underlying constitutional issue.

"A well regulated Militia, being necessary to the security of a free State, the right of the people to keep and bear Arms, shall not be infringed." That's the text of the Second Amendment; and here's the question that seems to have perplexed the Supreme Court for more than 200 years: Does the right to keep and bear arms, as laid out in the Second Amendment, belong to each of us as individuals, or does it belong to us collectively as members of the militia?

59

Here's the answer: The Second Amendment, like the First and Fourth Amendments, refers explicitly to "the right of the people." No reasonable person can doubt that First Amendment rights—speech, religion, assembly, and redress of grievances—belong to us as individuals. Similarly, Fourth Amendment protections against unreasonable searches and seizures are individual rights. We secure "the right of the people" by guaranteeing the right of each person. In the context of the Second Amendment, it does not protect the state, but each individual *against* the state—that is, the amendment is a deterrent to government tyranny.[11]

Some would insist, although the threat of tyrannical government has not disappeared, it is less today than it was when our republic was experiencing its birth pangs. Perhaps so. Tyranny may well be a lesser threat now, but incompetence by the state in defending its citizens against criminals is a greater threat. The demand for police to defend us increases in proportion to our inability to defend ourselves. That's why disarmed societies tend to become police states. Witness law-abiding inner city residents, many of whom have been disarmed by gun control, begging for police protection against drug gangs despite the terrible violations of civil liberties that such protection entails—like curfews, anti-loitering laws, civil asset forfeiture, even nonconsensual searches of public housing.

So even if a reduced threat of government tyranny no longer requires an armed citizenry, an unarmed citizenry could well create the conditions that lead to tyranny. The right to bear arms is thus prophylactic rather than remedial—it reduces the demand for a police state. George Washington University law professor Robert Cottrol puts it this way: "A people incapable of protecting themselves will lose their rights as a free people, becoming either servile dependents of the state or of the criminal predators who are their de facto masters."[12]

More than 60 years ago, in 1939, the Supreme Court looked at the question of individual right or collective right in *United States v. Miller*.[13] The statute in *Miller* was the 1934 National Firearms Act, which required registration of machine guns, sawed-off rifles, sawed-off shotguns, and silencers. First, said the Court, "militia" is a term of art that means "the body of the people capable of bearing arms."[14] That suggested a right belonging to all of us, as individuals. But the Court also held that the right to bear arms extended only to weapons rationally related to the militia—not a sawed-off shotgun, which was at issue in *Miller*.

That mixed ruling has puzzled legal scholars for six decades. If military use is the decisive test, then one would think today's citizens can possess rocket launchers, missiles, and even nuclear arms. Obviously, that's not what the Court had in mind. Because the Court's opinion in *Miller* is so murky, argues George Mason University law professor Nelson Lund, maybe the only lesson we can draw is that the case must be interpreted narrowly, allowing restrictions on those types of weapons covered by the 1934 Act—weapons like machine guns and silencers, which are of slight value to law-abiding citizens, and of high value to criminals.[15]

Apparently, that's the position that a few renowned, liberal law professors are now taking. It started with a famous 1989 article, "The Embarrassing Second Amendment," by professor Sanford Levinson in the *Yale Law Journal*.[16] For the first time, a prominent liberal acknowledged that the Second Amendment should be treated as something more than an inkblot. Evidently, the liberal apostasy has caught on. Harvard professor Laurence Tribe and Yale professor Akhil Amar concede that there's an individual right to keep and bear arms, albeit limited as in *Miller* by "reasonable regulation in the interest of public safety."[17]

In effect, they argue that the Second Amendment, like the First Amendment, is not absolute. "Reasonable" restrictions—for example, on the types of weapons that can be purchased—may be justified on cost-benefit grounds. On the other hand, Tribe and Amar imply that the Fourteenth Amendment binds the states, not just the federal government, to honor the Second Amendment. In that respect, the two professors go further than our federal appellate courts, which have taken a states' rights approach to the Second Amendment—rubber-stamping state gun prohibitions without subjecting them to rigorous constitutional scrutiny.

That difference between federal and state treatment is important in answering one of the arguments frequently raised against the Second Amendment by anti-gun advocates. For example, the Center to Prevent Handgun Violence makes this argument: When our nation was founded, many states had communal storage of guns and restricted their use to white males only. Maryland actually seized guns that weren't used in the militia; Pennsylvania denied firearms to 40% of its citizens for lack of virtue. Therefore, the framers could not have intended an individual right to keep and bear arms. But here's the missing link: Until 1868 when the Fourteenth Amendment was ratified, the Bill of Rights constrained only the federal government. What the states did prior to that time is not directly relevant from a constitutional perspective.

With that brief background, let's turn next to an important new case, *United States v. Emerson*, in Lubbock, Texas, which could be the first Second Amendment case to reach the Supreme Court in more than six decades.[18] In Texas, like many other states, spouses involved in divorce proceedings can be placed under a court order restraining them from harassing, stalking, or threatening their partner. A federal statute makes it illegal for anyone under that type of restraining order to possess a gun. Emerson was indicted under the federal statute, although there was no proof that he planned a violent act against his wife. He contested his indictment on Second Amendment grounds. In April 1999 a federal judge dismissed the indictment, agreeing with Emerson that the statute violated the Second Amendment. The government appealed; the case has been argued and a decision is now awaited from the U.S. Court of Appeals for the Fifth Circuit.

The trial judge, Samuel Cummings, didn't equivocate. He said: "If the amendment truly meant what the collective rights advocates propose, then the text would read, 'A well regulated Militia being necessary to the security of a free State, the right of the *states* [or the militia] to keep and bear arms shall not be infringed.'"[19] Cummings might have added that a collective right, if conferred on the states, would permit "state governments [to] maintain military organizations independent from the federal military, and to arm those organizations with nuclear weapons or whatever else the state may choose."[20] A states' rights approach would also suggest that "Supreme Court decisions recognizing that the federal government has final authority over the deployment and use of the National Guard must be incorrect."[21]

When Cummings parsed the two clauses of the Second Amendment, he concluded that "The function of the subordinate clause was not to qualify the right, but instead to show why it must be protected. . . . If this right were not protected, the existence of the militia, and consequently the security of the state, would be jeopardized."[22] In other words, the second clause ("the right of the people to keep and bear Arms, shall not be infringed") is operational; it secures the right. The first clause ("A well regulated Militia, being necessary to the security of a free State") is explanatory; it justifies the right. That syntax was not unusual for the times. For example, the free press clause of the 1842 Rhode Island Constitution states:[23] "The liberty of the press being essential to the security of freedom in a state, any person may publish his sentiments of any subject." That provision surely doesn't mean that the right to publish protects only the press. It protects "any person"; and *one* reason among others that it protects any person is that a free press is essential to a free society.

In a similar vein, Article I, section 8 of the U.S. Constitution gives Congress the power to grant copyrights in order to "Promote progress of Science and useful Arts." Yet copyrights are also granted to *Hustler* magazine, to racist publications, even to literature that expressly seeks to retard science and the useful arts.[24] The proper understanding of the copyright provision is that promoting science and the arts is one justification—but not the only justification—for the copyright power. Analogously, the militia clause helps explain why we have a right to bear arms, but it's not necessary to the exercise of that right.

As you might guess, that was not the position of the Clinton administration. Consider this exchange at the oral argument before the Fifth Circuit in the *Emerson* case:[25]

Judge William L. Garwood: "You are saying that the Second Amendment is consistent with a position that you can take guns away from the public? You restrict ownership of rifles, pistols, and shotguns from all people? Is that the position of the United States?"

Deputy U.S. Attorney General William Meteja: "Yes."

Garwood: "Is it the position of the United States that persons who are not in the National Guard are afforded no protections under the Second Amendment?"

Meteja: "Exactly."

Meteja later explained that even Guard members are protected by the Second Amendment only when and to the extent that their weapon is used for Guard business.

For those who believe that the Constitution means what it says, here's another text-based argument: The term "well-regulated," in its 18th century context, didn't mean *heavily* regulated, but rather *properly, not overly* regulated. Looked at in that manner, the Second Amendment ensures that the militia would not be improperly regulated, even weakened—say by disarming the citizens who would be its soldiers.[26]

Bear in mind that Article I, section 8 gives Congress, not the states, the power to call forth and "provide for organizing, arming, . . . disciplining . . . and for governing" the militia. State powers are limited to appointing officers and training. The framers feared and distrusted standing armies; so they provided for a federal militia—all able-bodied males over the age of 17—as a counterweight against potential tyranny. But the framers also realized, in granting Congress near-plenary power over the militia, that a select, armed militia subset—like today's National Guard—could be equivalent to a standing army. So they wisely crafted the Second Amendment to forbid Congress from disarming other citizens, thereby certifying that the militia would be "well-regulated."[27]

Consider also these three changes made by the 1789 Congress when it drafted the Amendment: First, a provision excusing conscientious objectors from military service was eliminated—making it clear that the Second Amendment is about firearms, not about military service. Second, the term "well-armed" was stripped as a modifier of "militia"—again clarifying that the arms were those of the people, not those of the military. Third, the phrase "for the common defense" was dropped after the words "to keep and bear arms"—no ambiguity there; the intent was to provide an individual right of defense, not common defense.[28]

Finally, it's worth noting that there are at least three other constitutional arguments against gun control, apart from the Second Amendment: (1) Many gun regulations are too vague and thus don't provide citizens with adequate notice of the particular acts that are illegal. That offends the Due Process Clause. (2) Some federal controls may intrude on matters traditionally subject to state supervision, or may exceed the powers of Congress enumerated in Article I, section 8. That would violate the Tenth Amendment. (3) An individual right to keep and bear arms could well be among the unenumerated rights secured by the Ninth Amendment.

Litigation Tyranny

Now let's switch gears—from constitutional law to tort law—as we turn to the deluge of lawsuits against the gun industry: first, the federal government claims, which the Bush administration will probably not pursue, then the litigation by more than 30 cities and counties as well as by New York state.

Federal Claims

At the federal level, Clinton's HUD secretary, Andrew Cuomo, had a plan to change the way the nation's gun makers do business. Already smothered by litigation from dozens of cities and counties, the gun industry would have been crushed under the weight of legal action from a horde of 3,200 housing authorities synchronized by HUD. The government wanted to hold gun makers responsible for defraying the cost of security guards and for alarm systems installed to curb violence in public housing.[29]

Like the cities, HUD said it was not interested in money damages. Maybe so, but Cuomo and his acolytes understood very well that the small gun industry couldn't afford to defend itself—even against unfounded suits—in the face of such overwhelming firepower. A *Wall Street Journal* story emphasized that very point: "As with the municipal suits, one filed on behalf of housing authorities would be groundbreaking and certainly not a sure bet to succeed in court. But a suit by a large group of housing authorities could [exhaust] gun companies' resources in pretrial maneuvering—by making demands for documents concerning industry distribution practices in hundreds or thousands of localities."[30] That's no better than thinly veiled blackmail.

In justifying HUD's litigation plans, Cuomo contended that "only one percent of the dealers are selling over 50 percent of the guns used in crimes."[31] But if crimes were linked to guns sold by particular dealers, why weren't the underlying data turned over to authorities whose duty it is to shut down dealerships that break laws against those sales—laws that are on the books in all 50 states? Instead, Cuomo sought to compel gun makers to become police, judge, and jury—to ferret out "bad" dealers, some of whom were entirely innocent, and deny to those dealers, without due process of law, the merchandise that they sell for a living.

That was just the beginning. Cuomo also demanded safer guns. "We have safety caps on aspirin," he says, so why not safety locks on guns?[32] Well, let's see, there are a couple of relevant differences between guns and aspirin. The requirement for safety caps on aspirin arose out of legislation, not judicial mandate. Aspirin is legally accessible to kids; guns aren't. Furthermore, not many people when confronted with an emergency will turn to a bottle of aspirin for protection. Use of a gun for self defense could be dangerously compromised if the gun is locked. Listen to Sammy "The Bull" Gravano, the Mafia turncoat, quoted in *Vanity Fair*: "Safety locks? You . . . pull the trigger with a lock on, and I'll pull the trigger [without one]. We'll see who wins."[33]

Actually, if Cuomo was concerned about unsafe public housing, he should have sued his own agency.[34] HUD is responsible for housing authorities—including their location, selection of tenants, eviction policies, even inadequate policing. But rather than admit to the abject failure of public housing, Cuomo instructed his minions to plan lawsuits, modeled after those filed by cities and counties from coast to coast. Here are the two principal legal theories.

Negligent Marketing

The city of Chicago, and other cities following its example, accused gun makers of "negligent marketing"—flooding the suburbs, where gun laws are relaxed, with more guns than suburban residents will buy, knowing that the excess guns will find their way to the inner city, where gun laws are more restrictive.

Simple economic logic puts the lie to Chicago's negligent marketing claim. If gun makers reduce the supply of firearms sold to suburban dealers, the market price of guns will rise. Consumers with the most "elastic" demand—that is, consumers who are most sensitive to price changes—will reduce or eliminate their purchases. The evidence is clear: Those price-sensitive consumers are typically law-abiding citizens. By contrast, criminals' demand for guns is highly "inelastic." They operate in a "survival at any price" environment—which is why crooks are willing to pay inflated black-market prices for firearms. Perversely, by restricting the legal supply of guns and raising prices, manufacturers will put relatively more weapons in criminals' hands and relatively fewer in the hands of honest citizens.

Besides, any coordinated industry response to a negligent marketing claim would surely run afoul of the antitrust laws. Manufacturers that supposedly overproduce would have to collude in order to reduce production jointly. Yes, Smith & Wesson knows how many of its guns are going to, say, Maryland. But those guns, by them-selves, don't come close to saturating the Maryland market. And Smith & Wesson has no idea how many Maryland guns are shipped by Colt, Beretta, Glock, Ruger, or any other manufacturer. Because brands are more or less interchangeable, no single gun maker would agree to cut back production for fear that other manufacturers would simply take up the slack. An antitrust suit is sure to follow.

Compare the gun model with dram shop laws, which hold bar-tenders liable when they continue to ply an obviously drunk patron with liquor knowing full well that the customer could kill himself or others when he drives home. Whatever the merit of those laws, the analogy in the gun context is not to hold the bartender, or even the bar owner, responsible. Instead, it's the equivalent of holding Seagrams or Anheuser Busch accountable for the ensuing drunk driving fatality.

An obvious solution to Chicago's problem, said the judge who dismissed the city's case in September 2000,[35] would be for the police to enforce laws that already prohibit sales to minors, felons, the mentally incompetent, and anyone else without a state-issued fire-arm owner's ID card. Instead, Chicago sued gun makers—who law-fully sell to wholesalers who, in turn, sell to licensed retailers. The city wants to hold gun makers liable for the violent acts of criminals, most of whom did not buy from licensed retailers and over whom the manufacturers have no control. As the Seventh Circuit held in a 1989 case, *Bloomington v. Westinghouse*,[36] a manufacturer is not liable for creation of a nuisance by the buyer unless the manufacturer participated in the conduct.

The chain of causation is broken when a criminal act intervenes between a gun maker's original sale and an injury arising out of the gun's violent use. That time-honored principle of law, by itself, is sufficient to dismiss these cases. A gun maker is liable only if the risk of injury was foreseeable. And when the law says "foreseeable," it doesn't mean merely possible; it means that the intervening crimi-nal act was the natural and probable outcome of the gun maker's sale.[37] Yes, Americans own roughly 250 million guns and commit about 500,000 gun-related crimes each year.[38] But even if a different gun is used in each of those crimes, only two-tenths of 1% of all guns are involved in criminal activity in any given year. That negligi-ble chance of criminal conduct surely doesn't cross the "natural and probable outcome" threshold.

The manufacture, sale, and ownership of handguns are highly regulated. If a gun dealer knowingly condones so-called straw purchases—that is, those made by legal buyers, but on behalf of criminals—the dealer can be prosecuted under current law. As of April 2000, 17 months after Chicago filed its lawsuit, only four of the retailers targeted by the city's undercover "stings" had been charged. In the one case to go to trial, the jury took but 10 minutes to find the defendant not guilty.[39] If the behavior of those dealers was as egregious as the city's complaint suggests, why were there only four indictments and zero convictions?

More generally, gun control authorities David Kopel and Richard Gardiner point out that

> Handguns are the only consumer product which an American consumer is forbidden to purchase outside his state of residence. They are the only mass consumer product for which retailers, wholesalers, and manufacturers all require federal licenses. They are among a tiny handful of consumer products for which the federal government regulates simple possession, and further regulates the terms of retail transactions, going so far as to require (for handguns) that police be notified and given an opportunity to disapprove the sale before being allowed to consummate the transaction.[40]

Nationwide, thousands of laws regulate everything from who can own a gun and how it can be purchased to where one can possess or use it.[41] Yet, in 1998, thousands of guns were brought illegally onto school grounds; there were only eight federal prosecutions.[42] From 1992 to 1999, according to a Syracuse University study, federal gun prosecutions declined by 43%.[43] Over the two years ending in mid-1999, half of the guns used in crimes were traced by the Bureau of Alcohol, Tobacco and Firearms to 389 dealers, but only 19 had their licenses revoked.[44] Julius Wachtel, who retired after 23 years as a BATF agent, remarked that he and his co-workers had a saying: "No cases, no waves; little cases, little waves; big cases, big waves."[45]

A BATF study released in June 2000 documented 1,700 federal and state gun-law prosecutions from July 1996 through December 1998.[46] On a per-year basis, that's 680 prosecutions—a trivial number when contrasted with roughly 500,000 gun crimes committed in the United States each year.

The effect of more rigorous law enforcement and stiffer penalties is apparent from Richmond's experience with Project Exile—a federal program that, in part, mandates a five-year minimum sentence in federal prison for any felon caught carrying or trying to buy a gun. Richmond reported a 36% decline in gun homicides and a 37% drop in armed robberies for the 1997 calendar year.[47] When the National Rifle Association sought to expand Project Exile, it received little support from the Clinton administration until September 1999, at which time the president requested an inconsequential budget increase of $5 million. Congressional Republicans had wanted $25 million, albeit targeted at cities in states where the senators on the Appropriations Committee served, not at cities where crime rates were highest.[48]

To be sure, the states, and not the federal government, exercise general police power. Why should federal courts be turned into what one federal judge in Richmond characterized as "police courts"[49]? Far better for the states to stiffen their own penalties than to federalize yet more crimes. Indeed, the federalization of most gun crimes cannot be squared with the Tenth Amendment, which instructs that the federal government may exercise only those powers that are enumerated in the Constitution and delegated by it to the United States. Still, many federal criminal laws would qualify as a legitimate exercise of state police power. In any event, nonenforcement—whether state or federal—cannot be laid at the doorstep of gun makers.

Naturally, if existing laws are not being enforced, the best bet, if you believe the politicians, is to pass more laws. In the Chicago suburbs, the legislative unit is Cook County, which could have enacted more restrictive gun laws. For whatever reasons, it chose not to do so. Instead, Cook County signed on as coplaintiff in Chicago's lawsuit. It wanted the judicial branch to do what the county elected not to do. Think about it: Cook County's complaint to the court, quite literally, is that the county has itself failed to pass appropriate legislation. In effect, Cook County's plea is "Stop me before I don't legislate again," which must be a first in American jurisprudence.[50]

Defective Product

Apart from negligent marketing, the second major claim among cities suing the gun industry is that firearms are "defective and unreasonably dangerous" as they are currently manufactured. How are the firearms defective? Do they misfire, or fire inaccurately? Not at all. Even the *Washington Post* has editorialized: "As a legal matter, it is hard to see how companies making lawful products can be held liable when those products perform precisely as intended."[51] No matter. First New Orleans, then other cities, insisted that guns are defective if they are sold without devices that prevent discharge by unauthorized users. On that ground, the cities hope to drag gun makers to the settlement table—turning the law of product liability on its head.

True enough, some guns have features that are particularly attractive to criminals. But that may be because criminals value many of the same features that appeal to law enforcement officers. Legislatures across the nation have regulated virtually every aspect of gun design and distribution. If a determination is to be made that guns are unreasonably dangerous, the legislature, constrained by the Constitution, must make that determination, not the courts. Here's how a federal judge in Massachusetts put it in a 1996 case, *Wasylow v. Glock*: "Frustration at the failure of legislatures to enact laws sufficient to curb handgun injuries is not adequate reason to engage the judicial forum in efforts to implement a broad policy change."[52]

Even Brooklyn's Jack Weinstein, the favorite federal judge of the plaintiffs' bar, had this comment about the safety of guns: "Whether or not . . . products liability law would require an anti-theft safety mechanism as part of the design of handguns requires a balancing of the risk and utility. . . . Plaintiffs have not shown that such a device is available, nor have they asserted the possibility of showing at trial that such a device would satisfy the . . . risk-utility test." Weinstein added, "The mere act of manufacturing and selling a handgun does not give rise to liability absent a defect in the manufacture or design of the product itself."[53]

When it comes to guns, New Orleans city officials are singularly unsuited to be the guardians of public safety. In 1998 the city's police department traded more than 8,000 confiscated weapons—40% of which were semi-automatic—to a commercial dealer in return for Glocks. Nearly half of the traded guns would have been characterized as "unsafe" in the city's lawsuit against gun makers—including TEC9s, AK47s, and Uzis, banned unless made before 1994. Only one-fourth of the guns had safety locks. Still, Mayor Marc Morial signed and approved the deal, paving the way for resale of those guns across the nation.[54] Ironically, New Orleans could end up as a defendant in other cities' suits.

Under pressure, Morial suspended the swap program.[55] But New Orleans wasn't the only hypocritical plaintiff. Police departments in Boston, Detroit, Oakland, Miami, St. Louis, and Bridgeport also traded-in "unsafe" guns, which are now back on the street, even while suing gun makers for marketing a defective product.[56] Undoubtedly as a result of the bad publicity, several police departments announced that they would explore a lease program, rather than trade-ins, with Glock.[57] Yes, that might relieve the city of direct responsibility for providing unsafe guns for commercial resale. But the revised contractual arrangement is mere camouflage for basically the same deal—that is, a so-called defective product is first used by the police and then recycled for use by private citizens.

Whether the claim is a defective product, negligent marketing, or public nuisance, these lawsuits are rubbish. Five of them have reached final judgment and all five were fully or partially dismissed.[58] In October 1999, an Ohio state judge threw out Cincinnati's claims. He wrote that gun makers are not responsible for the criminal misconduct of customers. "The city's complaint is an improper attempt to have this court substitute its judgment for that of the legislature."[59] The "design, manufacture and distribution of a lawful product" is not a public nuisance.[60]

Bridgeport's and Miami's suits were also dismissed in December 1999. Miami's judge observed that the city cannot use the courts to regulate; that's the job of the legislature.[61] A Florida appeals court upheld the Miami ruling, calling the lawsuit "an attempt to regulate firearms . . . through the . . . judiciary." "Clearly this round-about attempt is being made because of the County's frustration at its inability to regulate firearms," the appeals court wrote. "The County's frustration cannot be alleviated through litigation."[62]

In Chicago on September 15, 2000, a judge threw out that city's negligent marketing claim saying that statistical evidence of causation wasn't good enough, and that individual instances of illegal sales were a matter for the police to counter.[63] Then, on December 21, 2000, a federal judge dismissed Philadelphia's claims, describing the city's charge of public nuisance as "a theory in search of a case," and rejecting the negligence claim "for lack of proximate cause."[64]

Nevertheless, the trial lawyers press forward. Sooner or later they're likely to find, somewhere, a sympathetic judge who's willing to ignore the law in order to effectuate his personal policy preferences. It's called forum shopping, and it's a favorite tactic of the plaintiffs' bar. In fact, the major reason each city has sued its local dealers as well as gun manufacturers is so the plaintiff and at least one defendant reside in the same jurisdiction. That way the case cannot be removed to federal court, where the rule of law generally prevails—outweighing provincial prejudices.

While the search for friendly forums moves ahead, pending lawsuits are having predictable effects: Smaller gun makers are going out of business; two California dealers have declared bankruptcy; Colt announced a layoff of 300 workers, then said it would withdraw from the consumer handgun business, focusing instead on military weapons and collectibles.[65] Prospective litigation costs are showing up in higher gun prices. Top quality handguns are now priced in the $350 to $550 range, and fewer guns are available for less than $100.[66] Not surprisingly, higher prices have less impact on criminal demand than on the demand from price-sensitive, law-abiding citizens—especially those living in the inner cities.

On a parallel track, threatened litigation by the federal government and actual litigation by dozens of cities were used as a bludgeon to force the industry's largest manufacturer, Smith & Wesson, into a settlement. Despite countervailing pressure from its customers and other gun makers, Smith & Wesson threw in the towel—explaining that $100 million or more in damages, sought by several of the larger cities, exceeded the company's profits for the entire past decade. Moreover, the company protested, it cost $1 million to defend against each government-sponsored claim.[67] Smith & Wesson simply didn't have the resources to fight multiple lawsuits across the country. Accordingly, on March 17, 2000, it surrendered.

Smith & Wesson Settlement

Essentially, the Smith & Wesson deal is no better than a shakedown. Various government entities—HUD at the federal level, New York and Connecticut at the state level, and 13 cities—agreed not to pursue their baseless but costly litigation against the company. Other cities and counties offered to review their suits, but made no formal commitment to exclude Smith & Wesson.[68] In return, the gun maker pledged, first, to impose the following restrictions on its dealers and distributors: (a) No sales of any manufacturer's guns unless the buyer has passed a safety course and cleared a background check—even if the check takes longer than the three-day period required by law. (b) No sales at any gun show unless all sales at the show are subject to a background check.[69] (c) No sales of Smith & Wesson guns if a "disproportionate number of crimes" are traced to guns sold by a dealer or distributor.[70] (d) No purchase by one person of more than one gun at a time unless the buyer is willing to wait 14 days before picking up the rest.[71]

Second, Smith & Wesson agreed to childproof all of its handguns within a year, presumably by using features like a heavier trigger pull or a magazine disconnect, which prevents a gun from firing once the magazine is removed. Under terms of the settlement, every Smith & Wesson handgun would also be equipped with an external lock within 60 days and an internal lock within 24 months.[72]

Third, each gun would have a hidden serial number to facilitate tracing the weapon if it were used in a crime.[73] Fourth (reminiscent of the tobacco settlement that forced manufacturers to fund anti-smoking programs), Smith & Wesson promised to "work together to support legislative efforts to reduce firearm misuse" and contribute 1% of its revenue toward an "education trust fund" to inform the public about the risk of firearms.[74] The specific content of the anti-gun campaign will be determined by a five-member Oversight Committee in each settling city. That same committee—comprising one Smith & Wesson official and one representative each from the city, county, state, and federal government—will monitor and supervise all provisions of the settlement.[75]

Those terms and conditions obscure what is actually driving the settlement. From the government's perspective, the settlement was a means to bypass state and federal legislatures that had been singularly unresponsive to a variety of gun control proposals. Moreover, the settlement circumvents court review in many jurisdictions. Judicial approval would be required only in jurisdictions where lawsuits had already been filed and were to be dismissed as a condition of the settlement. That excludes the suits threatened but not filed by HUD and various cities and states.

From the company's perspective, the settlement represented an opportunity to avoid the cost, time, and uncertainty of overhanging litigation. That opportunity took on special meaning in the case of Smith & Wesson, which is owned by a United Kingdom company that was looking to sell its investment.[76] The market for acquisitions is materially diminished, however, when lawsuits lurk menacingly in the background.

To sweeten the deal further, President Clinton sought to assemble the Communities for Safer Guns Coalition, an alliance of local governments, along with HUD, that would refrain from buying police firearms manufactured by any company that didn't sign the settlement. That commitment to favor Smith & Wesson was not embedded in the text of the settlement agreement, but communicated informally by Clinton.[77] Perhaps that's because he knew that a refusal to deal might violate local and federal procurement regulations, discriminate against law-abiding gun makers, and deny disfavored companies the right to pursue a legitimate business.

In June 2000 the House of Representatives attempted, unsuccessfully, to pass a bill prohibiting enforcement of the Smith & Wesson settlement. But the House did approve a provision that would prevent spending in support of Clinton's coalition, which ultimately comprised 600 localities that agreed, first, not to sue Smith & Wesson and, second, to favor the company in police gun buys.[78] That was followed a month later by Senate approval of a bill barring federal procurement preferences for Smith & Wesson.[79] With a change in administration, the settlement probably will not attract other gun makers as cosigners, nor is the settlement likely to benefit Smith & Wesson, which announced this past June that it was closing two of its plants for a month, partly due to adverse customer reaction.[80]

As the real terms of the settlement (including preferential contracting) became clear, seven gun makers and their trade association, the National Shooting Sports Foundation, filed suit against HUD Secretary Cuomo, New York Attorney General Eliot Spitzer, Connecticut Attorney General Richard Blumenthal, and 14 mayors for conspiring to violate the constitutional right of the gun makers to engage in trade. The plaintiffs asked a federal court to forbid new gun regulations that were not authorized by Congress.[81] By August 2000, however, it was apparent that the buying preferences had not materialized. Police departments, for obvious reasons, wanted the best weapons available. Even HUD bought guns from Glock,[82] which did not sign the settlement yet continued to supply roughly two-thirds of police weapons nationwide.[83] In January 2001, NSSF and the seven gun makers dropped their suit.[84]

On another front, to intensify the pressure for a settlement, Cuomo, Spitzer, and Blumenthal threatened an antitrust suit against Smith & Wesson's rivals for organizing a boycott against that company's products. Blumenthal issued subpoenas for documents, despite no "solid evidence" other than a post-settlement industry meeting attended by a number of gun makers, who expressed criticism of Smith & Wesson and the settlement.[85] Spitzer pulled no punches. The goal, he gloated, is to "squeeze [gun] manufacturers like a pincers"[86]—proving once again that unprincipled politicians are more than willing to use the antitrust laws as a club to force conformity by companies that refuse to play ball.

Guns, Crime, and Accidents

Paradoxically, politicians who are busily abusing the rule of law, and zealots so eager to put gun makers out of business, overlook compelling statistics suggesting that the anti-gun crusade, if successful, would leave Americans more, not less, susceptible to gun violence. Three thousand criminals are lawfully killed each year by armed civilians. By comparison, fewer than 1,000 criminals are killed annually by police.[87] Guns are used defensively—often merely brandished, not fired—over two million times per year.[88] That's far more than the 483,000 gun-related crimes reported to police in 1996.[89]

Our country's most permissive gun carry laws are in Vermont, which has a very low crime rate.[90] Nationwide, as Yale scholar John Lott has demonstrated, the higher the number of carry permits in a state, the larger the drop in violent crime.[91] Half of our population lives in 31 states that have "shall issue" laws, which mandate that a permit be granted to anyone above the age of 21 who is mentally competent, has no criminal record, pays the requisite fee, and passes a gun safety course. Those states haven't turned into Dodge City, writes columnist Jonathan Rauch, "with fender-benders becoming hailstorms of lead."[92]

Actually, data show that Dodge City was safer than today's Washington, D.C.,[93] which has the highest gun murder rate in the United States, accompanied by the strictest gun control. Is that because guns are readily available in nearby Virginia? Then why is the District of

Columbia murder rate 57 per 100,000 while Arlington, Virginia, an urban community just across the river, has a rate of 1.6 per 100,000?[94] Social pathologies in the District of Columbia promote crime; guns in Virginia deter crime.

The reality is that less than 5% of the population take out concealed handgun permits.[95] The rest of us benefit because the criminals don't know which 5% are armed. Laws permitting the carrying of concealed handguns reduce murder by about 8% and rape by about 5%.[96] Police carry guns; mayors and bodyguards carry guns; why not law-abiding residents of high crime areas?

In May 2000 the House of Representatives passed—by voice vote with almost no debate—a bill permitting federal judges (including bankruptcy judges and even some retired judges) to carry concealed guns in any state, despite state laws to the contrary. A Florida federal district judge, Harvey Schlesinger, had this to say: "If a judge is in danger, the fact that he or she is in one state or the other does not eliminate the danger."[97] He might have made the same statement about any person at risk.

It's a myth that high gun ownership is a cause of the high murder rate in the United States. In Australia, for example, the population was disarmed in 1998. Since then, homicides are up by 3.2%, assaults are up by 8.6%, and armed robberies are up by 44%. For 25 years, armed robberies and homicides committed with firearms in Australia had declined.[98] The Swiss, Finns, and New Zealanders each have an ownership rate similar to ours, but we have a far higher murder rate.[99] In Israel, gun ownership is 40% above the U.S. rate, but the murder rate is far lower.[100] When all countries are studied, there is no correlation between gun ownership and murder rates.

Interestingly, in Israel, armed teachers are common,[101] and the terrorist threat is pervasive; but there are few terrorist attacks at schools. That's because armed civilians deter crime. An armed gun-store employee in Santa Clara, California, shot a customer who had threatened to kill three others. Armed citizens prevented massacres in Anniston, Alabama; Pearl, Mississippi; and Edinboro, Pennsylvania.[102] Yet the response of some politicians is to disarm those citizens. Meanwhile, madmen in Rwanda murdered almost a million people in less than four months using nothing but machetes.[103]

Gun control advocates reject that analysis and point instead to a study by Arthur Kellerman, who concluded that families possessing a gun are 22 times more likely to kill a family member or acquaintance than to kill in self-defense.[104] But what is not factored into the Kellerman equation is that guns are rarely fired; the value of the gun is to deter, not to kill. Moreover, 85% of the deaths that Kellerman cites are suicides.[105] He explains that suicides are five times more likely if there is a gun in the home.[106] But that has the causal relationship exactly backwards: It isn't possession of a gun that causes someone to decide on suicide; instead, emotionally disturbed people acquire a gun precisely because they intend, or may be psychologically prone, to commit suicide.

Again conflating cause and effect, Kellerman notes that a handgun in the home raises the risk of death by 3.4 times.[107] Yet he misses the obvious link: People at risk buy guns; the risk motivates the purchase, not vice versa. By analogy, a storeowner might decide to put iron bars on his store windows if the store were located in a high crime area. Surely, no one would suggest that the store would be safer if it removed the bars. Nor would a family in a high-risk inner-city environment be safer if it got rid of its handgun. The gun, like the bars, serves to safeguard lives and property.

Remember that each individual could well be the sole means of his own defense. In the words of Kopel and Gardiner:

> Governments are immune from suit for failure—even grossly negligent or deliberate failure—to protect citizens from crime. Similarly, governments are immune from suit for injuries inflicted by criminals who were given early release on parole. Accordingly, it would be highly inappropriate for the government, through the courts, to make it . . . impossible for persons to own handguns for self-defense because, supposedly, ordinary Americans are too stupid and clumsy to use them effectively. If the Judiciary will not question the government's civil immunity for failure to protect people, the courts certainly should not let themselves become a vehicle that deprives people of the tools they need to protect themselves.[108]

Ask yourself whether you'd be willing to put a sign on your house stating, "This home is a gun-free zone"[109]—especially if you lived in the inner city.

While we're on the topic of the inner city, National Association for the Advancement of Colored People head Kweisi Mfume acknowledges that there are "pathologies in any society that contribute to violence"[110]—for example, teenage pregnancy, dysfunctional schools, drug and alcohol abuse, and a welfare system that subsidizes illegitimacy and unemployment. And Professor Cottrol reminds us that late-19th-to-early-20th century state gun control laws were aimed specifically at keeping guns away from ex-slaves, other blacks, and recent immigrants.[111] Cottrol, a self-described Hubert Humphrey Democrat, also writes that "Bans on firearms ownership in public housing, the constant effort to ban pistols poor people can afford—scornfully labeled 'Saturday Night Specials' and more recently 'junk guns'—are denying the means of self-defense to entire communities in a failed attempt to disarm criminal predators."[112]

Or listen to Gregory Kane, an African-American columnist for the *Baltimore Sun*: "The NAACP should be assuring that every law-abiding citizen in America's black communities has a safe, affordable handgun. . . . These young men are smart enough to know that the combined forces of city and state governments, Bill Clinton, the police, the NAACP, and the outrage of gun controllers won't protect them."[113] Civil rights activist Charles Evers was even more blunt: "I put my trust in God and my .45 . . . and not always in that order."[114]

One would have thought that, before filing its lawsuit, the NAACP would have examined the historical record. In 1967, a 13-year-old could buy a rifle from most hardware stores or even through the mail. Very few states had retail age restrictions for handguns. Until 1969, most New York city high schools had a shooting club; students regularly competed in shooting contests; and the federal government paid for rifles and ammunition.[115] Federal and state gun laws today are far more restrictive than they were three decades ago. Yet, until the 1990s, more laws went hand in hand with an explosion of violent crime.

When gun ownership rates were constant during the 60s and 70s, violent crime skyrocketed. With ownership rates growing during the 90s, we have seen dramatic reductions in crime.[116] Recent statistics from the Bureau of Justice Statistics show that gun deaths and woundings declined by 33% from 1993 through 1997, with the decline continuing in 1998. Over the same interval, the number of circulating guns in the United States grew by 10%.[117] In short, despite misleading reports from the media, there is no evidence to suggest that gun ownership and violent crime are directly linked.

And speaking of the media: Is it likely that the press would have been so interested in Buford Furrow—the neo-Nazi who killed a mailman and wounded five others at a Los Angeles Jewish Center—if he weren't a poster boy for gun control? Jeff Jacoby, columnist for the *Boston Globe*, offers this answer: On May 3, 1999, Steven Abrams decided to "execute" children on a playground in Costa Mesa, California. He floored his 1967 Cadillac, plowed through a chain link fence into the crowd of children, killing two and injuring five others—a toll more grisly than Furrow's. The Associated Press ran a story two days later; six papers ran a follow-up four days afterward. That was it; no drumbeat of national news; no editorials or op-eds—and, of course, no gun.[118] Less than one year later, gun hysteria seemed to have gripped the nation: From the *Washington Post* in April 2000 we read, "Four 6-year-old boys were suspended from school for pointing fingers at one another as mock guns in a game of 'cops and robbers' on the playground."[119]

For the five years ending in 1997, the Centers for Disease Control and Prevention reported a 21% decrease in violent crime, 21% decrease in gun-related deaths, and 41% decrease in nonfatal gun injuries.[120] Gun deaths and overall homicides reached their lowest level in more than 30 years.[121] Some experts cite tougher gun control and safety courses, but that doesn't explain why all violent crime decreased by the same percentage as gun-related crime. The more likely reasons for the parallel decline are more vigorous enforcement, a booming economy, the waning crack trade, and an aging population.

CDC also reports that violent behavior by adolescents is declining sharply, despite Columbine and other high-profile school incidents. That's confirmed by data from the U.S. Department of Education indicating that expulsions for bringing firearms to school during the academic year 1997–98 were lower by one third from the previous year.[122] And it's not only teen violence but also teen accident rates that are plummeting. The National Center for Health Statistics reports that fatal gun accidents in 1997 among children were at an all-time low, down by 75% since 1975. Out of more than 32,000 gun-related deaths, only 630 were kids under 15. Of those, 142 were accidental.[123] Predictably, that good news was met by this outcry from the *Washington Post*: Safety locks will "reduce this country's horrifying accidental-gun-death rate of children under 15."[124]

Horrifying? More kids under 15 are killed by bikes, swimming pools, and cigarette lighters than by gun accidents.[125] Will our city mayors be pursuing each of those industries? If gun manufacturers are responsible for violence, why not the makers of the steel used in the guns? Indeed, when an Ohio appellate judge upheld the dismissal of Cincinnati's gun suit in August 2000, he wrote: "Were we to decide otherwise, we would open a Pandora's box. The city could sue the manufacturers of matches for arson, or automobile manufacturers for traffic accidents, or breweries for drunken driving."[126]

If anything, the case for holding carmakers liable for drunk driving accidents is stronger than the case for charging gun makers for gun-related injuries. "In contrast to gun dealers, automobile [manufacturers] make no effort at all to ensure that the buyer is not a criminal. Nor do automobile manufacturers require that their dealers take even minimal steps to check if a prospective automobile purchaser has recent convictions for drunk or reckless driving, or even for vehicular homicide."[127] Moreover, "automobile manufacturers have much more ability than gun manufacturers to control dealer behavior, since most automobile manufacturers have exclusive, direct relationships with dealers. In contrast, the majority of gun dealers purchase inventory from wholesalers" without affording manufacturers a reliable means to track retail purchases.[128]

Before we compromise the Constitution—undermining the principles of federalism and separation of powers, violating rights recognized expressly in the Second Amendment and implicitly in the Ninth—we ought to be sure of three things: First, that we've identified the real problem; second, that we've pinpointed its cause; and third, that our fix is less intrusive than alternative fixes. The spreading litigation against gun makers fails all three tests. Guns do not increase violence; they reduce violence. Banning or regulating firearms will not eliminate the underlying social pathologies that cause violence. And a less intrusive remedy already exists: enforce existing laws.

There is a lesson to be learned from all of this. If we do nothing to rein in baseless, government-sponsored lawsuits, private attorneys and their accomplices in the public sector will continue to invent legal theories to exact tribute from friendless industries. In the latest rounds of litigation, law-abiding gun manufacturers may be forced to pay for the actions of criminals. That outcome will likely entice politicians unwilling to make tough choices and enrich trial lawyers, but there can be no pretense that litigation of that sort has any basis at all in the rule of law.

Clinton Administration Proposals

Apparently, that logic wholly escaped the Clinton administration. About to be drowned in litigation from cities, counties, and more than 3,000 housing authorities, the gun industry was finding it hard to attract private investors to fund research on "smart guns"— personalized weapons incorporating technology that permits firing only by authorized parties. Not to worry, said President Clinton in his January 2000 State of the Union address. He and Sen. Ted Kennedy (D-MA) favored a $10 million research subsidy to Smith & Wesson to develop a smart weapon,[129] which could then no doubt be sold to presently unarmed suburban moms. Kristen Rand, from the anti-gun Violence Policy Center, said, "It makes the lawsuits seem like a charade."[130] Gun control and corporate welfare do indeed make strange bedfellows.

The depth of the hypocrisy in Washington during the Clinton era was beyond belief. The president called for draconian gun controls after Columbine, but told his Hollywood supporters, "There's no call for finger-pointing here." Although some young people will be pushed over the edge by violent imagery, that "doesn't make anybody who makes any movie or any video game or any television program a bad person or personally responsible. . . . For most kids it won't make any difference."[131] Clinton said he didn't want to lecture the entertainment industry—an ongoing source of major bucks. Then, to satisfy critics, he recommended an 18-month study to see if the industry deliberately markets violence to kids. Carefully timed so that no legislation would be possible until after the 2000 election, the study was guaranteed not to embarrass either Clinton himself or Al Gore's fundraisers.[132]

Meanwhile, Clinton and his surrogates offered a variety of gun control proposals. After six kids were trapped in the crossfire between rival gangs at the National Zoo in Washington, D.C., Gore bemoaned the shootings, then announced to a shocked audience of Democratic donors, "We really have to have mandatory child safety locks."[133] Laws against murder and a ban on handguns in the nation's capital didn't deter the young hoods, but the former vice president supposed they would somehow be foiled by safety locks.

Let's look at that proposal along with a few others, and see why none of them will work.

Safety locks. Gun accidents are not a significant problem. Locks are cumbersome and slow in an emergency. They're already available on 90% of new guns sold.[134] They give parents a false sense of security. In recent tests, 30 of 32 models of safety locks were found to afford inadequate protection. That generated calls for government-imposed standards, notwithstanding that not a single reported injury has been traced to an ineffective lock.[135]

Smart guns. Colt has estimated that 60 million nongun owners would consider buying smart guns.[136] At the same time, a smart gun mandate for new guns would have no effect on 250 million guns already in circulation. Smart guns may prevent some unauthorized use, but they can be programmed for multiple users and will not, therefore, deter straw purchases. Moreover, suicides and homicides, not accidents, are the two leading causes of gun death,[137] and most suicides and homicides are committed by the gun owner. In 1997 only three-tenths of 1% of gun-related deaths were accidental. Many of those accidents involved owners cleaning their guns; and many others were preventable by existing technology like magazine disconnects and heavier trigger pulls.[138]

One gun per month. Interestingly, from 1996 through 1998 Virginia was one of three states (the others were Maryland and North Carolina) that limited buyers to one gun per month. But Virginia was third in the nation as a source of guns used by criminals in other states.[139] Currently, multi-gun sales must be reported to authorities for investigation. The "one gun" rule makes sales more difficult to trace. And the rule is easy for criminals to circumvent by using straw purchasers. Most important, advocates of one gun per month have produced no evidence to show that multiple gun purchases are responsible for an increase in illegal activity.

Age limit. Under current federal law, 21 is the minimum age to purchase a handgun; 18 is the minimum age to possess a handgun. Clinton proposed to ban possession by anyone under age 21.[140] That's a bad idea, says John Lott. "Laws allowing those between 18 and 21 years of age to carry a concealed handgun reduce violent crimes just as well as those limited to citizens over 21."[141] Yes, 18- and 19-year-olds commit gun crimes at the highest rates; but they are also

likely victims, who need protection from gang members. Furthermore, we allow 18-year-olds to vote, go to war, get married and
divorced, and have an abortion; surely they are sufficiently mature
to be able to defend themselves.

Gun shows. If gun shows seem to be a problem, it's because
current laws have raised the cost of a legitimate license. The number
of licensed dealers declined from 250,000 in 1993 to 83,000 six years
later.[142] Harvard researcher David M. Kennedy reports that sellers
"at gun shows are [often] people who have been forced to give up
their licenses."[143] Moreover, the Clinton administration has provided
no evidence that such shows are an important source of guns for
criminals.[144] In the mid-1980s, a survey of felons in 12 state prisons
indicated that fewer than 1% got their guns at gun shows. A 1997
Department of Justice study came up with 2%.[145] And those figures
include straw purchases, which are already illegal, and purchases
through licensed dealers, which are already subject to background
checks. According to a BATF study, during the 30 months ending
in December 1998, 26,000 guns used in crimes were purchased at
gun shows.[146] That's 10,400 guns per annum, which is only 2.1% of
the roughly 500,000 gun-related crimes each year.

Background checks. Checks are already required for all dealer
sales, including those at gun shows. Clinton would have extended
the requirement to nondealer sales at gun shows. That's the rule
Maryland has already adopted. Not surprisingly, Maryland now
wants to go further and ban gun shows on public property and
property that receives taxpayer support.[147] The NRA's chief lobbyist,
James Jay Baker, observes: "Our opponents say that all we want to
do is close the loophole, but they're never satisfied."[148] Perhaps the
slippery slope argument isn't illusory after all.

The NRA has agreed to background checks at gun shows, provided the check could be completed within 24 hours. But proposed
legislation in the Senate contained a three-business-day time frame,
presumably because most gun shows occur over a weekend. House
Majority Whip Tom DeLay (R-TX) asked, quite logically, why the
FBI couldn't be open during weekend hours.[149]

In the House of Representatives, the corresponding bill included
nearly all of the items that the Democrats had demanded—a requirement for safety locks, a prohibition on youth possession of semi-
automatic weapons, a ban on large capacity ammunition clips, and

a lifetime ban on gun possession by anyone convicted of a felony as a juvenile. But the background check provision incorporated the NRA's proposal for a 24-hour time limit. House Democrats killed the bill[150]—apparently more interested in an election issue than real gun reform.

The National Instant Check System, implemented under the 1994 Brady Act, now has data on 38 million Americans. Expert witnesses testified before Congress in June 2000 that system glitches have delayed or blocked fully one-fourth of all lawful purchases.[151] Who knows how many of those purchases might have prevented gun violence. John Lott reports that "the national waiting period [under the Brady Act] had no significant impact on murder or robbery rates and was associated with a small increase in rape and aggravated-assault rates."[152] Criminals are not deterred; law-abiding citizens who want to defend themselves are told to wait.

Researchers at Georgetown University and Duke University identified 32 states that adopted Brady style restrictions when the Act was passed in 1994, and compared those states with 19 others that already enforced similar restrictions. Writing in the *Journal of the American Medical Association*, the researchers found that the decline in gun homicide rates was the same for the two groups of states, thus belying the contention that the Brady Act reduced gun murders. There was "no evidence that implementation of the Brady Act was associated with a reduction in homicide rates."[153] The only contrary statistic was a larger drop in gun suicides for people above age 55 in the 32-state group. The authors explained, however, that there was an offsetting increase in nongun suicides within the 32-state group.[154]

Notwithstanding Clinton's litany of gun control proposals, none would have prevented any of the recent spate of gun-related violence. In Illinois and Indiana, Benjamin Smith, a white supremacist, age 21, who went on a shooting rampage, bought two guns from an unlicensed dealer, but not at a gun show. He had previously failed a background check and was not prosecuted.[155] In Atlanta, a commodities trader killed nine people, but his purchase of four handguns would not have violated any of the proposed new laws. Likewise for Buford Furrow, who bought seven guns legally before assaulting children at a Jewish day care center in Los Angeles.[156] In Conyers, Georgia, the gun was stolen from the killer's stepfather.[157] In Michigan, a six-year-old also stole a gun. He lived without his mother or father in a crack house, where the loaded gun was easily accessible.[158]

More recently, in a Chicago suburb, a deranged former employee killed five people and wounded four others at a Navistar plant. He was armed with an AK47, pump shotgun, rifle, and revolver— purchased using a firearm owner's identification card issued by the state two weeks before he was convicted of a sex felony. Despite state law to the contrary, no one demanded that he turn in the ID card.[159] And this past March, in a suburban high school near San Diego, a 15-year-old boy killed two people and wounded 13 others using his father's handgun, which he had extracted from a locked cabinet and brought to school in violation of California law. The troubled teen, who dabbled in marijuana, acid, speed, and alcohol, had announced his plan for mass murder, but no one took him seriously.[160] California's gun laws—among the strictest in the nation—didn't help at all. Unsupervised juveniles can't possess a handgun or live ammunition; a background check is required on all gun sales; new residents must register their guns; purchases are finalized only after a 10-day waiting period; training is mandatory; and buyers are limited to one gun per month.[161]

The highest profile incident occurred at Columbine High School in Littleton, Colorado. There, the girlfriend of one of the killers, age 18, bought two shotguns and a rifle. She would have passed a background check. The killers' semi-automatic TEC9 was already illegal, as were the pipe bombs and grenades that they possessed. Both shooters were reputed to have idolized Hitler; they wore trench coats and metal-tip boots with swastika emblems, made bombs in their parents' garage, and stored guns in their bedrooms.[162] A degree of parental supervision might have uncovered a serious psychological problem before it became fatal.

The Columbine outcome might also have been different if more guns had been present—in the hands of security guards or perhaps even teachers or an armed principal. Maybe a dress code with stricter discipline might have mattered. But, observes federal appellate judge J. Harvie Wilkinson, "We are now in a society which freely and instinctively litigates routine public school decisions in the federal judiciary."[163] In public schools, avoiding lawsuits takes precedence over discipline; effective education is too often sacrificed at the altar of students' rights.

Our ex-president may well have had a hidden agenda to deal with future Columbines: federal registration, the ultimate in gun control short of prohibition. Despite repeated denials by Vice President Gore and others, Clinton asked rhetorically, "Should people . . . have to register guns like they register their cars? Do I think that?" He then answered, "Of course I do."[164] Never mind that registration would mean a national database containing names and addresses of every law-abiding, peaceful gun owner. Never mind that car registration—by states, not by the federal government—is primarily for revenue. And never mind that some government officials and private groups want to use registration to attain their ultimate objective, which is outright confiscation of handguns. Indeed, Pete Shields, the founding chair of Handgun Control, acknowledged that "The first problem is to slow down the number of handguns being produced and sold. . . . The second problem is to get handguns registered. The final problem is to make possession of all handguns . . . totally illegal."[165]

The evidence—or more precisely the lack of evidence—is compelling in those states that already require registration. There are no serious studies that link registration to a reduction in gun-related violence. To the surprise of no one except gun-control zealots, criminals will not register their firearms. Only law-abiding citizens will comply with registration requirements.

Conclusion

Legislatures have a duty to secure the constitutional legacy of Americans to defend themselves—by frustrating ineffective gun control proposals, preventing registration, and blocking the more radical calls for gun confiscation. Yet, even if the legislatures behave responsibly, courts are the final bulwark in safeguarding our right to keep and bear arms. Courts may not be used as a means around the legislative process.

The American public—especially voters and jurors—must be warned that our tort system is rapidly becoming a tool for extortion by a coterie of politicians and trial lawyers. Sometimes they seek money; sometimes they pursue policy goals; often they abuse their power. Take it from former labor secretary Robert Reich, certainly not renowned for his opposition to imperious government. Reich tells us that his ex-boss in the White House, President Clinton, launched "lawsuits to succeed where legislation failed. The strategy may work," Reich adds, "but at the cost of making our frail democracy even weaker. . . . This is nothing short of faux legislation, which sacrifices democracy to the discretion of administration officials operating in utter secrecy."[166]

Reich has it just about right. But the problem outlives the Clinton White House. It infests many of the state houses and city halls. Like most infestations, this one can be fumigated. When we condone the selective and retroactive application of extraordinary legal principles, intended specifically to transfer resources from disfavored defendants to favored plaintiffs—or even worse, to the public sector—we substitute political cronyism for fundamental fairness, profane the rule of law, and debase personal freedom.

4. More Tobacco, Lead Paint, Fatty Foods, and Alcohol

Beginning in 1994, state attorneys general from across the country sued major tobacco companies to recover Medicaid expenditures for smoking-related illnesses. By retroactively altering conventional rules of tort law, the states effectively foreclosed any defense by the industry against liability. Under duress, the cigarette giants decided to negotiate rather than litigate. That's how the tobacco settlement came to pass, as chronicled in Chapter 2. But it's not the whole story. There's a little-known but important sequel.

The same tobacco companies that more than tripled cigarette prices so they could cough up a quarter-trillion dollars in "damages" under the November 1998 Master Settlement Agreement still have more than 90% of the market. Consumers and companies that didn't sign the MSA now realize that the entire deal is a protectionist racket designed to prevent price competition. That appalling scheme is documented in the first four sections of this chapter.

Next, in the two following sections, we turn to the Justice Department's landmark litigation against the same tobacco companies. Two years ago, a supposedly confidential departmental memo related that government lawyers were about to abandon the federal lawsuit. The Bush administration apparently had doubts about the legal merits of the underlying claims and, in any event, did not want to include in its budget the $58 million in litigation expenses estimated for the ensuing year.

Dumping the federal court case would have been good riddance. Like the state Medicaid suits, it's based on bad law and bad public policy. But what a difference a couple of years makes. Today, after a U-turn by Attorney General John Ashcroft, the administration has decided that the costs of $58 million are a mere pittance when you can wring $289 billion in phony damages from the cigarette giants. So the litigation has been reborn.

Sad to say, the tobacco model only primed the pump for more extortion. Gun makers became immediate victims (see Chapter 3). Soon enough, the "slippery slope" stretched to at least three other industries. First, lead paint manufacturers were sued by the usual suspects—an alliance of government officials and private contingency-fee attorneys. Second, fatty food distributors came under fire, supported by a university seminar to teach lawyers how the profitable lessons of the cigarette wars could be exploited. Then, most recently, plaintiffs' attorneys found yet another "sin industry" prey: brewers and distillers of alcoholic beverages.

Those fresh targets will be discussed in the final sections of this chapter. But we start with an update on the tobacco wars.

Nurturing the Tobacco Cartel

MSA: The Mother of All Antitrust Violations*

The nasty little secret of the nationwide tobacco settlement is that it violates both the antitrust laws and the Constitution. The settlement transforms a competitive industry into a cartel, then guards against destabilization of the cartel by erecting barriers to entry that preserve the market dominance of the tobacco giants. Far from being victims, the big four tobacco companies are at the very center of the scheme. In collaboration with state attorneys general and their trial lawyer friends, the four majors managed to carve out a protected market for themselves—all at the expense of smokers and tobacco companies who did not sign the November 1998 Master Settlement Agreement.

To be sure, the industry would rather have prevailed in their state Medicaid recoupment suits; then a settlement would not have been necessary. But that outcome was foreclosed by the perverse legal rules under which the Medicaid suits were proceeding. So, to cut their losses, the tobacco giants negotiated something pretty close to a sweetheart deal. The incredible tale of that scheme, and its pernicious consequences, has yet to be told.

---

*An abbreviated version of this section, with other minor revisions, was originally published under the title, "A Tobacco Cartel Is Born, Paid for by Smokers," *Wall Street Journal*, May 1, 2000, p. A35, coauthored with Thomas C. O'Brien, former assistant general counsel, Corning Incorporated.

Here's the story in a nutshell: The 1998 tobacco settlement fills state coffers, pads the wallets of trial lawyers, and shields the big cigarette makers from would-be rivals, while foisting onto smokers the quarter-of-a-trillion dollar cost of the agreement. The MSA forces *all* tobacco companies—even not-yet-formed companies and companies that did not agree to the settlement—to pay "damages," thus preventing them from cutting prices. For the tobacco giants, those "damages" were not based on any assessment of injuries caused by cigarettes, but on a careful calculation of the price increases that could be sustained without significant loss of sales.

Because they would be raising prices substantially to cover their MSA payments, Philip Morris, Reynolds, Lorillard, and Brown & Williamson were concerned that smaller domestic manufacturers, importers, other discounters, and new tobacco companies that didn't sign the agreement would gain market share by underpricing cigarettes. To guard against that likelihood, the big four and their state collaborators added these provisions to the MSA:

- If the aggregate market share of the four majors were to decline by more than 2%, then their "damages" payments would be reduced by three times the excess over the two-percentage-point threshold. Any such reduction would be charged against only those states that did not adopt a "Qualifying Statute," attached as an exhibit to the MSA. Naturally, because of the risk of losing enormous sums of money, all of the states enacted the statute.
- The Qualifying Statute requires any tobacco company that does not sign the MSA to post pro-rata damages—based on cigarette sales—in escrow for 25 years to offset any liability that might be assessed. That's right—no evidence, no trial, no verdict, no injury, just damages. In fact, because the escrow payments are nondeductible against income taxes, they are actually about 1½ times what the majors would pay per cigarette.
- That was the stick. Next came the carrot. If a nonsettling tobacco company agreed to participate in the MSA, the Qualifying Statute would not apply. Then the new participant would be allowed to increase its market share up to a whopping 1¼ times its 1997 level. Bear in mind, none of the nonsettling companies had more than 1% of the market in 1997. Essentially, the big four companies guaranteed themselves virtually all of the market in perpetuity.

91

Thus have the dominant tobacco companies purchased (at virtually no cost to themselves) the ability to exclude competitors and raise prices with impunity. Smokers, who are the medical victims, receive nothing of value; yet they bear the entire cost of the agreement. Nonparticipating cigarette companies, current or future, are victims too, because they are precluded from lowering prices by the bogus "liability" that the agreement imposes on them.

Meanwhile, the settlement has led to massive and continuing shifts of wealth from millions of smokers to concentrated pockets of the bar. Predictably, part of that multibillion-dollar booty has started its roundtrip back into the political process—to influence state legislators, judges, attorneys general, governors, city mayors, and maybe some federal officials. With all that money in hand, the political influence of trial lawyers will grow exponentially. And with every passing day, the MSA becomes more firmly entrenched—tightly cementing the Machiavellian relationship between trial attorneys and their allies in the public sector. The billion-dollar spigot must be turned off before its corrupting effect on the rule of law is irreversible.

One way to turn off that spigot is to challenge the legality and constitutionality of the MSA. Without question, the agreement violates the antitrust laws, the Commerce Clause, and the Compacts Clause. Indeed, what could be more blatant than the MSA in violating the Compacts Clause, which provides in Article I, section 10 of the Constitution that "No State shall, without the Consent of Congress, . . . enter into any Agreement or Compact with another State." The MSA is a multi-state agreement, negotiated without congressional consent, which preempts key federal functions like taxation and regulation of interstate commerce. Those points have been all but absent from the debate.

The MSA authorizes states to exercise powers they could not otherwise exercise—for example, the collection of "damages" based on sales in other states, the interstate regulation of cigarette advertising, and the exaction of penalties against out-of-state companies that do not sign the agreement. In essence, the MSA sets up a national regime for regulating the tobacco business and fixing prices.

The exercise of those powers by the states is clearly unconstitutional—and, what is worse, the parties to the MSA knew it all along. That's why the MSA contains this explicit disclaimer: "Each Participating Manufacturer . . . acknowledges . . . that certain provisions of this Agreement may require it to act or refrain from acting in a manner that could otherwise give rise to state or federal constitutional challenges." By signing the document, each manufacturer expressly waived "any and all claims that the provisions of this Agreement violate state or federal constitutions." Those imminent constitutional violations also explain the establishment by the MSA of a $50 million enforcement fund, in part to defend against challenges to the settlement. Insidiously, the fund is underwritten by smokers, who are potential claimants against the settlement.

That's the story. Now what can we do about it? For starters, injunctive relief is available in private lawsuits brought directly by injured parties, including smokers and nonparticipating tobacco companies, which can also sue for treble damages under the antitrust laws. Yes, monopolies that arise out of state action—public utilities, for example—are ordinarily exempt from private antitrust prosecution, at least when the state acts as sovereign in regulating an industry. But here, because they are violating the Constitution, the states cannot be acting in their sovereign capacity.

If the MSA is allowed to stand, it will create and finance a rich and powerful industry of lawyers who know how to manipulate the system and are not averse to violating the Constitution or the laws. In short, the MSA should be dismantled, the legal fees refunded, price increases canceled, and competition restored. Naturally, any challenge to the MSA will be contested by virtually all of the states, the major tobacco companies, and the instant billionaires among the plaintiffs' bar. The only way to confront that formidable cabal is to mount a coordinated effort in the courtroom and in the media. That's a tall order, but the stakes are immense.

Selling Antitrust Immunity: Bedell v. Philip Morris*

Can states sell immunity from the federal antitrust laws? That's the issue the U.S. Court of Appeals for the Third Circuit will soon

---

*This section, with minor revisions, was originally published under the title, "The Gang That Couldn't Deal Straight: Multi-state Tobacco Settlement Is Violating Laws and Constitution," *Legal Times*, December 11, 2000, p. 61, coauthored with Thomas C. O'Brien, former assistant general counsel, Corning Incorporated. See also Robert A. Levy, "The Golden Goose: Far from Crippling Cigarette Giants, States Save Them," *Investor's Business Daily*, July 11, 2001, p. A20. [Author's note: Events have of course overtaken parts of this section, which was first published four years ago. Those events are recounted in later sections of this chapter.]

decide in *Bedell v. Philip Morris*. If you think a federal court shouldn't be wasting its time on self-evident questions of law, think again. The sale of antitrust immunity is precisely what an unholy cabal of tobacco companies, state attorneys general, and trial lawyers was up to when it negotiated the multi-state tobacco settlement in 1998.

The tobacco settlement has created a half dozen billionaires. They didn't earn their money by building commercial empires, like Sam Walton, or by developing new technologies, like Bill Gates. That's the conventional way of getting super rich. The modern formula, pioneered by the tobacco lawyers, is to find a well-heeled industry that wants or needs an antitrust exemption, then broker the sale of the exemption for, say, a quarter of a trillion dollars, and collect a fat contingency fee based on the sale price. That's how the tobacco lawyers made their billions.

The alluring thing about that business is that everybody goes home a winner—or almost everybody. The state attorneys general—who are the sellers of immunity—collect $206 billion that they can spend on their favorite "smoking-related" programs like sidewalk improvements, reduced college tuition, and flood control; the cigarette companies get to raise prices as high as their addicted customers can tolerate, unhindered by competitors; and the lawyers get $750 million per year for the first five years, and $500 million per year thereafter, in perpetuity. Only smokers are losers. They don't receive a penny for their smoking illnesses—past, present, or future—and they pay for the entire deal. Smokers, of course, were not represented at the bargaining table. In a nutshell, that's the tobacco settlement. Never mind that the whole scheme is unconstitutional and illegal.

It doesn't take a constitutional scholar to see that individual states are collecting payments (euphemistically labeled "damages") on cigarette sales in other states. In effect, the attorneys general arrogated unto themselves the power to regulate interstate commerce in tobacco. Recall, however, that the Constitution—more specifically, the Commerce Clause in Article I, section 8—assigns regulation of interstate commerce to Congress. And another provision of the Constitution—the Compacts Clause in Article I, section 10—prohibits the states from entering into multi-state compacts or agreements that could infringe on the powers of the federal government without the consent of Congress. It is difficult—in fact, preposterous—to deny that the multi-state tobacco settlement is an agreement among the states or that it infringes on the powers of the federal government. It is and it does.

Revealingly, the states asked for congressional approval of an earlier version of the tobacco settlement in June 1997. Congress declined. Then Sen. John McCain (R-AZ) introduced his version in May 1998. Congress rejected it. No matter; the tobacco companies, attorneys general, and contingency fee lawyers went ahead with the current deal anyway. This time, they didn't even bother asking for congressional consent. Evidently the money was just too tempting for them to be concerned with the Constitution.

If not deterred by the Constitution, how about the antitrust laws? Under the settlement, nonsigning tobacco companies that later elect to be bound by the agreement have to make pro-rata "damages" payments if their cigarette sales exceed (approximately) 1997 levels. And any nonsigning companies that reject the settlement have to make similar, but non-tax-deductible contributions into an escrow fund for 25 years. Those expenditures prevent nonsigners from cutting prices and capturing market share from the tobacco giants. Essentially, the settlement guarantees the four majors virtually all of the market forever—protected by the state attorneys general and immune from the federal antitrust laws. That's what the majors bought for a quarter of a trillion dollars.

Of course, the value of an exemption from the antitrust laws is astronomical. After nearly a year under the settlement, the tobacco companies were able to raise prices with impunity and increase their profits by more than twice the amount of their so-called damages payments.

That brings us to the *Bedell* case. A.D. Bedell Wholesale Company is an independent wholesaler that would like to compete in the sale of discount-priced cigarettes. Prior to the multi-state tobacco settlement, Bedell was able to purchase those cigarettes from a number of small manufacturers as well as from the majors. Following the tobacco settlement, virtually every tobacco manufacturer raised its prices in lockstep, effectively eliminating the discount trade. Those price increases were triggered by the multi-state tobacco settlement, which required all cigarette companies to restrict their sales or pay "damages," regardless of whether they were sued by the states or had any liability whatsoever. The result is that Bedell can no longer obtain discount cigarettes and is thus foreclosed from price competition.

Under the tobacco agreement, state attorneys general have agreed to use their criminal enforcement powers to limit existing and potential competitors of the tobacco giants. The result is to replace a competitive tobacco industry with a four-company cartel by erecting barriers to price competition. That's justified, say the attorneys general, because discounting by small manufacturers and wholesalers like Bedell could undermine the deal. Obviously, the states love the tobacco deal; and they want to do more deals like it.

The Third Circuit Court of Appeals may have a different plan, however. No doubt, the three-judge panel will grasp that the real persons paying the "damages"—namely, smokers—were not parties to the litigation or present at the negotiating table. In fact, the whole notion of settlement has little meaning when it requires one party (the states) to suspend the antitrust laws so that the other party (the tobacco giants) can pay the freight using someone else's money. But then, that is the beauty—or the outrage—of an exemption from the antitrust laws; and that is why it is so expensive.

The key question for the Third Circuit is whether state attorneys general have the right to sell immunity from the antitrust laws. In their *Bedell* court papers, the tobacco companies assert that their cartel and its anti-competitive actions are inoculated from the antitrust laws because the states are their partners, and the states are exempt under a doctrine called "state action immunity," originally set out in a 1943 Supreme Court case, *Parker v. Brown*. But that argument is nonsense when it's applied to the multi-state settlement.

The state action doctrine has been limited by the Supreme Court to "acts of government" taken by the state as "sovereign." Those are two specific criteria, both of which must be satisfied as preconditions to state action immunity. The tobacco deal cannot satisfy either of them. In lay terms, a state is "sovereign" when and where its actions are not subject to a superior legal authority. For example, a state would not be acting in its sovereign capacity in authorizing a corporation in another state to conspire with competitors to fix prices. Nor would the state be acting as sovereign in contracting with other states to enforce anti-competitive laws affecting interstate commerce without congressional approval. In the former instance, the state would be acting outside of its borders where another state or the federal government has sovereign power. In the latter situation, the state would be violating both the Compacts Clause and the Commerce Clause of the Constitution. Those circumstances are exactly the circumstances of the tobacco settlement agreement.

The second precondition for state action immunity is that the state must be carrying out an "act of government." That means the particular act must qualify as an official undertaking of the state in its governmental capacity—that is, it cannot be the unauthorized act of a state or nongovernmental official. Although the tobacco lawyers dressed up the tobacco settlement to look like an "act of government" by involving all three branches of state government in the agreement, they could not sidestep this fundamental problem: The settlement is unconstitutional. Remember that the Commerce Clause prohibits states from regulating interstate commerce, and the Compacts Clause prohibits states from entering into interstate compacts that could infringe on the powers of the federal government without the consent of Congress. The settlement agreement does both of those things.

Thus, it is not merely that the states improperly exercised a legitimate state power. Rather, they totally lacked the power to enter into and implement the agreement in the first place. A long-established Supreme Court rule from *Ex Parte Young* (1908) provides that "the use of the name of the state to enforce an unconstitutional act . . . is a proceeding without the authority of, and one which does not affect, the state in its sovereign or governmental capacity. It is simply an illegal act upon the part of a state official." On that basis as well, therefore, the tobacco agreement simply does not qualify for state action immunity.

And there's more. The tobacco agreement also exceeds state sovereignty by interfering with federal legislation, which preempts any contrary state enactment. The Federal Cigarette Labeling and Advertising Act, for example, establishes "a comprehensive Federal program to deal with cigarette labeling and advertising with respect to any relationship between smoking and health." The act provides that "[n]o requirement or prohibition based on smoking and health shall be imposed under State law with respect to the advertising or promotion of any cigarettes the packages of which are labeled in conformity with the provisions of this chapter." Notwithstanding those provisions, the tobacco agreement imposes multiple prohibitions with respect to advertising and promotion of cigarettes—thus violating the clear text of the federal statute and frustrating its explicit overall purpose.

A second cigarette-related statute, the Tobacco Control Act, actually permits selected compacts among tobacco-producing states, but Congress expressly disavowed "any compact for regulating or controlling the production of, or commerce in, tobacco for the purpose of fixing the price thereof, or to create or perpetuate monopoly, or to promote regimentation." The tobacco agreement effectuates precisely what the Tobacco Control Act forbids.

Thus, the multi-state action embodied by the tobacco agreement exceeds the bounds of state sovereignty in a variety of ways: It constitutes extraterritorial action with respect to neighboring sovereign states; it encroaches upon Congress's enumerated power to regulate interstate commerce; it interferes with congressional legislation governing the interstate tobacco trade; and it violates the constitutional prohibition against interstate compacts or agreements not approved by Congress. For each of those reasons, the tobacco agreement is not a valid "act of government" imposed by a state "as sovereign," and thus cannot immunize the conduct of the cigarette companies in violation of the Sherman Act.

The tobacco cartel also claims immunity based on a legal doctrine that allows competitors to petition for an antitrust exemption without incurring liability for the petitioning act itself—the *Noerr-Pennington doctrine*, first articulated by the Supreme Court in *Eastern Railroad Presidents Conference v. Noerr Motor Freight, Inc.* (1961) and *United Mine Workers v. Pennington* (1965). But petitioning means soliciting government officials to perform, or not to perform, specified acts. If the petition is not granted, or if government officials are legally or constitutionally disabled from granting the petition, then the attempt to obtain an exemption from the antitrust laws is ineffectual. Yes, the Noerr-Pennington doctrine may immunize the solicitation, but it does not immunize the subsequent anti-competitive conduct. Otherwise, prospective price fixers could avoid antitrust liability simply by asking for permission.

The decision in *Noerr* itself was predicated upon—and cited *Parker* for—the determination that there can be no Sherman Act violation "where a restraint upon trade or monopolization is the result of valid government action." And *Noerr* expressly recognized that the cases insulating government action "rest upon the fact" that the government's prerogative to pass and enforce an anti-competitive law exists only "so long as the law itself does not violate some provision of the Constitution." Thus, if the state action resulting from the petition is itself invalid, and hence unable to confer Parker immunity, the mere fact that it was procured through petitioning the government does not independently confer immunity. At most the Noerr-Pennington doctrine immunizes the request for action, not the result.

The *Bedell* case, therefore, is about a company victimized by a private cartel and its government allies, who seek to absolve themselves from liability for illegal conduct by exploiting two legal doctrines that simply do not apply. Ordinarily, the Justice Department or the state attorneys general would prosecute such antitrust infractions vigorously. In this instance, however, there seem to be no law enforcement officials willing to enforce the law. Perhaps we should not be surprised. Because the state attorneys general negotiated the tobacco deal, and because it has enriched their states' coffers to the tune of billions of dollars, they have a profound conflict of interest when it comes to prosecuting an antitrust claim against the cigarette makers. Likewise, the Clinton administration has commenced a lawsuit to garner a piece of the action; and the major contributors to Clinton's party are the contingency fee lawyers, who get a boatload of money from the settlement.

Still, private companies, like Bedell and small manufacturers, who are excluded from the market or must pay inflated prices, and smokers, who are footing the bill, can challenge the deal on antitrust and constitutional grounds. To be sure, litigation is an uphill battle. The clever lawyers who crafted the tobacco agreement buried a $50 million war chest in it for just such an occasion—to litigate against anybody who challenges or refuses to abide by the tobacco agreement. Without ever having to go to their legislatures for funding, the state attorneys general and their tobacco company partners can litigate until the opposing party runs out of money.

At Bedell, hopes are high that the Third Circuit will see through this insidious scheme. That would bring an end to the peddling of antitrust exemptions by state officials. Anyone who owns a bagel shop and conspires with his competitor to fix prices for an extra hundred dollars per week can go to jail. Surely, if a state attorney general or a tobacco lawyer sells phony antitrust immunity for $250 billion to giant cigarette companies who palm off the cost to their innocent customers, his culpability is immeasurably greater.

Poking a Hole in the MSA*

Trial lawyers and 46 states are scheduled to receive nearly a quarter of a trillion dollars over the next 22 years under the terms of the Master Settlement Agreement signed in November 1998 by the four tobacco giants. Not surprisingly, the lawyers and state attorneys general would rather have the money now than later—to avoid any chance that the whole deal could come undone. So they're busily assigning their rights under the MSA to institutional investors— getting cash up front in return for letting the institutions collect from the cigarette makers. Naturally, investors charge a price for bearing the collection risk: They will only sign up if they get an ample discount off the face amount of the settlement proceeds.

That discount could be heading much higher. On June 19, 2001, the U.S. Court of Appeals for the Third Circuit unanimously dismissed an antitrust challenge to the MSA by A.D. Bedell Wholesale Companies. Yet that apparent loss may turn into a resounding victory for Bedell and other plaintiffs who seek to have the MSA invalidated. In *Bedell v. Philip Morris*, the Third Circuit left a gaping hole in the MSA's structure. According to *The Bond Buyer*, a leading trade publication, the court's ruling "has caught the attention of the bond market." One portfolio manager observed that "the aggregate of the risks appears significant enough that at this point, we are not participating in tobacco bond deals." Until now, those deals have been proliferating—$900 million in New York, $500 million in Washington, D.C., $400 million in California, and nearly $1 billion in South Carolina. The *Wall Street Journal* reports that a group of lawyers agreed to a 70% discount on $1 billion in settlement fees due over 12 years.

If the financial implications are huge, the legal and public policy implications are even greater. The tobacco companies asserted that their cartel and its anti-competitive acts are inoculated from the antitrust laws under two related legal doctrines. First, the *Noerr-Pennington* doctrine—originated by the Supreme Court in *Eastern Railroad Presidents Conference v. Noerr Motor Freight, Inc.* (1961) and

---

*An abbreviated version of this section, with other minor revisions, was originally published under the title, "Crashing the Cartel: Tobacco Settlement's Victory Carries Seeds of Defeat," *Legal Times*, November 5, 2001, pp. 50–51. See also Robert A. Levy, "Risk of Investing in Tobacco Settlement Bonds," *Pensions & Investments*, September 17, 2001, p. 12.

United Mine Workers v. Pennington (1965)—allows competitors to petition the government for an antitrust exemption without incurring liability for the petitioning act itself. Second, "state action immunity"—set out by the Court in *Parker v. Brown* (1943)—exempts states from antitrust violations when they are performing acts of government in their sovereign capacity (for example, authorizing and regulating a public utility monopoly). A state thus immunized can transfer its immunity to the regulated industry.

In a bizarre opinion, the appellate court held that the tobacco companies are indeed immunized from an antitrust claim by the *Noerr-Pennington* doctrine, but not by the *Parker* state action doctrine. Here is the thrust of the court's analysis: First, *Noerr* stands for the proposition that "parties are immune from liability arising from antitrust injuries caused by government action which results from . . . petitioning. . . . Where the restraint upon trade . . . is the result of valid governmental action, as opposed to private action, there is immunity." Second, "the right to petition extends to all departments of the Government, including the judiciary." Third, the parties to the MSA successfully petitioned the judiciary to approve their settlement. Therefore, the parties are entitled to *Noerr* immunity.

By contrast, the court rejected *Parker* immunity on these bases: First, "only an affirmative decision by the state itself, acting in its sovereign capacity, and with active supervision, can immunize otherwise anti-competitive activity." Second, the test is "whether the antitrust injuries were more attributable to private parties than to government action." Third, although state attorneys general negotiated the MSA, state legislatures passed the related statutes, and state courts approved the settlement, "these acts by the governmental parties were not the direct source of the anti-competitive injuries." The injury resulted from conduct (price-fixing) after implementation of the MSA—"acts involving private parties" operating pursuant to a joint settlement with the states.

For *Parker* immunity to apply, concluded the court, the anti-competitive acts must be "actively supervised by the state." But the MSA "empowers the tobacco companies to make anti-competitive decisions with no regulatory oversight. . . . Specifically, the defendants are free to fix and raise prices, allegedly without fear of competition." To be sure, the States "are involved in the maintenance of the scheme, but they lack oversight or authority over the tobacco manufacturers' prices and production levels. These decisions are left entirely to the private actors." Thus, the parties are not entitled to *Parker* immunity.

Clearly, the court's *Noerr* analysis cannot be reconciled with its *Parker* analysis. In granting *Noerr* immunity, the court notes that immunity vests only "where the restraint upon trade . . . is the result of valid governmental action, as opposed to private action." Yet, if the MSA is not state action under *Parker* because there is no pricing supervision, and if the MSA's injuries are, in the court's own words, "more attributable to private parties," then *Noerr* immunity cannot apply. That inconsistency is the main basis for Bedell's petition for certiorari to the Supreme Court.

But there's another intriguing possibility that could transform the Third Circuit's opinion from a defeat for Bedell into a stunning victory. The Third Circuit concluded that *Parker* is not a valid defense to antitrust claims against the MSA. That suggests a second antitrust suit—one against the states rather than the tobacco majors. *Noerr*, which was invoked by the court in dismissing the current suit, is not applicable to the states. They do not petition themselves, of course. Therefore, the MSA can be defended by the states only if they are entitled to antitrust immunity under *Parker*. But the highest federal court in the Third Circuit has held that *Parker* is not available.

That means an antitrust challenge to the MSA against one or more states is an odds-on bet. Even if sovereign immunity shuts off recovery of damages against the states, injunctive relief is available against state officials. The end result could be invalidation of the anti-competitive statutes that force nonsettling tobacco companies to pay royalties into escrow. With the demise of those statutes, competition will reign and the entire MSA scheme will unravel. And without the expected windfall from the settlement, some states will have to cancel their pet "smoking-related" projects, like sidewalk improvements, reduced college tuition, and flood control.

The prospect that a $250 billion spigot might be turned off must be very unsettling—not only to the states, which have already planned to spend money they don't have, but also to the trial lawyers. Why, then, did the Third Circuit proceed to address *Parker* after concluding that *Noerr* was an adequate antitrust defense for the tobacco companies? Two answers come to mind. First, a cynic might conclude that the three-judge panel didn't want the political burden of overturning the MSA, but believed it should be overturned, and wanted to provide Bedell and other potential plaintiffs with a road map to pursue their claims to the full court or to the Supreme Court. Second, perhaps the panel wanted the high court to grant certiorari, and therefore reached the *Parker* issue to ensure that no base would remain uncovered. Conceivably, if an alternative theory of the case were not addressed by the appellate court, the Supreme Court might be disinclined to grant certiorari merely to issue an advisory opinion.

Whatever the reason that the Third Circuit ventured, on its own volition, into the *Parker* arena, the upshot could be an ignominious end to the mother of all antitrust violations. The MSA—an unholy alliance of private lawyers and state attorneys general, who abused the legal process by selling immunity from our antitrust laws to the tobacco giants for a quarter of a trillion dollars—could come tumbling down.

MSA Update

In January 2002 the U.S. Supreme Court declined to review the dismissal of Bedell's challenge to the MSA.

That triggered a second line of attack—an antitrust suit against a state rather than the tobacco majors. The *Noerr-Pennington* doctrine, it was thought, would not be applicable to a state that, after all, does not petition itself. So in October 2001, in *Mariana v. Fisher*, several smokers sued Pennsylvania attorney general Mike Fisher to invalidate the MSA, once again on antitrust grounds.

Regrettably, the trial court dismissed the case in June 2002 and the U.S. Court of Appeals for the Third Circuit affirmed in July 2003. Yes, said the appellate court, the MSA definitely violates the antitrust laws. But *Noerr-Pennington* immunity applies to the states as well as to the tobacco companies. In effect, the state attorney general functions as ombudsman for state residents when he petitions the state courts and legislature to advance his constituents' goals by approving the MSA. In February 2004, the U.S. Supreme Court decided not to review the *Mariana* case.

At about the same time, however, the outlook for the MSA became much smokier. In January 2004, the U.S. Court of Appeals for the Second Circuit took a position opposite from the Third Circuit on the *Noerr-Pennington* doctrine in a similar case. The Second Circuit unanimously reversed a trial court and reinstated a Sherman Act challenge to the MSA in *Freedom Holdings v. Spitzer*. Freedom Holdings imports cigarettes for resale in New York from foreign manufacturers who are not parties to the MSA. Eliot Spitzer is New York's attorney general.

Judge Ralph Winter wrote that the "anti-competitive market structure created by the [MSA]" constitutes a "per se violation of the Sherman Act," which preempts state statutes. Moreover, he remarked, the states cannot be immunized when they fail to regulate or even supervise the pricing conduct of the cigarette manufacturers. *Noerr-Pennington* "cannot sensibly protect the resultant anti-competitive legislation" from federal preemption. The right of a private party to petition the government "does not . . . protect the ultimate legislative result from Supremacy Clause analysis." MSA opponents cheered Winter's opinion. Now, in light of the split between two federal appeals courts, the Supreme Court may have to decide whether the Second Circuit or the Third Circuit got it right.

Federal Assault on the Tobacco Industry

*Clinton Wants a Piece of the Pie**

"Tonight I announce that the Justice Department is preparing a litigation plan to take the tobacco companies to court and, with the funds we recover, to strengthen Medicare." With that State of the Union bombshell by President Clinton, the chickens came home to roost for the tobacco industry.

First, the industry rolled over for state Medicaid suits; then it volunteered to waive its First Amendment right to advertise, submit to Food and Drug Administration regulation, and persuade customers not to buy its product. In other words, rather than go to war against the government's money grab, the tobacco companies tried to bribe the politicians. That capitulation—the unprincipled surrender of its right to market a legal product—has spawned Mr. Clinton's new assault on the industry: a proposed tax hike of 55 cents per pack and federal litigation to recoup health costs connected with smoking.

When Mr. Clinton needs money, he calls for Philip Morris. He simply bypasses the legislative process—not to mention the Constitution—and asks federal courts to create new laws. Never mind

*This section, as revised, was originally published under the title, "Clinton's Illegal Assault on the Tobacco Industry," *Wall Street Journal*, February 8, 1999, p. A23.

that the Justice Department has said repeatedly that the federal government has no statutory authority to bring a direct suit to recover smoking-related damages. When the objective is to replenish depleted Medicare coffers, anything goes—including the rule of law.

The feds are entitled to recoup Medicare outlays when a tobacco company causes a smoker's illness. To recover, the government must prove its case just as would the smoker suing on his own. And if the smoker knew about the risks of tobacco but elected to smoke anyway, then tobacco companies would win in court—as they had won consistently for four decades.

Mr. Clinton understood that principle perfectly well: It's called assumption of risk. His former Veterans Affairs secretary, Jesse Brown, invoked it when the government was threatened with liability suits for having provided millions of smokers with cigarettes over the years. It would be "borderline absurdity" to pay for "veterans' personal choice to engage in conduct damaging to their health," he said. "If you choose to smoke, you are responsible for the consequences of your act."

Of course, when the government becomes the plaintiff, it would prefer to ignore such defenses. That's what most of the states did in their Medicaid recovery suits. Florida worked its magic by statute, abolishing assumption of risk for purposes of the state's tobacco litigation. Other states copied the Florida statute, but many decided to make their appeal directly to state judges rather than go the legislative route.

For its part, the Justice Department has already divulged that it will model its suit after Florida's, with or without help from Congress. That means the government will claim it can recover by suing tobacco companies directly, without stepping into the shoes of each smoker and having to prove that smoker's case. The argument, just like Florida's, will be that the government never smoked, therefore it couldn't have assumed the risk. In effect, Justice will assert that it can recover merely because smoking injured someone protected by Medicare—even though that person, having assumed the risk, would have no right to recover on his own.

Also following the Florida model, the feds will ask the court to ignore the traditional requirement that causation be demonstrated on a smoker-by-smoker basis. Instead, the Justice Department will want to produce only aggregate statistics, indicating a higher incidence of certain diseases among smokers than nonsmokers. That means the government could sue for tobacco-related health expenditures on behalf of Medicare recipients without disclosing the names of the recipients or which of them smoked. The industry could neither challenge improper payments made by Medicare nor establish that its product was ever used by a recipient.

Even if the administration's latest litigation scheme could somehow be squared with the rule of law, another tax on cigarettes makes no sense. It's not just the destructive effect of black markets, or the brutal regressivity of price hikes, or the inequity when 44 million adult smokers have to fork up because some retailers violate unenforced laws and sell cigarettes to one million minors. It's also the judgment, by every scholar who has examined the data, that existing excise taxes more than cover the social costs of smoking. The uncomfortable truth is that federal and state governments have benefited handsomely from tobacco taxes, and therein lies one reason they have been unwilling to make cigarettes illegal.

Our adversarial system works quite well when smokers, insurance companies, and the industry fight it out in court, applying settled principles of tort law. The Medicare program can recover like any other insurer, but it should not be exempt from assumption of risk, it should have to prove case-by-case causation, and it must demonstrate actual damages.

That approach will work, and it's equitable. By contrast, the Clinton administration is embarked on yet one more raid on private wealth—a bald attempt to fatten the federal treasure chest without regard for individual liberty, personal responsibility, or the rule of law.

What Are They Smoking at the Justice Department?*

The ink had barely dried on the Master Settlement Agreement, negotiated between the major tobacco companies and 46 state attorneys general, when the Clinton Justice Department filed a federal suit against the same defendants. The complaint alleged, in part, that industry executives lied about the dangers of their product,

---

*This section, as revised, was originally published under the title, "Call Off the Anti-Tobacco Crusade," *National Post* (Canada), April 9, 2003, p. FP13. See also Robert A. Levy, "When Theft Masquerades as Law," *Cato Policy Report*, vol. XXII, no. 2, March/April 2000, p. 1.

manipulated nicotine content, and aimed ads at kids. Apparently no one at the Justice Department realized the irony—indeed the unbounded hypocrisy—of the Clinton administration pursuing anyone for lying under oath.

After the Republicans took over, Attorney General John Ashcroft, who opposed the suit when he was in the Senate, decided not to fund the litigation because it was too weak for trial. Evidently he has changed his mind: No explanation, no new legal claims, just an astonishing demand for $289 billion in damages—with a trial planned for September 2004 if the industry hasn't caved by then.

Never mind that the MSA already punished the industry's past misbehavior and forbade any future transgressions. Never mind that the so-called kiddy ads—in adult magazines like *Sports Illustrated* and *People*—promote brand allegiance, not the conversion of nonsmokers into smokers. None of that mattered. The federal litigation was part of an all-out strategy to plunder big tobacco—while keeping it alive for future plundering, of course.

The Justice Department's legal strategy, modeled after the states' lawsuits, was to seek reimbursement for billions of dollars in health care expenditures presumably related to smoking. Like the states, the federal government argued that it could sue tobacco companies without allowing them to assert that smokers were aware of the danger. That way, the Justice Department would not be subject to the "assumption-of-risk" defense that had been a consistent winner for the industry over four decades.

To supplement its bizarre tort theories, the Justice Department relied on three statutes: the Medical Care Recovery Act, the Medicare Secondary Payer Act, and the civil provisions of the Racketeer Influenced and Corrupt Organizations Act. In September 2000 federal judge Gladys Kessler dismissed most of the lawsuit out of hand. But she allowed a claim to go forward under the RICO act, despite expressing some reservations about the government's ability to prove damages. RICO was designed to be invoked against organized crime, but nowadays it's a standard bullying tactic by plaintiffs' attorneys. This time, however, the Justice Department had to deal with an embarrassing admission, tucked away in the final sentence of the press release that announced its lawsuit: "There are no pending Criminal Division investigations of the tobacco industry."

After a five-year, multimillion dollar inquiry by two dozen prose-cutors and FBI agents, the government came up with one misde-meanor plea against an obscure biotechnology company. The government dissected allegations that tobacco executives perjured themselves when testifying before Congress. Prosecutors plowed through documents for evidence that cigarette makers manipulated nicotine levels. Whistle-blowers and company scientists testified before grand juries. The outcome: not a single indictment of a tobacco company or industry executive.

Nonetheless, President Clinton collared his attorney general and she, somehow, conjured up a RICO complaint that accused the indus-try of the same infractions for which grand juries could not find probable cause. Among 116 counts against the industry, Janet Reno and her minions included all sorts of foolishness to ratchet up the pressure for an exorbitant financial settlement. Here's one example, count number three: In November 1959 the industry "did knowingly cause a press release to be sent and delivered by the U.S. mails to newspapers and news outlets. This press release contained state-ments attacking an article written by then-U.S. Surgeon General Leroy Burney about the hazards of smoking." There you have it— racketeering, in all its sordid detail.

The Justice Department's claims under the Medical Care Recovery Act weren't much better. The MCRA, passed in 1962, was intended to circumvent a 1947 Supreme Court case that denied a right of recovery under the common law for government medical outlays to pay for a soldier's injuries that were caused by a defendant's negligence. In no instance has the MCRA ever been used to reclaim Medicare expenditures. Indeed, because MCRA was enacted three years before Medicare, it could not have been within the contempla-tion of Congress that Medicare costs would be recoverable. Nor is there anything in MCRA suggesting that multiple claims can be aggregated as in the Justice Department's suit. Nor can the govern-ment recoup from tobacco companies the costs of treating a smoker's illness when the smoker himself could make no showing that his illness was due to the companies' negligence.

As a fallback, the department also claimed under the Medicare Secondary Payer Act. That 1980 statute expressly covers Medicare expenditures—implicitly confirming that the earlier MCRA did not do so. But MSPA is invoked against an injured party or his private insurer, not against a wrongdoer. The purpose of the statute is to prevent an injured party from recovering twice—once from a private insurer and a second time from Medicare—or to ensure that a private insurer isn't let off the hook for a legitimate claim just because the claim might otherwise be covered by Medicare. MSPA has never been employed to establish liability for an injury; it was designed for cost recovery only after liability had been determined.

Clinton insiders knew the charges were trumped up. Former Clinton aide Rahm Emanuel put it this way: "If the White House hadn't asked [Reno, she] would never have looked at it again." So it's politics and money, not law, that is driving this litigation. And what is worse, the entire scheme is cynically promoted as a way to protect the health of our children. Yet now that the loot is rolling in from the multi-state settlement, we know that kids' welfare is far down the list of priorities. Less than 5% of the money is being used for tobacco control programs.

Even prior to the November 1998 settlement, for every pack of cigarettes sold domestically, the industry earned about 23 cents, the feds got 34 cents, and the states averaged 37 cents. Thus, government got 71 of every 94 cents of pretax profits. In effect, the feds and the states were 76% stockholders in an enterprise that, according to government reports, kills 400,000 Americans every year. If indeed there's been a RICO conspiracy, government has been the major co-conspirator.

The American public—voters and jurors—need to know that our legal system is rapidly becoming a tool for extortion. Sometimes the politicians seek money; sometimes they pursue a policy agenda; too often they abuse their power. When Clinton was unable to persuade Congress to enact another tax on smokers, he simply bypassed the legislature and asked a federal court to impose damages in lieu of taxes. Bush can do much better. Yes, he's absorbed with establishing the rule of law around the globe, but the president needs to remind his Justice Department that the campaign begins here, at home. It is time to call off the federal government's anti-tobacco crusade.

Turning Lead into Gold*

Trial lawyers, their insatiable appetites whetted by a generous share of the quarter-trillion-dollar spoils extorted from smokers,

---

*This section, as revised, was originally published under the title, "It's Elemental: Pb + Lawyers = Au," *Mealey's Litigation Report: Lead*, vol. 10, no. 20, July 25, 2001. That article, in turn, was based in part on "Turning Lead into Gold," *Legal Times*, August 23, 1999, p. 21. See also Robert A. Levy, "Lawyers Greedily Trying to Turn Lead into Gold," *Houston Chronicle*, May 29, 2001.

have targeted their next two victims. Not surprisingly, the firearms industry was chosen to follow the tobacco bonanza. Responding to a string of mass shootings and egged on by the usual suspects in the contingency fee bar, nearly three dozen states, counties, and municipalities have gun makers in their crosshairs.[1]

Until recently, speculation about the third industry to be gouged had centered on the makers of beer, booze, and fatty foods. But prominent tobacco attorney John Coale assured us that he and his pals are "not going after alcohol and hamburgers. We like 'em too much."[2] Sad to say, there's no shortage of other prey, including pharmaceuticals, chemicals, sporting equipment, even automobiles.

It looks like the guessing game can end, however. According to the *Washington Post*, "trial lawyers and politicians locally and across the nation are gearing up to mount a major assault on the former makers of lead paint, which was banned in residences in 1978 but still poisons children in older buildings."[3] In 1999, Rhode Island's attorney general Sheldon Whitehouse (D) filed the first government-sponsored lawsuit.[4] Now, reports the *Houston Chronicle*, there's "a potential flood of lead paint litigation from school districts across Texas," patterned after the Rhode Island filing.[5] Milwaukee has also entered the fray,[6] with other cities and states waiting in the wings.

Texas attorney general John Cornyn (R) has declined so far to join his counterpart in Rhode Island. Cornyn has also criticized the tobacco settlement—especially the colossal $3.3 billion in legal fees that the states' trial lawyers collected.[7] But other Texas officials are less hesitant. Frank Sanders, chief of the litigation bureau in Harris County, has already sued. He gloats that outside lawyers will assume the costs even if the case fails. "We've got a situation we can't lose," he told the *Chronicle*.[8] Some might disagree. Surely, the politicization of the courts must be counted as a loss.

Rhode Island's Whitehouse admits that the multi-state tobacco settlement inspired him to file suit.[9] In fact, Rhode Island is being represented by Ness, Motley, Loadholt, Richardson & Poole, one of the law firms that was pivotal in rounding up states to sue cigarette makers.[10] The state hopes to replenish its coffers, purportedly depleted by public outlays for illnesses caused by lead paint and expenditures to remove lead from housing that hasn't been properly maintained. Rhode Island's sights are set on an industry that has never paid a cent in damages. For years, trial lawyers representing kids have sued landlords over lead poisoning and, in some cases, have won large judgments. But unlike landlords, the paint and pigment companies remain unscathed.

The industry has successfully argued that lead was a useful component of paint, helping to hide the previous color of surfaces to be re-covered; that paint makers voluntarily stopped using lead in interior paints in the 1950s, once it was known to be harmful; that the industry supported the 1978 federal ban; that recurring problems are the result of poor maintenance by homeowners (indeed, well-maintained surfaces covered with lead paint are not a danger); that lead poisoning arises from many products besides paint; and that it is impossible in any event to prove whose paint was on which wall.

That last argument, especially, has been a big stumbling block for plaintiffs' attorneys. The Pennsylvania Supreme Court, a New York appellate court, and federal appellate courts in the First, Third, and Fifth Circuits have required plaintiffs to show a causal link between their alleged injury and a particular manufacturer's paint. Those courts rejected plaintiffs' attempts to apportion liability based on "market share."[11] Nevertheless, enticed by the prospect of colossal fees like those looted from the tobacco companies, trial lawyers have fanned out in a frenzied search for attorneys general and mayors who are less concerned about the rule of law than about advancing their political aspirations at the expense of another hapless industry.

The complaints against lead paint makers are a near-perfect fit for the new litigation model: Costly lawsuits filed in multiple jurisdictions, spearheaded by private lawyers who stand to collect a hefty piece of the action, based on perverted rules of tort law applied retroactively in an attempt to circumvent the legislative process. That's the game the lawyers are playing. But here are the facts, as related in an editorial from the *Providence Journal-Bulletin*:

> [I]n 1955, the American paint industry voluntarily removed lead from its interior wall coverings in response to concerns expressed by the American Academy of Pediatrics. That was 23 years before Congress instituted a ban [supported by the industry] on lead in all paints. Lead was most commonly used in housepaint in the 1920s, and for many years, the federal government recommended its use because of lead's superior pigmentation. In other words, the paint industry sought to provide the best possible product to customers, and when the health hazards of lead became known, it took lead out of the paint—on its own initiative.[12]

Critics respond that paint manufacturers were aware early in this century that lead pigment used in residential house paint was hazardous to children, yet they conspired to market their product for decades without informing the public of its risks. Quite simply, that argument is implausible. Many hundreds of paint makers were in business at one time or another during the early 1900s. For a conspiracy theory to be credible, those companies—diverse and fiercely competitive—must have jointly suppressed actual knowledge of lead's harmful effects for half a century.

If it can be proven that a manufacturer knew of the danger and failed to notify its customers, there's an argument for liability in that particular case. But to hold an entire industry accountable without such proof is unconscionable. Therein lies the fundamental problem with these lawsuits: Specific causation—when a defendant's conduct results in a plaintiff's injury—has not been demonstrated. And that's why both private and government plaintiffs want to use market share liability: to bypass conventional notions of cause and effect.

Essentially, juries will be asked to presume that the companies being sued caused the alleged harm in proportion to their companies' sales of lead paint. That theory was originally applied in the DES (diethylstilbestrol) case.[13] A woman with a rare form of cancer sued the manufacturers of DES, which was administered to her mother during pregnancy to prevent miscarriage. Many daughters of women who took DES later contracted the same cancer. Because DES was sold by multiple manufacturers as a generic drug, and because of the long lead time between the use of DES and the onset of cancer, it was virtually impossible to determine precisely which company caused the disease in which women. Therefore, said the California Supreme Court, the apportionment of damages based on market share would ensure that culpable defendants could not evade liability.

Whatever the validity of market share liability in the DES case, its application to lead paint makers is plainly inappropriate. In the DES case, a few drug makers supplied almost the entire market; that contrasts with hundreds of paint manufacturers. All of the DES companies were deemed to be culpable; but nobody has determined which if any of the paint makers withheld information about known risks of lead-based paint. DES was the only cause of a rare form of cancer; by comparison, lead poisoning can arise from contaminated water and soil, lead pipes, hair dyes, some imported pottery, vitamin preparations, and dust from automobile emissions when leaded gasoline was sold. Injury from DES developed over a well-defined nine-month interval of pregnancy; injury from lead poisoning could arise at any time, decades after multiple applications of various paint products from numerous manufacturers.

Many of those manufacturers are no longer in existence, so historical share-of-market statistics are incomplete. Current statistics, of course, are irrelevant. Finally, an intervening causal factor—poor maintenance by the property owner—is an important consideration in assessing liability for lead poisoning; no such intervening factor complicated the DES case. The conclusion is inescapable: Market share liability should not be applied to allocate damage awards among lead paint makers. Indeed, without persuasive evidence of causation, coupled with defendant's willful failure to warn of known risks, damage awards cannot be justified.

On December 30, 1999, in dismissing a private lawsuit against pigment makers, a New York appellate court offered this cogent summary:

> [L]ead pigments other than white lead carbonate are used in lead-based paint; white lead carbonate is used for products other than interior residential paint; plaintiffs assert that they cannot determine when the lead-based paint was applied to their apartment; lead pigments are found in products other than lead-based paint; lead-based paint is not fungible; the manufacturers of white lead carbonate were not in exclusive control of the risk posed by lead-based paint; there is no signature injury associated with lead poisoning; and there is no indication by the Legislature that there should be a remedy for lead poisoning.[14]

Forget those facts. If the blandishments of the trial lawyers prove difficult to resist, states will be arguing, not that the owners or landlords of aging, substandard homes should have maintained them more diligently, but that lead poisoning in the 21st century should be blamed on the makers of paint that was used in the 1920s through the mid-1950s. That's the absurd argument now directed against innocent companies that produce useful products, employ thousands of people, and have not used lead for half a century.

Fat City for Trial Lawyers*

The race for the next litigation jackpot has officially begun—driven by trial lawyers funded by billions of dollars freshly extorted from hapless smokers. Caesar Barber, a 272-pounder, has sued the major fast-food chains because he is obese. "They said, '100% beef,'" Barber whined. "I thought that meant it was good for you. Those people in the advertisements don't really tell you what's in the food. It's all fat, fat and more fat."

Barber's case is just the beginning. In November 2002 his attorney, Samuel Hirsch, announced that he was putting the Barber suit on hold while he filed a second suit—a class action by parents on behalf of their obese teenagers. One of the moms, Roberta Pelman, was interviewed about the case on the Dr. Phil Show in September 2002. Here's how the dialogue unfolded: Dr. Phil: "Did you choose the food?" Ms. Pelman: "Yes, I did." Dr. Phil: "And did you serve it to your child?" Ms. Pelman: "Yes, I did." Dr. Phil: "So [your daughter] could sue you for putting it in front of her?" At that point, attorney Hirsch chimed in, "Yes, she could." That's the absurd logic of these lawsuits.

Ms. Pelman's daughter is 14 years old, under 5 feet tall, and weighs 170 pounds. She ate at McDonald's three or four times every week since age five. A second mom, Ms. Bradley, has a 19-year-old daughter who is 270 pounds, and ate at McDonald's twice a day for the past four years. Ms. Bradley says she never saw McDonald's posters containing nutritional information. Maybe so. But didn't she have a clue once her daughter exceeded, say, 200 pounds? How could those final 70 pounds—from 201 to 270—materialize without mom knowing something was wrong with her daughter's diet?

In January 2003 a federal judge threw out the Pelman-Bradley class action. But he suggested an amended complaint focused on whether McDonald's products had been so altered that their unhealthy attributes were not understood by consumers. Attorney Hirsch filed his amended complaint the next month, but it too was dismissed for lack of evidence in September 2003. Even so, if the tobacco litigation model holds up, a few states, then a few more,

*This section, as revised, was originally published under the title, "Where's the Beef? Fat City for Trial Lawyers Taking on Big Food," *South Florida Sun-Sentinel*, August 23, 2002, p. 29A.

will sue to recover their obesity-related Medicaid expenditures—another round of bogus legal theories contrived by clever private attorneys working as subcontractors to the state for a percentage of the loot. The entire scheme will be eagerly and greedily embraced by pals of the trial lawyers in state government. Contingency fee contracts will be awarded, mostly without competitive bidding, to law firms who bankroll state political campaigns.

Paranoia? Not at all. The Physicians Committee for Responsible Medicine warns that meat consumption is responsible for $61 billion each year in U.S. medical costs. "It's time we [held] the meat producers and fast-food outlets legally accountable. Without their powerful influence, America would have a healthier diet and a healthier national treasury." This fall, Northeastern University law professor Richard Daynard is holding a strategy session for nearly 100 lawyers interested in suing "Big Food." There's not much question what Daynard will be promoting: another shakedown without any concern for personal accountability, sanctioned by a nanny state with an insatiable appetite for social engineering.

If a corpulent plaintiff can prove that he was defrauded, that he relied on deceptive advertising despite an avalanche of contrary nutritional information, and that fatty foods caused his weight-related problems, then he might have a chance in court. But time-honored principles of tort law suggest that these lawsuits are frivolous, shamelessly designed to blackmail deep-pocketed companies. For starters, there are nondiet factors—heredity and lack of exercise, among others—inextricably linked to obesity. Under those circumstances, the science is highly suspect. Epidemiological studies are notoriously unreliable whenever the relationship between two variables (say, fatty foods and obesity) is complicated by so-called confounding factors.

Then there's the raging debate over which foods are harmful. When I was a kid, the nutritional gurus were pushing lots of steak and eggs. That regimen was overturned by supposedly wiser authorities, who substituted potatoes and pasta. Now we're told that high doses of carbohydrates in today's government-recommended diets may be the cause of recent waistline distention across America. So whom to sue: Dr. Atkins or the Pritikin Center? Kansas beef cattlemen or Idaho potato growers? Burger King or the Thai rice restaurant? Naturally, the lawyers have a ready response: Sue 'em all.

115

That's fine, for those who have little respect for the rule of law. Otherwise, here's the governing principle: If a consumer elects to gorge on foods known to be high-calorie, then he is accountable for the consequences. He cannot hold food companies responsible, least of all on a retroactive basis. By condoning these ridiculous lawsuits, we will send our children messages far more destructive than Big Macs. First, it's okay to change the rules after the game has begun. Second, you can engage in risky behavior, then force someone else to pay the bills.

If fatty foods are so injurious, let's make sales to kids illegal like we do with cigarettes. Require proof-of-age at retail stores. Prosecute retailers who break the law. Prohibit vending machine sales where underage consumers congregate—like in schools and arcades. For good reasons, those proposals are unlikely to attract wide support. Parenting is, after all, the job of moms and dads, not food companies and certainly not state governments.

Five years ago I predicted, without much risk of being wrong, that tobacco lawyers would soon be attacking other products deemed by our moral overseers to be bad for us. There would be no shortage of candidates, but the immediate target would probably be the food industry—sugar, dairy products, red meat, and French fries— because obesity allegedly causes 300,000 deaths each year. The anti-tobacco crowd laughed off the slippery slope argument, but now we know the risk is real and imminent. Yesterday it was tobacco, then guns. Today it's fatty foods. Tomorrow it could be skis, motor-cycles, cars, you name it—litigation lottery.

Intoxicating Lawsuit*

Hardly a week passes without a reminder that the state tobacco lawsuits have had an enduring and corrupting effect on the rule of law. The legal travesty *du jour* involves yet another "sin" industry. This time the trial lawyers are hounding the purveyors of alcoholic beverages because of ads ostensibly targeted, "deliberately and reck-lessly," at underage consumers.

Here's the cast of characters: The plaintiffs are a class of parents and guardians of kids too young to drink but exposed to the ads.

*This section was originally published under the title, "Liquor and Beer Ads Are Not the Problem," *Chicago Tribune*, December 8, 2003.

Representing the class are a pair of law firms: one headed by David Boies, the eminent litigator hired by the Justice Department to go after Microsoft; and a second headed by his son, David Boies III. The defendants include the Beer Institute and a number of large distillers and brewers such as Coors, Heineken, and Brown-Forman. Interestingly, the two largest domestic beer producers, Anheuser-Busch and Miller, a client of Boies senior, are not among the defendants.

Supposedly, the offending companies advertise in magazines "disproportionately read" by young people, place their products in movies seen by teens, make their Web sites accessible to minors, allude to college activities like "spring break," and use cartoon characters—probably the same way that MetLife uses Snoopy to hoodwink all those gullible adolescents into buying insurance policies.

Never mind that our drinking laws are absurd. An 18-year-old is presumably mature enough to sign contracts, get married, have an abortion, go to war, and decide who is going to run the country. But he's three years away from coping with the weighty implications of consuming a can of beer. Nor can a person of age 20, according to the Boies team, possibly resist the allure of a movie star enjoying a brew in a PG-13 film. In the end, how does a brewer or distiller, or a jury for that matter, distinguish an ad that would be suitable for a 21-year-old from an ad that might be construed as impermissibly "targeted" at a 20-year-old?

It's not as if this issue has escaped scrutiny. The Federal Trade Commission's *2003 Report on Alcohol Marketing and Advertising*, approved by the commission without dissent, looked at nine major companies and analyzed their ads, marketing plans, and consumer research. The Report "found no evidence of targeting underage consumers" in the increasingly popular market for flavored malt beverages, which combine beer and distilled spirits. Moreover, studies from other sources have concluded that liquor advertising doesn't affect aggregate consumption. The purpose of ads for alcoholic beverages, like ads for automobiles, is to encourage brand shifting, not to convert nondrinkers into drinkers.

There's another key concern when courts are asked to prevent private companies from exercising their commercial speech rights. In a 1983 case, *Bolger v. Youngs Drug Prods. Corp.*, the Supreme Court remarked that government must not "reduce the adult population ... to reading only what is fit for children." Then, 13 years later, the Court held that even "vice" products like alcoholic beverages are entitled to commercial speech protection (*44 Liquormart, Inc. v. Rhode Island*). Indeed, our Constitution protects Ku Klux Klan speech, flag burning, and gangsta rap, which is targeted directly at teenagers. Yet if Coors wants to advertise Keystone Light in *Sports Illustrated*, Mr. Boies and his team of lawyers would bring the boot of government down hard on the company's neck.

Ads are not the problem and their prohibition is not the solution to teenage drinking. The sale of alcoholic beverages to minors is illegal in every state. Those laws should be vigorously enforced. Retailers found to have violated the law should be prosecuted. But ultimately the responsibility rests with the family. However serious the problem of underage consumption of beer and liquor, and however heartrending that youngsters may injure themselves and others while driving under the influence of alcohol, there are countervailing values that are implicated when speech restrictions are proposed.

The choice between preserving core First Amendment values and regulating ads for alcoholic beverages is a particularly easy one when there is little evidence of any connection between those ads and the aggregate level of underage drinking. We need not sacrifice commercial free speech to reduce alcohol consumption by minors. Nor should we sit back and allow the trial lawyers to add one more notch to their expanding tobacco belt. Their message is simple: The doctrine of personal accountability is out the window. In its place is the insidious notion that you can engage in risky behavior, then force someone else to pay for your mistakes. That message is far more pernicious than any beer or liquor commercial.

5. Can Tort Reform and Federalism Coexist?*

Introduction

"A billion here, a billion there, and pretty soon you're talking about real money." When the late Sen. Everett M. Dirksen from Illinois offered that famous quip 40 years ago about government spending, no one imagined that the same words might be used today to describe damage awards in tort cases. Yet in 2003 a Florida jury somehow conjured up punitive damages of $145 billion for a class of plaintiffs. The year before, a California jury recommended a $28 billion treasure trove for a single claimant. And in 1998 four major cigarette companies agreed to the grandmother of all awards—a quarter-trillion-dollar settlement supposedly to reimburse the states for the Medicaid costs of smoking-related illnesses.

So it goes. Not just tobacco; but guns, asbestos, and a cross section of American industry that has morphed into the Mass Tort Monster: "DDT, Bendectin, DES, swine flu vaccine, Copper-7, PCBs, the Dalkon Shield, Shiley heart valves, heart catheters, pickup-truck fuel tanks, blood products, silicone breast implants, pedicle screws, penile implants, intraocular lenses, . . . lead pigment, latex, dietary supplements, fen-phen, Rezulin, L-tryptophan, Duract, Parlodel, Synthroid, Propulsid, and so forth almost *ad infinitum*."[1]

According to the U.S. Chamber of Commerce, our tort system is wrecking our economy. Since 1930 growth in litigation costs has been four times that of the overall economy. The chamber reports that federal class actions tripled over the past 10 years, while similar filings in state courts ballooned by more than 1,000%.[2] One chamber official estimates that the annual cost of the tort system translates into $809 per person—the equivalent of a 5% tax on wages.[3] The

*Originally published, with minor revisions, as Cato Institute Policy Analysis no. 514, April 14, 2004, coauthored with Michael I. Krauss, professor of law, George Mason University.

share going to trial lawyers—roughly $40 billion in 2002—was one-and-a-half times the annual revenues of Microsoft or Intel and twice those of Coca-Cola.[4] The estimated aggregate cost of the tort system in 2002 was $233 billion, says Tillinghast-Towers Perrin, a respected actuarial firm. That cost represented 2.23% of the U.S. gross domestic product.[5] Over the next 10 years, the total "tort tax" will likely be $3.6 trillion.[6]

When costs explode, proposals for reform are never far behind—especially when the electoral season is upon us. Thus, we have been deluged by congressional schemes to curb class action litigation, ban lawsuits against gun makers and fast food distributors, cap medical malpractice awards, and otherwise enlist the federal government in the battle against allegedly biased state judges and juries.

Our primary objective in this paper is not to document that tort reform is necessary or desirable. That task has been ably and effectively performed by several others.[7] Instead, we seek to explore the methods by which reforms might be implemented—especially the extent to which various proposals are compatible with our system of dual-sovereignty federalism. Our underlying premise is straightforward: No matter how worthwhile a goal may be, if there is no constitutional authority to pursue it, then the federal government must step aside and leave the matter to the states, or to citizens in the private ordering of their affairs.

Congress can proceed only from constitutional authority, not from good intentions alone. That means we must find a source of constitutional authority for each proposed tort reform. One possible source, which we examine in the next section, is the all-encompassing Commerce Clause. As the country grew and some people believed that all of its problems required national regulatory solutions, Congress sought to earmark a specified constitutional power that would justify an ambitious federal agenda. The Commerce Clause became the vehicle of choice.

Yet the central reason that the clause appeared in the Constitution was quite different. Under the Articles of Confederation of 1776, the national government lacked the power to regulate interstate commerce. Each state was free to advance local interests and to create barriers to trade, without regard to possible prejudice to out-of-state interests. That process devolved into what Justice William Johnson characterized as a "conflict of commercial regulations, destructive to the harmony of the States."⁸ The solution: a constitutional convention at which, according to Justice Johnson, "If there was any one object riding over every other in the adoption of the constitution, it was to keep the commercial intercourse among the States free from all invidious and partial restraints."⁹

Today, instead of serving as a shield against interference by the states, the commerce power has become a sword wielded by the federal government in pursuit of a boundless array of socioeconomic programs. But the mere fact that goods and services subject to tort litigation are transported across state lines and sold to customers in several states does not justify federal intervention under the Commerce Clause. To legitimately invoke the commerce power, Congress must show that federal tort reform is "necessary" *and* that it is "proper"—that is, it does not violate other constitutional principles—to ensure the free flow of interstate commerce. As we shall see—on the basis of examples involving fast food distributors, the firearms industry, and medical malpractice—substantive federal reform is neither necessary (procedural remedies would do the trick) nor properly harmonized with traditional concepts of federalism.

Following our look at the Commerce Clause, we turn to an alternative source of constitutional authority, the Due Process Clause of the Fourteenth Amendment. Ratified in 1868, the Fourteenth Amendment states, in relevant part, that no state shall "deprive any person of life, liberty, or property, without due process of law." If confiscatory state court decisions have the effect of denying due process to defendants in tort litigation, federal courts are empowered by the Fourteenth Amendment to intercede. And section 5 of the amendment authorizes Congress "to enforce, by appropriate legislation" the Due Process Clause.

The question, then, is whether state courts have gone so far as to deprive tort defendants of due process. If so, federal remedies might be in order. Perhaps, for example, a damage award is so excessive that it breaches constitutional safeguards. Then again, perhaps "due process" imposes no substantive limits on state tort awards, just procedural guarantees such as advance notice of the existence of a rule and an opportunity to defend oneself against a claim. Or perhaps substantive and procedural protections merge when damage awards are so capricious and unpredictable that defendants cannot know with any assurance how to conform their conduct to the dictates of the law.

In our section on the Fourteenth Amendment, we weigh those issues by analyzing the Supreme Court's recent decision in *State Farm Mutual Automobile Insurance Co. v. Campbell*.[10] That case specifically addressed punitive damages, although many of the principles debated by the Court are applicable to tort reform more broadly. In dissecting *State Farm*, we discuss the purpose of punitive damages, the need for reform, past efforts at reform, and the current controversy over so-called judicial activism and substantive due process.

Although we recognize the limitations of what is known as substantive due process, and in fact urge the Court to reconsider the Privileges or Immunities Clause of the Fourteenth Amendment as an alternative justification for striking down certain state laws, we nonetheless conclude that the majority in *State Farm* was correct in curbing punitive damages. That said, we proceed in the following section, "Reconciling Tort Reform and Federalism," to recommend a series of reforms that avoid the inconsistencies of substantive due process while respecting the notion that states should serve as experimental laboratories of competing tort systems.

First among our suggested reforms are those that can be implemented at the state level. We begin by offering several solutions to the problem of excessive punitive awards. Then we advocate state-based reforms in other areas, like curbing joint and several liability, shifting attorneys' fees when government is the losing party in a civil lawsuit, prohibiting contingency fee contracts between government and private lawyers, and restraining litigation by government to recover expenditures made on behalf of private parties.

Switching to federal reforms, we support two changes that are procedural in nature.[11] The first change is federal reform of state "long-arm" jurisdiction—the rules that determine whether an out-of-state entity can be sued in a local court. A sensible application of the Due Process Clause would exempt businesses from local court jurisdiction unless they have sufficient dealings within the state. Currently, out-of-state businesses find it exceedingly difficult to avoid oppressive state tort regimes.

The second federal reform that we endorse is a change in "choice-of-law" rules, which determine which state's laws control a suit involving litigants from more than one state. Frequently, tort defendants will be disadvantaged when plaintiffs select jurisdictions that have plaintiff-friendly choice-of-law rules. The concern is that the tort laws of some states discriminate against out-of-state corporate defendants. If that were to happen on a large scale, it could impede interstate commerce—the very problem that the Commerce Clause was intended to redress. By establishing a federal choice-of-law rule—a procedural solution that does not intrude on state sovereignty, because it leaves underlying state substantive law in place—the federal government can effect meaningful tort reform without trampling on principles of federalism.

Tort Reform, Federalism, and the Commerce Clause

Background

Our review of the federal government's venture into tort reform starts with recent efforts by Congress to expand its already copious power to regulate interstate commerce. A few examples:

1. Legislation that would cap medical malpractice awards and limit attorney fees cleared the House 229 to 196 on March 13, 2003.[12] That was the seventh attempt at federal malpractice reform since Republicans took over the House in 1995.[13]
2. In the aftermath of the September 11, 2001, terrorist attacks, Congress passed the Air Transportation Safety and System Stabilization Act, which created a federal cause of action for property and personal injury claims related to 9/11. At the same time, the act capped the airlines' liability at the amount of their insurance coverage.[14]
3. In 2001 the House and Senate passed separate versions of the Patients' Bill of Rights, which provided for an expansion of patients' right to sue health plans in state courts while limiting damages for pain and suffering and punitive damages.[15]

On the subject of tort reform, hypocrisy on both sides of the aisle is thick enough to slice. Democrats opposed to federal tort reform suddenly profess abiding faith in federalism. Yet those same Democrats were beside themselves when the Supreme Court held in 1995 that federal power to create criminal law is not plenary.[16] Meanwhile, Republicans, self-styled ardent defenders of decentralization, now argue that malpractice (for instance) is a "national problem." But under our federal system, every *national* problem does not ipso facto become a *federal* problem.

Several commentators have proposed that state tort rules should give way to uniform national rules in order to help federal courts cope with ever-increasing mass tort cases.[17] Legislators have proposed several bills that would alter "diversity jurisdiction," allowing federal courts to hear tort class actions even if some plaintiffs reside in the same state as some defendants.[18] Some observers have suggested that federal law alone should govern punitive damages.[19] Federalization of tort law is also occurring indirectly through executive branch agencies. That means defendants in tort suits may be able to avoid liability by arguing that they have complied with all applicable federal statutes and regulations, which would preempt irreconcilable state rules.[20]

In the face of those pressures to federalize tort law, our constitutional principles must be recalled and enforced. The general principle cannot be repeated often enough: *Our federal government is one of limited and enumerated powers.* The making of tort law is not one of those powers. The Constitution *does* provide, as we have noted, that Congress can "regulate Commerce . . . among the several States."[21] Over the past 65 years, courts have read the Commerce Clause very broadly, using it to uphold federal legislation concerning noncommercial activity.[22] In so doing, the courts have allowed Congress to turn the commerce power on its head. Instead of using it to strike down state barriers to interstate trade, Congress has in fact *erected* federal barriers that prevented free trade.

To be sure, state laws, including tort rules, often "affect" commerce. But that is not enough to justify federal intervention unless the flow of trade among the states is impeded by such laws. In 1995 the Supreme Court took a step toward reaffirming that important principle. In *United States v. Lopez*, the Court held that the Gun-Free School Zones Act of 1990, which purported to ban the possession of guns within 1,000 feet of any school, exceeded Congress's authority under the Commerce Clause, in part because Congress made no finding that the possession of firearms near schools affected interstate trade.[23] In 2000 the Court extended *Lopez* in *U.S. v. Morrison*, which held that a statutory federal tort suit for sexual battery under the Violence Against Women Act was unconstitutional, even though Congress had issued fig-leaf findings that sexual assaults affected interstate commerce.[24]

State laws regularly affect interstate commerce without raising constitutional concerns. California, for example, requires special catalytic converters on cars sold in that state. That's a permissible use of California's police power that doesn't directly affect interstate trade.[25] But if California tried to regulate catalytic converters on every car that crossed its state boundary, that would provoke stronger Commerce Clause questions. Cars traveling interstate would have to stop at the border and turn back—clearly a burden on interstate commerce.

Can federalism be squared with Washington's current tort reform proposals? In a word, no. Federal intervention is rarely authorized for the purpose of altering substantive rules of state tort law. Most tort suits involve "internal" activities, like negligent driving,[26] doctoring, lawyering, and so forth, and pit an in-state individual plaintiff against an in-state individual defendant. When litigated in a state court before a local jury, that type of case creates no intrinsic predisposition against either party. What is sometimes termed a "public choice" problem[27] is absent: The plaintiff cannot persuasively ask the jury to bring "outside" money into the locality without harming anyone locally. Even when parties are insured, both in-state and out-of-state insurance companies are exposed to the same liability regime.

Other, noncommercial kinds of bias (against the social class or race of either party, for example) are of course possible in those cases, as in all lawsuits. Such biases might raise Fourteenth Amendment concerns. However, race and class biases are not intrinsic to a party's status as plaintiff or defendant. In any case, parties can attempt to guard against those biases through challenges to the jury selection.[28] Thus, there is no valid structural reason for the federal government to intervene in the ordering of behavior through state tort law.

A second type of tort suit—exemplified by negligence claims invoking *respondeat superior* (suits against an employer for damages caused by wrongful behavior by its employee)[29]—usually sets in-state *individual* plaintiffs against in-state *corporate* defendants. Because juries are always composed of individuals and never of corporations, corporate defendants might experience systemic prejudice here: A jury may be tempted to transfer wealth from an entity that does not "feel pain" to a suffering real person with whom it can identify. But such temptations may be offset by the jury's desire to maintain employment and economic activity in its own locality, especially if the defendant corporation maintains a large local presence. It is hard to predict how those offsetting incentives will ultimately unfold in a specific case.[30] In any event, those problems derive from the *corporate* nature of the defendant, not its state of domicile. Thus, state tort law can alleviate any anti-corporate biases that may exist. Few states want existing employers to pack up and leave.

To the extent that abusive state tort rules operate like a tax on productive activity, the greater the abuse, the greater the decline in productivity or wealth. Customers will pay more for in-state services if the providers of those services have to pay for injuries they did not wrongfully cause. Physicians will avoid practicing in jurisdictions with unreasonable malpractice rules. Local children and their parents will suffer if playgrounds cannot be built without the park authority being held liable for inevitable accidents. Those costs produce powerful in-state lobbies for tort reform. Predictably, since the so-called torts crisis of the mid-1980s, almost all 50 states have enacted some form of tort reform for intrastate activity.[31]

The reforms have varied substantially—from caps on punitive damages to the creation of statutes of repose (limiting the time period within which claims can be filed) to the modification of joint and several liability (whereby each one of multiple defendants is held liable for the entirety of a plaintiff's damages, irrespective of the extent of the individual defendant's culpability).[32] Some state reforms have arguably been misguided—and more than a few have been declared by state supreme courts to violate state constitutions[33]— but misguided or nonexistent state reform is no justification for federal lawmakers to intervene. When voters realize that they pay a price if their state persists in applying dysfunctional tort rules, state lawmakers have every incentive to respond. The same types of incentives that dissuade states from imposing exorbitant income or sales taxes can operate to create a rational tort system.

Early product liability suits tended to be of the intrastate kind. Most products were manufactured near their place of consumption, as transportation costs made far-flung markets unreachable. Thus, many lawsuits concerning allegedly defective products were filed by local individual plaintiffs against local corporate defendants.[34] But with the advent of "paradigm shifters"[35] such as assembly-line production, interstate highways, and electronic auctions, markets for goods (though not yet services) have today become largely national.

Modern product liability suits characteristically set in opposition an *in-state* individual plaintiff and a corporate *out-of-state* defendant.[36]

In a typical product liability suit today, a consumer purchases a product, is allegedly injured while using it, and sues its far-off manufacturer[37] to recover damages. Most purchases take place close to home; almost all product use takes place near the home or the workplace;[38] and no state is home to a majority of manufacturers' head offices or factories. The confluence of those factors means that a plaintiff ordinarily files a product liability suit in his home state, which is also the state where he was injured and where he purchased the allegedly defective product. In the vast majority of cases, however, the product was designed and manufactured in another state.

Assume for a moment that the victim sues in his home state. There, the court agrees it has jurisdiction to try the suit and concludes that its own product liability law applies to resolve the dispute. Such a suit would now pit a local individual against an out-of-state corporation, in the local plaintiff's court and subject to the local plaintiff's state law. That situation creates a risk of bias that is unlikely to be remedied by political and economic forces within the state. Such a situation is ripe for federal tort reform. Even then we will conclude that *substantive* (as opposed to procedural) federal tort legislation is neither needed nor beneficial.

First, however, we look at pending federal tort reform proposals in three industry-specific areas—fatty foods, guns, and medical malpractice. None of these reforms is authorized by the Commerce Clause, and each offends basic tenets of federalism.

The Case against Substantive Federal Tort Reform: Three Examples

Fatty foods. The most recent area where preemptive federal legislation has been proposed is that of fatty foods. Sen. Mitch McConnell (R-KY) drafted a bill that would ban certain liability suits against food sellers and manufacturers.[39] In the House, Rep. Ric Keller (R-FL) introduced the Personal Responsibility in Food Consumption Act.[40] His bill would forbid civil suits, in both federal and state courts, against food manufacturers, distributors, or restauranteurs for obesity or other supposed deleterious effects of eating noncontaminated food. The bill has 108 cosponsors and, of course, the backing of industry groups.

Because the fatty food lawsuits are groundless,[41] we understand and sympathize with the objectives of both bills. Still, good intentions are not a substitute for constitutional authorization. Moreover, it's easy to exaggerate the litigation problem. A 2003 case brought by obese New York teenagers against McDonald's claimed that the restaurant should be responsible for the plaintiffs' health problems.[42] In another case, Oreo cookies and Big Daddy ice cream were alleged to have misled customers about their products' nutritional content.[43] But those suits have not succeeded.[44] Indeed, every court that has considered similar litigation has refused to allow it to go forward.[45] Nonetheless, one day a sympathetic state court will likely be found, perhaps in one of America's "judicial hellholes."[46] Senator McConnell's and Representative Keller's bills are meant to nip those future decisions in the bud.

Yet where in the Constitution does the federal government find authority to ban lawsuits against fast food manufacturers? According to McConnell's bill, the answer is—to no one's surprise—the all-purpose Commerce Clause. In a nutshell, fatty food suits are said to hinder interstate commerce in ingredients, and therefore to invite federal intervention. Undoubtedly, frivolous lawsuits against food manufacturers would jeopardize legitimate businesses that may be important to our national economy. The geographic scope of the problem does not, however, demand that it be resolved by Congress. Lawsuits against food manufacturers affect commerce in multiple states. But so does just about every state regulation or court decision. The Commerce Clause would not permit the federal government to override state minimum wage laws, for example, even if high in-state wages discourage out-of-state employers from setting up shop.

Procedural choice-of-law rules, as we will explain below, can resolve interstate problems that might be caused by baseless state fatty food liability decisions—without sacrificing state sovereignty over the substantive rules of tort law. The fatty food legislation must be trimmed.

Guns. The same considerations underlie our view of federal proposals to ban state and local suits against firearm manufacturers. But here there is one additional factor: The right of individual and collective self-defense, enshrined in the Second Amendment, may be undermined by undue state interference with firearms manufacturers. Accordingly, we distinguish between federal intervention under Commerce Clause auspices, which would not be justified, and federal intervention to secure the rights guaranteed by the Second

Amendment—as applied to the states through the Fourteenth Amendment—which may be justified, depending on the specific provisions of the legislation authorizing the intervention.

Let us make clear at the outset that most lawsuits against firearms manufacturers for anything other than manufacturing defects[47] are barely disguised extortion attempts. Here are the two principal legal theories recently asserted by dozens of municipalities against gun makers:

1. "Negligent Marketing." According to this newfangled theory of tort law, gun manufacturers "flood" suburban jurisdictions with more guns than are "legitimate" for local suburban demand, knowing that dealers will connive to sell illegally the excess supply to criminals from the inner city, where gun laws are typically more restrictive.
2. "Design Defect." Under this theory, guns are defective and unreasonably dangerous because they do not have design features that would minimize their use by criminals.

Both theories are shot full of holes.[48] Courts across the nation—without the help of Congress—have concluded that gun makers are not the proximate cause of, and therefore not responsible for, the criminal misconduct of a very small percentage of their customers.[49] Those are the right results. But wrong results might one day occur.[50] Would that justify federal intervention? Yes, it might—*unlike* the fatty food example—but only if one condition were satisfied. If the federal government declared forthrightly that gun ownership by law-abiding citizens was a guaranteed Second Amendment right, which Congress could therefore protect from undue state encroachment by virtue of the Fourteenth Amendment, federal intervention could be appropriate. But if protection of firearm manufacturers is premised on Commerce Clause grounds, then the idea of federal intervention is flawed. If Congress's Commerce Clause authority is misused to allow the federal government to impose rules that restrict state gun lawsuits, it could one day similarly be misused to impose federal rules that impose more severe liability on gun manufacturers and distributors.

The National Rifle Association, which has vigorously backed a federal ban on firearms lawsuits, would not like that. NRA attorneys would argue that the Commerce Clause was intended to ensure free trade, not to establish a federal police power. How do we know that would be the NRA's view? Because in 1995, after Congress enacted the Violent Crime Control and Law Enforcement Act of 1994,[51] the NRA sued, contending that Congress exceeded its powers under the Commerce Clause when it prohibited the manufacture, transfer, and possession of semi-automatic weapons.[52] It cannot be that the Commerce Clause did not authorize a federal ban on the sale and manufacture of assault weapons in 1995—a position we certainly endorse—while in 2004 that same Commerce Clause permits the federal government to commandeer state courts and tell them what kind of product liability suits they can entertain.

Federal intervention is not needed to rein in municipal litigation against gun makers. Since the first of the state firearms suits was filed, 33 states[53] have enacted legislation that prevents such suits. In those jurisdictions where the suits have not been barred, the firearms industry has not lost a single case.

On October 7, 1999, Ohio Judge Robert Ruehlman dismissed with prejudice Cincinnati's suit, calling it "an improper attempt to have this court substitute its judgment for that of the legislature, something which this court is neither inclined nor empowered to do."[54] On December 10, 1999, Superior Court Judge Robert F. McWeeny threw out the city of Bridgeport's suit, writing: "[T]he court finds as a matter of law that the plaintiffs lack standing to litigate these claims; thus, the court is without jurisdiction to hear this case."[55] On December 13, 1999, Florida Circuit Judge Amy Dean dismissed Miami-Dade County's lawsuit against the industry with a similar decision, stating, "Public nuisance does not apply to the design, manufacture, and distribution of a lawful product."[56]

Here are three other examples of state supreme court rulings against frivolous firearms lawsuits:

1. On April 3, 2001, the Louisiana Supreme Court voted 5 to 2 to dismiss the City of New Orleans' suit, the first of its kind to be filed, upholding the state law that forbids municipalities in Louisiana from bringing those types of suits. In October 2001 the U.S. Supreme Court allowed the Louisiana court's decision to stand, by refusing to review the case on appeal.[57]

2. On August 6, 2001, the California Supreme Court issued a 5-to-1 ruling that gun manufacturers cannot be held responsible

when their products are used to commit crimes. The decision referred to a 1983 California law prohibiting that type of lawsuit.[58]

3. On October 1, 2001, the Connecticut Supreme Court upheld the 1999 ruling that dismissed Bridgeport's suit because the city lacked "any statutory authorization to initiate ... claims" of liability against the firearms industry.[59] After the rejection of the New Orleans suit, Bridgeport's mayor Joseph Ganim told the Associated Press that an appeal of his city's suit to the U.S. Supreme Court was "probably not a likely route for us" and "[i]t's not likely we're in a very strong position."[60]

Clearly, state legal and political processes have produced the correct outcomes—both in the courts and in the legislatures. To the extent that the mere filing of lawsuits, and the attendant cost of litigation, is a burden on the firearms industry, that problem can be remedied by procedural reforms, which we discuss at greater length in our section on "Reconciling Tort Reform and Federalism."

When the bill to ban selected lawsuits against the gun industry was first introduced in the 107th Congress,[61] its only constitutional pedigree was the Commerce Clause. By the time the bill was reported in the House nearly 17 months later, it included a finding that "[c]itizens have a right, under the Second Amendment ... to keep and bear arms." And one of the expressed goals of the legislation was to "preserve a citizen's access to a supply of firearms and ammunition for all lawful purposes." Later, in the 108th Congress, the Second Amendment justification was preserved in S. 659,[62] along with the original Commerce Clause rationale. S. 659 contained this finding, which reflects both sources of constitutional authority:

> The possibility of imposing liability on an entire industry for harm that is solely caused by others is an abuse of the legal system, erodes public confidence in our Nation's laws, *threatens the diminution of a basic constitutional right and civil liberty*, invites the disassembly and destabilization of other industries and economic sectors lawfully competing in the free enterprise system of the United States, and constitutes an unreasonable burden on interstate and foreign commerce of the United States.[63]

Because our focus is on the Commerce Clause, we do not intend to parse the specific provisions of S. 659 to determine whether each

131

type of lawsuit that it attempts to ban would, if litigated, offend the Second Amendment. Yet we do argue that securing Second Amendment rights is the only legitimate basis on which federal intervention might be justified.

With respect to the Commerce Clause rationale, it's time for Congress, the NRA, and the Supreme Court to draw a line in the sand. Plain and simple, an outright ban on selected state tort lawsuits is not a regulation of interstate trade.

Interestingly, at this writing, the Senate has done the right thing; it has overwhelmingly rejected S. 659. The bill's own sponsors turned against it, as did its NRA supporters. But, sad to say, the senators were not suddenly concerned about the bill's Commerce Clause or federalism implications. Rather, they voted the bill down because opponents had added "poison pill" amendments, including one that would have extended a soon-to-expire ban on so-called assault weapons.[64]

Very likely, the industry's supporters in Congress will mount another effort to immunize gun makers from unfounded litigation. That may be warranted from a public policy perspective. But public policy arguments cannot confer federal authority where none exists. Under our Constitution, the commerce power was meant to ensure the free flow of interstate trade, not to dictate substantive product liability rules in each and every state. Yes, municipal lawsuits against gun makers have been baseless and extortionate. But that, in and of itself, does not make the substantive rules of state tort law the business of Congress.

Medical malpractice. When it comes to federal incursions into traditional state functions, it's not only the legislative branch that has overreached. President Bush used his support for federal malpractice tort reform measures to distinguish himself from Al Gore during the 2000 presidential campaign. And he's doing so against his Democratic opponents in 2004. Of course, the president is a former governor who says he is committed to principles of federalism. Yet he defends the federalization of malpractice law: "People say, well, is [medical malpractice] a federal responsibility?" "It's a national problem," he responds, "that requires a national solution. The federal government ought to set a minimum federal standard to reform the medical liability system."[65] Again, however, the fact that a problem exists in more than one state does not make it a *federal* responsibility.

The administration's legal strategy in defense of federal intervention appears to be twofold.[66] First, federal limitations on medical malpractice suits are supposedly warranted because the federal government spends money on health care, and the Constitution's spending power[67] presumably allows Congress to impose conditions on parties that benefit from those expenditures. Not only does the federal government fund Medicare and Medicaid, it also provides direct care to members of the armed forces, veterans, and patients served by the Indian Health Service, as well as tax breaks to workers who obtain health insurance through their employers. The administration projects savings of at least $25 billion a year if its proposed medical malpractice reforms are put in place. "[A]ny time a malpractice lawsuit drives up the cost of health care, it affects taxpayers. It is a federal issue," the president declared in a North Carolina speech.[68]

In essence, the argument is that Washington pays the states for *a lot* of health care; therefore Washington can enforce state malpractice reform, which would affect how *all* health care money is spent. But the Supreme Court has invalidated conditions imposed on the recipients of federal spending unless, among other things, the conditions are unambiguous and reasonably related to the aim of the expenditure.[69] In this instance, Congress has not linked the receipt of federal health funding to malpractice reform, nor has the federal government shown that the goals of Medicare and Medicaid depend on such reforms. Moreover, the scope of proposed federal malpractice intervention extends, though it need not logically do so, to all health care lawsuits—not just those brought by or against parties who receive federal funds.

Second, the administration posits a Commerce Clause argument.[70] Physicians are "forced" to move to another state, or to retire from practice altogether (thus removing their services from the "stream of interstate commerce"), by hikes in malpractice premiums.[71] At the margin, malpractice abuse has surely steered some patients across state lines to find better health care. But intrastate regulation of in-state conduct is simply not interference with interstate commerce—otherwise there is no area immune from federal jurisdiction. Naturally, there's an effect on commerce when any individual or company withdraws from a state. But if the withdrawal is related to unjust in-state negligence claims, without discrimination against out-of-state defendants, then the effect is not uniquely related to the *interstate* aspect of commerce.

In objecting to the president's assertion of federal jurisdiction, we do not dismiss potential problems associated with excessive medical malpractice decisions in certain states. Fear of malpractice liability may lead doctors to order redundant and expensive diagnostic tests[72] and operations.[73] High malpractice insurance premiums may encourage competent physicians to retire prematurely, leaving whole geographic areas underserved.[74] On the other hand, those allegations are disputed. Indeed, some well-respected academic sources suggest that there may be too little medical malpractice liability.[75]

But we need not enter the substantive debate on medical malpractice reform here. It is sufficient to show that federal intervention is neither necessary nor proper. The two litigants in a medical malpractice suit are usually a local (in-state) plaintiff and a local (in-state) physician. As a result, excessive liability will be directly felt in the local state, where it will translate into high insurance premiums for doctors and high costs for patients. Doctors can of course retire from practice or relocate to other states if they find liability too onerous. That will exert pressure on both juries and legislatures to temper excesses.

State medical malpractice reform is ubiquitous.[76] More than three dozen states have passed damage caps. All 50 states have passed or considered some kind of medical malpractice reform.[77] If a state legislature has chosen not to enact medical malpractice reform—and to suffer an increase in the cost or a decline in the quantity of medical care, or both, from a presumed "optimal" level—that is not a federal crisis. Rather, that is a matter for the state's voters to resolve.

Nonetheless, H.R. 5 and S. 607, the Help Efficient, Accessible, Low-Cost, Timely Healthcare (HEALTH) Act,[78] set damage caps and limited attorney fees, among other things. Rep. Tom Feeney (R-FL), usually a defender of federalism, claims to have "wrestled with the issue."[79] But he and his fellow Republicans seem to have concluded that a partial federal takeover of state tort law is necessary.

Yet there is no constitutional right to health care. Moreover, the Commerce Clause rationale invoked by H.R. 5 and S. 607 is unconvincing. Shocking malpractice damage awards, if indeed they are systemically too high, are not commerce and seldom interstate.

Tort Reform, Federalism, and the Fourteenth Amendment

Because the Commerce Clause has been distended to accommodate all manner of federal mischief, some proponents of federal tort reform have endorsed an alternative source of constitutional authority, the Fourteenth Amendment. Here's their argument: Advocates of states' rights too often have a crabbed, essentially mistaken conception of federalism. Federalism is not just about states' rights. To be sure, the framers originally established a federal government of enumerated powers. And the Tenth Amendment, ratified in 1791, provided that those powers not delegated to the United States were reserved to the individual states or to the people. But in 1868, when the Fourteenth Amendment was ratified, the relationship between federal and state governments was fundamentally restructured. And those politicians who rail against federal legislative incursions and judicial activism may not have fully grasped the significance of the post–Civil War transformation.

The Fourteenth Amendment to the federal Constitution addresses the violation of constitutionally guaranteed rights by state governments. Both the legislative and judicial branches of the federal government are empowered to remedy those violations. And within that framework, the U.S. Supreme Court may prevent a state court from denying rights to citizens inside and, a fortiori, outside the state. That is not mere activism—at least not in the sense of fabricating entitlements never grounded in the Constitution. Rather, it is judicial responsibility, allegiance to the law and to the Constitution, rooted in a theory of rights. Arguably, one of those rights, enshrined in the Due Process Clause of the Fourteenth Amendment, is protection against grossly excessive or arbitrary punishments. We turn next to that topic, in the context of punitive damage awards.

Punitive Damages: A Case for Federal Reform

Perhaps the most business-friendly of the Supreme Court's recent opinions was its 2003 reversal of a bloated $145 million punitive damages award against State Farm Insurance.[80] Ironically, that holding overcame separate dissents from the Court's conservative stalwarts, Justices Antonin Scalia and Clarence Thomas. Justice Ruth Bader Ginsburg also dissented. The same three justices had dissented from the Court's 1996 decision overturning a punitive damage award against BMW.[81] In that case, Chief Justice William H. Rehnquist dissented as well. But in *State Farm*, he switched sides without explanation.

The odd lineup of the justices is a healthy sign, say many Court watchers. It suggests that law and politics operate within separate realms. An alternative explanation, however, is that the current Court has no coherent jurisprudential compass. *State Farm* may simply be the latest case in which the Court has struggled to reconcile traditional state-based lawmaking—in this instance, tort law—and federalism. Once again, the Court had to grapple with federal intervention, through the Fourteenth Amendment's Due Process Clause, to prevent states from violating substantive rights that some people believe are secured by the U.S. Constitution.

Contrasting the majority opinion in *State Farm* with the terse dissents by Scalia and Thomas, we hope to shed light on the battle between conservatives who want to rein in runaway punitive damage awards and other conservatives who reluctantly find no federal judicial power to do so. First, we set the stage with a few comments on the nature of punitive damages, the need for reform, and the Court's major stab at the problem in the case of *BMW v. Gore*. Then we analyze the *State Farm* opinion and explore the controversy over the Court's substantive due process jurisprudence.

Our conclusion: *State Farm* was a close call, but the majority successfully made its case for federal judicial intervention. Nevertheless, there are better approaches to tort reform. We will address those approaches in a later section on "Reconciling Tort Reform and Federalism."

Nature of punitive damages. Compensatory damages are supposed to redress any loss that the plaintiff suffers because of the defendant's wrongful conduct. Punitive damages serve a different purpose. They "are aimed at deterrence and retribution."[82] The logic goes like this: A defendant whose misbehavior causes injury will neither be adequately punished nor deterred from similar misbehavior in the future if he is held accountable only for the losses he causes. That's because some wrongful acts, especially premeditated and intentional ones, are concealed or for some other reason never litigated. Therefore, proper deterrence requires hiking up the compensatory award.[83] Still, advocates of tort reform argue that judges and juries have allowed punitive damage awards to explode without regard to their harmful impact on the economy and without a rational link to the real need for deterrence. The evidence seems to support that view.

Need for reform. Consider the recent *Engle* tobacco class action litigation,[84] in which an inflamed Florida jury resolved to assess $145 billion in punitive damages against cigarette manufacturers. Trial judge Robert Kaye, notwithstanding an advisory opinion to the contrary from the state's attorney general, permitted the jury to quantify punitive damages for the entire class, after hearing evidence on only three of the claimants and before *any* tort liability to the remaining claimants had been established.[85]

No one knew the names of the other class members. No one even knew how many smokers were in the class; estimates ranged from 30,000 to nearly a million. No one knew anything about their alleged injuries or how much if any compensatory damages might be warranted. Yet Judge Kaye approved an award of punitive damages in the aggregate, as if it did not matter whether 50,000 plaintiffs had a raspy throat or 500,000 died from lung cancer, whether they started smoking as kids or as consenting adults, and whether they were ever influenced by the industry's so-called deceptive ads. Ultimately, a Florida appellate court decertified the class and reversed the punitive damages award because there had been no prior determination of compensatory damages. The *Engle* case demonstrates the enormous potential for mischief when local juries impose punitive damages on out-of-state defendants.

But the *Engle* fiasco is not the only evidence that punitive damage awards are dangerously out of control. According to the *National Law Journal*, the largest punitive award in 2002 was $28 billion. Five verdicts exceeded $500 million and 22 exceeded $100 million. The total of the top 100 verdicts for 2002 was nearly three and a half times the total for 2001. Longer term, 38 verdicts topped $20 million in 1991; 66 verdicts were over $20 million in 1996. But in 2002, $20 million did not make the top 100 list.[86] No doubt nine U.S. Supreme Court justices were aware of that general trend. Perhaps that's why, seven years ago, the Court took a first step toward reform.

BMW v. Gore. When Dr. Ira Gore discovered that his new BMW had been repainted before delivery, he sued BMW of North America for fraud. The distributor conceded that its policy was not to notify consumers if repairs for predelivery damage to a new car cost less than 3% of the suggested retail price. Gore's car, scratched during shipment and touched up at a cost of approximately $600, had sold for $40,000. On the basis of testimony that a repainted car loses 10% in value, an Alabama jury found BMW liable for $4,000 in compensatory damages, then imposed an additional $4 million in punitive damages, computed by multiplying the compensatory award by roughly 1,000 similar repairs nationwide. On appeal, the Alabama Supreme Court concluded that only in-state sales should have been considered, then reduced the punitive award to a "mere" $2 million, without explaining how it arrived at that figure. The U.S. Supreme Court declared that state sovereignty and comity prevented one state from imposing its policy choices on other states. In remanding the case, the Court held that the punitive award violated BMW's rights under the Due Process Clause of the Fourteenth Amendment.

The Court noted, first, that Gore's loss was purely economic. None of the aggravating factors associated with reprehensible conduct causing physical injury were present. Second, the ratio of punitive damages to compensatory damages was 500 to 1, which the Court felt was clearly outside any acceptable range. Third, Alabama's statutory penalty for retailer fraud was only $2,000—an amount so much lower than the punitive award that out-of-state defendants would not have had fair notice of their exposure to a multi-million dollar sanction.

Gore's three-part test—"the degree of reprehensibility . . .; the disparity between the harm . . . suffered [and the] punitive damages award; and the difference between this remedy and the civil penalties authorized or imposed in comparable cases"[87]—provided the business community with some minimal predictability and offered hope that the punitive damages crisis was defused. Regrettably, it did not turn out that way. During the seven years after Gore, punitive awards continued their upward spiral. State Farm v. Campbell was a poster child for what could go wrong.

State Farm v. Campbell. Curtis Campbell, trying to pass six vans on a two-lane highway, faced a head-on collision with an oncoming car driven by Todd Ospital. To avoid a collision, Ospital swerved, lost control of his car, and hit Robert Slusher, who suffered permanent disabling injuries. Ospital was killed. Campbell was unharmed. Slusher's and Ospital's estates sued.

Campbell's insurer, State Farm, rejected settlement proposals for the policy limit of $50,000. Instead, State Farm decided to litigate, assuring Campbell and his wife that their "assets were safe," they had "no liability," and they did not need separate counsel.[88] The jury had other ideas, however, and found the Campbells liable for roughly $186,000. Initially, State Farm refused to cover the excess liability of $136,000; Campbell had, after all, purchased only $50,000 of coverage. Somewhat callously, State Farm advised the Campbells to "put 'for sale' signs on your property to get things moving."[89] The Campbells then hired their own lawyer to appeal the jury verdict against them. They lost in the Utah Supreme Court. At that point State Farm changed its mind and agreed to pay the entire judgment.

Still, the Campbells sued State Farm for bad faith, fraud, and intentional infliction of emotional distress. Because State Farm had ultimately paid the full $186,000 award, a Utah trial court threw out Campbell's new suit. That ruling was overturned on appeal, however, and the case was returned to the trial court, which then determined that State Farm's refusal to settle had been unreasonable.

Next, the trial court was to address fraud, emotional distress, and damages. But meanwhile the U.S. Supreme Court had decided *Gore*. In that case, to recall, the Court disallowed evidence of out-of-state conduct that was lawful where it occurred and had no effect on in-state residents. On the basis of *Gore*, State Farm asked the trial court to exclude evidence of conduct in unrelated cases outside Utah. The court denied that request and proceeded to weigh State Farm's alleged fraudulent practices nationwide. The jury awarded the Campbells $2.6 million in compensatory damages and $145 million in punitive damages, which the judge reduced to $1 million and $25 million, respectively. That satisfied no one; both the Campbells and State Farm appealed to the Utah Supreme Court.

Purporting to apply *Gore*'s three guideposts, relying on evidence about State Farm's nationwide practices, and considering State Farm's "massive wealth," the Utah Supreme Court reinstated the $145 million punitive damages award.[90]

The reinstatement was short-lived. Justice Anthony Kennedy, writing for a six-member majority of the U.S. Supreme Court, put it bluntly: "[T]his case is neither close nor difficult. It was error to reinstate the jury's $145 million punitive damages award."[91] The high court returned the case to Utah with this advice: "An application of the *Gore* guideposts to the facts of this case, especially in light of the substantial compensatory damages awarded (a portion of which contained a punitive element), likely would justify a punitive damages award at or near the amount of compensatory damages."[92]

Then Kennedy proceeded to address in some detail the first two guideposts of *BMW v. Gore*—the reprehensibility of the conduct and the ratio of punitive to compensatory damages. He also discussed at length the propriety of evidence related to the defendant's out-of-state conduct and net worth. As to *Gore*'s third guidepost, comparable fines, Kennedy dismissively noted, "The most relevant civil sanction under Utah state law for the wrong done to the Campbells appears to be a $10,000 fine."[93]

Regarding reprehensibility, Kennedy concluded that the Utah courts were justified in awarding punitive damages, but "a more modest punishment for this reprehensible conduct could have satisfied the State's legitimate objectives."[94] That conclusion stemmed in major part from the state courts' misplaced reliance on State Farm's dissimilar out-of-state conduct. Such conduct should not itself be punished, declared Kennedy, even if it was unlawful.[95] Nonetheless, he added, it may assist the judge or jury in assessing the reprehensibility of similar *in*-state conduct for which the defendant may be liable.[96] The key to Kennedy's reprehensibility analysis is the similarity between in-state and out-of-state acts. The Campbells had shown no conduct by State Farm similar to that which harmed them.

Turning to the 145-to-1 ratio of punitive-to-compensatory damages, Kennedy made it clear that the Utah courts had overreached. He did not impose a bright-line ratio, but he did volunteer that, "in practice, few awards exceeding a single-digit ratio between punitive and compensatory damages ... will satisfy due process."[97] That guideline is somewhat elastic. "[R]atios greater than those we have previously upheld may comport with due process where 'a particularly egregious act has resulted in only a small amount of economic damages.' ... When compensatory damages are substantial, then a lesser ratio, perhaps only equal to compensatory damages, can reach the outermost limit of the due process guarantee."[98]

Applying that framework to the injuries suffered by the Campbells, Kennedy wrote:

> The compensatory award in this case was substantial; the Campbells were awarded $1 million for a year and a half of emotional distress. This was complete compensation. The harm arose from a transaction in the economic realm, not from some physical assault or trauma; there were no physical injuries; and State Farm paid the excess verdict before the complaint was filed, so the Campbells suffered only minor economic injuries for the 18-month period in which State Farm refused to resolve the claim against them. ... Much of

the distress was caused by the outrage and humiliation the Campbells suffered. . . . Compensatory damages, however, already contain this punitive element.[99]

Future plaintiffs will find little to cheer about in Kennedy's explanation. But he did hint at one qualification: The Court was dealing with a case in which only economic, not physical, harm had occurred. That suggests the Court might condone a more generous allowance for punitive damages in product liability cases involving injury or death.

One other aspect of the *State Farm* opinion has especially cheered defense attorneys: The Court's reluctance to consider the defendant's net worth as an appropriate ground for measurement of punitive damages. As Justice Kennedy wrote, "[T]he presentation of evidence of a defendant's net worth creates the potential that juries will use their verdicts to express biases against big business, particularly those without strong local presences."[100] He also noted that State Farm's assets are what other insured parties in Utah and elsewhere must rely on for payment of claims. Accordingly, he concluded, "The wealth of a defendant cannot justify an otherwise unconstitutional punitive damages award."[101]

By declaring that a defendant's wealth cannot justify an "otherwise unconstitutional" punitive damages award, the Court left ample wiggle room for trial courts and juries. Even if Kennedy's 10-to-1 ratio of punitive-to-compensatory damages were a rigid upper constraint, an award somewhere between zero and ten times a dollar amount that included both economic losses and retribution for pain and suffering might still be deemed constitutional. Within that expansive range, evidence of net worth can legitimately be used by a jury to decide on a specific punitive award.

Judicial Activism? That brings us to the dissenting opinions. We begin with Justice Ginsburg, who balked at the Court's substitution of its judgment for that of Utah's decision makers.[102] If the Utah legislature or the Utah Supreme Court had decided to set single-digit and 1-to-1 punitive damage benchmarks, that would have been within their purview, she stated. But "a judicial decree imposed on the States by this Court . . . seem[s] to me boldly out of order."[103]

Concern over federal judicial usurpation of state authority is more often associated with conservatives who rail against "judicial activism." Columnist George Will, for example, put it this way: "What, other than the justices' instincts, provides criteria of proportionality and arbitrariness? . . . And what principle makes the justices' instincts superior to the jury's . . .? Furthermore, even if the jury's award was unjust, the idea that 'unjust' and 'unconstitutional' can be synonymous gives [the Court] a license to legislate."[104]

Literally applied, the Ginsburg-Will formulation could preclude judicial review. Obviously, *some* unjust outcomes *are* unconstitutional. Judicial restraint does not consist in deferring to a legislature that has exceeded its constitutional authority. Statutes that are unconstitutional cannot stand, nor should unconstitutional outcomes imposed by trial judges or juries. Intervention by the U.S. Supreme Court is our final shield against abuse of government power and our final bulwark against violation of individual rights.

The crucial question, therefore, is whether the legislative enactment or the common-law-based verdict of a federal or state court violates the U.S. Constitution. In deciding such questions, Supreme Court justices should not impose their own policy preferences; rather, they should apply the Constitution according to a proper theory of that document grounded in the framers' notions of limited government, separation of powers, federalism, and individual liberty.

If an egregious punitive damages award breaches constitutional safeguards, then the justices are authorized to do something about it. Their remedy might be couched in the broadest terms, as in *Gore*, or it might be somewhat more concrete, as in *State Farm*. Indeed, *State Farm* affords a particularly strong argument for judicial benchmarks. No statute dictated the outcome—just an unprecedented application of the common law of tort by judge and jury. An appellate court is uniquely qualified to review the common-law decision of a lower court. So the real debate in *State Farm* centers not on separation of powers but on federalism. And that debate, in turn, recalls the muddle over substantive due process—the doctrine intermittently invoked by federal courts to prevent states from violating substantive rights presumably secured by the U.S. Constitution and applied to the states via the Due Process Clause of the Fourteenth Amendment.

Substantive Due Process

The Court should not have imposed its judgment on Utah "under the banner of substantive due process," insisted Justice Ginsburg.[105]

Her concern over the scope of that doctrine was echoed by Justices Thomas and Scalia, both of whom cited Scalia's earlier dissent in *Gore*.

Thomas's *State Farm* dissent is little more than one sentence: "[T]he Constitution does not constrain the size of punitive damage awards."[106] Scalia's dissent, in relevant part, is not much longer: "[T]he Due Process Clause provides no substantive protections against 'excessive' or 'unreasonable' awards of punitive damages."[107]

In short, Scalia believes the U.S. Constitution guarantees defendants that the *process* followed in determining a punitive award, including judicial review, will be reasonable but not that the award itself will be reasonable. Assurances regarding the appropriate size of an award must come, if at all, from state courts, state statutes, and state constitutions.

At first blush, the 1993 majority opinion by Justice John Paul Stevens in *TXO Production Corp. v. Alliance Resources Corp.*, upholding an enormous punitive damages award, seemed to agree.[108] But Justice Stevens distinguished semantically between "unreasonable" awards, which are not foreclosed by the Constitution, and "grossly excessive" awards, which are foreclosed.

> Justice Scalia's assertion notwithstanding, we do not suggest that a defendant has a substantive due process right to a correct determination of the "reasonableness" of a punitive damages award. . . . [S]tate law generally imposes a requirement that punitive damages be "reasonable." A violation of a state law "reasonableness" requirement would not, however, necessarily establish that the award is so "grossly excessive" as to violate the Federal Constitution.[109]

Stevens reminds us that "our cases have recognized for almost a century that the Due Process Clause of the Fourteenth Amendment imposes an outer limit on such an award."[110]

Revealingly, Justice Kennedy's *TXO* concurring opinion rejected the distinction between "reasonable" and "grossly excessive" in no uncertain terms:

> To ask whether a particular award of punitive damages is grossly excessive begs the question: excessive in relation to what? . . . [W]e are still bereft of any standard by which to compare the punishment to the malefaction that gave rise to it. A reviewing court employing this formulation comes

143

> close to relying upon nothing more than its own subjective reaction to a particular punitive damages award in deciding whether the award violates the Constitution.[111]

Instead of a "grossly excessive" standard, Kennedy preferred to focus on the jury's reasons for an award—that is, whether the "award reflects bias, passion, or prejudice on the part of the jury, rather than a rational concern for deterrence and retribution."[112] Fast forward one decade. In *State Farm*, Kennedy now opts for benchmark ratios and cites binding precedent that the "Due Process Clause of the Fourteenth Amendment prohibits the imposition of grossly excessive or arbitrary punishments."[113]

Kennedy's earlier apprehension about unmanageable standards like "grossly excessive" remains Scalia's concern today, and Thomas's as well. Still, both Scalia and Thomas have by and large honored the doctrine of *stare decisis*—that is, respect for past decisions now well settled in law. In that light, their peremptory refusal to invoke substantive due process in *State Farm* is difficult to square with a case dating back to 1907 holding that Due Process imposes substantive limits "beyond which penalties may not go"[114] or a 1915 case in which the Court actually set aside a penalty because it was so "plainly arbitrary and oppressive" as to violate the Due Process Clause.[115]

Moreover, Scalia and Thomas might have sidestepped substantive due process by authorizing federal intervention on procedural rather than substantive grounds. Arguably, remedies have as much to do with procedure as with substance, in the following sense: Proper procedure requires advance notice of the law. Private parties must be able to determine what behavior is required to comply with the law, and legal outcomes must be reasonably predictable. As the Court stated in *State Farm*, "Elementary notions of fairness enshrined in our constitutional jurisprudence dictate that a person receive fair notice not only of the conduct that will subject him to punishment, but also of the severity of the penalty that a State may impose."[116] By violating those norms, outrageous punitive damages do not provide adequate notice and therefore offend *procedural* due process.

If the Court's conservatives are serious about resolving the substantive vs. procedural quandary implicit in the Due Process Clause, maybe it is time for them to revisit the Fourteenth Amendment's nearly forgotten Privileges or Immunities Clause. Indeed, Justice

Thomas and Chief Justice Rehnquist have indicated a willingness to do so "in an appropriate case."[117] Other conservatives, like former judge Robert Bork, demur because "we do not know what the clause was intended to mean."[118] Yet that critique is no more persuasive when applied to the Privileges or Immunities Clause than it would be if applied to the General Welfare Clause, the Necessary and Proper Clause, or the Commerce Clause. A compelling case can be made that the Court has misinterpreted every one of those clauses, but to our knowledge, no one has suggested that they not be interpreted at all.

An excellent discussion of the Privileges or Immunities Clause appears in a 1998 Cato Institute monograph by professor Kimberly Shankman and Cato scholar Roger Pilon. Here's their recap of the rise and fall of the clause:

> Shortly after the Civil War, the American people amended the Constitution in an effort to better protect individuals against state violations of their rights. Under the Privileges or Immunities Clause of the new Fourteenth Amendment, constitutional guarantees against the federal government could be raised for the first time against state governments as well. . . . But . . . in 1873, in the infamous *Slaughter-House Cases*,[119] a deeply divided Supreme Court effectively eviscerated the Privileges or Immunities Clause. Since then courts have tried to do under the Due Process and Equal Protection Clauses of the amendment what should have been done under the more substantive Privileges or Immunities Clause.[120]

If *Slaughter-House* is overturned and the Privileges or Immunities Clause is revived, a more coherent doctrine of the Fourteenth Amendment and federalism is likely to emerge. Along the way, the debate over the substantive content of the Due Process Clause will inevitably diminish.

Reconciling Tort Reform and Federalism

While we wait patiently for an "appropriate case" to revisit Privileges or Immunities, the general problem of tort reform and the specific problem of confiscatory state punitive damage awards need not be irreconcilable with dual-sovereignty federalism. First, various remedies can be implemented by the states themselves, without federal involvement. Second, federal reform of long-arm jurisdiction and choice-of-law rules will curb tort law abuse yet fit comfortably within a federalist regime.

State-Based Reforms

One cure for inflated punitive damage awards might be to take the dollar decision away from the jury. For example, the jury might be instructed to vote "yes" or "no" on an award of punitive damages, with the amount then set by a judge in accordance with preset guidelines. If the judge complied with the guidelines, an appellate court would grant deferential review. But should the trial court exceed the guidelines, appellate review would be more rigorous. The rationale for a diminished jury role, from a 1989 article by our current solicitor general, goes like this:

> Juries are well constituted to perform as factfinders and determiners of liability. But here they are being given in effect the public function of sentencing—of deciding how high a penalty someone should pay for violating a public standard. Juries are remarkably ill-equipped for that task because they sit in only one case, hear evidence only in that case, and are then given very vague guidance with which to form a judgment. . . . Jurors are drastically swayed by such factors as the wealth, success, or personal demeanor of a defendant, even how far away the defendant lives from the location of the litigation. The jurors are frequently told to send a message back to such and such a corporate headquarters. After being instructed to set aside emotion, bias, and prejudice, juries are bombarded with arguments that are based almost exclusively on emotion, bias, and prejudice.[121]

A similarly skeptical view of jurors' competence to assess punitive damages comes from attorney Mark Klugheit, who specializes in class actions and mass tort litigation.

> Jurors are hardly expected to be experts in social engineering or economic analyses. They are not likely to understand, let alone apply, any kind of reason-based analyses to punitive damage determinations. Yet in most jurisdictions the law requires lay jurors to decide claims involving millions, or sometimes billions, of dollars with virtually no guidance about how to translate abstractions like the need for punishment or deterrence into an appropriate verdict. Instructions

predicated on amorphous concepts like "punishment," "deterrence," and the "public good," ... make the imposition of punitive damages a standardless, if not haphazard, exercise.[122]

A second suggestion for reform at the state level is to limit punitive damages to cases involving intentional wrongdoing or gross negligence. In fact, an even higher standard has had a salutary effect in Maryland, where punitive damages are permitted in a tort case only if the plaintiff has proved that the defendant acted with actual malice.[123] Whatever the heightened standard, the idea is that accidental injuries arising out of ordinary, garden-variety negligence are unlikely to require the deterrence for which punitive damages are designed.

Third, states might effect procedural guarantees similar to those inherent in criminal law. In *State Farm*, Kennedy observed that punitive awards "serve the same purposes as criminal penalties [but] defendants subjected to punitive damages in civil cases have not been accorded the protections applicable in a criminal proceeding."[124] Among the protections that might be offered:

- A higher burden of proof than the usual civil standard, which is preponderance of the evidence. Thirty-one states now require clear and convincing evidence for punitive awards.[125]
- No double jeopardy. Current rules allow "multiple punitive damages awards for the same conduct; for in the usual case nonparties are not bound by the judgment some other plaintiff obtains."[126] Victor Schwartz, a noted torts scholar, has proposed that "punitive damage awards be reduced by the sum of all previous awards for the same misconduct. The result would be what amounts to a single 'rolling' award."[127]
- No coerced self-incrimination, which criminal defendants can avoid by pleading the Fifth Amendment. In civil cases, however, compulsory discovery can be self-incriminating.

Fourth, the states could codify the Eighth Amendment's prohibition of excessive fines and apply it to punitive damages. At present, because the Eighth Amendment is primarily directed at prosecutorial abuse, the excessive fines provision does not cover civil damages. That principle was spelled out in the *Browning-Ferris* case.[128] But Justice Sandra Day O'Connor's dissent,[129] covering the history of fines, convincingly showed that punitive damages, unless they were merely symbolic, were always treated as fines. Moreover, after *Browning-Ferris*, several states modified their statutes to provide that punitive damages would be, in part, payable to the state.[130]

A fifth possible reform is making punitive awards payable to the state. Because the purpose of punitive damages is deterrence, not compensation for injury, the identity of the recipient is irrelevant to that purpose, and receipt by the plaintiff is beyond what is necessary to make him whole. We recognize, of course, that states would become an interested party in tort suits if they stood to receive punitive awards. That could exacerbate the expansion of tort liability. Perhaps the experience in states that are implementing this solution will help us determine whether that happens.

If punitive damages are received by the state rather than the plaintiff, adequate incentive must be provided for the plaintiff's attorney to seek those damages. That incentive might be in the form of court-ordered attorneys' fees with the amount set by a judge. Much of the abuse that now exists can be traced to enormous contingency-based fees paid not to "public officials, who are accountable to the citizenry . . . but private citizens and lawyers whose only interest is the size of the award they can bring in."[131]

Sixth—broadening our focus to cover not just punitive damages but the larger area of tort law—states ought to dispense with joint and several liability. That's the "deep pockets" rule that permits plaintiffs to collect all of a damage award from any one of multiple defendants, even if the paying defendant was responsible for only a small fraction of the harm. The better rule is to apportion damages in accordance with the defendants' degree of culpability—especially if the state has adopted a comparative negligence standard, which holds that the plaintiff himself is not "jointly liable" when he too is negligent. What's sauce for the goose is sauce for the gander.

Seventh, government should pay attorneys' fees when a governmental unit is the losing party in a civil lawsuit. Recall the discussion of that point in Chapter 3, which we repeat here:

> [C]oordinated actions by multiple government entities can impose enormous legal fees on defendants. As a result, those actions have been used to extort money notwithstanding that the underlying case is without merit. Just listen to former Philadelphia Mayor Edward G. Rendell (D) calling for dozens of cities to file concurrent suits against gun makers: They

"don't have the deep pockets of the tobacco industry," Rendell explained, and multiple lawsuits "could bring them to the negotiating table a lot sooner."[132] Never mind that the suits are baseless. We're not dealing with law, but with extortion masquerading as law.

One effective way to stop that thievery is by implementing a "government pays" rule for legal fees when a governmental unit is the losing plaintiff in a civil case. In the criminal sphere, defendants are already entitled to court-appointed counsel if needed; they're also protected by the requirement for proof beyond reasonable doubt and by the Fifth and Sixth Amendments to the Constitution. No corresponding safeguards against abusive public-sector litigation exist in civil cases. By limiting the rule to cases involving government plaintiffs, access to the courts is preserved for less affluent, private plaintiffs seeking redress of legitimate grievances. But defendants in government suits will be able to resist meritless cases that are brought by the state solely to ratchet up the pressure for a large financial settlement.

Also from Chapter 3, we restate below an eighth suggestion for state-based reform that contingency fee contracts between private lawyers and government entities should be prohibited:

When a private lawyer subcontracts his services to the government, he bears the same responsibility as a government lawyer. He is a public servant beholden to all citizens, including the defendant, and his overriding objective is to seek justice. Imagine a state attorney paid a contingency fee for each indictment that he secures, or state troopers paid per speeding ticket. The potential for corruption is enormous. Still, the states in their tobacco suits doled out multi-billion-dollar contracts to private counsel—not per-hour fee agreements, which might occasionally be justified to acquire unique outside competence or experience, but contingency fees, a sure-fire catalyst for abuse of power. And those contracts were awarded without competitive bidding to lawyers who often bankrolled state political campaigns.[133]

Government is the single entity authorized, in narrowly defined circumstances, to wield coercive power against private citizens. When that government functions as prosecutor or plaintiff in a legal proceeding in which it also dispenses punishment, adequate safeguards against state misbehavior are essential. That is why in civil litigation we rely primarily

> upon private remedies with redress sought by, and for the benefit of, the injured party and not the state. As the Supreme Court cautioned more than 60 years ago, an attorney for the state "is the representative not of an ordinary party to a controversy, but of a sovereignty whose obligation to govern impartially is as compelling as its obligation to govern at all."[134]
>
> Put bluntly, contingency fee contracts between government and a private attorney should be illegal. We cannot in a free society condone private lawyers enforcing public law with an incentive kicker to increase the penalties.

From a federalism perspective, it's instructive to examine an alternative proposal to deal with scandalous attorneys' fees—almost all of which were contingency based—that were collected by private lawyers who represented the states in their Medicaid recovery suits against the major cigarette companies. The Hudson Institute's Michael Horowitz reports that some attorneys stood to make $200,000 an hour for late-filed, copycat suits that never went to court.[135] To reclaim some of that money for the taxpayers, Horowitz would treat all attorneys receiving contingency fees in large class action litigation as fiduciaries under the Internal Revenue Code, then limit their fees to amounts that are "reasonable and risk-based"— perhaps as high as six times normal hourly rates. Any excess would be either refunded to the states or taxed by the federal government at a 200% rate.

However well-intentioned, that remedy raises more problems than it solves.[136] Most important for purposes of this paper, Horowitz's scheme would flout principles of federalism. Some 70 years after the New Deal Court eviscerated the constitutional doctrine of enumerated powers, the Rehnquist Court has begun reviving it. That revival, long overdue, would be dealt a body blow if conservatives, supposed champions of federalism, vested the national government with extended powers merely because the outcome might be congenial to business interests and adverse to the hated trial lawyers. Where in the Constitution is there an express or implied power to manipulate the Internal Revenue Code to punish disfavored groups?

Moreover, why should the federal government—or even state government for that matter—be regulating contingency fees paid by private parties? If the right to contract and respect for free markets mean anything, they mean that private parties should be able to negotiate fee arrangements for legal representation without government interference. Otherwise we should not be surprised when fiduciary standards are extended to the fees charged by doctors, accountants, architects, investment managers, you name it. The contingency fee contracts that must be regulated—indeed prohibited—are those between *government* and private lawyers. And the purpose of the prohibition is to remove incentives that might otherwise lead to the abuse of public power.

Finally, in the area of state-based tort reform, legislators should consider the Fairness in Litigation Act, a model statute proposed by the American Legislative Exchange Council.[137] The act provides that the same legal rules applicable to a private claim by an injured party will also be applicable if the government sues to recover indirect economic losses related to the same injury. Recall the states' lawsuits against the tobacco industry to recoup Medicaid outlays for smoking-related illnesses. For more than 40 years, cigarette companies had regularly prevailed against smokers' claims—by disputing that tobacco was the cause of a particular person's ailment and by demonstrating that the plaintiffs had assumed the risk of smoking, in which case they were personally responsible for the adverse health effects.

That set the stage for some legal legerdemain—a fresh wave of litigation by state attorneys general, beginning in 1994, grounded in a new claim that gave the states more legal rights than any aggrieved smoker. Florida became the first state to codify the new claim by amending its Medicaid Third-Party Liability Act in 1990 and 1994.[138] First, "causation and damages . . . may be proven by use of statistical analysis" without showing any link between a particular smoker's illness and his use of tobacco products. Second, "assumption of risk and all other affirmative defenses normally available to a liable third party are to be abrogated to the extent necessary to ensure full recovery by Medicaid from third-party resources."

Before the new dispensation, the state could assert only those theories of recovery against cigarette makers that an injured patient could assert. But that had not worked for smokers, so the states simply wiped that rule off the books and then, for good measure, made the new rules apply retroactively to illnesses supposedly caused by cigarettes sold decades earlier. As the president of the

Maryland Senate blurted to the *Washington Post* in an unguarded moment: "We agreed to change tort law, which was no small feat. We changed centuries of precedent in order to assure a win in this case."[139]

Under the proposed Fairness in Litigation Act, the same rules of evidence, the same standards of responsibility, and the same burden of proof would apply to the state standing in a plaintiff's shoes as to a plaintiff suing on his own behalf.

Federal Reform of Long-Arm Jurisdiction

In addition to state-imposed tort reforms, there are at least two areas where the federal government can intervene without intruding on long-established state prerogatives. A guiding principle is that federal legislatures and courts are authorized to act when there is a high risk that state legislatures or courts will systematically appropriate wealth from the citizens of other states. One federal reform that is consistent with that principle is to amend the rules that control state exercise of so-called long-arm jurisdiction over out-of-state businesses.

Rather than apply the Due Process Clause to control, for example, the size of a punitive damages award, a federal court could instead use that same clause to preclude a local court from hearing a case unless the defendant engages directly in business activities within the state. Sensible rules should protect a firm from being hauled into court unless the firm does in-state business. Those rules would give firms an exit option—that is, if they withdrew from a state, they could avoid the risk of an unrestrained in-state jury. Unfortunately, federal limits on state long-arm statutes remain lax or ambiguous.

Law and economics scholars Paul Rubin, John Calfee, and Mark Grady outline the problem:

> If Alabama juries demonstrate bad judgment in pharmaceutical cases, manufacturers might refuse to sell in Alabama, denying Alabamians drugs that expose the manufacturer to inappropriate punitive damages awards. Middlemen, however, might fill this lacuna by purchasing and reselling drugs in Alabama at a higher cost to compensate for liability, and manufacturers might not be able to escape liability under existing long-arm statutes.[140]

An overhaul of the Court's jurisdictional rules would entail a significant shift in its prior case law. First, under *International Shoe*

Co. v Washington,[141] the Court held that an out-of-state corporation could be sued within the state if the corporation had "minimum contacts" in state. International Shoe was sued in Washington even though it had no office and made no contracts there to buy or sell merchandise. Because the company employed salesmen who resided and solicited business in Washington, it was subject to the jurisdiction of the state's courts.

Encouragingly, 35 years later, in *World-Wide Volkswagen Corp. v Woodson*,[142] the Court signaled that state jurisdiction triggered by nominal ties might violate the Due Process Clause. The Robinsons purchased an Audi from a New York dealership that had acquired the car from a regional distributor. Later, the Robinsons were injured when their car was involved in an accident in Oklahoma, where neither the dealer nor the distributor did business. The Court said the defendant might have foreseen that an automobile bought in New York would be driven through Oklahoma, but noncommercial contact with Oklahoma was insufficient to confer jurisdiction on that state's courts.

That hopeful outcome was mostly undone by the Court's 1987 opinion in *Asahi Metal Industry Co., Ltd. v. Superior Court of California*.[143] Valves made by Asahi, a Japanese corporation, were installed by another company on Taiwanese tires that were involved in a California accident. The Court refused to confer jurisdiction on the California courts, mainly because the burden on Asahi of litigating in California outweighed the state's interest in adjudicating the case. But Justice O'Connor could not command a majority of the Court to support this more restrictive proposition: "[A] defendant's awareness that the stream of commerce may or will sweep the product into the forum State does not convert the mere act of placing the product into the stream into an act purposefully directed toward the forum State."[144] If that rule had won the day, exit from a state with a confiscatory tort regime would be feasible. But only three other justices agreed with O'Connor.

Rubin, Calfee, and Grady conclude that "the economically harmful effects of excessive punitive damages awards by unrestrained juries in particular states could ... largely be ameliorated by a clear and realistic 'minimum contacts' doctrine. Justice O'Connor's opinion in *Asahi* suggests how such a doctrine could be formulated, but the Court has not accepted her approach."[145]

By tightening state long-arm jurisdiction, the national government would simultaneously be broadening the procedural guarantees of the Due Process Clause and encouraging nondiscriminatory tort laws that promote interstate commerce.

Regrettably, because the Supreme Court continues to apply capacious jurisdictional rules, oppressive state tort laws remain a threat to out-of-state defendants. Thus, the expansion of product liability arises in part, not because of increased wrongdoing by defendants or increased risk aversion on the part of plaintiffs, but because some states' legal arrangements are intrinsically biased in favor of local plaintiffs suing nonresident defendants.[146]

If manufacturers could avoid unfair tort regimes—for example, by not doing business in a particular state—juries would not be able to impose liability and damage awards extraterritorially. Then consumers in each state would decide whether they wanted confiscatory tort law or plentiful goods and services. But to the extent that manufacturers cannot avoid a state's jurisdiction—because long-arm statutes overreach—a different remedy is necessary. The remedy that raises the fewest federalism concerns is a federal choice-of-law rule,[147] which would allow manufacturers to exert some control over governing law.

Federal Choice-of-Law Rules

Basically, choice of law is the doctrine that determines which state's laws control litigation when litigants from more than one state are involved. If a suit is filed in state court, there are a number of different and complex rules used by that court to decide choice-of-law questions. If the suit is filed in federal court, or removed to federal court at the request of the defendant, the federal court will apply the choice-of-law rules of the state in which the federal court is sitting. Federal courts may exercise so-called diversity jurisdiction over tort suits even when they involve questions of state law. Basically, the prerequisites for diversity jurisdiction are that the plaintiffs be from different states than every defendant and that the amount in controversy exceed $75,000 per plaintiff.[148]

Whether the forum turns out to be a federal court or a state court, the underlying substantive tort law will be state law, not federal.[149] The Supreme Court recognized that it must preserve state law even in federal diversity cases. Otherwise, diversity jurisdiction would effectively nationalize areas of law that were meant to be left to the states. In other words, federal diversity jurisdiction provides procedural protection to out-of-state litigants but not substantive uniformity across states. A citizen of one state is not immune from the laws of another state, but his out-of-state citizenship should not subject him to prejudice from a state court.[150]

That still means that plaintiffs will select the most favorable forum state, basing their choice in part on the choice-of-law rules of each state. The resultant tort law will no doubt be least hospitable to the defendant and might even be contrary to the defendant's home-state law in important respects. The defendant, in essence, will be at the mercy of the plaintiff.

Of course, there would be no involuntary extraterritoriality and less of a liability crisis if consumers and sellers could choose both their forum and their law by contract. Transacting parties should be able to designate the state whose laws will govern any disputes arising out of their agreements. Unfortunately, however, many trans-actions are not covered by written agreements, and choice-of-law clauses in consumer contracts are generally unenforceable.[151]

Accordingly, if the forum state's rules call for applying the law of the state where injury occurred, out-of-state manufacturers will have difficulty avoiding oppressive regimes. But suppose a federal choice-of-law rule were enacted for those cases in which the plaintiff and defendant are from different states. Suppose further that the applicable law were based on the location where the product was originally sold. A manufacturer could thus stamp products by state of sale and price them differentially to allow for anticipated product liability verdicts.

Naturally, prices would be higher in plaintiff-friendly states than in defendant-friendly states. The price premium would be similar to buying product liability insurance—but instead of paying for an insurance policy that would reimburse the buyer for injuries suf-fered, the higher price would pay for a "better" set of legal rules if a dispute over such an injury were to arise. Of course, differential pricing may be costly and cumbersome to manufacturers, and the federal government would have to mandate common labeling requirements so that original and subsequent purchasers would know where the product was first sold.

To bypass those complexities, the applicable law might instead be that of the state where the manufacturer was located or had the largest number of employees.[152] That would obviate the need to price differentially or to identify where the sale occurred. A manufacturer would decide where to locate, and its decision would dictate the applicable legal rules. Consumers, in turn, would evaluate those rules when deciding whether to buy a particular manufacturer's product.

Would there be a race to the bottom by manufacturers searching for the most defendant-friendly tort law? Perhaps. Then again, states might balance their interest in attracting manufacturers against the interest of in-state consumers who want tougher product liability laws to ensure adequate redress for injuries.[153] In effect, healthy competition among the states would enlist federalism as part of the solution rather than raise federalism as an excuse for failing to arrive at a solution.

In any event, as federalism scholar Michael Greve has observed, it might be impossible to precisely mimic a neutral, competitive world in which each state structures its legal arrangements as if it were a self-sufficient and independent nation.[154] The search for perfection is beside the point. "The sensible question," continues Greve, "is whether a competitive products-liability world, operating under approximately efficient (if imperfect) choice of law rules, will be preferable to the existing game of mutually assured regulatory aggression and, at the other extreme, to any set of monopolistic, national rules that are likely to emerge." Greve concludes that "the answer to that question is almost certainly in the affirmative."

The central constitutional concern, according to Greve, is not the prospect of federal intervention to resolve the choice-of-law question but rather the prospect of federal abdication. He finds it anomalous, as do we, "that the field should have been ceded in the first place to state courts and their choice-of-law rules, which are systematically biased against sister-states and their citizens."[155]

In essence, the choice-of-law inquiry is, Whose law governs in disputes involving more than one state? By its very nature, that inquiry is a *federal* question; no state has the authority to create binding law for a neighbor state. Moreover, the Privileges and Immunities Clause of Article IV forecloses discrimination by a state in favor of its own citizens. The Full Faith and Credit Clause, also in Article IV, gives Congress the authority to prescribe the effect that each state's public acts and judicial proceedings will have in every other state. And the Commerce Clause of Article I authorizes federal choice-of-law rules in multi-state litigation if states use tort law in a manner that impedes the free flow of trade across state borders.

Each of those constitutional pedigrees circumvents the difficult controversy over substantive due process. And each is perfectly consistent with the time-honored principles of federalism.

The touchstone of federalism is not states' rights but dual sovereignty—checks and balances designed to promote liberty by limiting excessive power in the hands of either state or federal government. When a state exercises jurisdiction beyond its borders to impose grossly excessive damages on out-of-state businesses, and applies tort laws that deny both procedural and substantive protection against quasi-criminal punishment, the federal government not only may but must intervene. Otherwise, federalism becomes a pretext for constricting rather than enlarging liberty.

Conclusion

Defenders of modern tort law would have nearly every "victim" compensated by corporate America. Such theories have penetrated deeply into the psyches of many judges and jurors. As a result, the cost of insurance and of goods and services now includes a "tort premium" that far exceeds the true costs of corporate misbehavior. And those who produce the goods and services that make the American economy strong have come to believe that no matter what they do, no matter how responsibly they behave, they are going to be held liable for the negligence of others.

Those problems are indeed real. But however real the problem, if there is no constitutional authority, Congress may not intercede. States have reformed, and can continue to reform, their own tort law. When and where they have not done so, the federal government may occasionally act, but only if state substantive rules violate a substantive federal constitutional right, or are so capricious that they rise to the level of a due process violation—that is, they deny to defendants sufficient notice of the law to conform their conduct to its dictates.

157

Otherwise, time-honored principles of federalism command that the states continue to exercise dominion over the substantive rules of tort law. To ensure that state sovereignty does not extend beyond a state's borders, the federal government may and should enact procedural reforms that tighten state long-arm jurisdiction and implement federal choice-of-law rules.

PART TWO

ANTITRUST LAW AS CORPORATE WELFARE
FOR MARKET LOSERS

6. Introduction to Part Two: Antitrust Law as Corporate Welfare for Market Losers

In Part Two, the spotlight shifts from tort law to antitrust—specifically, the Microsoft case. The central thesis of Part Two, as developed in Chapters 7 through 10, is that the concept of antitrust is flawed to the core. Markets move faster than antitrust officials could ever move. The assumption of would-be regulators—that inefficiencies, especially in high-tech markets, can lock a company into a position from which it cannot be unseated—is a myth. Consumers rule, not producers. And consumers can unseat any product and any company no matter how "powerful." Antitrust, if it were ever needed, is now obsolete.

Battle of the Browsers

In May 1998 the Justice Department and 20 state attorneys general filed two antitrust suits against Microsoft in the U.S. District Court for Washington, D.C. The two suits were consolidated and assigned to federal judge Thomas Penfield Jackson. He was to resolve, among other contentious issues, whether Microsoft engaged in illegal tying arrangements in the sale of its Windows operating system, entered exclusionary contracts with Internet service and content providers, and colluded to divide markets with Netscape, a rival manufacturer of Internet browsers.[*]

Thus began the browser wars, although the seeds of the conflict were sown years earlier in 1991, when the Federal Trade Commission first investigated claims that Microsoft monopolized the market for PC operating systems.[†] That allegation, and others raised in the

---

[*]For those readers unfamiliar with the jargon of personal computers and the Internet, see Appendix A to this chapter for a mini-glossary.

[†]See Appendix B to this chapter for a condensed timeline of the Microsoft litigation.

Justice Department challenge, are examined in Chapter 7. The threshold question posed by the Microsoft case—Do our antitrust laws still make sense, if they ever did?—is answered with a resounding "no."

Today's software industry, where innovation proceeds at an astonishing pace, stands in stark contrast to the stagnation that occurs when government removes the incentives that lead to new and improved products. In the textbook world of "perfect competition," and in the real world of planned economies, the actions of market participants are determined by surrounding circumstances, leaving no room for imaginative, entrepreneurial vision. By comparison, in a modern industrial free-market economy, the impetus for growth comes from vigorous exertions by producers struggling to establish market power. That power is invariably short-lived—unless government-created barriers, arising out of special-interest legislation or misguided regulations, prevent competitors from entering the market. The obvious remedy is not more government in the form of antitrust enforcement, but rather for government to stop creating barriers to entry.

There were, and are, no legal barriers to prevent competitors from dislodging Microsoft as the market leader. Rivals must first, however, persuade customers that their product is superior—an assessment that will be based not only on technical features but also on ease of use, quality, price, service, and other factors. Whether a product is inferior or superior is a matter to be decided by consumers, not by "experts" at the Justice Department.

Despite intense competition in the information technology market, the federal government and some state attorneys general persisted in their crusade to force Microsoft to offer two versions of its Windows operating system—one with its Internet browser, one without—even if both versions were identically priced. That option, according to the Justice Department, would have resolved the main dispute between the litigants. Yet if Microsoft could have dispelled the department's concerns by offering a stripped product, at no reduction in price, which consumers would likely reject, then the government's position was quite simply unfathomable.

In the end, taxpayers and consumers paid for the litigation. Companies devoted more of their resources to politicking, and less to building the kinds of integrated products that, until recently, characterized the software industry. That misuse of the political process—which economists call rent-seeking—was both facilitated and made necessary by an amorphous set of antitrust statutes that delegated too much discretion to Justice Department officials and federal judges. Potential defendants, like Microsoft, simply could not know the rules that presumably governed their conduct.

Broader Implications of the Microsoft Case

Chapter 8 welcomes the reader to the post-modern world of high-tech antitrust—where big is once again bad, lofty profit margins are a wakeup call to government regulators, executives are brought to heel for aggressively worded e-mails, pricing too high is monopolistic, pricing too low is predatory, propping up politically wired competitors is the surreptitious aim, bundling products that consumers want is illegal, and successful companies are rewarded by dismemberment. That was the Orwellian world in which Microsoft found itself, a year into the most important and least justified antitrust crusade of our generation.

Antitrust law aside, the principle of the matter is simple: Microsoft created its operating system and has a right to sell the system as it sees fit. But antitrust law pays little attention to such niceties as property rights. Instead, the reigning shibboleths are economic efficiency and consumer welfare. The questions for antitrust advocates, therefore, are whether Microsoft has an illegal monopoly, whether consumers have been harmed, and whether government can find a cure that isn't worse than the disease. The answers are no, no, and no.

Microsoft behaves not like a monopolist but like a company whose very survival is at stake. Its prices are down. Its technology is struggling to keep pace with an explosion of software innovation. And it faces an avalanche of competition from new operating systems, consumer electronics, and Web-based servers. Yet antitrust officials are preoccupied with antiquated notions—tying arrangements, exclusionary contracts, predatory pricing, and a host of other purported infractions—all irrelevant, unless the real purpose, of course, is to pacify rivals trying to attain in the political arena what they have been unable to attain in the market.

Meanwhile, government lawyers with marginal understanding of how businesses operate, and even less understanding of the technical subject matter, were bamboozled into bringing the Microsoft antitrust case by rent-seeking executives. Disgruntled rivals played on the naiveté of Justice Department officials and persuaded them that Microsoft's aggressiveness could be scripted into an antitrust suit. Those rivals convinced bureaucrats to do their competitive dirty work at taxpayer expense—unwilling to acknowledge that antitrust doctrine is bankrupt, and destructive to a modern Internet economy.

Appealing Arguments

Judge Thomas Penfield Jackson categorically rejected the legal, economic, and policy arguments expounded in Chapters 7 and 8. Indeed, his final judgment in the Microsoft case indicated that he had fallen hook, line, and sinker for the government's unsubstantiated claims. But on appeal, Chapter 9 predicts, a higher court would not be so accommodating. Originally written after Judge Jackson's decision, but before the U.S. Court of Appeals for the District of Columbia Circuit reversed certain of his key holdings, Chapter 9—co-authored with economist Alan Reynolds—rebuts the entirety of the Justice Department's case. We forecast (accurately, as we now know) that the trial judge's opinion would crumble as a result of procedural errors, flawed fact finding, wrongheaded legal conclusions, and Jackson's preposterous plan to break up the software company most directly responsible for America's high-tech revolution.

Among the more flagrant procedural errors were these: Jackson expanded the scope of the trial to include charges that were not part of the government's initial complaint. He conducted the trial on an accelerated timetable that did not allow Microsoft sufficient opportunity to prepare its defense. He embraced the government's proposed remedies without any hearing whatsoever. He relied on post-trial evidence that was not part of the record. Lastly, both during and after the trial, Jackson granted media interviews, contravening an explicit canon of judicial ethics.

Still worse, Jackson's findings of fact could not bear up under serious scrutiny. Those findings were the shaky foundation on which he constructed his conclusions of law. And when the foundation is unsound, the resultant structure collapses. Consequently, Jackson's legal conclusions on Microsoft's tying arrangements, first-screen restrictions, and so-called exclusionary contracts, were quite simply incorrect.

Yet the government's proposed remedies, rubber-stamped by Jackson, may well have been the most destructive aspect of this case. Jackson's final remedies were wholly disassociated from any of Microsoft's alleged transgressions. If one didn't know better, his ruling to split Microsoft into two companies seemed crafted to inflict as much damage as possible, not just on Microsoft but on the broader high-tech marketplace. Company employees, like expendable chess pawns, would have been deployed to advance the dismemberment scheme. Bureaucrats would have supervised the allocation of those employees—sales, marketing, programming, product development, research, procurement, legal and accounting—as well as the allocation of physical plant, equipment, and intellectual property.

Real people were injured by Jackson's folly. After the announcement of his proposed remedies, Microsoft's shareholders—including millions of retirees and mutual fund investors—saw their stock value erode by hundreds of billions of dollars.

Triple Jeopardy

Ultimately, the Justice Department's case against Microsoft came tumbling down because its foundation was paper thin. In June 2001, even though the Court of Appeals concurred that Microsoft had maintained its Windows monopoly by anti-competitive means, the court reversed Judge Jackson's other holdings. And citing his extrajudicial comments, the appellate court also rejected Jackson's order to split up Microsoft, then remanded the remedies question for more hearings under a different judge, Colleen Kollar-Kotelly.

Five months later, the Justice Department and nine of the state attorneys general agreed to settle with Microsoft. Among the key provisions of the settlement: Microsoft must allow PC makers both to hide certain bundled products, like the Internet Explorer browser and Windows Media Player, and install competing products. Microsoft must also disclose selected software code to companies producing larger-scale server computers.

In December 2001 the remaining nine states and the District of Columbia rejected the settlement and asked the court for different remedies. They wanted Internet Explorer to be placed in the public domain, Microsoft Office to be made compatible with non-Microsoft operating systems, and Windows to be produced in a modular package that facilitates removal of selected middleware and other applications. That was bite number two at the Microsoft apple—a rear-guard attempt by nine attorneys general, acting on behalf of Microsoft's competitors, to replace the United States as enforcer of federal antitrust laws.

Chapter 10 begins with an interpretation of the Court of Appeals decision and the Justice Department settlement. Then it continues with a commentary on allowing a handful of self-selected state law enforcement officials to dictate Microsoft's nationwide product design and restrict the company's business dealings in every state in the union.

To her credit, Judge Kollar-Kotelly resisted the blandishments of the attorneys general. In November 2002 she approved the Justice Department settlement with a few modifications, and rejected the remedies proposed by the nonsettling states. Two of those states, Massachusetts and West Virginia, appealed Judge Kollar-Kotelly's ruling. West Virginia later withdrew from the appeal, and the Massachusetts challenge was unsuccessful. Both Kollar-Kotelly's approval of the settlement and the failed Massachusetts case are summarized in Chapter 10.

Yet that is not the end of the story. Microsoft's rivals still had an ace in the hole. In 1998 Sun Microsystems had filed an antitrust complaint against Microsoft with the European Union. And in March 2004 the EU finally issued its ruling, which addressed the same concerns that were first raised by the Justice Department, then raised and rejected after a separate hearing instigated by nine states before a federal judge. The EU ordered Microsoft to pay a $613 million fine, disclose additional source code to ensure server interoperability, and provide an unbundled version of Windows XP, without Media Player, to PC makers in Europe. Microsoft has announced that it will appeal the EU ruling.

The penultimate section of Chapter 10 assesses the global implications of the EU's intervention—a third bite at the Microsoft apple—and concludes that it represents yet another step toward transforming antitrust law into a corporate welfare program for market losers.

Finally, Chapter 10 closes by recapping the major themes of earlier chapters and offering an eight-part justification for repeal of the antitrust laws. Antitrust is thought by some to be the bulwark of free enterprise. Without the continued vigilance of the Justice Department and the Federal Trade Commission, so the argument goes, large corporations would ruthlessly destroy their smaller rivals and soon raise prices and profits at consumers' expense. When megamergers grab headlines and a federal judge decides that the nation's leading software company should be dismembered, the importance of vigorous antitrust law enforcement seems to be obvious. But antitrust has a dark side. The time for modest reform of antitrust policy has passed. Modern scholarship has shown over and over again that antitrust has become a playground for special pleaders. Root-and-branch overhaul—even better, repeal—is the requisite remedy.

Appendix A

Mini-Glossary*

API: Application Programming Interface. **Software** that allows the **application program** to interact with the **operating system**.

Application program: **Software** that performs a specific task for the computer user, as contrasted with software that handles the internal functions of the **PC**. Most people buy PCs so they can run application programs like **word processors**.

Browser: An **application program** used for **surfing** the **Web** or for connecting to a particular **Web site**. Examples include Microsoft's Internet Explorer and Netscape's Navigator.

Consumer electronics: In the context of this paper: hand-held computers, digital TVs with set-top boxes, sub-notebook computers, and other new devices that offer an alternative to the standard **PC** for processing information and communicating with the **Internet**.

Desktop: The first screen displayed when a **PC** is started. It contains **icons** that can be used to start **application programs** and other **operating system** functions.

DOS: Disk Operating System. An IBM **operating system** that preceded **Windows**.

Download: To copy files from a distant to a local computer via a **network** or **modem**.

E-commerce: Electronic commerce. Transactions in goods and services that take place over the **Internet**.

E-mail: Electronic mail. A way of sending messages to and receiving messages from other **PC** users.

Hardware: The physical components of a computer and its connected devices.

*Extracted August 25, 1999, from www.users.bigpond.com/jenkos/G.htm, with extensive changes and additions.

Home page: The computer screen chosen by the user as the location from which other pages are accessed; ordinarily displayed when a user first enters the **Web**.

Icon: A small picture displayed on the screen, intended to depict a task graphically. A user can execute the task by clicking on the icon with a **mouse**.

Internet: A worldwide computer **network** through which you can send a letter, chat with people electronically, or search for information on almost any subject. A "network of computer networks," the Internet was first conceived in the early 1960s under the leadership of the Defense Department. It was intended to promote the sharing of super-computers among researchers, and to avoid overreliance on one supercomputer that might fail or be destroyed.

Internet content provider (ICP): A company that maintains a presence on the **Internet** through which it provides users with goods or services. Examples include Amazon.com, Travelocity.com, and CNN.com.

Internet service provider (ISP): A company that provides communications by means of which **PCs** can connect to the **Internet**.

Java: A modern programming language developed in 1995 by Sun Microsystems. Java programs are intended to run on stand alone **PCs** or across the **Internet**, and to be compatible with different types of computers (e.g., IBM PCs, Apple Macintoshes).

Linux: A variant of the **Unix operating system** developed by Helsinki student Linus Torvalds, distributed without charge to **software** developers and **OEMs**. Software support is available, for a price, through Red Hat Software and others.

MacOS: A graphical **operating system** developed by Apple.

Modem: A device that converts information from analog form (like telephone sound waves) to digital form (zeroes and ones), which computers can understand. Modems are used to send information over phone lines from one computer to another.

Mouse: A common pointing device used to invoke certain computer tasks by clicking on displayed graphics or text rather than entering instructions via the keyboard.

MS-DOS: Microsoft Disk Operating System. Microsoft's version of the **DOS operating system**.

Network: A number of computers linked by wires and cables by means of which information is exchanged and common resources are shared.

Network computer: Low-cost **personal computers** touted by some as the ultimate replacement for today's **PCs**. In a network computing environment, **software** applications reside on, and are accessible from, the **Internet**, which substitutes for the PC's hard disk. The network computer is thus more of a communications device than it is an independent processor.

OEM: Original Equipment Manufacturer. The company that manufactures the **PC**.

Online service provider (OLS): A company that offers both access to the **Internet**, like an **ISP**, with information content that is accessible online without using the Internet. Among the popular OLSs are America Online (AOL) and the Microsoft Network (MSN).

Operating system: Software that is responsible for running the **PC**—controlling and utilizing the processor and its peripheral devices, like printers.

OS/2: A graphical **operating system** developed by IBM.

Personal computer (PC): Broadly, a computer designed to be used by one person at a time. More narrowly, the term PC is sometimes used to mean personal computers with microchips manufactured by Intel—a restriction that would exclude Apple computers and many **consumer electronics** products.

Portal: A **Web site** that serves as a gateway to other services on the **Internet**, and frequently as a **home page** or **search engine** as well. Among the popular portals are Netscape.com, Microsoft.com, and Yahoo.com.

Search engine: A **Web site** that provides a means of searching other Web sites for specified content. Among the popular search engines are Google and Yahoo!.

Server: Computer **hardware** and accompanying **software** that distributes processing between two or more computers on a **network** in a manner that makes most efficient use of each and facilitates multiple access to **application programs**.

Software: A series of instructions, sometimes called a program, that causes a **PC** to perform a task. The **operating system** is an example of systems software. A **word processor** is an example of an **application program**.

Surf: A popular activity by users connected to the **Internet**—looking around the **Web**, jumping from one location to another, sampling the various sites that are available.

Unix: A modern **operating system** intended to be portable—that is, capable of running on different computers without compatibility problems.

Web site: A group of **Web** pages or screens, developed to display related information that collectively represents a particular individual or entity.

Windows: The graphical **operating system** developed by Microsoft to overlay and later replace **DOS**. Widely used **PC** versions, chronologically, include Windows 3.1, Windows 95, and Windows 98. Another version, Windows NT, is run primarily by larger users on **networks** and **servers**.

Word processor: An **application program** used mainly for creating text-based documents like letters, reports, legal documents, and so on. Popular word processors include Microsoft Word and its principal competitor, WordPerfect.

World Wide Web (WWW) or, simply, the **Web**: Originally used to denote a subset of **Internet** sites that featured graphic displays and icons with links to related content on other screens and other sites. Today, the term Web is roughly synonymous with the term Internet.

Appendix B

Condensed Timeline*

Key dates and events in the legal battle between Microsoft and the U.S. Department of Justice:

1991: The Federal Trade Commission (FTC) begins to investigate claims that Microsoft monopolizes the market for PC operating systems.

1993: The FTC deadlocks on two votes to file a formal complaint against Microsoft for antitrust infringements, and then closes its investigation; but Department of Justice (DOJ) antitrust investigators begin their own independent probe.

July 1994: Microsoft and DOJ sign a consent decree with a provision that prevents Microsoft from requiring PC makers (OEMs) who

---

*Extracted August 25, 1999, from www.microsoft.com/presspass/doj/time line.htm, with modifications. Updated by the author for events from July 1999 through June 2004.

license Windows to also license another software product. The consent decree explicitly states, however, that the provision "shall not be construed to prohibit Microsoft from developing integrated products."

August 1995: The consent decree signed by Microsoft and DOJ is approved by the U.S. District Judge Thomas Penfield Jackson.

October 1997: DOJ files a petition in U.S. District Court claiming that Microsoft's browser, Internet Explorer, is a product separate from, not integrated with, the Windows operating system. The government argues that Microsoft, by requiring OEMs to take the browser when they acquire Windows, is in contempt of the consent decree.

December 1997: Judge Jackson denies DOJ's petition for a contempt citation against Microsoft, but issues a preliminary injunction, tentatively accepting DOJ's characterization of Internet Explorer as a "separate product." The injunction requires Microsoft to offer a version of Windows without Internet Explorer.

January 1998: Microsoft reaches agreement with DOJ regarding the company's compliance with the preliminary injunction until an appeal is resolved. Basically, Microsoft will offer OEMs the option of removing or hiding browser functionality while leaving essential Internet Explorer code intact.

May 1998: The U.S. Court of Appeals, District of Columbia Circuit, grants Microsoft's motion for a stay of the preliminary injunction insofar as it applies to Windows 98. The court's ruling clarifies that the release of Windows 98, scheduled for June 1998, will not be affected.

May 1998: DOJ and 20 state attorneys general (South Carolina has since withdrawn) file two antitrust suits in U.S. District Court. The suits are consolidated and assigned to Judge Jackson. The government charges Microsoft with attempted collusion to divide markets with Netscape, illegal tying arrangements in the sale of Windows to OEMs, and exclusionary contracts with Internet service and content providers.

June 1998: The Court of Appeals overturns the December 1997 preliminary injunction, stating that Microsoft had plausibly demonstrated that consumers will benefit from the integrated design of Windows 95 with Web browsing functionality. In effect, the court rejects the claim that Windows and Internet Explorer are separate products under the terms of the consent decree.

October 1998: Microsoft's antitrust trial begins.

June 1999: Microsoft's antitrust trial ends.

November 1999: Judge Jackson issues his findings of fact. He concludes that Microsoft is a monopoly, has stifled innovation, and harmed consumers.

April 2000: Judge Jackson issues his conclusions of law. He concludes that Microsoft, in violation of the Sherman Act, maintained monopoly power by anti-competitive means, attempted to monopolize the browser market, and unlawfully tied its browser to the Windows operating system.

June 2000: Judge Jackson issues his remedies opinion. He holds that Microsoft must alter its conduct in a variety of ways and be split into two companies—one to produce the Windows operating system, another to produce applications programs.

June 2001: The U.S. Court of Appeals for the District of Columbia Circuit agrees that Microsoft maintained its Windows monopoly by anti-competitive means. But the court reverses Judge Jackson's other holdings. Citing his extrajudicial comments, the appellate court also rejects Judge Jackson's order to split Microsoft in two, and remands the remedies question for more hearings under a different judge, Colleen Kollar-Kotelly.

October 2001: The U.S. Supreme Court decides not to review the Court of Appeals opinion.

November 2001: The Justice Department, nine states, and Microsoft agree to settle their antitrust case. Among the key provisions: Microsoft must allow PC makers to hide certain bundled products like the Internet Explorer browser and Windows Media Player, and to install competing products. Microsoft must also disclose selected software code to companies producing larger-scale server computers.

December 2001: The remaining nine states and the District of Columbia reject the settlement and ask the court for different remedies. They want Internet Explorer to be placed in the public domain, Microsoft Office to be made compatible with non-Microsoft operating systems, and Windows to be produced in a modular package that facilitates removal of selected middleware and other applications.

March 2002: Judge Kollar-Kotelly commences proceedings under the Tunney Act to decide whether the court will approve the settlement, as well as hearings on the remedies proposed by the nonsettling states.

November 2002: Judge Kollar-Kotelly approves the settlement with a few modifications, and rejects the remedies proposed by the non-settling states.

December 2002: Two of the nine nonsettling states, Massachusetts and West Virginia, file an appeal of Judge Kollar-Kotelly's ruling. West Virginia later withdraws from the appeal.

March 2004: The European Union issues its ruling in an antitrust case against Microsoft that arose out of a 1998 complaint by Sun Microsystems. The EU orders Microsoft to pay a $613 million fine, disclose additional source code to ensure server interoperability, and provide an unbundled version of Windows XP, without Media Player, to PC makers in Europe. Microsoft announces that it will appeal the ruling.

April 2004: Microsoft and Sun Microsystems sign a broad cooperation agreement and settle their private antitrust litigation.

June 2004: The European Union postpones its penalties pending hearings on appeal in late summer 2004.

June 2004: The U.S. Court of Appeals for the District of Columbia Circuit unanimously rejects Massachusetts' appeal of Judge Kollar-Kotelly's November 2002 ruling.

7. Microsoft and the Browser Wars: Fit To Be Tied*

Introduction

America's century-old antitrust law, whatever its original rationale,[1] is increasingly irrelevant to our modern global information technology market. That, at least, is the rallying cry of the "techno-optimists," who claim that efforts by government to promote competition by restraining high-tech firms that acquire market power will only stifle competition. The pace of innovation is so rapid, they add, that a firm like Microsoft will simply lose its customers if it does not offer the very best products. Some analysts disagree. They concede that dynamic technology makes it tough to sustain market power. Still, consumers will want compatible equipment, which will lead them to buy whatever product other consumers are using, even if the product is inferior. Consequently, insist those analysts, there is a continuing need for aggressive antitrust enforcement in a high-tech world.[2]

Then there is Sen. Orrin Hatch (R-Utah), prominent among a contingent of politicians from both parties who have rediscovered the virtues of antitrust law as applied to information technology. Not so long ago, Republicans attacked the Clinton administration for trying to hobble Microsoft, the symbol of American dynamism. But now Hatch—whose home state is the headquarters of Microsoft rival Novell, Inc.—assails the company for attempting to dominate the Internet. Explaining his turnabout, Hatch observes that "we're witnessing a historic technological revolution. Congress has to strengthen the antitrust laws from time to time, and this could be one of those times."[3]

The range of views extends, then, from the optimists who think that ever-changing technology obviates the need for antitrust, to

*Originally published, with minor revisions, as Cato Institute Policy Analysis no. 296, February 19, 1998.

middle-of-the-roaders who think that antitrust has always been and still is an important weapon in the government's arsenal, to legislative activists like Hatch who think that the new technology is yet another reason for strengthening the government's hand. That leaves just one position, the thesis of this paper: Antitrust laws were both wrong and counterproductive when they were first enacted in the late 1800s; they remain so today. As Federal Reserve Board chairman Alan Greenspan concluded more than 30 years ago, "The entire structure of antitrust statutes in this country is a jumble of economic irrationality and ignorance."[4]

Telecommunications and information technology have indeed brought about quantum changes in many fields, but new technology has neither extinguished nor revitalized the rationale for antitrust. That rationale was always illusory. To be sure, there are monopolies that government ought to control—the very monopolies government created in the first instance. It is government, and only government, that confers and perpetuates monopoly power by erecting and maintaining barriers to market entry, ordinarily in response to political pressures from special interests. We can hardly justify government imposition of antitrust laws on private parties when the underlying problem is government itself.

To explore those issues in a contemporary context, let us begin by tracing the latest dispute between Microsoft and the Department of Justice—its origin, its current status, and the arguments advanced by both sides. That dispute revolves around Microsoft's "tie-in" of its browser (Internet Explorer) with its operating system (Windows 95)—a tie-in that poses no greater threat to competition, in my view, than the packaging of tires with automobiles, cream with coffee, laces with shoes, even left gloves with right gloves. We will then examine the issue of market power, the law and economics of tying arrangements, and the theory of "network effects." That theory, a fresh addition to the arsenal of antitrust proponents, holds that consumers can be duped into buying mediocre or substandard products whenever those products already have a large base of users.

As we shall see, tying arrangements are often pro-competitive; network effects are at worst a transitory phenomenon; and market power, when properly evaluated, is an indispensable stimulus in extending what Senator Hatch has called our "historic technological revolution."

Department of Justice v. Microsoft

In 1991, during the Bush administration, the Federal Trade Commission began its investigation of Microsoft's market power in the sale of operating systems for personal computers. That investigation was later co-opted by DOJ and pursued vigorously by Clinton appointee Anne Bingaman, then head of the Antitrust Division.[5] After an extensive inquiry, DOJ uncovered one practice it deemed worthy of challenge: Microsoft licensed its Windows software for multiyear periods on a "per processor" basis.

To help prevent software piracy, Microsoft insisted that computer makers pay a royalty to Microsoft for each computer they shipped, whether or not Windows was installed as the operating system. DOJ was not persuaded by Microsoft's contention that physical machines can more easily and reliably be counted than can intangible copies of computer software. Nor was DOJ convinced that customers might actually favor long-term contracts to guard against unpredictable price increases and other uncertainties. Instead, the controversy centered on this loaded and, ultimately, unanswerable question: Did Microsoft exploit its dominant market position by "insisting" on "unfair" licensing arrangements?

Never mind that Windows became the industry standard because PC makers thought it was a "superior" product—an assessment that surely took into account the entire array of product features, not only technical features but also ease of use, quality, price, service, and contract terms. Never mind that consumers shared that view. Never mind that there were no barriers to entry that would prevent a competitor from ousting Windows as the market leader. Those considerations, apparently, did not impress DOJ's Antitrust Division.

Quite to the contrary, DOJ threatened costly and protracted litigation, which Microsoft opted to avoid, not surprisingly, by signing a consent decree in 1994. Effective in 1995, the decree prohibited Microsoft from using "per processor" licenses, shortened the initial term of each license from two years to one, and implemented other technical changes of presumably lesser significance—one of which, however, would become the subject of DOJ's current crusade.

Thus, after a five-year investigation costing millions of dollars, the Antitrust Division found little that could be characterized as anti-competitive. But that did not stop the government. Not only did DOJ subsequently file an antitrust suit that prompted Microsoft to cancel its planned acquisition of Intuit, manufacturer of a popular personal finance program, but the department also threatened to halt the release of Windows 95, Microsoft's upgraded operating system. Bingaman was reportedly concerned about the link between Windows 95 and the Microsoft Network, an Internet service provider intended to compete against America Online, Compuserve, and others. Whenever a user started a Windows 95 system, an MSN icon appeared; then one click of the mouse connected the user with the MSN service. That packaging, according to DOJ, gave MSN an unsporting edge over its online rivals.

As it happens, a few more mouse clicks enabled any Windows 95 user to bring up an AOL or Compuserve icon, which would appear automatically thereafter, at the same time as the MSN icon. Evidently content with its discovery that MSN's edge could be thus neutralized, the Antitrust Division abandoned its threat to block Windows 95. In retrospect, however, Bingaman's concern was just plain silly. MSN now loses an estimated $200 million annually providing service to fewer than 3 million customers. AOL, by contrast, has 9 million subscribers and will add nearly 3 million more with its acquisition of Compuserve's consumer business.[6] Although rivals whined that bundling MSN software with Windows 95 would swamp competition, Microsoft's feared clout has not materialized. Whatever competitive advantage Microsoft may enjoy in the sale of operating systems, the company has been singularly ineffectual in leveraging that advantage. Customers refuse to buy a product they do not like.

That lesson, however, was completely lost on DOJ operatives. The Antitrust Division, now headed by Joel Klein, has raised the bundling issue yet again, this time objecting that Windows 95 and Internet Explorer are two separate products, not one integrated product. On that distinction turns a great deal; the 1995 consent decree that Microsoft signed forbids any tie-in between Windows 95 and a separate software product. Is the Internet Explorer a "separate" product, as Klein contends? Or are the two products "integrated," as Microsoft contends? (The consent decree provides expressly that the prohibition on tying separate software products "shall not be construed to prohibit Microsoft from developing integrated software products.") Because DOJ denies that Windows 95 and Internet

Explorer are "integrated," Klein proposed to fine the company $1 million a day until the two products are unbundled.

In its defense, Microsoft maintains that Windows 95 cannot perform several crucial tasks—like word processing, imaging, and drawing—if all Explorer files are deleted.[7] Moreover, states the company, the control panel, which governs such devices as modems and printers, will not work without Explorer, nor will "thousands" of other products developed by other companies for Windows machines. DOJ rejoins that Microsoft did not have to make Windows dependent on the browser and could easily have allowed computer manufacturers to "uninstall" Explorer without compromising the operating system.[8]

What then did the consent decree mean by explicitly sanctioning "integrated software products"? That question will probably be resolved in court. For now, federal judge Thomas Penfield Jackson has granted DOJ's request for a preliminary injunction that directs Microsoft to offer PC manufacturers the option of installing Windows 95 without Internet Explorer. While the judge declined to hold the company in contempt or impose a fine, he concluded, "The probability that Microsoft will not only continue to reinforce its operating system monopoly by its licensing practices, but might also acquire yet another monopoly in the Internet browser market, is simply too great to tolerate indefinitely until the issue is finally resolved."[9] Jackson appointed a "special master" to evaluate the legal and factual questions, then report back to the court. The judge will then consider whether a permanent injunction should be issued.

In its initial response to the preliminary injunction, Microsoft offered PC makers two versions of Windows 95 without the browser. One version excluded all of the browser files; as a result, it did not work. A second version dated back to 1995, before Microsoft bundled Internet Explorer with Windows; it worked but did not include more recent enhancements. Predictably, DOJ was not happy with the company's response. Accusing Microsoft of a "naked attempt to defeat the purpose of the court's order," DOJ asked once again for a contempt citation and a fine of $1 million a day.[10]

Microsoft replied that its offer of a dysfunctional or an obsolete system complied with the letter of the judge's order. According to the company, "Microsoft has done precisely what the DOJ requested and what the court ordered [but] now that the DOJ understands the implications of its prior position, it wants to play by a new set of rules."[11] True enough, while hearings proceeded on the second contempt petition, DOJ expressed a new willingness to live with removal of Explorer's icon from the Windows desktop—an alternative that leaves most of the Explorer program on the system. And Judge Jackson signaled that he, too, would be amenable to that solution—having discovered on his own that a court employee was able to "uninstall" the browser in only 90 seconds.[12]

Consequently, to avoid a possible contempt citation, Microsoft agreed to comply with the preliminary injunction by offering computer makers two new options: (1) use the Windows 95 "uninstall" function to remove the Internet Explorer icon but leave related software in the operating system, thereby making Explorer harder—but not impossible—to access, or (2) remove both the icon and most of the related software, thereby making Explorer inaccessible to the ordinary user, without impairing other features of the operating system.[13] Amazingly, neither the judge nor DOJ acknowledged what should have been obvious from the judge's own "uninstall" experiment: The immense power of the federal government surely need not be invoked to ameliorate a "problem" that virtually any consumer can resolve in 90 seconds.

From the skirmishing over the preliminary injunction, it seems that Microsoft intends to play political and legal hardball. The company might have avoided much of the confusion over interpretation of the injunction by seeking clarification from the court. But Microsoft decided, apparently, that it had no interest in or responsibility for coaching the government on how to inhibit its business practices—and certainly no desire to have bureaucrats design its software. One spokesman acknowledged that the company's hard-line approach might be risky, might be pilloried by the press, and might be lambasted by some denizens of Silicon Valley. But Microsoft decision makers evidently believe that the long-term health of the software industry justifies their aggressive stance.[14] Or they might just believe that DOJ's bullying attitude and tactics need to be resisted as "un-American."

Thus, Microsoft has appealed the preliminary injunction, contending not only that the judge engaged in extrajudicial fact finding but also that he treated the case as an antitrust infraction rather than a contempt petition for violating the 1995 consent decree. According to Microsoft, by expanding the case beyond the scope of the government's complaint, Judge Jackson denied the company adequate notice and an opportunity to defend itself.[15]

In addition, Microsoft has objected to the appointment of Harvard University law professor Lawrence Lessig as special master, claiming that his mandate is too broad, that Microsoft should have been allowed to review the qualifications of candidates for the job, and that Lessig is biased in favor of a rival company, Netscape.[16] Judge Jackson dismissed those objections as "trivial" and "defamatory," and the company appealed that decision as well.[17] Meanwhile, Lessig will not be allowed to continue his work until the appellate court can examine his role more carefully.[18]

Microsoft's real concern, however, may be with Jackson's extension of the injunction to apply to "any successor version" of Windows 95. Microsoft insists that its new operating system, Windows 98, scheduled for release by the middle of 1998, will have a browser that is totally integrated—that is, the browser and the operating system will be technically and functionally interdependent. Some industry observers think the company will have to alter its plans. Others argue—more persuasively in my view—that the new system will qualify under the exception in the decree for "integrated software products." A former DOJ official put it this way: "The prohibition is against tying, not against selling a different operating system."[19]

Still, satisfying the consent decree is one thing, complying with the antitrust laws quite another. Klein has warned that DOJ intends "an active and continuing investigation into several Microsoft business practices," including the company's stake in new video technology and its recent investment in Apple Computer.[20] The government may also challenge Microsoft's contracts with Internet service providers if they give preferential treatment to Internet Explorer, and DOJ lawyers are "poring over hundreds of contracts Microsoft struck in the past two years with major providers of information or entertainment on the Internet."[21]

Why the frenzy of antitrust activity after three years of relative peace? Reporters for the *Wall Street Journal* speculate that Microsoft, "by its effort to defer compliance and its aggressive—some say arrogant—posturing in the case, has committed what is widely seen as a colossal public relations blunder, angering ... the antitrust regulators."[22] If that is the explanation for DOJ's fulminations, the department is doubtless more of a menace than Microsoft. When public policy is rooted in the petulance of government officials, we are all at risk. Microsoft has an obligation to its shareholders and an absolute right under the law to defend itself vigorously, no matter how testy the reaction of DOJ attorneys. How refreshing, in a world of corporate capitulation to government threats, that the company, so far, has exhibited some backbone.

Those are some of the larger, longer-range issues—substantive, procedural, and political. Before discussing them in greater detail, however, it may be well to explain a few essentials in the current dispute about software. Here then is a bare-bones framework for grasping the technical questions that are likely to arise as the Microsoft litigation winds its way through the legal system.[23]

The term "software" includes applications programs (like games and word processors) and systems programs (like Windows and Java), which control the computer's hardware and provide a platform on which to run the applications.[24] Each type of program includes "enabling files," which support both systems and applications tasks. Operating systems like Windows also come with mini-applications, called "applets," which provide basic functionality without requiring the installation of full-blown applications. For instance, calculators and simple text editors are applets; they are neither wholly integrated nor sold as separate applications.

Internet Explorer is more than a bunch of enabling files and more than an applet. It is an intricate, elaborately embellished Web browser, capable of standing alone; in fact, it was originally sold by Microsoft as a full-featured, independent application. Nevertheless, contends Microsoft, similar products, also tied to Windows, have survived government scrutiny. MSN, for example, is a full-featured, independent application, yet DOJ ultimately allowed it to be packaged with Windows as a joint product.

Apparently, DOJ's new rule—unsupported by economic analysis—is that products initially distributed in separate boxes must be permanently distributed in separate boxes. It is as if air conditioning, once sold as an option to be installed later on cars, must be forever so sold. If that indeed is the current doctrine, observes legal scholar Peter Huber, it would force Microsoft and other companies to upgrade their products infrequently, by whole rewrites, rather than more often by add-on improvements. Furthermore, notes Huber,

> Almost every new feature added [to Windows] was sold by some other vendor in a separate box first. Modem drivers (Hayes' Smartcom, $155 in 1988); memory management (a Quarterdeck product, $79 in 1991); CD-ROM drivers (Corel's SCSI, $99 in 1993); drive compression; fax utilities; disk defragmenters.... All of these, and countless other now-standard features, once came in separate packages. Most of them originally cost more than the whole of Windows costs today.[25]

Microsoft also argues that DOJ knew of plans to package Internet Explorer and Windows even before Microsoft signed the 1995 decree. Two years later, according to the company, the government inexplicably contends that Microsoft will be violating the decree merely by doing precisely what it told DOJ it was going to do.

For its part, DOJ denies that it was aware of Microsoft's intent to integrate a browser with its operating system. As proof, the department cites intracompany e-mail from a Microsoft executive stating in June 1994 that the company did not then plan to include Mosaic, a browser that Microsoft had licensed, with Windows 95. Another e-mail message described a browser as "stuff you need to obtain from 3d parties."[26] A third message, from a Microsoft senior vice president in December 1996, suggested that executives were still debating at that time whether to combine the two products.[27]

The company counters that DOJ's own earlier statements reflect its understanding of what the parties meant by "integrated." During the debate over the 1995 consent decree, a graphics company complained about Microsoft's plan to incorporate 3-D technology into Windows. DOJ rejected the complaint with the explanation that "incorporating new features into the operating system is what Microsoft has done for 14 years." That statement, says the company, indicates that DOJ condoned the same behavior it is now asking the court to halt.[28]

More important, insists Microsoft, two products can be "integrated" even if they are not technically interdependent. The products need not function *only* in combination, nor be marketed *only* as a package. To be characterized as "integrated," they just need to be combined in a manner that creates synergism—a whole that is better than the sum of its parts. According to Microsoft, that characterization applies no less to the current product package than it did in the

1980s when operating systems first included software that allowed interaction with hard disk drives, or later when operating systems began supporting local area networks.

Today, fax modems and electronic mail—once available only as separate products—are essential ingredients of an operating system. Any system without those functions would be incomplete. And in an environment where the shibboleth is "Internet access," browser software is no less essential. That is why IBM and Sun Microsystems, like Microsoft, have packaged browsers with their operating systems. That is also why IBM, Hewlett-Packard, Compaq, and other computer manufacturers have bundled *both* Internet Explorer and its principal competitor, Netscape Navigator, with Windows 95. Indeed, to ensure Internet users have maximum flexibility, Netscape has itself tied a wide range of other software products—for example, e-mail, security systems, and graphics—to its browser. Such decisions, argues Microsoft with unassailable logic, are better left to computer companies than to government lawyers.

Microsoft's Market Power

Whether Microsoft's browser is integrated with or separate from its operating system is perhaps more easily resolved by semanticists than economists. But that question is peripheral to the larger battle. Over the longer term, constraints on the company's behavior will arise under established antitrust law, not the consent decree. That was the implication of Judge Jackson's December 1997 opinion. He did not limit his inquiry to the functional seam between the browser and the operating system, as Microsoft had asked. Instead, he inquired whether the browser was marketed separately and whether it had separate consumer demand. Those are antitrust criteria.[29] Thus, the foundational questions are, at one level, does Microsoft exercise its market power in an anti-competitive manner and, more broadly, do the antitrust laws, with their prohibition of tying arrangements, make any sense?

A principal objective of those laws is to foreclose arrangements that "restrain" trade and harm consumers. But trade is not restrained just because a consumer agrees to pay a price for Windows that exceeds some lower price that he would have preferred. Nor is *aggregate* trade diminished when Netscape does less business and Microsoft does more. Moreover, there is no harm when a computer maker packages Internet Explorer with Windows in response to consumer demand. In fact, few manufacturers could risk offering a PC without Internet Explorer. If they did, rival manufacturers might be tempted to entice customers by bundling Explorer free of charge.[30] That is probably why Micron Technologies announced that it would not remove the Microsoft browser even if a customer wanted it removed.[31]

Some analysts predict that DOJ's temporary success in court will embolden PC makers to demand compensation from Microsoft in return for installing its browser. In all likelihood, those analysts are wrong. Indeed, major manufacturers—including Compaq, Hewlett-Packard, Dell, and Packard Bell NEC—have already indicated that they will continue installing Internet Explorer. "PC makers don't appear interested in having a choice," reports the *Wall Street Journal.*[32]

Nonetheless, Attorney General Janet Reno declared that "[f]orcing PC manufacturers to take one Microsoft product as a condition of buying a monopoly product like Windows 95 is not only a violation of the court order, it's plain wrong."[33] The attorney general does not tell us how she has determined that Windows is a monopoly product—about which more in a moment—or why the company's behavior is plain wrong, or precisely who has suffered as a result. Surely consumers are no worse off. They are getting browser software—often the Netscape Navigator as well as Internet Explorer—at no extra cost.

And because high-tech giants like Microsoft and Intel have aggressively introduced new and better products, consumers can now purchase for about $2,800 a PC with a Pentium II microprocessor and Windows 95 software that can carry out 600 million instructions per second. Ten years earlier, by comparison, mainframe computers were one-sixth as fast and cost more than $1 million per installation. Not even the supercomputers of the early 1980s, which cost upwards of $10 million, could match the power of a Pentium II today.[34]

Maybe Attorney General Reno was concerned about the impact on Microsoft's competitors when she bemoaned the company's "plain wrong" conduct. If so, she conflates preserving competition, the asserted rationale for our antitrust laws, with protecting competitors, which all too frequently entails companies attempting to procure through the political process what they have been unable to achieve in the marketplace.

Microsoft chief Bill Gates poses this analogous question: Would DOJ require the *New York Times* to eliminate its business section in order to protect the *Wall Street Journal*?[35] Why should the answer to that question be any different if the *Times* were to sell its business section separately, or if the *Times* sold 90% of the newspapers in New York? Our antitrust laws were not intended to prop up competitors but "to ensure that consumers benefit from the widespread availability of goods and services at fair prices."[36]

Even if competitor protection were a legitimate objective of the law, there is no justification for the government's intervention in the browser wars. Yes, Netscape's share of the market has dropped from more than 90%[37] to roughly 60%[38]; but the company's browser is still the market leader, and its 1997 sales—in the face of a massive marketing effort by Microsoft—are expected to increase sharply over 1996, despite large fourth-quarter losses.[39] Rather than badgering Microsoft, DOJ ought to be thanking the company for challenging Netscape's "near monopoly" in the sale of browsers; and consumers should be grateful to Microsoft for provoking Netscape to reduce its price.[40]

It is not just in the browser market that Microsoft is battling. The company's so-called monopoly in the sale of operating systems has come under intense pressure as well. Rivals have joined forces in an attempt to oust Windows as the industry standard. IBM, Netscape, Novell, Oracle, and Sun Microsystems, in a collaborative venture that somehow has eluded DOJ scrutiny, are reported to be "cooperating"—but apparently not "conspiring"—in three new areas of technology: Java software, developed by Sun, that can be transported from computer to computer without major incompatibilities; a low-cost network computer[41] pushed by Oracle; and a programming technique known as Corba for building Lego-like blocks of software.[42]

Perhaps most intriguing, hardware giant Intel, with more than 85% of the market for PC microchips, is developing a low-cost alternative to personal computers that will use operating systems from IBM, Novell, Oracle, and others, in addition to Microsoft. And Microsoft, underscoring that its interests are not always aligned with those of Intel, has proposed several PC alternatives, some of which do not require the Intel chip.[43] One *Washington Post* reporter sizes up the situation like this:

> [T]he high-technology world is on the brink of changes as profound as when the personal computer first emerged. . . . [T]he era of a single, dominant device is fading. . . . A smorgasbord of new devices—ranging from inexpensive hand-held machines to "network computers" to digital televisions—is appearing on the horizon. And Intel and Microsoft appear to be headed in different directions in their efforts to exploit these technologies.[44]

Thus, the two behemoths may find themselves butting heads—countervailing powers of the type that makes short shrift of a would-be industry czar. Microsoft's competitive advantage is likely a fleeting phenomenon. The company may now enjoy a 90% share of the operating system market; but entry into that market is unrestricted, and the technology is so dynamic that market dominance is probably not sustainable.

Furthermore, economists differ about what constitutes the "relevant market" for determining Microsoft's share. If the market is construed expansively as, say, "information technology," then Microsoft accounts for only 1% of the industry's $1.1 trillion in revenues. If the boundaries are more narrowly drawn to embrace only "software products," Microsoft has less than a 4% share. Indeed, IBM's 1996 software sales of $13 billion exceeded Microsoft's $11 billion[45]; 13 companies had 1996 annual revenues of $1 billion or more[46]; and the top 20 producers (including Microsoft) controlled just 42% of the market.[47]

Admittedly, in the context of antitrust law Microsoft's "relevant market" is not so sweeping as "information technology" or "software products." The Supreme Court has defined the term to cover "products that have reasonable interchangeability for the purposes for which they are produced."[48] Still, if "software products" are confined to those operating systems that are reasonable substitutes for Windows—that is, systems that run hand-held personal computers, portable and desktop PCs, and mainframes—Microsoft's market share is a mere 13%.[49]

Only if the relevant market is constricted to PC operating systems can Microsoft be said to dominate. And that definition, too, is somewhat equivocal. Browsers will soon, or may already, replace many of the functions served by operating systems. That appears to be the view held by Netscape, for example, whose general counsel maintains that Microsoft's tying arrangement is anti-competitive "because the browser threatens the operating system."[50]

Microsoft's aggressive quest for browser customers suggests that it shares Netscape's assessment. In any event, the potential for competition between browsers and operating systems reflects the ephemeral nature of market dominance in a high-tech world. Whether broadly or narrowly construed, Microsoft's relevant market requires invention and enterprise; it is an environment in which a single fresh idea can have enormous repercussions.

One such idea, initiated by Netscape, was to give away its browser, thereby spawning a generation of surfers on the World Wide Web. Now it is Microsoft, following Netscape's lead, that is packaging its browser at no additional charge. Not even the Antitrust Division has suggested that Netscape should be able to offer a free browser while Microsoft should not. Instead, Microsoft has been accused not of "predatory pricing"[51] but of denying consumers a choice. DOJ's complaint, in short, is that Microsoft forces consumers to take Internet Explorer—at a price of zero!

Astonishingly, DOJ concedes that Microsoft could fully comply with the consent decree by offering PC manufacturers two versions of Windows 95—one with and one without Internet Explorer— even if both versions were identically priced.[52] Naturally, few if any manufacturers or customers would prefer the stripped system. Yet that option, according to DOJ, would settle the current dispute. It is all quite remarkable; DOJ's stance is unfathomable. Essentially, DOJ is bent on forcing Microsoft to offer PC makers an inferior product. And consumers and taxpayers will foot the bill.

The "Problem" of Market Power

We turn now to a pair of economic questions with implications reaching far beyond the Microsoft case, even as they illuminate the real issues of that case. First, assuming that Microsoft has substantial market power, are there untoward consequences if that power is exercised? That in turn leads to a second question, discussed in the next section: Do tying arrangements allow a company to leverage its power in a manner that reduces aggregate welfare? Put another way, does the prohibition of tying arrangements increase the availability of goods and services, thus making us, on balance, better off?

Under "perfect competition," products are homogeneous, no single firm has a significant effect on the market, each firm takes the price as given, and each is able to sell all it can produce at that price, but not at a higher price. Any consumer who might have been willing to pay more secures a benefit, or surplus, equal to the difference between the value that he subjectively assigns to the product and the lower price that he actually pays.

When a firm acquires market power by differentiating its product, it becomes a price maker. As such, the firm can select the price it will charge, subject to expanding or contracting sales as prospective purchasers respond to the chosen price. Imperfect information usually prevents the firm from discriminating among its customers. That is, the firm rarely knows enough about consumer demand to be able to charge each customer a price that corresponds to the customer's subjective valuation of the goods or services offered. Moreover, a customer granted a lower price might find it profitable to resell the product in competition with the original supplier.

Because the firm is typically unable to discriminate, if it decides to reduce the price of a product, all buyers of that product will be affected—including those who would have paid more. Accordingly, marginal revenues (i.e., the increase in total revenues when one additional unit is sold) will decline at a steeper rate than price. Of course, the firm will produce only to the point where its marginal revenue equals its marginal cost; additional production would reduce the firm's profits. At that point, because price is higher than marginal revenue, the consumer will pay more and the seller will produce less than under "perfect competition." Effectively, some of the consumer surplus is expropriated by the producer through the higher price, and some is lost through the reduced quantity sold. The portion thus lost represents a reduction in aggregate welfare; it is, in theory, the economic cost of market power.

But what if that power results from a technological or other entrepreneurial innovation? And what if the innovation would not have materialized without the incentives that market power affords? Under those conditions, the quantity sold might actually be greater than if there were no such power. When the increase attributable to innovation exceeds the decrease attributable to market power, output will rise—notwithstanding the conventional wisdom that market power necessarily diminishes aggregate wealth. Thus, the proper standard of comparison is not the economist's utopian vision of what might have transpired had the same products been sold in a perfectly competitive environment. Instead, we must compare actual output against what would have occurred if anti-monopoly laws had eliminated the incentives that elicit new and improved products.

Professor Stephen C. Littlechild of the University of Birmingham (UK) illustrates this point by describing a businessman who charges a high price for a new product he has invented; the businessman prefers to maximize profits even though he will sell fewer units.

> It is true that he is restricting output compared to what he could produce, or compared to what would be produced if all his rivals shared his insight. But they do *not* share his insight; this is not the relevant alternative. . . . *[T]he relevant alternative to his action is no product at all.* It would therefore be inappropriate to characterise his action as generating a social loss. . . . On the contrary, *his action generates a social gain.*[53]

Arguing from a somewhat different perspective, F. A. Hayek noted long ago that in a dynamic marketplace—the marketplace of the real world—sellers are continuously seeking to carve out mini-monopolies; thus, disequilibrium is the perpetual state as profit incentives unleash entrepreneurial exertions that drive the economy forward.[54] By contrast, in a static environment (i.e., the perfect competition paradigm), no market participant can obtain a deal that is not obtained, at the same time, by countless others. There is simply no competition remaining under "perfect competition."

Even when one or more producers have market power, as long as there are no barriers to entry, there will be ongoing opportunities for businesspeople to make speculative decisions, some of which will bear fruit. The result is spontaneous ordering—seemingly chaotic, yet fed by, and responsive to, a continuing flow of information embedded in changing market prices. Thus, the market is a process of discovery rather than a method of producing specifically intended outcomes. If the market were to reach full equilibrium, the actions of market participants would be wholly determined by surrounding circumstances, just as they are in a planned economy, leaving no room for imaginative, entrepreneurial vision. In a nutshell, perfect competition is antithetical to innovation.[55]

190

For that reason, market power (even private monopoly) is not by itself a condition sufficient to invoke the antitrust laws.[56] "Predatory" or "exclusionary" conduct must also be present. Despite the professed ill effects of such conduct, market power creates the opportunity for extraordinary profits, however transitory, which stimulate risk taking, propel technology, and raise productivity. Should government, acting under the banner of antitrust, shackle that creativity and initiative, consumers will ultimately pay the price.

To be sure, a seller with market power will occasionally engage in "predatory" or "exclusionary" tactics intended to restrict competition. If that seller has a better product, he may succeed. Otherwise, the success of such tactics over time will depend on government-created and government-sustained barriers to entry—the outgrowth, more often than not, of special-interest legislation that should never have been permitted in the first place.

Regrettably, pundits and policymakers alike too frequently mischaracterize *legitimate* business dealings as anti-competitive conduct. For one such mischaracterization, let us look at tying arrangements— the antitrust infraction that the Microsoft consent decree was intended to proscribe. Tying arrangements are neither predatory nor exclusionary; instead, they protect against software piracy, facilitate lawful price discrimination, and may even expand aggregate output. Their impact is vertical rather than horizontal; that is, they are bargains between sellers and buyers, not collusion between competitors.

Tying Arrangements

Legal Background

A tying arrangement is "an agreement by a party to sell one product but only on the condition that the buyer also purchases a different (or tied) product."[57] While that definition seems straightforward, it has nonetheless generated considerable controversy among lawyers and economists—probably because of the murky provisions of the Sherman Act and the Clayton Act, each of which ostensibly justifies federal challenges to tie-ins. The Sherman Act provides, in part, that "[e]very contract, combination, . . . or conspiracy in restraint of trade or commerce among the several States, or with foreign nations is declared to be illegal."[58] Section 3 of the Clayton Act is more concrete, but it covers a tie-in only if the buyer is required to purchase the tied product *and* to abstain from purchasing a competitive product.

> It shall be unlawful ... to lease or make a sale or contract
> for sale of goods ... for use, consumption, or resale ... on
> the condition, agreement, or understanding that the lessee
> or purchaser thereof shall not use or deal in the goods ...
> of a competitor ... where the effect ... may be to substantially
> lessen competition or tend to create a monopoly in any line
> of commerce.[59]

Four years after the passage of the Clayton Act in 1914, the Supreme Court examined whether a tying arrangement might be used unlawfully to enlarge the scope of market power. In *United Shoe Machinery Corp. v. United States*,[60] a single company controlled over 95% of the shoe machinery market and refused to lease its equipment unless the lessee also bought supplies. Because of that tie-in, prospective competitors in the supplies market either had to produce their own machinery—an unlikely scenario, given United's dominant market position—or be denied access to 95% of the customer base. Accordingly, concluded the Court, the arrangement unlawfully insulated United from new entrants in the tied product market.

Over the next three decades, courts scrutinized various tying arrangements by applying a so-called rule of reason. Under that standard, to assess whether a tie-in was anti-competitive, courts weighed "the facts peculiar to the business to which the restraint is applied; its condition before and after the restraint was imposed; the nature of the restraint and its effect, actual or probable."[61] Then in 1947 a supplemental rule emerged in *International Salt Co. v. United States*,[62] purporting to set forth a brighter line. Tying arrangements would be deemed per se illegal if three conditions were met: (1) there must be two distinct products, with the seller conditioning the sale of one on the purchase of the other; (2) the seller must have market power in the tying product; and (3) there must be an effect on a "not insubstantial" volume of commerce in the tied product. Without any of those conditions, the courts would continue to apply a rule of reason test.

The new standard was aimed at providing both DOJ and private companies with more precise guidelines, thus discouraging flagrant misbehavior and increasing the predictability of dispute resolution.

Another objective was judicial economy. As the Court put it, tying arrangements meeting the threshold conditions

> are conclusively presumed to be unreasonable and therefore illegal without elaborate inquiry as to the precise harm they have caused or the business excuse for their use. This principle of per se unreasonableness ... avoids the necessity for an incredibly complicated and prolonged economic investigation into the entire history of the industry involved, as well as related industries.[63]

More recently, in 1984, the Court attempted to clarify its per se standard, observing that two products will be considered as one—thus not per se illegal—if there is insufficient demand for the tied good to offer it separately from the tying good.[64]

Notwithstanding the purported brighter line rule, court pronouncements have been inconsistent, leaving much uncertainty about whether in any particular instance an actionable tying arrangement exists. Thus, the Supreme Court allowed a newspaper to require that advertisers simultaneously purchase space in both the morning and evening editions: the dual editions were considered one advertising vehicle.[65] On the other hand, the Fifth Circuit treated automobiles and their air-conditioning units as two distinct products[66]; and the Ninth Circuit followed suit, disallowing a tie-in between a computer and its operating system.[67]

For an insight into what the Supreme Court's current view may be, consider a 1992 case involving Eastman Kodak.[68] Kodak had a practice of refusing to sell replacement parts for its copying equipment to independent service firms, which made it nearly impossible for those firms to compete with Kodak in servicing its equipment. Except for customers who repaired their own machines, Kodak said that if you wanted parts (the tying product) you had to purchase service (the tied product).

No party disputed Kodak's assertion that the copying equipment market was competitive. Kodak contended that interbrand competition in that market would automatically discipline intrabrand competition in the vertical markets for parts and service; that is, Kodak would not be able to force unwilling customers to purchase parts and service if the customers could easily select a different supplier of equipment. Undoubtedly, if Kodak's equipment had been the tying product, with parts and service as the tied products, the arrangement would have passed muster under the Court's per se rule because of healthy competition in the tying market. Taking note of that, Justice Antonin Scalia, joined in dissent by Justices Sandra Day O'Connor and Clarence Thomas, questioned why Kodak should be blameless if all three products were tied but not if parts and service alone were tied.

The majority disagreed and sent the case back to the lower court for additional evidence. Justice Harry Blackmun remarked, first, that Kodak controlled nearly 100% of the parts market for its copiers. Second, he suggested that Kodak's customers might find themselves locked into higher-than-expected prices for service: either the customers might not have obtained adequate information when they purchased the equipment, or the postpurchase cost to switch equipment might be exceedingly burdensome. Blackmun rejected the hypothesis that prospective buyers evaluate equipment, parts, and service as a package and that any lock-in would self-correct if Kodak sought to sell new customers, or resell existing customers, a noncompetitive package. He also rejected Justice Scalia's argument that consumers are to some extent locked in whenever they make large investments in durable goods—an event, Scalia observed, that "regularly crops up in smoothly functioning, even perfectly competitive, markets" without implicating the antitrust laws.[69]

The Case against Per Se Illegality

Against the background of the Kodak and Microsoft cases, each of which provides a useful framework for evaluating tying arrangements, let us examine the principal arguments for making such arrangements illegal. Courts, ignoring most economists, have proffered three interrelated reasons to invalidate tie-ins: (1) customer coercion, (2) leverage theory, and (3) creation of barriers to entry in the tied product market. Most courts have relied on leverage theory: the potential to garner power in the tied product market by extending existing power in the tying product market. I will argue, to the contrary, that neither leverage theory nor customer coercion is a proper ground to hold a tie-in unlawful. Only the creation of barriers to entry, in narrowly defined situations, may justify government intervention—invariably to counteract previous government intervention that produced anti-competitive effects in the first place.

Customer coercion. Proponents of per se illegality maintain that tying arrangements are inherently coercive. Supposedly, they force consumers to purchase a tied product that, at best, the consumer would prefer to buy from someone else and, at worst, the consumer does not want at all. But economists routinely dismiss customer coercion as a legitimate basis for opposing a tie-in.[70] They do not see voluntary contractual bargains as coercive, except in exigent circumstances—for example, a dying man, wandering in the desert, driven to negotiate with the region's sole supplier of water. Practically speaking, the product in which market power is presumed to exist is rarely if ever an essential good. Accordingly, the customer who is opposed to buying the tied product can simply decline to transact.

That is what Apple discovered in the 1980s when it refused to license its operating system. In effect, Apple conditioned the sale of its operating system on the purchase of an Apple computer. Unhappily for the company, too many customers decided that they did not want the tied package, and Apple's fortunes plummeted.

Similarly, a prospective purchaser of Kodak copying equipment was not compelled to buy parts and services from Kodak because, as a threshold matter, he need not have purchased the equipment itself. Only after buying the equipment would a customer be constrained to use Kodak parts, in which market the company had a virtual monopoly. But that customer—typically a business, not an inexperienced individual—should certainly have known that and taken it into account before making a purchase. To be sure, once purchases were made, Kodak's tying arrangement locked most purchasers into using the company for both service and parts. But no one forced the purchase. The customer had numerous options for copying equipment but elected Kodak despite the tie-in, which he either overlooked or thought unimportant. Whatever the purpose of antitrust law, it should not be to protect customers from unwise purchases; nor should antitrust policy presume that buyers are incapable of looking after their own interests.

The Microsoft case is different in one significant respect. Whereas Kodak had little market power in copying equipment, Microsoft has substantial market power in PC operating systems. Does that mean, therefore, that a PC buyer is coerced into purchasing Microsoft's browser? Of course not. First, no one is required to own a personal computer; millions of Americans do not. But even if PCs were essential and everyone had to own one, producers would no doubt seek to expand sales by installing multiple computers in each home or business. Competition for those follow-on, discretionary purchases would restrain any attempt to "coerce" first-time buyers.

Second, the corollary of Microsoft's 90% share of the operating system market is that 1 customer in 10 does not use Windows. Alternatives are available—MacOS, Unix, and OS/2, to name a few—and more are on the horizon.

Third, network computing technology, with its reliance on the Internet for software applications, will radically diminish the importance of the operating system. When it comes to PC software, market power is likely to be here today, gone tomorrow.

Fourth, even if a Windows customer is "forced" to accept the free Internet Explorer, he is not obligated to use it. Netscape and other browsers are readily available, and Microsoft imposes no restrictions on their purchase or use. A customer who so wishes is perfectly free to acquire Netscape's Navigator, which can also be obtained at no cost.

If that customer buys the bundled Microsoft product anyway, he has tacitly agreed to pay more for Windows than would a customer who assigns a value to Explorer greater than zero. Indeed, many tying arrangements are just an implicit price hike for the tying product. A $200 price for Windows plus a useless (to the customer) Explorer is not different in any material respect than a $200 price for Windows alone. Clearly, if there were no tie-in, but Microsoft raised the price of Windows without the browser from $150 to $200, DOJ would have no cause to object. Why should it react differently if Microsoft sweetens the deal by including another product that at least some customers want?

Leverage. A second objection to tying arrangements—not entirely unrelated to the "customer coercion" theory—is that tie-ins permit a company with market power in the tying product to extend that power and capture supercompetitive profits from the tied product. Did not Kodak, for example, using leverage from its virtual monopoly in parts, reap extraordinary profits by requiring customers to purchase high-priced service in order to obtain parts? Perhaps so, said the Supreme Court, citing that possibility as one reason not to approve Kodak's tying arrangement. But is it really feasible for a producer with market power to use leverage as a means of enlarging the scope of its power? Many commentators and economists think not,[71] and Justice O'Connor, concurring in the *Jefferson Parish* case, seems to agree:

> [T]he existence of a tied product normally does not increase the profit that the seller with market power can extract from sales of the tying product. A seller with a monopoly on flour, for example, cannot increase the profit it can extract from flour consumers simply by forcing them to buy sugar along with their flour.[72]

To explore Justice O'Connor's hypothesis, which may sound counterintuitive, consider this illustration: Mr. P produces a highly desirable product that he will sell for $1,000. In an attempt to extend his market power, he requires his customer, Mr. C, to purchase a worthless tied product for an additional $100. Assume further that the tied product is pure profit to P (i.e., his costs are zero) and pure loss to C (i.e., the product has zero value for use or resale). At first blush, those facts suggest that market power may have been impermissibly "exploited."

Note, however, that the $1,100 package price for the two products is precisely the same whether P chooses to allocate the proceeds entirely to the tying product or instead allocate $1,000 to the tying product and $100 to the tied product. In either case, C has two choices. He can accept the offer, which indicates that he values the tying product at $1,100 or more; or he can reject the offer, which indicates that he values the tying product at less than $1,100. Those two options are identical—with or without the tie-in. Since P is indisputably entitled to charge whatever he wishes for the single product (subject only to C's willingness to pay), there is no additional cost to C as a consequence of P's decision to include the tied product as part of the arrangement.

Now let us modify the illustration so that it corresponds more closely to Microsoft's tie-in of Windows and Internet Explorer. Suppose Microsoft offers Windows with its bundled browser for $200 and refuses to sell Windows separately. C thinks that the Internet Explorer is worth about $25—less than Microsoft's $50 stand-alone price. At a price of $50, C would rather buy the comparably priced Netscape browser. What are the various tradeoffs?

If C accepts the bundled product at $200, it means that he values Windows alone at $175 or more (i.e., the $200 package price minus the $25 value that he assigns to the Explorer). If C declines Microsoft's offer, it means that he values Windows alone at less than $175. Naturally, C's preference would be to buy Microsoft's operating system for $150 (i.e., the $200 package price less Microsoft's quoted price of $50 for its Explorer), then purchase Netscape separately for $50. But that is not an option because it is not an offer Microsoft is willing to make. Why then should Microsoft be forced by the Antitrust Division to make it an option? This is a simple marketing decision by Microsoft. Given that decision, C, having valued Explorer at $25, needs now to decide only whether the operating system is worth an additional $175.

Such tie-ins occur in the marketplace in infinite variety every day: toys with batteries, suit jackets with matching pants, cable TV with a basic package of channels, and on and on. Some sellers have substantial market power in the tying product; some do not. But in each case, sellers and buyers simply weigh the tradeoffs from their own perspectives before reaching agreement. Whatever those tradeoffs, tying arrangements neither diminish nor enlarge the scope of market power. The essence of that power is to facilitate pricing at a level that will generate profits exceeding competitive norms. When a second product is tied in, consumers will evaluate the price of the combined products with respect to their aggregate worth. If the consumer accepts the package, and if the tied product is priced above its competitive value, that simply indicates that the *tying* product is priced correspondingly below what the consumer would otherwise have paid. The pricing allocations are mere bookkeeping.

Yet even if Microsoft had a true private monopoly in the tying product—100% of the market for operating systems—and even if Netscape's browser could be used only in a Windows environment, Microsoft should still not be compelled to unbundle its browser and sell it separately. The company can refuse to sell Windows altogether, of course, no matter how badly that decision harms consumers or Netscape. So why should it be precluded from selling Windows conditionally—an alternative that, in this case, is more beneficial to consumers and Netscape both?

In reality, Microsoft does not have a true monopoly in operating systems, nor is Netscape's browser limited to a Windows environment. To prohibit Microsoft's tying arrangement in a competitive market—when there would be no basis for doing so even in a monopolistic market—makes no sense whatever.

Barriers to entry. Tie-ins are also opposed on the ground that they create barriers to entry to the market for the tied product. In *Kodak*, the defendant controlled nearly the entire market for parts (the tying product) and refused to sell those parts without service (the tied product), except to customers who repaired their own equipment. How, then, could a prospective entrant compete in the service market without access to parts? Similarly, how could Netscape, or any other browser manufacturer, compete against Microsoft, which packages Internet Explorer as part of an operating system that is sold to 90% of the users who might be interested in buying a browser? Kodak's and Microsoft's tying arrangements, it would seem, shield the two companies from new entrants in the tied product market.

In fact, there are four options that remain open to potential entrants. First, if the would-be competitor is a lower cost producer of the tied product, it might be able to sell its product to the tying company.[73] For example, Microsoft might elect to buy, then resell, Netscape's browser. Kodak might choose to contract for service from an independent firm, then provide the lower cost service to its customers. That would increase Kodak's profits; the new entrant would have a market for its service; and the customer would be no worse off. Naturally, if the prospective market entrant is a higher cost producer, then the tying arrangement is socially desirable; it discourages the would-be competitor from wasting resources in an ill-advised venture.[74]

Second, if Kodak decided to gouge its "locked-in" customers by charging an outrageous price for parts and service, an opportunity might arise for independent service firms to reverse engineer Kodak parts. That is not as far-fetched as one might think; Kodak did not manufacture most of its own parts but purchased them from other companies. The more dispersed a technology, the harder it is to protect against reverse engineering.

Third, competitors in the tied market could continue to offer their product, notwithstanding that the customer is paying for an equivalent product under the tying arrangement. That strategy works as long as the customer perceives the competitive product to be sufficiently better than the tie-in to justify the incremental cost. Prior to Netscape's recent announcement that it would be giving away its browser, the company had succeeded in convincing enough buyers to pay incrementally, despite Microsoft's tie-in.

Fourth, service organizations could contract with competitors of Kodak, much as Netscape could (and does) contract with competitors of Microsoft. That approach might eventually weaken the tying company's underlying market power. Indeed, it is power by the tying company in the *tying* market that is the purported problem. The tie-in itself is but a derivative concern.

To illustrate that final point, if Microsoft were to have a true monopoly in operating systems, it could ordinarily exploit that monopoly equally well with or without a tie-in. Even without a tie-in, the company could still price Windows at a super-competitive level, limited only by customer appraisal of the product's worth. Assume that Microsoft thereafter bundled Windows with Internet Explorer. The company could increase its price, but only by an amount equal to the competitive value of Explorer, no more. The browser would command precisely the same incremental price that it would command if sold separately in a competitive market. That is exactly what is now happening in the browser wars; Microsoft's tie-in adds nothing to its market power.

Hypothetically, a tying arrangement might expand the scope of a company's market power if all of these criteria were satisfied: (1) there were no suppliers in the tied market to establish a competitive price; (2) the tie-in created barriers to entry in that market, exacerbated by high costs or long lead times for entry or exit; and (3) the methods outlined above to circumvent those barriers were impracticable because of the tying company's overwhelming and persistent power in the *tying* market. In that limited case, the question is whether the government should intervene to reduce the tying company's power or make the tying arrangement illegal. In my view, the answer is still no, except under narrowly and carefully defined conditions.

The third of the three criteria is key: Without extraordinary power in the tying market—the quintessential ingredient of a sustainable tie-in—competition for the tying product will automatically discipline the tying arrangement. Only when that competition is somehow barred can a tie-in expand the scope of the tying company's power. In our largely—but not wholly—free-enterprise system, true barriers to competition come in two varieties.[75]

First, barriers can arise out of special-interest legislation or—which frequently amounts to the same thing—a misconceived regulatory regimen that protects existing producers from potential competition. When cable companies, electric utilities, and telephone companies are issued "certificates of public convenience and necessity" or their equivalent, monopolists are born and nurtured at public expense. When government offers tax benefits, subsidies, insurance, or loans to specific businesses, or erects trade barriers designed to protect a U.S. firm from foreign competition, the effect is frequently to foster the same sort of anti-competitive environment that the antitrust laws were meant to foreclose.

The obvious answer—which has little to do with the antitrust laws and nothing to do with tying arrangements—is for politicians to stop doing those things.[76] If the government does not take that sensible step, *and* if there is no actual or potential competition in the tied market, then the government should consider interceding to prevent a politically favored company from using a tying arrangement to exploit its government-conferred market power.

A second and quite different barrier to entry, likewise created by government, arises from the application of patent (and copyright) laws. The temporary market power that flows from those laws is the incentive that helps drive research and development. That incentive is available to all firms that meet prescribed standards for a patentable product. Thus, the laws—as distinct from the patents themselves—do not benefit a specified company. By contrast, special-interest legislation benefits particular firms, named or otherwise identifiable within the provisions of the law itself. For those privileged firms, which did not earn their competitive advantage in the marketplace, some tie-ins should be disallowed. But in the intellectual property context, where the grant of market power is a premium designed to encourage creativity, the crux of the matter is not whether a tying arrangement is good or bad but just how much incentive is necessary and proper to promote invention and innovation.

Some would argue that when a tying product is patent protected, government should intervene to prohibit the tie-in if above-normal profits in the tied product market are thought to constitute excessive compensation for the research and development that patents are intended to reward. But that would mean government regulation of profits on everything from patented drugs to machinery to you name it—a horrifying prospect worth avoiding at all cost.

201

Realistically, not even a patent can exclude competition from a modern, capitalist economy. Almost all patented products have close substitutes that are unprotected. Consumer preferences change. Technological obsolescence is always looming on the horizon. And every patent has a limited term.[77] The benefit in that rare instance in which public policy might be well served by prohibiting a tie-in is undeniably outweighed by the legal cost of identifying offending cases, the economic cost of false positives, the burden of oppressive regulation, and the uncertainty introduced by not having a bright line rule that says tie-ins are lawful.

In sum, government in a free society must honor and enforce private contracts unless they can be shown to violate rights. Because heavy-handed regulation has an immense potential for mischief, and because opponents of tying arrangements have not shown that such arrangements are coercive or otherwise harmful, they should be legal. Our existing standard—per se illegality if threshold conditions are met, backed up by a rule of reason otherwise—is misguided and destructive. Strictly speaking, therefore, it should not be necessary to set out the affirmative case for tie-ins. Nonetheless, there is a strong case to be made.

The Case for Legalized Tie-Ins

Most economists recognize not only that tying arrangements are not anti-competitive but that they have pro-competitive effects as well, even when not intended that way. First, if the tying and tied products are functionally related, there may be cost savings through economies of joint production or distribution. Second, if the tied product is integral to the operational efficiency of the tying product, or if the tying product is sensitive to the quality of the tied product, there are obvious performance advantages in avoiding inferior substitutes—especially when it is difficult for the consumer to determine whether operating problems are due to low-quality inputs.[78]

Third, in the software industry, tie-ins are particularly important insofar as they afford some protection against unauthorized copying of software and related intangible products. Although Microsoft has a property right in the software it creates—perhaps secured by copyright—as a practical matter, the company can enforce its right only against entities that openly and visibly distribute pirated copies. When an individual makes a copy of Windows or Internet Explorer for a friend, there is not much that Microsoft can do about it. But if Microsoft can convince a PC maker to package Windows with each computer sold, then any consumer who wants that PC and also wants Windows will have to pay for both; copying will save no money. The inclusion of the operating system makes the computer more valuable, and the higher price for the bundled product reimburses Microsoft for its software.[79] That process can be extended, of course, to encompass a second piece of software tied to the first—Internet Explorer tied to Windows 95, for example.

Fourth, tying arrangements provide a means by which a seller can engage in lawful price discrimination,[80] which in turn can raise the level of economic output. When a price-making seller is considering a price reduction but lacks sufficient information to identify those buyers who would continue to pay more than the contemplated lower price, the seller has two choices: either to extend the price concession to all buyers, which may lower his potential profits, or to make no such price concession, which forgoes additional sales to price-sensitive customers. Under the second scenario, the volume of production will be lower and prices higher than in a perfectly competitive environment. Lower output represents the economic cost of market power.

But production need not decline if the firm is able to discriminate among its customers, charging each a different price in accordance with his subjective valuation—that is, his willingness to pay. Since price discrimination can lead to more transactions and expanded output, any device that promotes such discrimination will have desirable economic effects, as long as the cost of the device does not exceed the gains from increased output. That, in essence, is what tying arrangements are all about. By facilitating three tools of price discrimination—metering, risk sharing, and optimal product bundling—tie-ins are a low-cost method of differentiating one customer's subjective valuation from another's.

Metering. Let us assume that Kodak sold copying equipment under a tying arrangement that required the customer to purchase ink, paper, and supplies from Kodak. The customer who intended to use the equipment regularly would be willing to pay more for the machine than the customer who intended to use it infrequently. But Kodak might find it prohibitively expensive to obtain sufficient information about each customer's intended volume of use. Instead,

Table 1
VALUE OF GOODS

Customer	W95	IE	Total
X	$150	$40	$190
Y	$125	$50	$175

the company could charge a low price for its machine—a price that most prospective users (low and high volume) are willing to pay. Then, in order to meter usage, Kodak could tie the purchase of high-priced supplies to the purchase of the machine. As larger users acquire more supplies, the company collects a premium, without pricing its machine out of reach of smaller users.[81]

Risk sharing. Suppose further that Kodak desires to lease its equipment to high-risk start-up ventures. The company does not know which of its potential lessees will be successful; but it does have a reasonable expectation that some portion will ultimately succeed. Risk sharing enables Kodak to charge a low enough lease fee to encourage all of the start-ups to participate. In order to extract higher payments from those that succeed, Kodak can tie in a variable input like paper and supplies. The lessee, if unsuccessful, will pay only the low lease fee on the copying equipment. Successful lessees will use more of the variable input, thus paying higher overall fees. Risk is pooled, with Kodak counting on the law of averages to ensure adequate total revenues.[82] At the same time, Kodak is providing its customers with an alternate means of financing. Instead of fixed lease obligations, the customer can substitute a variable stream of payments proportional to usage.

Optimal product bundling. Neither risk sharing nor metering applies in Microsoft's case because the tied product, the browser, is not used in variable quantity with each operating system. But a third method of price discrimination, optimal product bundling,[83] may well apply. Consider two goods, Windows 95 and Internet Explorer, and two customers, X and Y. Suppose the values of the two goods to the two customers are as shown in Table 1.

Given low marginal costs of production, the profit-maximizing prices of the two goods, if sold separately, will be $125 for Windows 95 and $40 for Internet Explorer. Both X and Y will buy; Microsoft's revenue will be $165 × 2, or $330; and consumer surplus will be

$35 (i.e., $25 for X, who values the two products at $190, and $10 for Y, who values them at $175). But what if Microsoft offers the products as a tied package, priced at $175? Again, both customers will buy; but revenue will increase by $20 to $350, and consumer surplus will decline by $20 to $15. Ten dollars of surplus will have been transferred from X to Microsoft and an equal amount will have been transferred from Y.

Of course, consumers have no vested right to surplus; they have a right only to refrain from buying if the purchase price exceeds their estimate of the product's worth. Otherwise we would have the Antitrust Division threatening litigation every time a producer raised its prices. The real issue, then, is whether the aggregate level of economic activity—that is, the volume of output—has declined. If so, the tie-in reduces economic efficiency. But if aggregate transactions have increased—the earmark of a more efficient economy—then fewer consumers are forgoing purchases of goods that they want.

Moreover, if Microsoft can collect a larger share of the surplus, it will probably produce more. That is, the company's output will likely be higher at a price of $175 for its tied package than $165 for two separate products. Here is why: As Microsoft expands output to serve more customers, its marginal costs will rise—not the modest production cost associated with another copy of the software, but the marketing cost that can escalate rapidly as potential customers become harder to identify and sell to. Obviously, if there is no decline in the number of units sold, then the higher the price for each sale, the higher the marginal revenue. When that happens, more money is available for marketing and more units can be produced and sold before marginal profits turn negative. In our hypothetical example, because neither customer will decline to pay the bundled price of $175, total output will increase.

Indeed, *more* customers may want the package at $175 than want the two separate products at $165 (i.e., $125 for Windows and $40 for Explorer). If the two products are sold separately, then no one who values Windows at less than $125 or Explorer at less than $40 will buy both. But if the products are packaged for $175, a customer who values Windows at, say, $120 will still buy as long as he values Explorer at $55 or more. Similarly, a customer who values Explorer at only $20 will still buy as long as he values Windows at $155 or more.

Thus, by paving the way for price discrimination—whether by product bundling, metering, or risk sharing—tying arrangements produce concrete economic benefits. Output expands, losses attributable to market power are thereby reduced, and aggregate wealth increases. From that perspective alone, tie-ins should be legalized.

Network Effects

That brings us, finally, to a relatively recent rationale purporting to support an activist antitrust agenda: the theory of network effects. Spawned by the computer revolution, the theory holds that competitors can be excluded from high-tech markets when customers, concerned about compatibility with other users, are seduced by a "first mover"—that is, a producer with an early or commanding market lead—into purchasing an inferior good. More generally, the term "network effect" (or "network externality") refers to the change in perceived value of a product that is caused by a change in the number of people who use it: as more people use the product, the theory says, the more its value rises, to the detriment of would-be competitors.

When prior acceptance of a product affects its perceived value, the theory continues, consumers' actions can become "path dependent"—meaning that a consumer can be locked in to an "objectively" second-rate product, despite known alternatives that are superior. Simultaneously, producers benefit from "increasing returns to scale"—due not to declining production costs but to higher revenues as the product becomes more valuable to each new consumer.[84]

In the Microsoft context, the claim is that customers cannot escape from the software path that Microsoft has been able to dictate because of its self-reinforcing market dominance. Before asking whether that claim is true, let us note that the history of Microsoft's ascendancy is inconveniently inconsistent with the theory of network effects.

Recall that Windows was not the first operating system; it was layered on top of a DOS platform, partly in response to the competitive threat posed by Apple. IBM adopted Microsoft's version of DOS in the early 1980s; but Apple's MacOS system, introduced in 1985, was thought by many to be functionally superior and easier to use. At that time, consumers considering a switch to Windows faced high switching costs. They were using either an incompatible MacOS system or an MS-DOS system with a totally different structure and work environment. Notwithstanding those costs—one aspect of network effects—consumers ultimately embraced Windows because they liked it.[85] They rationally predicted that many other consumers would feel the same. Intelligent buyers make such forecasts all the time, precisely to avoid locking themselves into incompatible products.[86]

No doubt, high-tech companies try hard to exploit network effects. That was surely Apple's intent when it offered its computers to schools at little or no charge—in an unsuccessful attempt to "lock" future consumers into Apple technology. Netscape employed much the same strategy with its early decision to give away its browser. Looking back, it is clear that consumers were not inveigled by either scheme. Nor were consumers prepared to anoint WordPerfect as ruler in perpetuity of word processing, or Novell as permanent king of network operating systems, or Lotus as spreadsheet leader forever, merely because usage of those products was ubiquitous.

On the other hand, consumers are usually the beneficiaries when software developers capitalize on network effects. Globally, millions of programmers have created thousands of compatible products—thanks in part to the standardized platform that Windows affords. The perverse outcome if DOJ forces Microsoft to offer customers dual versions of Windows—one with an integrated browser, one without—could well be higher prices and fewer product improvements. Consumers pay if computer manufacturers and software designers, faced with devising products that must interact with multiple operating systems, incur higher costs simply to ensure that Microsoft's competitors in the browser market are protected from it.

Fortunately for PC users, incompatibilities rapidly disappear in a high-tech world. That is exactly the process now unfolding in the personal computer industry with the development of transportable programming languages, like Java, and the adoption of the Internet's open architecture by makers of network computers. Sellers have an enormous incentive to dislodge the market leader when "increasing returns" and "path dependence" give birth to super-competitive profits. Rivals will advertise, reduce prices, offer bonus programs, and try a host of other marketing devices to persuade consumers to switch.

Naturally, not all consumers will be convinced, even if their original purchases turned out, in retrospect, to have been ill-advised.

More often than not, the regretted transactions had little to do with path dependence and everything to do with imperfect information at the time of purchase. Consumers do make mistakes, but those same consumers unquestionably know far more than does a government bureaucrat about what goods and services they want to buy. Before too eagerly substituting DOJ's political power for Microsoft's market power, we should carefully consider the consequences.

The very thought that the Antitrust Division might be entrusted with determining whether a consenting buyer, supposedly swayed by network effects, acquired an inferior product should be unsettling to anyone who values liberty. Economists James Buchanan and Gordon Tullock, in their pioneering work on the theory of public choice,[87] remind us that self-interest drives the actions of public officials no less than those of private entrepreneurs. In the private sector, however, markets discipline self-interest, channeling it in ways that promote the general good. No corresponding discipline exists in the public sector, where political power reigns and the abuse of that power is pervasive.

Recall, for example, that President Richard M. Nixon, when he wanted to browbeat the three major TV networks, used the threat of an antitrust suit as a sword of Damocles, hoping thereby to extort more favorable media coverage. In a conversation tape-recorded in 1971, but only recently released, Nixon told White House aide Chuck Colson: "Our gain is more important than the economic gain. We don't give a goddamn about the economic gain. Our game here is solely political. . . . As far as screwing them [the networks], I'm very glad to do it."[88] Yet in another conversation recorded that same year, indicating how political antitrust enforcement can be, Nixon barred "any more antitrust [action] as long as I am in this chair . . . goddamn it. We're going to stop it."[89]

Given Nixon's shifting predilections, the public was mostly unaware, until now, that politics, not economics, underlay DOJ's intimidation of ABC, CBS, and NBC—all innocent of any antitrust wrongs. If such invidious behavior were limited to one administration, that would be bad enough. But former *New York Times* and *Newsweek* reporter David Burnham warns that presidents from Kennedy through Clinton have routinely demanded that DOJ bend the law.[90] We can only guess the number of occasions on which an overzealous or malevolent public official misused the power of the antitrust laws to threaten a private business.

Still, proponents of antitrust enforcement assert that the possibility of government venality is outweighed by the iniquity of private monopoly power. That dubious proposition, even if it were true in some isolated context, has no credibility at all when applied to the software industry. There, notes Microsoft, productive capacity is infinite—not subject to ownership by anyone.[91] Unlike oil, utilities, railroads, and other capital-intensive ventures, software is based not on physical equipment but on ideas—human intellect, which economist Julian Simon has called the "ultimate resource."[92] No company can monopolize ideas.

The history of information technology in general, and software in particular, shows that better products prevail; manufacturers of those products are able to overcome any initial reluctance of customers to switch. Indeed, in major consuming companies the number of individual users is frequently large enough that the choice of technology is not governed by considerations of interfirm compatibility. And even smaller consumers, presumably "locked in" by high switching costs, may take matters into their own hands by entering into joint purchase agreements with other consumers to acquire a superior product.

Even more basic, by purchasing particular goods and services, consumers reveal their preferences in the marketplace. Yet advocates of network effects seem to believe that revealed preferences are not a reliable indicator of the products that "best" serve a consumer's needs. Instead, they would have us believe that there are objective measures that can tell us which products are technically "superior," a consumer's actual choices notwithstanding. If objective and subjective outcomes differ, they imply, the consumer must not have been truly free to choose—perhaps because he was locked in by a need for compatible products.

The problem with that argument, of course, is its presumption of an "objective" measure of quality—and its equally presumptuous dismissal of actual consumer preferences. It leads directly to government paternalism, to the idea than an elite group of government officials knows our interests better than we do—and can regulate affairs to satisfy those interests better than the market does.[93]

When we permit government to make such assessments, and we allow those assessments to trump the subjective choices of consumers, we are well on the road to tyranny. In the process, we will have reduced the mechanism by which a purchaser selects the goods he prefers to a formalistic appraisal centering on technical features alone—notwithstanding that products are also desired for their quality, price, service, convenience, and a host of other subjective variables.

None of this is to dismiss the essential premise of the network effects theory. Consumers of high-tech products undoubtedly do consider compatibility in their purchasing decisions. But it is not the only thing they consider. And because high-tech markets are incredibly dynamic, compatibility is assuredly not static—a view evidently shared by Nobel laureate Kenneth Arrow. While warning that we must be vigilant in maintaining open markets, Arrow nonetheless states,

> The history of market shares in PC application software has been marked by great volatility. Although first-mover advantages and increasing returns are important, there are many examples to show that such advantages are far from permanent. As examples, consider the fates of Wordstar, Apple Computer, and IBM itself. All were once dominant in critical PC-related product markets; yet each has experienced rapid loss of market shares.[94]

Today, Microsoft's commanding lead in PC operating systems is threatened on two main fronts. First, Sun's Java technology purports to offer a standardized, platform-independent environment for software developers. In a pre-Java world, a new operating system might have been hampered by a paucity of applications programs and a reluctance on the part of developers to depart from a Windows setting. But Java, when fully operational, promises an environment in which applications can be run both on stand-alone PCs and across the Internet without compatibility problems. Second, Netscape's browser may soon offer Internet users a means by which they can overlay and eventually replace major parts of Windows. The browser's Web-based user interface could become the principal working environment for creating new applications.

Together with low-cost network computers, Java and Netscape jeopardize Microsoft's control over PC desktops and over software development. Thus network effects, while they may slow competition over the short run, are not an effective barrier to longer term competition, nor, therefore, are they a valid excuse for government intervention in high-tech markets.

That assessment is even more compelling when we grasp the following realities: First, the barriers to entry that government should properly eradicate are those that government itself has created. Second, our economy suffers enormous damage when production is deterred by unnecessary regulation. Third, the right of a free citizen to enter into voluntary contractual arrangements cannot be squared with antitrust meddling. Fourth, we must not condone pernicious assaults by government on our nation's most innovative companies. Insofar as the antitrust laws are used to impose restraints through litigation against successful competitors, those laws sanction an indirect, anti-competitive subsidy to less successful firms. They are no different in principle than taxing winners in order to subsidize losers.

Industry consultant James F. Moore reminds us that leading information companies focus on how to solve important problems for consumers. The key is to build integrated systems, linking together what less creative firms look upon as separate technological elements. Companies like Microsoft understand that processors, software, keyboards, and video monitors can, in Moore's words, "be integrated into an appliance that people could use to improve their lives—an everyday tool for everyone."[95] It would be perverse indeed if government overreacted to putative network effects, or relied on groundless objections to tying arrangements, to assail companies that have been responsible for such extraordinary advances. As Alan Greenspan bluntly warned,

> Whatever damage the antitrust laws may have done to our economy, whatever distortions of the structure of the nation's capital they may have created, these are less disastrous than the fact that the effective purpose, the hidden intent, and the actual practice of the antitrust laws in the United States have led to the condemnation of the productive and efficient members of our society *because* they are productive and efficient.[96]

Conclusion

On the surface, the most recent attack against Microsoft revolves around the definition of "integrated" as that term is used in the 1995 consent decree signed by the company and DOJ. That decree, however, is of little lasting import: the soon-to-be-released update of Microsoft's operating system, Windows 98, will include a browser that is "fully" integrated. Accordingly, no matter how the court rules on the current dispute, the new system should qualify under the exception in the decree that allows Microsoft to develop "integrated software products."

But that will not necessarily take Microsoft off the hook, for Judge Jackson has suggested that the company could still be culpable under established antitrust law. The ongoing issues, then, are more basic and far weightier. They are, first, whether the government has any useful role to play in protecting American consumers against tying arrangements and, second, whether antitrust intervention is at all necessary to preserve competitive markets.

A tying arrangement allows a seller to discriminate among buyers on the basis of their willingness to pay. The effect may be to transfer some portion of consumer surplus to the producer, but that transfer does not, in itself, diminish aggregate welfare. A seller's ability to engage in price discrimination frequently increases overall output—the standard by which economic efficiency is measured. Further, tie-ins enable producers of intangible products like software to guard against piracy. By arranging for Windows to be bundled with a computer, then tying its browser to Windows, Microsoft obtains some protection against unauthorized copying of two software products. Moreover, tie-ins facilitate quality control and may even generate cost savings when products are jointly produced or distributed.

Given those considerable benefits, tying arrangements should be legal. The consumer need not enter into such an arrangement; by voluntarily purchasing a package of products, one of which he may not have wanted, he implicitly agrees to a price increase on the other product. He evaluates tied products with regard to their aggregate worth; price allocations are mere bookkeeping. From the selling company's perspective, if it has market power, it may try to extend the scope of that power by using a tying arrangement; but those attempts usually fail. A seller can enlarge its power only if shielded by effective barriers to entry in the tying market—barriers that are almost always transitory, and thus reversible, unless they are initiated and maintained by government.

More generally, DOJ intervention to safeguard competition is rarely if ever justified. Without government-sponsored barriers, free markets are sufficiently dynamic to ensure that market power cannot long subsist. In striving to build even a temporary power base, market participants engage in an intensely competitive process that fuels and expands the economy. Resourceful entrepreneurs struggling to carve out market niches provide the propulsion for growth. Nowhere is that more evident than in the computer software industry, where competition and innovation are extraordinarily vigorous.

From 1987 through 1994, U.S. software companies grew at seven times the rate of the economy as a whole; those companies currently provide 600,000 jobs.[97] If automobile and aerospace technology had exploded at the same pace as information technology, a new car would cost about $2 and go 600 miles on a thimble of gas, boasts Microsoft, and you could buy a Boeing 747 for the price of a pizza.[98] Indeed, the cost of computing was 10 thousand times higher in 1975 than in 1994, according to World Bank and International Monetary Fund data. Meanwhile, Microsoft does nothing to prevent IBM, Netscape, Oracle, Sun Microsystems, and countless other companies from developing products that could displace Windows 95 and Internet Explorer. In fact, those companies are aggressively pursuing that very course of action.

Despite that record of dynamism and progress, DOJ officials persist in the delusion and conceit that they can fine-tune the markets. Yet we will benefit no more today from their pursuit of Microsoft than we did not long ago from DOJ's 13-year trust-busting crusade against IBM. Writer Virginia Postrel described that debacle: "Millions of dollars were transferred from the taxpayers and stockholders to lawyers and expert witnesses. . . . The suit was a complete waste. Whatever quasi monopoly IBM had was broken not by government enforcers but by obscure innovators, working on computer visions neither IBM nor the Justice Department's legion of lawyers had imagined."[99] If anything, today's computer technology is more dynamic than ever, and today's dominant product could easily be tomorrow's relic.

If DOJ prevails in its attack against Microsoft, we will have sanctioned government scrutiny of any company that integrates previously distinct technologies, and we will have politicized competition by enlisting the public sector in pursuit of private, parochial interests.[100] Our recourse as responsible citizens—and as consumers most directly affected by the hubris of federal bureaucrats—is to insist that the Antitrust Division make better use of its employees' time and taxpayers' money. We must remember that the alternative to big companies is not small companies but big government—the most formidable and coercive monopoly of all.

8. Microsoft Redux: Anatomy of a Baseless Lawsuit*

Introduction

Let's begin our examination of the Microsoft case with a statement of first principles. They are simple, they are straightforward, and they handily resolve this dispute. Stating them is necessary because the Department of Justice, joined by 19 state attorneys general,[1] wants to transform Microsoft's private property into something that belongs to the public, to be designed by bureaucrats and sold on terms congenial to rivals who are bent on Microsoft's demise. Some reputed advocates of the free market endorse that foolishness, evidently oblivious to the destructive implications when private property is stripped of its protection against confiscation.[2]

The principles are these: No one other than Microsoft has a right to the operating system that it alone created. Consumers cannot demand that it be provided at a specified price or with specified features. Competitors are not entitled to share in its advantages. Those are core principles of individual liberty and a free society. Yet by insisting that the Windows desktop be exploited for the benefit of competitors—or even consumers—our politicians, some misguided businessmen, and not a few academics are helping those who debase private property, and doing an enormous disservice to those of us who have a healthy respect for free markets and a free society.

Even those who don't accept that argument should be appalled at the workings of the legal system in this case. The focus of the case—and necessarily, therefore, of this paper—is on three issues: Does Microsoft in fact have a monopoly? If so, has the company exercised its power in a manner that somehow coerces consumers into buying goods they do not want or would rather have acquired

*Originally published, with minor revisions, as Cato Institute Policy Analysis no. 352, September 30, 1999.

by different means? If so, does government have a solution that will make things better? That is, should we prefer political power under Bill Clinton to market power under Bill Gates? The answer to all three questions must be "yes" to justify a role for government. If the answer to any of the questions is "no," then the Antitrust Division of the Justice Department should step aside.

The theses set out below are, first, Microsoft has no monopoly as that term should be understood in the context of the antitrust laws; second, consumers have not been harmed—indeed they have benefited—from Microsoft's aggressive competition; and third, government doesn't have the foggiest idea how to redress a problem, if one existed, without butchering competition in the process. In making those points, we will be covering these related topics: existing and potential rivalry in the operating system market, tying arrangements, exclusionary contracts, proposed remedies, and the proper role of antitrust in a high-tech world.

Microsoft's Purported Monopoly

Price, Service, and Technology

Whether it's the post office, the local phone company, or an electric utility, the exercise of monopoly power is typified by rising prices, inferior service, and stagnant technology. Yet applying those criteria, it's evident that Microsoft doesn't conform to the monopoly mold. The price of Windows, on a comparable features basis, has plummeted. Windows 3.0, which required the added purchase of DOS, was introduced in April 1990 at a combined price of $205. More than eight years later, in November 1998, Windows 98, which does not require DOS, was introduced at a price of $169 for the full system and $85 for an update.[3] During that interval, countless features, once separately priced and packaged, became standard.[4] So prices are declining rapidly; and not only are they declining, they are low in absolute terms. A Windows update costs between 3 and 5% of the total cost of a personal computer.

Critics respond that the real test is not whether prices are increasing or decreasing, but whether they are higher than they would be in a competitive market. Conveniently for the critics, that question cannot easily be answered. Most industry analysts concede, however, that if Microsoft were a monopoly, it could and would charge far more than it does; and users would gladly pay the higher price.[5]

216

In an empirical study of software prices, economist Stan Liebowitz observes that prices rose 35% when WordPerfect (not a Microsoft product) was the dominant word processor, but fell 75% since Microsoft's Word took the lead.[6] More broadly, he states, there have been much sharper declines in markets where Microsoft has a product (−65%) than in markets where it doesn't (−15%).[7] It's fair to conclude: if price gouging is the mark of a monopolist, Microsoft just doesn't qualify.

Nor does Microsoft act like a monopoly in servicing its customers. In April 1998, when *Computer Reseller News* asked which firm provides the best training to its customers, 46% of the survey respondents identified Microsoft. Running a distant second place, IBM polled 14%, followed by Novell with 8%, and Sun Microsystems with 4%. Netscape Corporation, Microsoft's arch rival in the browser wars, didn't make the list.[8]

More important, many features now a standard part of Windows—like modem support, fax utilities, and CD-ROM drivers—originally cost more than all of Windows costs today. National Economic Research Associates reports that Windows 98 users will pay less than one-fifth of what they paid in 1989 for software that, at the time, had far fewer features.[9]

Competition in the Operating System Market

What about Microsoft's purported 85–90% share of the PC operating systems market? Doesn't that, by itself, signify monopoly power? The answer is "no," for five major reasons.

First, DOJ has stacked the deck by so narrowly circumscribing the relevant market that it appears as if Microsoft has it all. Economist Alan Reynolds points out that the government defines the market as operating systems for single-user desktop PCs that use an Intel-compatible microchip. Thus, Apple's market share, estimated at 10% in the fourth quarter of 1998, doesn't count because Apple uses a Motorola chip. Nor does Sun Microsystems' share—Sun's sales were up 30% in 1998—because Sun, too, isn't Intel-based, except Sun's Solaris system, which doesn't count because it isn't a single-user system. As for the Linux craze, it came too late to be included in DOJ's market share calculations. Then there are hand-held computer systems—sales climbed 61% in 1998—sub-notebooks, and set-top TV boxes, none of which count because each uses a non-Intel chip.

Finally, remarks Reynolds, 15% of PCs are marketed "naked"—that is, without an operating system. Reynolds estimates that Microsoft's share of all 1999 desktop shipments will be 70%. If that constitutes a monopoly, he notes, then DOJ better investigate Quicken and America Online, which have long enjoyed market shares exceeding 70%.[10]

Second, the corollary of Microsoft's supposed 85-to-90% market share—call it 87½%—is that 12½%, one customer in eight, does not use Microsoft. That's not a huge number, but neither is it trifling. Alternative operating systems are available—MacOS, Unix, and Linux, to name a few. Apple, with 13 million users, reports sharply rising iMac sales of which nearly half are new users or Microsoft converts.[11] And Linux, with up to 10 million users,[12] is now available on an Intel platform from more than 100 dealers worldwide.[13] In fact, Linux captured 17% of the server market in 1998,[14] and it's now exerting pressure on Microsoft in the PC market as well. Giant PC makers like IBM, Dell, Hewlett-Packard, and Silicon Graphics are all offering Linux on Intel-based machines.[15] Meanwhile, investment capital for Linux distributor Red Hat Software is cascading in from Microsoft's friends and rivals alike—including Dell, Compaq, IBM, Intel, and Netscape.[16] Thus far, an investment in Red Hat has paid off handsomely. One month after its August 11, 1999, initial public offering, Red Hat common stock has exploded to $120 per share from its offering price of $14. Apparently, investors who put their own or their clients' money on the line know something about the Linux phenomenon that has eluded Antitrust Division chief Joel Klein and his minions at DOJ.

Third, Microsoft's new Windows 98 must compete against operating systems offered by a company that controls nearly 90% of the market—namely, Microsoft itself. Even if Microsoft were to go out of business this afternoon, all of its installed systems would continue to function indefinitely. So to sell a new product Microsoft must convince customers to pay more money, learn the new system, and run the risk that existing applications software will be incompatible. That imposes a powerful discipline on Microsoft's behavior. It is utterly inconceivable that Microsoft would alienate the very consumers it must rely on for new sales. Roughly two million new PCs each month are sold with Windows 98 installed.[17] That's trivial compared to almost 300 million existing Microsoft users,[18] each of whom is

218

a primary prospect for an upgraded system. In short, the major competition for Windows 98 is Windows 95, just as the competition for Windows 95 was Windows 3.1. Accordingly, the more relevant market share isn't the 85-to-90% that Microsoft controls in the aggregate, but the 66% represented by Windows 95 and Windows 98 users. The other third of the market is still running Windows 3.1 or DOS or some other non-Microsoft system.[19] If Microsoft has such overwhelming market power, how come it couldn't persuade fully one-third of PC users to upgrade to its flagship product?

Fourth, it's not only existing but also potential competition that must be factored into an assessment of monopoly power. In that regard, Microsoft's dominance is threatened on many fronts: (1) Sun's Java programming language, if it's ever fully operational, promises an environment in which applications run both on standalone PCs and across the Internet without compatibility problems. (2) Low-cost network computers, with software downloaded from the Internet, could transform PCs into high-speed communications devices, thus jeopardizing Microsoft's control over the desktop. (3) Digital TVs, hand-held computers, and other consumer electronics devices have radically altered the scope, nature, and function of the operating system. (4) Mushrooming electronic commerce has shifted profit opportunities from the operating system to Internet portals, where Microsoft is already far behind AOL, whose merger with Netscape, first announced in November 1998, changed the competitive landscape overnight. More about that merger in a moment.

Fifth, Web-based software is perhaps the most formidable of Microsoft's potential competitors. That software runs on browsers, which have already overlaid, and may eventually displace, major parts of Windows. Here's how the *Wall Street Journal* described this new happening:

> The Internet is fueling a fundamental shift in software development, from PCs to machines called servers connected to the Web. . . . Instead of buying and selling programs, users increasingly can rent the same functions from Internet services—or get them free if they sit through advertising. . . . [S]ervers do the heavy duty processing, and the only essential user program is a Web browser. . . . If users don't need PCs with Microsoft's Windows operating system or Intel Corp. chips to use Web-based software, the vaunted market power of the duo called Wintel doesn't seem so unshakable.[20]

In the new Internet world, traditional application software developers are morphing into "applications service providers," or ASPs for short. They are rewriting popular software packages and creating new packages to run on Web-based servers. Thus, corporate users don't have to install and update large applications programs on each PC, nor rely on their own networks and servers. Instead, PCs will tap into the Internet to access customized corporate applications as well as standard programs such as word processing, spreadsheets, and presentation software.

"In the past six months, we have not seen a business plan for a conventional packaged software application," says James Breyer, a venture capitalist at Accel Partners. "It's the first time in our history I could say that."[21] For Microsoft, that means its putative "applications barrier to entry"—that is, the array of software programs written for Windows that might not be available to users of an upstart would-be Windows competitor—if it ever really kept rivals at bay, is unlikely to afford much protection in the future.

Indeed, to cite just one example of this new paradigm, on August 31, 1999, Sun Microsystems announced its acquisition of Star Division Corp., a company that makes StarOffice, a suite of software very similar to Microsoft Office. Sun insists, however, that it has no plans to go head-to-head against Microsoft. Rather, Sun will convert StarOffice into a free Internet-based service that can be run directly by any user with any Web browser.[22]

Sun CEO Scott McNealy writes that "a few years from now, savvy managers won't be buying many, if any, computers. They won't buy or build anywhere near as much software either. They'll just rent resources from a service provider."[23] McNealy, who may be Microsoft's most vitriolic critic, predicts that fewer than 50% of the devices accessing the Internet will be Windows-equipped PCs by the year 2002.[24] That forecast comes from the same antagonist who complains that "Microsoft operates beyond the constraints of market discipline."[25]

Of course, Web-based servers will themselves need an operating system. But that's a market where Linux leads the pack with a 31% share, and growing. Windows NT is second with 24%, followed by a trio of free operating systems—FreeBSD, NetBSD, and OpenBSD—developed at the University of California in Berkeley, with a total of 15%. In fact, the world's busiest Web site, Yahoo!, serving nearly

80 million people per month, is run by 1,000 computers using FreeBSD. Even Microsoft's own Web-based e-mail service, Hotmail, runs on FreeBSD and not on Windows NT.[26]

The antitrust implications are crystal clear, especially to McNealy if not to his collaborators at DOJ. Microsoft has zero leverage in a world where applications are written so that any browser can run them and any operating system can access them. Whether a user has MacOS, Unix, Linux, or any other system, as long as he is running a Web browser he has much the same capabilities as a Windows user. That exciting development is here today; it's not a "could happen in the future" item. There's a good reason only a few companies are clamoring to compete against Microsoft in the PC operating system market: It isn't a growth market anymore. That opportunity has passed. The future is elsewhere.

The AOL-Netscape Merger

When virtually no new application software is written using client-specific code, Windows is no threat to anyone with a browser. That may go a long way toward explaining AOL's willingness to fork up $10 billion for the company that controls 42% of the browser market.

After AOL announced its acquisition of Netscape, as well as its close working relationship with Sun Microsystems, federal judge Thomas Penfield Jackson acknowledged that the deal could have a major impact on the Microsoft case.[27] Ironically, the case itself probably delayed the merger. Why, after all, commit $10 billion to do battle against a rival that may be dissected by the government? And why not, at a minimum, wait until the government has irrevocably committed itself to the Microsoft litigation before announcing a merger that DOJ might otherwise have challenged?

The AOL-Netscape combination suggests that browsers and e-commerce—a $26 billion business in 1996, expected to grow to $1 trillion by 2005[28]—not operating systems, are where the greatest profit opportunities lie. Internet commercial traffic will be driven primarily by portals, or home pages; and when it comes to portals, AOL-Netscape is the leader, far ahead of Yahoo!, with Microsoft a distant tenth.[29] With Netscape's Netcenter portal, its e-commerce software, and its newly updated Communicator 5.0 browser, which will be shipped in December 1999 and bundled with AOL's software

CDs,[30] an AOL-Netscape-Sun alliance becomes a redoubtable competitor to Microsoft.

Despite pronouncements by Netscape CEO James Barksdale and AOL CEO Steve Case—in court and to journalists—that the AOL-Netscape-Sun alliance was not a threat to Microsoft, merger-related documents, subject to the anti-fraud provisions of the securities laws, said exactly the opposite.[31] The three companies intend to develop, jointly, a browser-based de facto operating system—yet another sign, for anyone who cares to look, of an explosive marketplace the contours of which change with every day's newspaper.

Microsoft's Tying Arrangements[32]

The government-defined market for operating systems—single-user desktop PCs running Intel chips—is in its death throes. Even Microsoft seems to think so. That's why it's putting most of its marbles into Windows NT 5.0 (renamed Windows 2000), which is primarily a server operating system.

That said, let's assume for argument's sake that Microsoft enjoys sustainable monopoly power within a market properly defined to include all reasonable Windows substitutes. By itself, monopolies are not illegal under the antitrust laws. The government is supposed to step in only if the alleged monopolist is misusing its power. Just what is it that Microsoft is doing to raise hackles at DOJ? For a clue, we turn to the government's 800-page proposed "Findings of Fact," which DOJ deposited with Judge Jackson on August 10, 1999. There we find the centerpiece of the government's antitrust case: "Microsoft substantially impeded the most effective channels of distribution ... and, ultimately, effectively eliminated Netscape as a platform threat."[33]

That may sound to some as if the government's central focus is safeguarding Netscape rather than protecting consumers, which is after all the purpose of the antitrust laws. To be sure, DOJ has tried mightily to link one objective to the other. But even the government's own witness, M.I.T. professor Franklin Fisher, when asked whether consumers have been harmed by Microsoft, responded, "On balance, I'd think that the answer is no."[34] Still, DOJ accuses Microsoft of barring consumers from access to Netscape, and vice versa, by a variety of exclusionary agreements.

On the facts, that claim is preposterous. More than 150 million copies of Netscape's browser were delivered in 1998 alone.[35] Over 65 million Internet users start up at Netcenter, which is the second most visited site on the Web after Yahoo!; Microsoft is far behind.[36] Over 400,000 Web sites link to Netscape's home page—more than twice the number of links to Microsoft's home page.[37] Netscape still controls 42% of the browser market and will soon control an additional 16%[38] through its new partner, AOL, which paid more than $10 billion to acquire a 4-year-old company purportedly mangled by Microsoft.

How, according to the government, did Microsoft banish Netscape from the market? DOJ claims that Microsoft told PC makers (original equipment manufacturers, or OEMs) they had to take its Internet Explorer browser or they couldn't have the Windows operating system—known as a tying arrangement. That assertion by DOJ is correct, but not germane to its charge of exclusionary contracting. Plain and simple, Microsoft's tying contracts with OEMs are not exclusionary. To require Internet Explorer is not to exclude Netscape. By analogy, consider the *Washington Post*, with a virtual monopoly in the Washington, D.C., newspaper market. The *Post* "ties" its business section to the rest of the paper; to get the *Post*, you must also buy the business section. But the *Post* doesn't insist that its subscribers not buy competitive independent business publications like, say, the *Washington Business Journal*. Imagine the reaction if the *Post* were forced by the government to untie its business section from the rest of the paper.

Tying can be exclusionary in two instances: a technological tie that disables other products or a contractual tie that forecloses other products by agreement. Microsoft uses neither. It uses bundling, which is nonexclusive. Microsoft merely prevents OEMs, by contract, from deleting the Internet Explorer browser. Microsoft does not prevent OEMs from using Netscape or any other browser; and many OEMs do just that.

Microsoft's nonexclusionary tying arrangements were not the cause of Netscape's decline. Nor has Microsoft been able to secure market leadership by bundling other products with Windows. For example, Microsoft Network (MSN) hasn't dented AOL's control of the online market. MSN loses about $200 million per year serving 2 million customers. AOL, with 15 million users, is making a ton of money.[39] So despite all the complaints, Microsoft's tie-ins proved impotent; consumers didn't like the Microsoft Network and they couldn't be forced to buy it. By contrast, when consumers decided that Microsoft's Internet Explorer was better than Netscape's browser, they switched.

That's the reason Netscape's browser share, once 90%,[40] declined to 42%. Remember, Netscape still controlled 90% of the browser market long after Microsoft began bundling its browser with Windows. Not until PC magazines, then consumers, discovered that newer versions of Internet Explorer were superior did Microsoft's market share explode.[41] A better product, not tying arrangements, won the battle for consumer acceptance. How else to explain the triumph of Microsoft's Word and Excel over their respective rivals, WordPerfect and Lotus, with users of Apple computers, where Windows was obviously not a factor?[42]

Meanwhile, as Microsoft improved Internet Explorer, Netscape made some key mistakes. First, it didn't offer software developers a viable platform onto which applications could easily be written. Then, it responded too slowly when its browser was outclassed; it twice spurned help from AOL; it was late in offering a free browser; and it took three years to exploit its Netcenter portal.[43] In a nutshell, that's how Netscape lost the browser wars—lost, that is, if you ignore the $10 billion payday from AOL. Perhaps Netscape's browser would still be the market leader if CEO Barksdale had spent more time on product development and less time cobbling together his anti-Microsoft coalition and pleading for government aid.

By the way, if DOJ were to look for an example of truly exclusionary behavior, it would find that Netscape, when it controlled the browser market, offered payment to OEMs if they would agree to ship computers without installing Internet Explorer. Microsoft countered with a three-part strategy: It expanded its research and development to create a better browser; it priced the browser at zero; and it bundled the browser with Windows, thereby guaranteeing that Internet Explorer would appear on the Windows desktop.[44] But Microsoft did not exclude Netscape. Nor did it try to "bribe" OEMs, as Netscape did. The end result: Netscape's near-monopoly crumbled; consumers benefited from zero price and a better product; competition thrived.

Paradoxically, DOJ appears to regard the dissipation of monopoly power as regrettable in the case of Netscape but eminently desirable in the case of Microsoft. Both firms stood to lose some portion of their dominant market shares as soon as a competent competitor surfaced. For Netscape, that competitor was Microsoft. But for Microsoft, no competent competitor emerged. Instead, IBM ineptly positioned its OS/2 system as a juiced-up version of Windows that needed more computer horsepower than users had or were willing to buy. And Apple blundered by forcing customers into a tying arrangement whereby they had to purchase Apple hardware if they wanted the MacOS operating system. Those wrongheaded management decisions backfired, but through no fault of Microsoft's.

We see, then, that consumers are free to reject tie-ins like Apple's MacOS and Microsoft's MSN. More often, however, tying arrangements are welcomed for their beneficial effects. First, they facilitate quality control by preventing the use of inferior substitutes, especially when users have difficulty tracing the cause of a technical problem. Second, tie-ins curb pirating by linking software to physical product. If a large distributor openly pirates Microsoft software, Microsoft will take remedial action; but if I copy Windows or Internet Explorer for my neighbor, there's little that Microsoft can do. By attaching Windows to every outgoing computer and attaching Internet Explorer to every copy of Windows, Microsoft forces pirates to pay for the software they get. Third and most important, tie-ins are economically efficient. Consumers want an integrated operating system, which provides more bang for the buck; it's easier to operate, document, and debug; it's less expensive to market and distribute; and it provides a uniform standard for software developers.

Even if it were possible, as the government contends, to erase Internet Explorer from Windows without affecting other operations, the same could be said for removing the speedometer from a new automobile. The key test is not whether two products can be separated but, in the words of the U.S. Court of Appeals, whether the product is integrated; that is, whether it "combines functionalities ... in a way that offers advantages unavailable if ... bought separately and combined by the purchaser." As the court concluded, Microsoft clearly met its burden to show "facially plausible benefits to its integrated design."[45]

Software vendors and their customers know that a system without truly integrated functions would be incomplete. That's why IBM and Sun, like Microsoft, package browsers with operating systems.

And that's why Netscape ties a wide range of software products—that is, security systems and graphics—to its browser. Indeed, when Netscape enjoyed its short-lived monopoly, it tied e-mail to its browser and almost destroyed a rival e-mail product offered by Eudora.[46] Still, Netscape's product design decisions, like Microsoft's, are better left to computer companies than to government lawyers.

Microsoft's Other Exclusionary Contracts

The government asserts that Microsoft has also employed nontying exclusionary devices in its contracting with OEMs. Supposedly, OEMs were coerced to "play by Microsoft's rules" by threatened price increases for Windows. IBM's Gary Norris, testifying for the government, complained that IBM faced retribution if it insisted on promoting competitive products, like OS/2 and Lotus.[47] Yet the resultant post-retribution price from Microsoft was no worse than the price other OEMs paid, even though IBM continued aggressively to market both OS/2 and Lotus. Similarly, DOJ charges that Compaq had to knuckle under to Microsoft in order to retain its discount price for Windows. But Compaq's general counsel has a different view: "Compaq is an independent company and we'll make our own decisions on products and services, and if they compete with Microsoft, so be it."[48] As already noted, both IBM and Compaq have invested in Linux distributors and are offering Linux on their PCs. Furthermore, Compaq installs a wide variety of other operating systems on its computers,[49] and makes Netscape's browser available on every PC it ships.[50] So much for being cowed by Microsoft.

DOJ points next to Microsoft's "exclusive" contracts with Internet service providers (ISPs), Internet content providers (ICPs), and online service providers (OLSs). Naturally, companies negotiate exclusive deals all the time, but those deals may run afoul of the antitrust laws if one of the companies is a monopolist. The question, then, is whether Microsoft tried to leverage its alleged operating system monopoly to obstruct ISPs, ICPs, and OLSs from doing business with Netscape.

Originally, in return for referring business to fewer than a dozen ISPs (among more than 4,000 firms offering ISP services),[51] Microsoft required that they use Internet Explorer as their default browser. In effect, Microsoft told its ISPs: "If Microsoft refers a customer to you, don't give that customer our competitor's browser." That arrangement gave way to a requirement for "parity of promotion" between Microsoft's browser and Netscape's. Later, Microsoft relaxed the deal still further, eliminating all restrictions. With Windows 98, Netscape can be the default, or even the exclusive, browser. At no time, however, did Microsoft insist that the favored ISPs totally exclude Netscape. Even when Internet Explorer was the default browser, ISPs could distribute non-Microsoft browsers to 25% of their users, and ISPs exceeded that cap without retribution from Microsoft. During the fourth quarter of 1997, one of the ISPs, Earthlink, actually distributed non-Microsoft browsers to 2.5 times as many users as received Internet Explorer.[52]

Microsoft's cross-promotional deals with ICPs were even less insidious. Prior to release of Windows 98, Microsoft had "Active Channels" that guided users to 24 selected content providers, such as MSNBC. Netscape had similar cross-promotional deals—with ABC News, for example. With one restriction, Microsoft's "preferred" ICPs were at liberty to promote Netscape on any Web page they wished. Only the single page to which Microsoft linked directly was off limits. More important, while they were in effect, Active Channel accesses to two-dozen ICP sites accounted for a minute fraction of total Web accesses to as many as 2.5 million sites, thousands of which are commercially significant.[53] Microsoft's ICP deals, by any rational standard, represented an infinitesimal "foreclosure" of Netscape's market penetration.

In its contract with AOL (an OLS), Microsoft provided for "preferential" promotion of Internet Explorer. To preserve its guaranteed position in Microsoft's online services folder, which is displayed on the Windows opening screen, AOL had to meet distribution targets—85% of AOL users had to use Internet Explorer, which was the default (but not the exclusive) browser. AOL's version of Internet Explorer was customized, however, to link to AOL's preferred sites, not Microsoft's. Moreover, AOL could have switched to Netscape after 1998 but chose not to do so—perhaps because Microsoft never enforced the 85% target, or perhaps because AOL's position in Microsoft's online services folder gave AOL leverage in negotiating for desktop space with OEMs.[54] Another possible reason, of course, is that AOL still considers Internet Explorer to be the better browser. In any event, AOL continues to offer Netscape to any user who wants it. Having now acquired Netscape, AOL will no doubt soon switch to its subsidiary's browser. The merger itself demonstrates, if nothing else, that AOL was not intimidated by Microsoft nor forced to use Internet Explorer.

There's another aspect to Microsoft's dealings with ISPs, ICPs, and OLSs that seems to have escaped the attention of DOJ officials. Take Microsoft's contracts with AOL and Intuit (an ICP), for instance. DOJ gripes that Microsoft offered those companies a place on the Windows desktop if they would sever their dealings with Netscape. True or not—and Microsoft vigorously disputes the allegations—such offers are wholly irrelevant to this case. Whatever monopoly Microsoft may enjoy in the operating systems market, it plainly did not exploit *that* monopoly in negotiating the AOL and Intuit contracts. In short, DOJ has identified the wrong market. Here's how the government missed the boat.

Remember, Microsoft did not tell AOL or Intuit that they could not purchase the Windows system. Instead, Microsoft is charged with refusing to provide space on the Windows desktop—the means by which those companies could advertise and distribute their products. So the pertinent market in which to look for monopoly power is not the operating systems market but the market for advertising and software distribution.

Consider the *Lorain Journal* case[55]—that's the case that former judge Robert Bork trots out in arguing, episodically, that the antitrust laws are good for us.[56] In that case, the *Journal* newspaper supposedly had a lock on advertising in Lorain, Ohio. When a radio station tried to compete for ad dollars, the *Journal* threatened not to accept advertising from any company that plugged its product on the radio—clearly an exclusionary deal. The Supreme Court ruled against the *Journal*, concluding that it had a monopoly—not in the news market but in the advertising market. To the extent that the *Journal* had any leverage over its advertisers, it was in withholding ad space, not in denying them the right to buy the daily paper. Similarly, Microsoft limits ads, not the purchase of Windows.

But DOJ, unlike in the *Lorain Journal* case, cannot reasonably claim that Microsoft has a monopoly in advertising or, for that matter, in software distribution. Vendors sell software through retail stores, over the Internet, by mail order, bundled with hardware, and through a variety of other channels. Internet service is advertised in newspapers and magazines, on radio and TV, by direct mail, on the Web, and so on. Not even the Windows desktop is controlled by Microsoft, which uses only 7 of 49 possible icons. In other words, 85% of the desktop space is available to OEMs and consumers, who can display icons for any products they wish, including software produced by Netscape and other Microsoft rivals. In order to show that Microsoft used monopoly power to "coerce" customers into signing exclusionary contracts, the government first must examine the relevant monopoly. It has not done so.

Miscellaneous Affronts

To win its case against Microsoft, DOJ must prove all of these points: (1) Microsoft is a monopoly, which can raise prices long-term without competitive consequences; (2) Internet Explorer is a separate product, tied by Microsoft to the Windows operating system without offering consumers any plausible benefit; (3) by tying and other exclusionary practices, Microsoft foreclosed Netscape's distribution of its own browser; and (4) in that manner, Microsoft has harmed consumers. Because it failed to prove any of those threshold points, much less all, the government has leveled a number of tangential charges, to which we now turn.

Specifically, the government alleges in its Proposed Findings of Fact that "Microsoft sought to curtail other actual or potential . . . threats to its operating system monopoly, including Sun's Java, Intel's Native Signal Processing (NSP), and Apple's Quick Time." DOJ adds that "Microsoft began its attack . . . by proposing to Netscape that it agree not to compete and to divide the browser market." In addition, says DOJ, Microsoft engaged in predatory pricing; it "gave its browser away for free, without any expectation or basis for believing that it could defray the huge development, promotion, and distribution costs associated with Internet Explorer." Finally, according to the government, Microsoft cemented its monopoly position by imposing unreasonable restraints on OEMs and users who might wish to alter the Windows opening screen. Let's briefly review each of those allegations.

Microsoft's "Assault" on Sun, Intel, and Apple

Sun Microsystems, which licenses its Java software to Microsoft, has claimed in a private lawsuit that Microsoft "polluted" the software—altering it in a manner that renders it incompatible with non-Microsoft systems. In response, Microsoft contends that its license agreement allows alterations as long as Microsoft also makes available a version of Java that is compatible with non-Microsoft systems for any user who prefers it. Initially, a federal district court issued a preliminary injunction that precluded Microsoft from distributing its version. But in August 1999, an appeals court reversed the injunction because the lower court had not shown that Sun would be irreparably harmed pending final resolution of the dispute.[57]

The essential point is this: Whether the Sun-Microsoft dispute involves a copyright violation—the "pollution" charge—or merely a contract question, the parties are quite capable of resolving their dispute through ordinary litigation without DOJ intrusion. On one hand, if Microsoft breached its license agreement, it should be enjoined from doing so, and held liable for damages; but that is no concern of the Antitrust Division, whose mission does not include intervening in private quarrels. On the other hand, if Sun inadvertently opened itself up for competition in the Java arena by sloppy contracting, Microsoft's exploitation of the advantage hardly rises to the level of an antitrust infraction.

In August 1995, asserts DOJ, Microsoft also made "vague threats" against Intel to discourage that company from developing NSP, a competitive multimedia platform. Microsoft maintains that its concern centered on NSP's incompatibility with Windows 95, not on the development effort itself. Ultimately, Intel went ahead with parts of NSP, belying the contention that Microsoft was somehow able to convince its giant Wintel partner to withdraw from a potentially lucrative market. Moreover, Intel supports a number of Microsoft rivals, including Unix, Java, Solaris, and Real Networks—all over Microsoft's vigorous objections.[58] Microsoft's discussions with Intel about NSP were known to DOJ when it filed its antitrust complaint in May 1998.[59] If those discussions had antitrust significance, surely DOJ would have questioned them in its initial court papers. NSP was not mentioned.

The government also protests Microsoft's relations with Apple Computer, which rejected Microsoft's request that it share the technical specifications for QuickTime, Apple's multimedia program. At one point there was speculation that Microsoft had sabotaged QuickTime by intentionally disabling the product on Windows-based PCs. It turned out, however, that the problem was Apple's bug, not

Microsoft's sabotage.[60] Then, DOJ explored whether Microsoft had leaned on Compaq not to install QuickTime on Compaq PCs. That investigation proved futile; Compaq explained that its abandonment of QuickTime had nothing to do with pressure from Microsoft and everything to do with Apple's new pricing of a product that formerly had been free.[61] Currently, both Microsoft and Apple continue to produce their own multimedia products.

Market Splitting

In June 1995, according to the government, Microsoft met with Netscape and proposed that the two companies split the browser market, in violation of the antitrust laws. Microsoft responds that the meeting was initiated not by Microsoft but by Netscape, and points to an earlier e-mail sent by Netscape's chairman, Jim Clark, to Microsoft. "We want to make this company a success," wrote Clark, "but not at Microsoft's expense. We'd like to work with you. . . . Depending on the interest level, you might take an equity position in Netscape."[62]

Was that meeting a setup? Hard to prove; but within 48 hours of the meeting, the government received detailed notes about it, recorded by Netscape officer Marc Andreessen, who had been present. Those notes were supplied to DOJ by Netscape's outside attorney, Gary Reback.[63] Yet, if DOJ possessed evidence of an illegal market splitting proposal by Microsoft, why did it take three years for the government to press charges? Whatever the answer to that question, DOJ has fallen far short of its burden under the antitrust laws to show that Microsoft extended to Netscape a clear and unambiguous invitation to engage in collusive, illegal acts. The charge of attempted market splitting is just one more unsubstantiated accusation DOJ has raised to embellish an otherwise vacuous lawsuit.

Predatory Pricing

When Microsoft isn't being accused of monopoly price gouging for charging too much, it is accused of predatory pricing for charging too little. When Microsoft followed in Netscape's footsteps by giving away its browser, the government cried foul. But the antitrust standards for "predatory pricing" are more complex than that. First, the accused company must be charging less than its marginal cost. Microsoft (supported by the U.S. Court of Appeals) treats Windows and Internet Explorer as a package, the aggregate price of which is far higher than Microsoft's near-zero cost to produce one additional copy of the software. Second, the accused predator must have the intent and realistic expectation of driving its victim out of business. Third, the predator must then intend to raise its price in order to recoup the losses it suffered during the predation period.

In this instance, Netscape has more than 40% of the browser market and close alliances with Microsoft's adversaries—Oracle, IBM, and Sun. Netscape's parent company, AOL, has an additional 16% market share. It's simply unthinkable that Microsoft would be able to drive Netscape out of business. And if it succeeded, Microsoft would find that Netscape's browser code is now part of the public domain, and there are three dozen other browsers that are both free and Windows-compatible.[64] That means Microsoft could not hope to raise its price and recoup its losses—assuming there were any.

Equally important, the payoff in browsers comes, first, from adding value to the operating system and, second, from revenues associated with advertising and electronic commerce on Web sites to which the browser directs the user. Like network TV and controlled circulation magazines, the browser can profitably be given away because it generates ancillary revenue. Essentially, the browser's marginal cost is negative. Thus, neither Microsoft nor Netscape—whose browser is also free—is engaged in predatory pricing: the browser's zero price is more than its marginal cost. That alone defeats a predatory pricing claim.

Whether the charge was predatory pricing or other illegal means of excluding Netscape from the market, DOJ's evidence consisted almost entirely of Microsoft's internal documents and e-mail. Out of 3.3 million pages of such documents, the government extracted a handful of statements—many from junior staff, some taken out of context. Bill Gates alone gets 37,000 e-mails each year; yet DOJ complained of his selective recall.[65] Moreover, aggressive language in e-mail or elsewhere is not an antitrust violation. The Sherman Act proscribes conduct, not mere intent.[66] Federal appellate judge Frank Easterbrook reminds us that "Vigorous competitors intend to harm rivals. . . . To penalize intent is to penalize competition."[67]

First-Screen Restrictions

Stretching to make its suit look plausible, DOJ argues finally that Microsoft uses its control over the Windows opening screen to dictate

Internet access and content. On initial boot-up, Microsoft uses about 15% of its opening screen to display selected icons. But OEMs may easily remove icons, add icons to the large part of the screen that Microsoft doesn't use, install rival software, even make Netscape the default browser. Users can do all of that as well, then go a step further. They can substitute a shell for the opening screen—all with a few clicks of the mouse—in which case the Internet Explorer icon will disappear altogether.

Ask yourself whether you would be upset if a car dealer preset the stations on your car radio. Obviously not, because you can easily change the presets. Microsoft's rules are even less restrictive than those imposed by your favorite restaurant. Try bringing your own dessert to a dining establishment. The rule is: "If you eat in my restaurant, you select from the items on my menu." Microsoft is more user-friendly. It displays its preferences, helps consumers get to preferred "desserts," but then allows the user to substitute his own dessert if he wishes.

If Internet restrictions are the issue, imagine the limitless control over access and content when the government begins to dictate what icons are to appear on Microsoft's opening screen.

No Injury, but Plenty of Remedies[68]

For nearly six months, DOJ and its hired gun, private attorney David Boies, hammered Microsoft witnesses in a futile attempt to show that the company's bad-boy tactics harmed consumers. Never mind that it's not consumers but competitors who are grousing. That may be true today. But tomorrow, DOJ warns, consumers will certainly be paying too much—or is it too little?—for computer software.

Sad to say, the government's gloomy forecast might well prove accurate. Boies and antitrust chief Joel Klein have floated a number of "structural" remedies, the unintended consequences of which are guaranteed to harm consumers. So the damage that Microsoft has been accused of inflicting on its customers may finally materialize— but only if Judge Jackson buys DOJ's pathetic proposal to punish vigorous competition by dismembering the winning competitor. We'll soon know. If Jackson holds that Microsoft has violated the antitrust laws, he has broad discretion to determine appropriate relief—guided, but not bound, by the government's recommendations.

For good reason, DOJ has all but abandoned the remedies it sought in its original complaint. At first the government wanted Microsoft to stop tying Internet Explorer to the Windows operating system. That approach was gutted by the U.S. Court of Appeals, which declared the browser and operating system to be a single, integrated product. Next the government asked that Microsoft revise its contracts with ISPs, ICPs, and OLSs. But Microsoft had already eliminated any vestiges of exclusionary language from those contracts. Not a single ISP, ICP, or OLS is prohibited from offering the Netscape browser. Then DOJ insisted that Microsoft give OEMs more control over the Windows opening screen. But it turned out that OEMs could alter most of the screen at will, and users could get rid of it altogether.

As events unfolded, DOJ's original remedies sounded sillier than ever. And so we are beginning to hear musings from the government on a variety of alternative, more draconian approaches. The first idea was to force Microsoft to publish its APIs—the software by which applications programmers interface with the Windows system. Nice try, but DOJ hasn't produced any evidence that Microsoft withholds its APIs. Even Sybase's then-CEO, Mitchell E. Kertzman—no fan of Microsoft—said, "They're very timely with sharing technology. They don't withhold it."[69]

Then Klein and Boies pushed for "transparent pricing"—that is, full disclosure of all terms and conditions that affect the price Microsoft charges OEMs. Supposedly Microsoft uses those arrangements to "control" its OEM clients. But virtually all of the major OEMs are now offering PCs loaded with the Linux operating system. Armed with new equity capital from Microsoft's rivals, Linux distributors are growing by leaps and bounds—fast enough to keep more than a few Microsoft executives awake at night.

That brings us to the latest round of so-called structural remedies. At first any conjecture that Microsoft might be dismembered was pooh-poohed as grandstanding by DOJ, smitten with itself after successfully demonizing Bill Gates. But now we're told that the 19 state attorneys general who are coplaintiffs, and thus must endorse any remedies proposed by DOJ, won't be satisfied with any outcome that doesn't essentially restructure Microsoft.[70] So here's a recap of the government's three favorite plans—from the moronic to the merely foolish.

The first option is vertical divestiture. Microsoft would be split into two or three parts. One company would keep the Windows operating system. A second company would get the application programs like Access, Excel, and Word. Perhaps a third company would take on the Internet and e-commerce products. Evidently, whoever designed that solution has never read DOJ's initial complaint, which after all is about a company that purportedly has a monopoly in PC operating systems. Normally one doesn't attack monopoly power by spinning off the monopoly into a separate company. But what is worse, vertical divestiture will require ongoing government decisions about whether a product is part of the operating system, or an application, or Internet related. Just look at the browser wars to see how difficult it is to compartmentalize a product within a nearly seamless operating environment. And look at the AT&T breakup to see how easy it is for a court to get bogged down in post-divestiture regulation.

DOJ's second trial balloon calls for horizontal divestiture. Each of several vertically integrated clones—"Baby Bills"—would receive full rights to Microsoft's source code and other intellectual property. They could then proceed to compete freely and fiercely against one another. May the better Bill win, at least until a new leader emerges, at which time DOJ will undoubtedly call for another divestiture to buy more time. No one seems to know which corporate Bill gets the real-life Bill, nor whether new operating system features have to be shared and, if so, why any company would continue to innovate, knowing that its competitors will reap the benefits.

The third structural remedy is actually a variation on horizontal divestiture, with all of its problems and then some. Basically, Microsoft would be forced to license the Windows source code to several other companies, each of which could develop and sell it independently, thereby creating instant competition in the operating system business. Are new features from Microsoft within the scope of the license? If the licensee improves the product, does Microsoft have equal rights to the improvement? There are no good answers to those questions. If new technology is to be declared public property, it will not materialize. If technology is to be proprietary, then it must not be expropriated. Once expropriation becomes the remedy of choice, the goose is unlikely to continue laying golden eggs.

Meanwhile, government-driven balkanization of operating system protocols will wipe out Microsoft's most important contribution to software markets: standardization. Like the Unix system, Windows will end up with a dozen or more variations—no common platform on which software developers can build. The result will be fewer application programs, increased costs of development, and higher user prices. Globally, programmers have developed thousands of compatible programs, thanks to the standardized platform that Windows affords. If the government gets its way, that enormous value will disappear in a twinkling.

One can only speculate about the motives underlying DOJ's destructive campaign. When the head of the Antitrust Division meets on numerous occasions to discuss this case with a disaffected Microsoft competitor, including breakfast at the latter's home,[71] the conclusion is all but inescapable that the antitrust laws are being used as an anti-competitive subsidy to prop up less successful or unsuccessful firms. Or perhaps the motives are slightly less insidious: ordinary empire building that has become standard operating procedure in Washington, D.C.

President Clinton has asked for a 17% increase in funding for the Antitrust Division to pay for 943 employees (up by 26% in two years) who will be working on 554 cases (up by 35% in two years).[72] Citizens Against Government Waste estimates that the Microsoft litigation has slapped taxpayers with a $30 million to $60 million bill.[73] To justify that expenditure and those increases, DOJ must provide the American public with dramatic evidence of its effectiveness. Hence, a high-profile case with sensational remedies as the exit strategy, played to the media and focused not on substantive legal issues but on public ridicule of a company and its chief executive. We deserve better.

What Role for Antitrust?

To uncover what's really driving the browser wars, read DOJ's complaint and accompanying legal memorandum. There you will find Netscape mentioned 130 times in 130 pages[74]—government resources co-opted for the welfare of a competitor, not consumers. Thankfully, the putative victim, only four years old, is feeling much better—evidently comforted by $10 billion from AOL. As for others in the industry, instead of focusing on new and better products, software executives find themselves having to consort with members and former members of Congress, their staffers, antitrust officials,

236

and the best lobbying and public relations firms that money can buy. Microsoft will learn to play that game and, of necessity, become adept at currying favor with politicians in Washington, D.C. Those who are fearful of Microsoft's competition in private markets should have ever-greater concern if the company decides that political clout better serves its interests.

The Supreme Court cautioned more than 60 years ago that an attorney for the state—whether a government employee like Joel Klein or a private subcontractor like David Boies—"is the representative not of an ordinary party to a controversy, but of a sovereignty whose obligation to govern impartially is as compelling as its obligation to govern at all."[75] That's because government is the single entity that may wield coercive power against private citizens. Therefore, in the criminal law context, adequate safeguards against abusive government conduct are essential—and so we have the Fifth and Sixth Amendments to the Constitution, and the requirement for proof beyond reasonable doubt. But in civil litigation—where private parties, adverse to one another, seek remedies that redress the injured party, not the state—we neither have nor do we need the same protection against abusive government. When the state stays out, the risk of abuse is diminished; when the state is a party, as it is in this case, we must insist on scrupulous adherence to the rule of law—not pandering to the press, not courtroom histrionics, not preferential treatment of favored constituents, and not public harassment of companies whose only offense is to prevail over their competitors by creating better value for consumers.

Microsoft neither has the leverage it is said to have nor did the damage it is said to have done. Instead, lawyers with marginal understanding of how businesses talk and operate, and even less understanding of the technical subject matter, were bamboozled into bringing this case by rent-seeking executives like McNealy and Barksdale, who knew then and know now that software markets are intensely competitive. Disgruntled rivals played on the naiveté and power lust of government officials and persuaded them that Microsoft's aggressiveness could be scripted into an antitrust suit. No doubt, McNealy and Barksdale are privately clucking because they see the fatuity of this lawsuit better than anyone. Yet they have succeeded in getting the government, at taxpayer expense, to do their competitive dirty work and, to boot, humiliate a rival whom they envy and despise.

The history of software is that better ideas mean better products, and better products win in the market. Most observers understand that excessive regulation can do great damage to that process. Yet government moves forward in the name of correcting "market failure," apparently giving little or no weight to the possibility of government failure. Economist Thomas Sowell put it this way: The St. Louis Cardinals don't send in a pinch hitter whenever Mark McGwire strikes out. They know that the pinch hitter will likely do worse.[76]

Joel Klein can profit from those insights. Indeed, he can profit from the words of his former coplaintiff, South Carolina attorney general Charles Condon, who withdrew from the Microsoft suit after AOL announced its acquisition of Netscape. Condon said: "Recent events have proven that . . . innovation is thriving. . . . Further government intervention . . . is unnecessary and . . . unwise. Consumers have not taken a leading role in this action. That's because there are no monopolies on the Internet."[77]

The government needs to rethink its entire approach to high-tech antitrust. What exactly will be accomplished by any of the proposed remedies? If the objective is to take away the "leverage" of Windows so that the industry isn't "forced" to live in a Windows world, well, the market has already attained that goal, without any "help" from DOJ. Yes, it will take a few years for the impact to play out fully, but that would be the case even if DOJ were to win its lawsuit. Years could elapse before a final disposition, and millions of users are not going to abandon Windows overnight.

Yet even assuming that DOJ had been correct on every point it has raised, the real-world case is over. What the government says it wants has already happened. Thus, the ineluctable conclusion must be that the whole concept of antitrust is flawed to the core. The market moves faster than antitrust could ever move. The assumption of would-be regulators—that inefficiencies, especially in high-tech markets, can lock a company into a position from which it can't be unseated—is a complete myth. Consumers rule; not producers. And consumers can unseat any product and any company no matter how "powerful." Antitrust, if it were ever needed, is as obsolete as Windows will soon be.

9. Microsoft's Appealing Case*

Introduction

We'll soon know whether the Department of Justice will be successful at dismembering what used to be the most valuable corporation in the world. If the government fails, it won't be for lack of trying. Instead, DOJ's case will come tumbling down because its foundation is paper thin. Despite an initial victory before federal district judge Thomas Penfield Jackson, the government cannot sustain its charges on appeal. The trial was incurably plagued by procedural irregularities, the judge's fact finding was clearly erroneous, his legal conclusions are unsupportable, and his brutal remedies are neither proportionate nor even related to the asserted infractions.

But first, some background. Here's how Microsoft—prodigy of the new economy, yet former neophyte in the ways of Washington—suddenly awakened to find that its very existence is under siege.

The Federal Trade Commission started the ball rolling against Microsoft in 1991 with a fruitless two-year investigation of claims that the software maker monopolized the market for PC operating systems. Then came another two years of scrutiny by DOJ, culminating in a 1995 consent decree. Two years later, the government claimed that Microsoft had flouted that decree by tying its Internet Explorer browser to the Windows operating system—that is, by requiring every buyer of Windows to take Internet Explorer as well. In the ensuing lawsuit, Judge Jackson agreed with DOJ, but he was reversed in mid-1998 by a higher authority, the U.S. Court of Appeals for the District of Columbia Circuit.[1]

That didn't stop DOJ. In May 1998 the antitrust division, joined by 20 state attorneys general (reduced to 19 after South Carolina pulled out), sued Microsoft for violating the Sherman Antitrust Act.[2]

*Originally published, with minor revisions, as Cato Institute Policy Analysis no. 385, November 9, 2000, coauthored with Alan Reynolds, director of economic research, Hudson Institute (now senior fellow, Cato Institute).

After an eight-month trial, Jackson released his findings of fact in November 1999, once again deciding for the government on virtually every issue. Those fact findings essentially dictated the outcome, laying the groundwork for the judge's legal verdict. Predictably, when Jackson issued his conclusions of law in April 2000, he held that Microsoft had indeed violated the Sherman Act. Then came the bombshell. Less than a month later, on April 28, Jackson proposed an array of conduct-related and structural fixes, including a breakup of Microsoft into two separate companies, without a minute of hearings on remedies.

Naturally, Microsoft has appealed—to the D.C. Circuit Court, which had ruled its way two years earlier. To show how important the case is, and to signal its willingness—indeed, eagerness—to decide the case, the D.C. Circuit set an accelerated briefing schedule and an early hearing. And although a three-judge panel typically hears appeals, the Circuit agreed to have the entire court hear the case.

This time, however, DOJ and Judge Jackson tried an end run around the appeals court, asking the U.S. Supreme Court to take the case directly. The government hoped to avoid a repeat of its previous reversal by the D.C. Circuit. But the Supreme Court wasn't required to take the case, and elected not to, voting 8-to-1 with only Justice Breyer dissenting. Evidently the justices did not want to immerse themselves in a trial record that is both voluminous and complex. They decided it would be better for the appellate judges first to sharpen the issues. No doubt the justices were also aware that they could be wasting their valuable time should a Bush administration decide to settle the litigation in 2001. Possibly, the Supreme Court also wanted to ensure that the Circuit Court would have an opportunity to rebuke its own trial judge, given his glaring procedural and substantive blunders.

Meanwhile, pending appeal, the remedies ordered by Judge Jackson—both conduct-related and structural remedies—have been put on hold. Originally, DOJ had asked the judge for a narrowly tailored court order that would enjoin Microsoft from engaging in four allegedly anti-competitive activities. Specifically, Microsoft was not to: (1) enter into new contracts or enforce existing contracts with Internet service providers or content providers that would foreclose distribution or promotion of Netscape's competing Internet browser;

(2) technologically tie its own browser to its operating system, unless it gave users a practical means to untie the two products and offered the stripped operating system at a reduced price; (3) treat Netscape's browser any differently than Internet Explorer with respect to inclusion or exclusion from the Windows package; or (4) retaliate against any original equipment manufacturer (OEM) that chose to remove Internet Explorer from Windows 98.

That was the relief sought by DOJ in court filings as late as September 1998. But once the trial ended a month later, those requests somehow morphed into a barrel-full of remedies that extended far beyond anything DOJ had initially considered necessary to address Microsoft's supposed misbehavior. In the end, here are the remedies that the government proposed—by-and-large rubber-stamped by Judge Jackson in his final order.

First, the conduct-related remedies. Microsoft would have to: (1) refrain from exclusionary contracts with Internet service providers and content providers; (2) refrain from tying contracts with OEMs; (3) sell an unbundled version at a lower price if products are bundled (thus, Microsoft might not be able to give away its browser); (4) agree not to "penalize" companies for supporting rival software; (5) charge uniform operating system prices to its largest customers, even if those customers offered a better product, or better service, or helped control software piracy; (6) disclose to software developers its applications programming interfaces—not just instructions regarding use of the interfaces, but actual source code; (7) disclose sufficient source code to enable OEMs to redesign the Windows opening screen, in effect devaluing the Windows brand name and infringing Microsoft's copyright protection; (8) continue to license earlier versions of its operating system on the same terms for three years after a new version is released; (9) retain all executive e-mail pertaining to platform software for four years; and (10) establish what Loyola economics professor Thomas DiLorenzo has called a "creepy and totalitarian . . . Gestapo-style monitoring system" whereby the government has ongoing access to inspect and copy virtually all of Microsoft's records, and Microsoft's employees are able to report violations of government regulations "on a confidential basis."[3]

Neither DOJ nor Judge Jackson was content with those directives, so then came the coup de grâce: structural remedies. Microsoft would be split into two companies—an operating systems company, which would get a one-time license for Internet Explorer, and an applications company, which would otherwise retain all rights to Internet Explorer. The operating system company could not develop a modified version of the browser, even though browser functionality is now integral both to Windows and to rival operating systems, which would face no such restrictions. For 10 years, the operating system and applications companies could not recombine, invest in one another, cross-license products on an exclusive basis, or engage in joint ventures. For the first three of those years, all of the conduct-related remedies would remain in force for both companies. Any contract between the two companies would have to be on terms no more favorable than those available to third parties. That same "most favored company" provision would also apply to technical disclosures between the two firms.

Will Microsoft win its appeal? It should, given the procedural irregularities, factual errors, and mistaken legal conclusions plaguing the case due to Judge Jackson's handling of it.

Procedural Irregularities

When a party to litigation is systematically deprived of due process, and the deprivation is egregious, as it was in the Microsoft case, the court's substantive findings and legal conclusions cannot be sustained. A new trial is frequently necessary. Here, because the procedural errors were so stark, it's conceivable that the appellate court will direct Judge Jackson to recuse himself from any subsequent proceedings.

Among the more flagrant errors were these: Jackson expanded the scope of the trial to include charges that were not part of the government's initial complaint. He conducted the trial on an accelerated timetable that did not allow Microsoft sufficient opportunity to prepare its defense. He embraced the government's proposed remedies without any hearing whatsoever. In rationalizing his wholesale adoption of the government's remedies, he relied on post-trial evidence that was not part of the record, then applied criminal sentencing guidelines to a civil antitrust case. Lastly, during and after the trial, Jackson granted media interviews, contravening an explicit canon of judicial ethics.

Expanded Scope of the Trial

In May 1998 when DOJ first filed its antitrust complaint against Microsoft, the centerpiece of the government's case was its allegation that the company had illegally tied its operating system and its browser. A month later, the D.C. Circuit Court of Appeals effectively wiped out that claim. The government responded by raising new allegations, dramatically expanding the scope of its case. Suspecting—incorrectly, as it happens—that Judge Jackson would feel bound by the higher court's ruling, DOJ turned its attention to a variety of peripheral issues, none of which had appeared in its May complaint.

Over the company's repeated objections, the government decided to explore Microsoft's attempt to dominate the server market as well as its relationships with Intel, Apple, RealNetworks, and IBM. DOJ also took the side of Sun Microsystems in a pending lawsuit in which that company had charged Microsoft with "corrupting" Sun's Java programming language by creating a Windows-specific version that was incompatible with Sun's own version.[4] Java and Netscape's browser were two essential components of the "middleware" market—software that would bridge the gap between users and their operating systems, thereby enabling applications to run on multiple platforms, not just on Windows.

DOJ characterized middleware as a potential threat to Microsoft. Ultimately Jackson would assert that Microsoft had exploited its dominant Office Suite software to stifle the middleware market. Inconveniently for Jackson, that charge had first been brought against Microsoft by the attorneys general, who later dropped it when their lawsuit was consolidated with DOJ's. No matter. Jackson shrugged off that minor predicament by enlarging the litigation as if all of the charges against Microsoft appeared in the consolidated complaint. Despite the amplified charges, he did not require the government to file an amended complaint. Instead, he simply assured Microsoft that he "would not be making any findings" and "would not predicate any relief" on the new allegations.[5] In the end, those assurances meant nothing.

Speed of the Trial

Faced with defending allegations that appeared out of nowhere, Microsoft sought extra time to prepare its case. After all, an antitrust suit against the largest company in the world was no small matter. Yet Jackson had scheduled the trial to begin on September 8, 1998, only three and a half months from the date of the complaint. And he limited each side to 12 witnesses, each of whom would be required to submit testimony in writing, not on the witness stand. Oral presentations would be limited to cross-examination and rebuttal.

That timetable and format was unprecedented for a major antitrust case. So when the judge allowed DOJ to augment its complaint, digging into all sorts of new charges, Microsoft was sure it would be granted some scheduling leeway. It was not. Despite the complexity of the case, the expanded allegations, and the need for extensive discovery, Microsoft was given less than five months to prepare for trial on the original accusations, and a much shorter time to defend against the trumped up charges that DOJ managed to tack on with Jackson's indulgence.

Remedies Hearing

If the quickness of the main trial was extraordinary, the rush to judgment at the remedies hearing set a new speed record. Perhaps more than any other event, the remedies hearing—or more precisely, the want of a remedies hearing—revealed Jackson's mindset. When he was first asked whether he contemplated further proceedings to address remedies, Jackson responded, "I would assume that there would be further proceedings."[6] He added that he might "replicate the procedure at trial with testimony in written form subject to cross-examination."[7] He apparently had second thoughts.

On June 7, 2000, Jackson endorsed the government's proposed final judgment and its suggested remedies without a single material change. Not only was Microsoft to be drawn and quartered, but its conduct was to be circumscribed step-by-step and inch-by-inch— all without issuing findings, developing an evidentiary record, or even granting the company further discovery on the remedies issue. After pledging to Microsoft that it would have an opportunity to be heard, Jackson reversed himself with the incredible excuse that "testimonial predictions of future events" are "less reliable even than testimony as to historical fact."[8] Evidently, the judge forgot that his entire case rested on "testimonial predictions" about the competitive implications of Microsoft's alleged misconduct.

Even more astonishing, Jackson conjured up this rationalization for anointing the government's final judgment: "I am not an economist. I do not have the resources of economic research or any significant ability to be able to craft a remedy of my own devising."[9] That might explain why Jackson couldn't formulate remedies without expert advice, but it certainly does not explain why he chose DOJ as his sole adviser. Here's his answer:

> Plaintiffs won the case, and for that reason alone have some entitlement to a remedy of their choice. Moreover, plaintiffs' proposed final judgment is a collective work product of senior antitrust law enforcement officials of the United States Department of Justice and the Attorneys General of 19 states, in conjunction with multiple consultants. These officials are by reason of office obliged and expected to consider—and act in—the public interest; Microsoft is not.[10]

Never mind that public officials, no less than private companies, act in their self-interest. That's why the Framers devised a system of checks and balances—to rein in the penchant for political society to overrun civil society. The principal difference between public and private actors—about which Judge Jackson is oblivious—is that private companies are guided "as if by an Invisible Hand" to behave in the public interest. By contrast, although self-interest leads to benign outcomes in the marketplace, it frequently yields perverse outcomes when it comes to political decisions. The constituency of a private company is the public, which buys its product. The constituency of a public official is too often the special interests that disproportionately control the political process.[11]

That elemental lesson of public choice theory is lost on Judge Jackson. So too is a sober conception of due process. Consider these fantastic statements on his refusal to hold hearings on remedies: First, it's "procedurally unusual to do what Microsoft is proposing— are you aware of very many cases in which the defendant can argue with the jury about what an appropriate sanction should be? Were the Japanese allowed to propose the terms of their surrender? The government won the case."[12] Second, "I am not aware of any case authority that says I have to give them [Microsoft] any due process at all. The case is over. They lost."[13]

Due process, turned on its head by Thomas Penfield Jackson. First, says the judge, decide who wins; then decide what process was due. The Queen in *Alice in Wonderland* couldn't have said it better.

Post-trial Justifications

Maybe Judge Jackson recognized that he had not adequately explained his uncritical acceptance of DOJ's remedies. Surely the judge knew, however, that his explanation would be subject to even greater scorn if it were based on evidence that was not part of the official record. Nonetheless, to buttress his case, Jackson curiously relied on post-trial e-mails, which had never been proffered as testimony or exposed to the rigors of cross-examination. That belated evidence supposedly proved that Microsoft, notwithstanding the ongoing litigation, was still trying to leverage its monopoly position. Only harsh remedies, so the argument went, could cure such grave wrongdoing.

But the e-mails, unaccountably, concerned matters not before the court. According to one set of messages, Bill Gates had tried to persuade manufacturers of hand-held computers (personal digital assistants, or PDAs) to use a Microsoft operating system called Windows CE. Unless the manufacturers complied, Microsoft would code new features in its applications software so that they would run only on PDAs made by Microsoft itself.[14] But Jackson had already defined the relevant market to include only single-user desktop PCs that used Intel chips. That crabbed view of the market excluded PDAs, Windows CE, and applications software. Even if the definition could somehow be stretched to cover applications software, Microsoft's new features did not confer monopoly power that could be leveraged—at least not as long as versions of the same software without the new features were available.

Taking a different tack at validating his remedies, Jackson observed that they had crystallized only after Microsoft had shown itself "unwilling to accept the notion that it broke the law or accede to an order amending its conduct."[15] In other words, it was Microsoft's lack of remorse that prompted such severe remedies. That unbelievable assertion, coming as it did before Microsoft had exercised its indisputable right to appeal, meant that Jackson required the company to admit fault or face the consequences.

True enough, federal sentencing guidelines in criminal cases provide for reduced punishment if a convicted defendant accepts responsibility for his criminal acts. But Microsoft was sued under the civil, not criminal, provisions of the Sherman Act. Courts are not authorized in civil cases to punish antitrust violators. Relief must be remedial, not punitive.[16] Still, in a post-trial luncheon speech to an antitrust seminar, Jackson told his audience that a "structural remedy was never my remedy of choice." It was "a last resort, and in my judgment Microsoft's intransigence was the reason."[17] There you have it; the decision to gut a half-trillion-dollar corporation hinged on the petulance of a federal judge.

Media Interviews

In a tribute to his candor, if not to his legal acuity, Jackson conceded in that same luncheon speech that "Virtually everything I did may be vulnerable on appeal."[18] Perhaps that realization—that his legal insights would not convince an appellate court—explains Jackson's media crusade to make his case public. Both during and at the conclusion of the trial, he granted "friendly, informal and unstructured" interviews to the *New York Times*. He also spoke with the *Wall Street Journal, Washington Post, Newsweek,* and CNN, commenting on Microsoft's legal strategy and the credibility of its witnesses.[19] It's interesting to compare Jackson's public pronouncements with the near-total silence maintained by respected appellate judge Richard Posner, who was asked by Jackson to help negotiate an out-of-court settlement. Despite constant pleas from the media to assess the likelihood of a resolution, Posner said nothing.

That is what we should expect from a federal judge, who is charged under Canon 3A(6) of the *Code of Conduct for United States Judges*[20] to "avoid public comment on the merits of a pending or impending action." The Code goes on to advise against public comment "until completion of the appellate process." In this instance, Jackson's remarks came before Microsoft had appealed; indeed, the *New York Times* interview was conducted during the trial over which Jackson himself was presiding. Not only was the case pending, but it was pending *before him* and might even, after appeal, land back in his court for further proceedings.

The only statements to the media condoned by the *Code of Conduct* are those connected with the judge's official duties, his explanation of court procedures (e.g., "the next step is for defendants to file a notice of appeal"), or scholarly presentations for educational purposes. None of Jackson's comments fit the exceptions. Moreover, Jackson was well aware of the rules. In 1991, an appeals panel found that Jackson had improperly spoken at the Harvard Law School about a pending case involving Washington, D.C., mayor Marion Barry.[21] That's the same judge, plainly unrepentant, who now accuses Microsoft of insufficient remorse and of not accepting responsibility for its previous acts.

Erroneous Fact Finding

To be sure, procedural errors, even if they were to result in a new trial, might simply postpone Microsoft's agony. If Judge Jackson continued to preside, there's little reason to presume—without an appellate reversal on substantive issues—that his findings and conclusions would be significantly different a second time around. For that reason alone, it's important to scrutinize not only procedural irregularities but substantive issues as well. So we turn now to Judge Jackson's findings of fact and then to the conclusions of law that flowed from those findings. It will shortly be evident that the judge's substantive errors are every bit as troubling as his procedural errors.

Findings of fact are supposed to constitute a judge's assessment of what was discovered during the trial. Regardless of Judge Jackson's colorful language about Microsoft's "immense profits"[22] and "oppressive thumb,"[23] nothing in his wordy document is intended to prove that any law was broken. The findings are just the foundation for the conclusions of law, which in turn become the basis of any remedies.

Microsoft's critics tend to treat Judge Jackson's findings as sacred text, which a higher court could never question. Yet some central "facts," and even some legal conclusions, are nothing more than heroic forecasts about technology. "While some consumers may decide to make do with one or more information appliances," opines the judge, "the number of these consumers will, for the foreseeable future, remain small in comparison to the number of consumers deciding that they will still need an Intel-compatible PC system."[24] On the contrary, technological forecasters from International Data Corporation, among others, expect that sales of non-PC Internet devices will outnumber sales of PCs within a few years.[25]

Those devices include wireless PDAs and cell phones from such industry leaders as Palm and Nokia; Linux-based Internet devices from AOL-Gateway; powerful Internet-ready game consoles from Sony, Nintendo, and Sega; AOL's hard-drive-equipped interactive TV, and more. Because the judge totally ignored the *non-Microsoft*

248

browsers in all those millions of Internet devices, no appellate court could possibly affirm his legal conclusion that Microsoft had a "dangerous probability" of monopolizing the browser market.[26] And for the same reason, the judge's speculation that "Internet Explorer is not demonstrably the current 'best of breed' Web browser, nor is it likely to be so at any time in the immediate future"[27] must be duly dismissed on appeal.

Within the judge's litany of facts, the few findings that appear to be based on quantitative data are often seriously inaccurate. For example, here is his mistaken recitation on Microsoft's market share, which has been widely echoed by the media as being all the proof needed that Windows has a monopoly:

> Every year for the last decade, Microsoft's share of the market for Intel-compatible PC operating systems has stood above ninety percent. For the last couple of years the figure has been at least ninety-five percent, and analysts project that the share will climb even higher over the next few years.[28]

Those seemingly precise figures were lifted uncritically from the government's Exhibit One.[29] They are not facts at all, but outdated estimates and projections published in early 1997—*before* "the last couple of years"—by IDC. At that time, IDC analysts thought Apple's Mac OS system would slip into oblivion, and they could not imagine that Linux would be popular enough even to warrant a separate mention.

In June 2000 IDC estimated that various versions of Windows, including NT for workstations, accounted for 87.7% of "new license" (wholesale) shipments of "client" operating systems in the previous year. Mac accounted for 5%, according to IDC, and Linux 4.1%. IDC analysts now project that Windows' share will fall to 85% by 2004, and possibly much lower if the exciting new Unix-based Mac OS X catches on ("Apple could always opt to bring OS X to Intel platforms," notes IDC).[30]

Rather than Windows' share being 95% and rising, as the judge stated, his own source now says Windows' share is below 88% and falling. That is still a large number, of course, but we are about to explain why it is much *too* large. To be sure, the newest IDC estimates, based on shipments rather than the installed base of old and new computers, are an improvement over the 1997 figures. Yet the new estimates still involve serious exaggerations arising from what is included in Windows' share (such as Windows NT for Workstations), and what is excluded from competitors' sales (such as retail sales of Linux and computers sold with no operating system).

At the outset, it helps to keep in mind that there are three distinct versions of Windows, not just one. Windows CE, now called Pocket PC, is mainly used on handheld computers in competition with companies such as Psion and Palm. IDC estimates that Windows CE has less than 10% of that market. Windows NT, now called Windows 2000, is used on servers and on high-powered desktops called workstations. In the server market, Windows NT/2000 competes with versions of Unix, including Linux, and with Novell Netware. IDC estimates that Windows NT has 36% of that market. Clearly, Microsoft has a modest share of the lucrative computer markets in which Windows CE and NT struggle to compete. Moreover, the lines between those submarkets are blurry, particularly when it comes to workstations and to laptops, which are marketed in all three versions of Windows (and with competing systems such as Mac, Linux, and Psion).

In order to demonstrate that Microsoft's market share was much larger than those figures suggest, Judge Jackson resorted to the simple expedient of narrowing the defined market. He included only single-user desktop computers, in which Microsoft has an edge, limiting the trial testimony as well as his own findings to Windows 95 and 98. (Nonetheless, he proceeded to apply his proposed remedies to Windows CE and NT as well.) Unlike the trial testimony, however, IDC's definition of Windows' share of the "client" market is *not* confined to Windows 95 and 98. On the contrary, the apparent Windows share of nearly 88% is substantially inflated by including Windows NT for Workstations, now called Windows 2000 Professional edition. Including NT might have been perfectly reasonable if the judge had defined the "relevant market" to include the operating systems of *all* workstations, but that is not what he did.

Judge Jackson chose to define the relevant market to include only "Intel-based" computers. That means the market was confined to "IBM clones"—that is, computers originally designed to run on Microsoft operating systems, just as Apple computers were designed to run the Mac OS and Sun computers to run Solaris. The wonder is not that most Intel computers use Windows, but that other operating systems, such as Linux, BeOS, and the Intel version of Solaris (and possibly of Mac OS X), have been cleverly adapted to operate on the "Wintel" architecture.

When the government proposed, as part of its Microsoft breakup scheme, to create a separate operating systems company, astute journalists made the undeniable observation that the new company's major competitors in the operating system business would include Sun Microsystems, Novell, Apple, and Palm.[31] Yet Sun, Apple, and Palm were totally excluded from Judge Jackson's definition of the "relevant market" because they are not "Intel-based." Apple and Palm use Motorola microprocessors, while Sun builds its own. Defining the market to include only Intel-based computers provided the magic by which the government managed to completely ignore Apple, the sixth largest producer of computers in the United States, as though "Apple products" are not really computers.[32] Novell's networking software was arbitrarily excluded too, because IDC counts only "single-user" computers. That single-user limitation also eliminates, by definition, all network or "thin client" computers from IBM, Sun, Compaq, and others that use non-Microsoft operating systems.[33] In fact, most of Microsoft's leading competitors were simply *defined* out of existence by Judge Jackson.

And in the workstation market, limiting competitors to those that produce Intel-based systems completely excludes Sun Microsystems—lately the world's largest seller of workstations.[34] Sun workstations, which start at less than $2,000, can even run Windows software by plugging in a card for that purpose. The exclusion of Sun, by itself, invalidates the government's use of IDC's measure of market share. Recall that IDC includes Windows NT workstations that compete directly with Sun. Because the government chooses to exclude Sun workstations, as they are not "Intel-based," Windows workstations should surely be excluded too. *If we exclude NT workstations, then the IDC estimate for Windows 95 and 98 drops from 88 to 66% of the "licensed shipments" of "client" operating systems.* Yet the problems do not end there. Licensed shipments do not include retail sales, downloads, and computers shipped with no operating system. And IDC's "single-user" client computers do not include computers linked to a server in a local network.

Counting licensed systems alone, as IDC does, seriously understates the use of Linux. Licensed sales ignore sales in retail stores, where Linux is very strong, not to mention millions of free (not licensed) Linux downloads. When retail sales were included, according to a report in a leading newspaper, Linux accounted for 23.6% of all operating systems sold, while Windows supposedly had a 71.4% share.[35] Walk through any store selling software, and you will see many boxes of Linux, most of which (notably, Corel Linux) are aimed at desktop users rather than servers. Yes, looking at retail sales alone would clearly *underestimate* Windows and Mac, because those systems are more often sold wholesale, by bulk licensing of the operating system to computer makers. Yet it is just as misleading to base market share on licensed shipments alone. Doing so ignores the remarkable success of Linux in retail stores.

Even if someone counted both licensed and retail sales, that would still ignore "naked" computers shipped without a new, commercially available operating system. Naked computers account for 15% of the market, according to government expert Frederick Warren-Boulton.[36] Whatever sort of operating system is most often installed on naked computers (including free operating systems and older software), it will not be a new version of Windows. Anyone who wants Windows 98 or 2000 knows it is much cheaper and easier to have it preinstalled by the manufacturer than to pay retail for a boxed CD with instructions. If few naked computers use new versions of Windows, that fact alone could shave as much as 15 percentage points from Windows 98's market share, which has already been shown to be much smaller than the judge believed. At the very least, uncertainty about naked computers further detracts from the spurious precision of Judge Jackson's allegation about some undefined version of Windows having a 95% share of some unexplained market.

No higher court is likely to accept as fact the government's archaic and selective estimates of Microsoft's share of an artificially defined market of "Intel-compatible" computers that are neither small enough to use Palm's system nor powerful enough to use Sun's. In fact, judges in the nation's higher courts have become increasingly sophisticated about economics in recent years, which means they (like economists) are unlikely to accept *any* measure of market share as a viable measure of monopoly.

To illustrate just how misleading market share can be, consider the Microsoft Office suite. It has a very high market share but certainly no monopoly. Many popular computers come preloaded with rival office suites. WordPerfect is installed on CyberMax, Quantex, NuTrend, and ABS. Lotus Smart Suite comes with IBM and Polywell. And Sun's Star Office is preloaded on eMachines. If consumers don't like the office software that comes with their computer, they can easily switch to another as an inexpensive upgrade, or download Star Office for free. Monopoly means no consumer choice; it does not mean that consumers freely choose one product over others, even when the others are free. Similarly, the fact that the Windows operating system is currently more popular than systems from Apple, Sun, or VA Linux does not mean Windows has a monopoly. It means that Windows is the consumers' choice. Although the Internet may make consumers relatively less concerned about which operating system they use, they will never be wholly indifferent to the features and ease of use that an operating system affords.

While Judge Jackson's reliance on, and treatment of, market share data raises serious concerns, some of his other findings of fact are equally dubious. In particular, there is his emphasis on the pure number of games and other software applications, old and new, that supposedly create an insurmountable "applications barrier" to entry. Rival operating systems are prevented from competing, insists the judge, because they cannot offer the huge array of software programs that are available on a Windows platform. "Although Apple's Mac OS supports more than 12,000 applications," he says, "even an inventory of that magnitude is not sufficient to enable Apple to present a significant percentage of users with a viable substitute for Windows."[37] This "relative dearth" of software for Apple was the judge's implausible excuse for excluding Mac from the relevant market (although Linux, with far fewer applications than Mac, was *not* excluded).

The judge asserts that the large stockpile of Windows and DOS applications must make it impossible for non-Microsoft operating systems to gain a "significant" number of customers. Yet Mac, Linux, Palm, and Sun's Solaris are all doing quite well. In reality, few computer users want more software than is contained in the competent office suites that are readily available for all operating systems. Economist Richard McKenzie has estimated that a credible challenge to Windows could be mounted with no more than a few hundred key applications.[38]

WordPerfect, Star Office, and Applix offer free or inexpensive office suites for Linux (which is why Lotus and Microsoft do not), but that does not make Linux any easier to install or use. IBM's OS/ 2 system ran all Windows software in the early nineties, but OS/ 2 was nevertheless an overpriced system that required expensive hardware. Microsoft Office has always been available for Mac, but that did not make Apple's pricey computers any more affordable. Plainly, factors other than the availability of applications software dissuaded consumers from buying those rival systems.

Furthermore, the Justice Department grounded many aspects of its case on a debatable interpretation of a technological forecast. According to DOJ, applications will be gravitating away from local PC hard drives toward the Internet. Perhaps so, but that does not prevent a wide range of Internet browsers from accessing the Internet and interacting with the service providers that will be providing the new applications. Still, the government assumed that only Netscape would be able to reach and communicate with applications service providers.

That was the logic underlying the government's muddled argument for protecting Netscape's "usage share" from competition. Judge Jackson, agreeing with that argument, evidently ignored two countervailing facts. First, several dozen browsers all read the same languages (mainly html) and can all link to Internet-based applications. Second, a "network-centric" delivery system for software, if it ever catches on, would make it irrelevant how many programs were once available on floppy discs and CD-ROMs. In other words, Microsoft's applications barrier, if it existed at all, would afford no competitive protection in an Internet-dominated world.

Legal Issues

Judge Jackson's findings of fact were the foundation on which he constructed his conclusions of law. When that foundation is unsound, the resultant structure inevitably collapses. Still worse, in this case much of Jackson's legal structure collapses even if we accept his factual foundation. To illustrate, we next examine Jackson's critique of Microsoft's tying arrangements, first-screen restrictions, and so-called exclusionary contracts.

Tying Arrangements

In December 1997 Judge Jackson preliminarily enjoined Microsoft from tying the Internet Explorer browser to the Windows operating system in violation of the 1995 consent decree between the company and DOJ. Microsoft then pressed its case with the U.S. Court of Appeals for the District of Columbia Circuit. Six months later, the appellate court, not wanting to be in the "unwelcome position of designing computers,"[39] reversed the trial court and vacated the injunction.

DOJ had advised the D.C. Circuit to look to antitrust law for guidance in interpreting the consent decree. The Circuit Court took that advice but, to DOJ's dismay, expressly rejected the antitrust standard that the government preferred. Specifically, the appellate court declined to apply a 1984 Supreme Court case, *Jefferson Parish Hospital District No. 2 v. Hyde*,[40] which held that tying two products is impermissible, even though the products may be functionally integrated, if there is sufficient consumer demand to constitute a separate viable market for the second product. Based on that case, DOJ maintained that Windows and Internet Explorer were illegally tied as long as Internet Explorer could profitably have been sold by Microsoft as a separate product.

Instead of following *Jefferson Parish*, the D.C. Circuit treated the Microsoft package not as a contractual tie but as a physical or "technological" tie—principally because Internet Explorer and Windows were combined in a manner that precluded removal of the browser. The appropriate benchmark, said the court, must be one based on "plausible benefit" to the consumer. Under that standard, a tying arrangement would survive antitrust scrutiny if it resulted in a "product that combines functionalities . . . in a way that offers advantages unavailable if . . . bought separately and combined by the purchaser."[41] In essence, the court concluded that Microsoft's packaged product, including both Windows and Internet Explorer, was better for customers than buying the two components separately and trying to put them together. Accordingly, the D.C. Circuit remanded the case to Judge Jackson for reconsideration of his injunction, but warned DOJ in no uncertain terms to abandon the suit. "The Department may well regard further pursuit of the case as unpromising," instructed the court.[42]

We now know, of course, that neither DOJ nor Judge Jackson took the appellate court's admonition very seriously. DOJ went forward with its antitrust suit, repeating its allegation that Microsoft's tying arrangement violates the Sherman Act. And Jackson in his final judgment effectively lectured the D.C. Circuit on the law—ignoring the higher court's plausible benefit rule in favor of his own formulation based on the *Jefferson Parish* standard that the Circuit had considered and rebuffed. Even Harvard professor Lawrence Lessig, handpicked by Jackson to file a friend-of-the-court brief, acknowledged that the government had not made out a claim of technological tying. Although Lessig thought the Circuit should have applied a different rule, he said bluntly: "Under the Court of Appeals test, Microsoft must prevail."[43]

Indeed, Microsoft should prevail no matter which standard is applied. In a nutshell, the company could not have been acting anti-competitively if its actions were in response to similar actions by its rivals. Jackson found, for example, that "consumers in 1995 were already demanding software that enabled them to use the Web with ease." Moreover, "IBM had announced in September 1994 its plan to include browsing capability in OS/2 Warp [IBM's operating system, which was then the principal challenger to Windows] at no extra charge." Jackson also found that "Microsoft had reason to believe that other operating-system vendors would do the same."[44] Combining Internet functionality with an operating system was just one more instance of product improvement through integration. That pro-competitive practice—the norm in high-tech industries—could not, therefore, violate the antitrust laws.

For once, Jackson got it right when he said that "the inclusion of Internet Explorer with Windows at no separate charge . . . contributed to improving the quality of Web browsing software, lowering its cost, and increasing its availability, thereby benefiting consumers."[45]

First-Screen Restrictions

In its complaint, the government rebuked Microsoft for insisting that OEMs not delete certain icons from the Windows opening screen. In that manner, argued DOJ, Microsoft used its control over the desktop to dictate Internet access and, to some extent, content. On initial boot-up, Microsoft uses about 15% of its first screen to display selected icons. But OEMs can easily remove most icons (although not Internet Explorer); they can add icons to 85% of the screen that Microsoft doesn't use, install rival software, even make Netscape the default browser.

Microsoft *never* restricted any OEM from installing a rival browser and displaying its icon on the startup screen. Consumers could go a step further; they could delete the Internet Explorer icon or even substitute a shell for the first screen—all with a few clicks of the mouse—in which case the icon would disappear forever. Thus, Microsoft's restrictions are no more burdensome than, say, those imposed by an automobile dealer who presets the stations on your car radio or refuses to remove the hood ornament.

Judge Jackson seemed to agree. He found that "Microsoft's license agreements have never prohibited OEMs from preinstalling programs, including [Netscape's] Navigator, on their PCs and placing icons and entries for those programs on the Windows desktop."[46] Despite that apparent endorsement of Microsoft's first-screen policy, the judge held that the company's license agreements with OEMs violated the Sherman Act insofar as they required Microsoft's permission before an OEM could delete specified icons from the desktop. Not only did Jackson's holding elevate a trifling contractual restriction—which bound OEMs but not consumers—to the level of an antitrust violation, but it also precluded Microsoft from exercising its rights under federal copyright law. Companies that hold valid copyrights are entitled to demand of distributors that copyrighted products be delivered to customers in the form prescribed by the creator.[47]

"Exclusionary" Contracts

DOJ also contended that Microsoft's contracts with Internet service providers and Internet content providers were exclusionary—that is, they were designed to prevent ISPs and ICPs who dealt with Microsoft from also dealing with Netscape. Naturally, companies negotiate exclusive contracts all the time, but those contracts can run afoul of the antitrust laws if one of the companies is a monopolist. The question, then, is whether Microsoft tried to leverage its alleged operating system monopoly to obstruct ISPs and ICPs from doing business with Netscape, thereby foreclosing Netscape from using that channel to market its browser.

In assessing DOJ's exclusive dealing claim, Judge Jackson reached two contradictory conclusions. First, he held that the various ISP and ICP agreements "did not foreclose enough of the relevant market to constitute a § 1 [Sherman Act, section 1] violation." But second, he declared that Microsoft's absolution under section 1 "in no way detracts from the Court's assignment of liability for the same arrangements under § 2."[48] Those two holdings simply cannot coexist. If Microsoft is exonerated of a section 1 charge, covering conspiracies in restraint of trade, then a section 2 charge, covering attempts to monopolize, must also fail. Foreclosing Netscape's distribution channels was a central element of both violations. If Microsoft had indeed attempted to exclude Netscape from the ISP and ICP channels, and if Microsoft enjoyed the overwhelming monopoly power that Jackson asserts, then surely Microsoft would have succeeded. Yet Jackson himself concedes that it did not.

Draconian Remedies

Piling error upon error—procedural gaffes, factual inaccuracies, and wrong-headed legal analysis—Judge Jackson's final remedies are undoubtedly his most pernicious blunder. In some respects wholly disassociated from any of Microsoft's alleged transgressions, in other respects lopsided when weighed against his findings and conclusions, Jackson's remedies—if one didn't know better—seem crafted to inflict as much damage as possible, not just on Microsoft but on the broader high-tech marketplace.

Seemingly separate charges—maintaining a monopoly in operating systems, attempting (unsuccessfully) to monopolize browsers, illegally "tying" Internet Explorer to Windows, and behaving in a "predatory" manner—all come down to essentially the same thing. Stripped of irrelevant gobbledygook about "bullying," which is neither definable nor illegal, the essence of Microsoft's alleged infractions was, first, making it possible to use the Internet with browsing software included in Windows at no extra charge and, second, offering software developers a faster, Windows-specific version of the Java programming language licensed from Sun.

The thrust of the judge's conclusions of law, in his own words, is that Microsoft's misconduct purportedly foiled "Netscape's Navigator Web browser and Sun's implementation of the Java technology."[49] Nearly all of the many companies recruited to complain in court about their dealings with Microsoft were participants in a circus sideshow having nothing to do with those accusations.

The government's role in protecting Netscape and Java—in effect, taking sides in the now-obsolescent, prewireless "browser wars"— was central to the case from beginning to end. That was always a curious obsession because browsers have mostly been free, ever since Mosaic in 1993, and have long been bundled with most operating systems (OS/2, Linux, BeOS, EPOC), most Internet services (AOL) and some office suites (Star Office, WordPerfect 7 and 8). When it came to remedies, however, the government quickly lost its previous passion for helping out Netscape and Java, both of which are doing fine despite being "pummeled" by Microsoft. Instead, DOJ hired new experts to spin new theories about, say, the hypothetical wonders of providing Microsoft Office for Linux, a system the judge dismissed as a trivial niche product. Citing new theories and post-trial evidence, the government appeared to be groping for any sort of rationale to justify its elaborate plans for restructuring and regulating the company.

Anyone who believes that Microsoft's vigorous competition with Netscape and Sun was illegal would surely expect the judge's remedies to focus on those issues, such as "untying" Internet Explorer (thereby imposing a hugely irritating inconvenience on consumers), and prohibiting Microsoft from offering its own version of Java. But the actual remedies have little to do with those alleged offenses, nor even with the judge's poorly supported claim that Windows 98 has a monopoly (which is not itself illegal).

Surely, if the problem were a Windows 98 monopoly, the spinoff of a separate Windows company would do nothing to change that. The newly created Operating System (OS) company would still have the same large market share for Windows 98 and small shares for Windows NT and CE. And the Applications (APPS) company would still have the most popular office suite, while struggling valiantly against Quicken and Turbo Tax in financial software. In fact, any company that sold nothing but Windows would be in a stronger position to raise its price: The company would no longer be concerned that a higher price for the operating system would shrink the market for applications.

The only rationale for separating OS from APPS was a claim from the software lobby that intimate knowledge of Windows is what gives Microsoft an edge in applications. Yet no shred of evidence was presented at the trial to substantiate that claim. In fact, the government's most theatric "remedy"—separating OS from APPS—is entirely unrelated to *any* complaint aired at the trial. There is simply no link between the breakup scheme and any specific legal transgressions ostensibly in need of a remedy.

Naturally, one effective way to reduce the market share of a product as popular as Windows is to make that product less attractive to consumers. That is where the so-called conduct remedies come in. They would indeed prevent Windows from becoming more useful to consumers. Because those restrictions were designed to last for 10 years if the company is not split in two, and because court-ordered divestiture is highly unlikely, the heart of the U.S. software industry would be transformed into a regulated utility for a fatally long time. Consider, for example, the way the following regulation, from the judge's final judgment, redefines and redistributes the property rights to Windows:

> Microsoft shall not restrict . . . an OEM from modifying . . . [any] aspect of a Windows Operating System Product to . . . display icons or otherwise feature other products or services . . . display any user interfaces, provided that any icon is also displayed that allows the user access to the Windows user interface, or . . . launch automatically any non-Microsoft Middleware, Operating System or applications.[50]

That "remedy" effectively gives computer manufacturers carte blanche to expropriate the Windows trademark. OEMs would be free to hide the Windows screen, have a different operating system launch automatically (whether consumers want one or not), and transform the desktop into an advertising billboard. That remedy is also a recipe for balkanization: Consumers buying a computer with "Windows" would have no idea what that means until they turned on the machine. Standardization, arguably Microsoft's most important contribution to software markets, would be no more.

Further compromising Microsoft's intellectual property rights, Judge Jackson would mandate that the company invite OEMs, other hardware vendors, and competing software vendors to scrutinize the inner workings of Windows whenever they see fit—that is, "to study, interrogate, and interact with relevant and necessary portions of the source code, and any related documentation of Microsoft Platform Software."[51]

Finally, lurking among Judge Jackson's more harmful remedies is this one—destructively if unintentionally designed to completely paralyze innovation:

> Microsoft shall not, in any Operating System Product . . . bind any Middleware Product to a Windows Operating System

unless . . . all means of End-User Access to the Middleware Product can readily be removed by OEMs . . . [and] by end users. When an OEM removes End-User Access to a Middleware Product . . . the royalty paid by the OEM for that copy of Windows is reduced.[52]

Requiring that the price of Windows be reduced if the browser or other "middleware" is removed is just a devious way of prohibiting Microsoft from including Internet Explorer for free, and from adding other free features such as voice recognition, Web security, or virus protection. Since AOL-Netscape and others could continue offering integrated products—with some add-ons priced at zero—Microsoft's OS company would be put at a hopeless competitive disadvantage.

Because "middleware" can include just about everything,[53] Microsoft could not integrate any features in Windows that could not, as a technical matter, be easily removed. And because Internet Explorer would be owned by a separate APPS company, which would be prohibited for years from dealing with the OS company, the browser currently built into Windows could only be improved by leasing a newer browser from, say, AOL-Netscape. Like most of the proposed remedies, that one would be good news for competitors but bad for competition.

Lessons to Be Learned

Judge Jackson's final judgment indicates—if there was ever any doubt—that he has fallen hook, line, and sinker for the government's flawed arguments. As a result, real people will be, and have been, injured by this foolishness. Microsoft's shareholders suffered an erosion of market value measured in hundreds of billions of dollars, adversely affecting other tech stocks and the economy in general.[54] If Jackson's remedies are effectuated, company employees, like expendable chess pawns, will be deployed to advance DOJ's dismemberment scheme. Bureaucrats will supervise the allocation of those employees—sales, marketing, programming, product development, research, procurement, legal, and accounting—as well as the allocation of real estate and intellectual property.

Billionaire businessmen—like Larry Ellison of Oracle and Scott McNealy of Sun Microsystems—have skillfully yet wrongly used government in an attempt to bring down a competitor.[55] Consumers pick up the tab when those companies devote more of their resources to politicking, and less to the kinds of integrated products that, until now, have characterized the software industry. That misuse of the political process—which economists call rent-seeking—is both facilitated and made necessary by an amorphous set of antitrust statutes that delegate too much discretion to DOJ officials and federal judges. Potential defendants, like Microsoft, simply cannot know the rules that presumably govern their conduct.

Meanwhile, the Clinton administration doesn't comprehend this basic tenet of economics: In the real world, producers seek to carve out market niches in order to have some influence over the terms on which they sell their product. The profits that arise when they succeed propel economic growth. Rather than measure high-tech markets against the textbook model of perfect competition—a model better suited to an agrarian economy—we need to concern ourselves with the sterile marketplace that will evolve if vigorous antitrust enforcement extinguishes the incentives for new and improved products. Without those incentives, Microsoft would not spend 17% of its revenue on research and development. Its rivals—Oracle, Sun, IBM—spend between 6 and 10%.[56]

Sad to say, Microsoft has learned to play the political game in a hurry. For many years conspicuous by its absence from Washington, D.C., Microsoft has now expanded its D.C. office from four people in 1994 to 14 in April 2000. Between January 1999 and February 2000, Microsoft's political action committee ladled out $278,000 to 149 congressional incumbents in both parties. The company expects to spend more than a million dollars this election cycle.[57]

It's even worse among Microsoft's rivals. A single Silicon Valley fundraiser in April brought in $1.3 million to Democratic Party coffers.[58] TechNet, the brainchild of politically connected financier John Doerr, has made Silicon Valley an official new participant in the Washington problem. Rather than make principled arguments regarding the proper role of government, TechNet, with great enthusiasm, has advocated industrial age government intervention against too-successful high-tech competitors. Ultimately, that political agenda will destroy what it sets out to protect. Because politicians are basically order takers, we get the kind of government we ask for—including oppressive regulation. To their lasting regret, some in Silicon Valley may soon get the kind of government they are requesting. The lesson is straightforward: Rent-seeking businessmen had better rein in their appetite for government largess before they begin to reap the unwelcome fruits of their unwholesome labors.

10. It's Microsoft Redux All Over Again

Maybe the fat lady hasn't crooned the final note, but the petite lady who carried the most weight, U.S. District Judge Colleen Kollar-Kotelly, wrote the denouement to the Microsoft antitrust fiasco. In November 2002 she approved the Justice Department settlement and rejected the demands of nine recalcitrant attorneys general. Massachusetts—alone among the states that contested the settlement—unsuccessfully pursued yet another appeal. The Massachusetts crusade was as futile as a high-tech company trying to comply with the Sherman Act.

Imagine that it's 1993 and the Federal Trade Commission has just opened its antitrust investigation of the company that dominates the market for desktop operating systems. Now fast forward roughly 11 years. The same company still dominates the same market. But new products and new technologies, inconceivable in 1993, are attacking the desktop market in ways that government bureaucrats could never have dreamed. Linux is making inroads against Windows. Palm sells most of the handheld computers. Sun and Oracle are major players in server systems. AOL controls online access. RealNetworks is a leading multimedia provider.

Those companies challenged Microsoft and carved out their market niches. But that wasn't good enough. The challengers decided that litigation, greased by political clout, was the road more easily traveled. Unfortunately, when software executives spend more time suing and less time innovating, the tab is ultimately paid by consumers, employees, and shareholders. That's part of the reason for the tech sector's dismal stock market performance over the several years preceding the settlement.

Thankfully, Judge Kollar-Kotelly has penned the coda to the antitrust dud of the decade—at least the U.S. rendition. That still leaves the European Union, which is evidently oblivious to the damage that its latest antitrust silliness will cause to the global marketplace. The ultimate remedy is to get government out of the business of managing private markets to prop up unsuccessful competitors. Toward that end, the final section of Chapter 10 repackages the arguments made throughout Part Two of this book—arguments that lead inescapably to this conclusion: The best antitrust laws are those that are repealed.

But before defending that assertion, let's bring the browser wars up to date. The opening section below discusses the decision by the U.S. Court of Appeals for the District of Columbia Circuit, which affirmed one holding by trial judge Thomas Penfield Jackson and reversed or remanded the rest. Then we turn to the Justice Department settlement, the first light at the end of the long Microsoft tunnel. That's followed by an analysis of the wasteful and duplicative suit by nine state attorneys general, who decided they knew better than the Justice Department about federal antitrust enforcement.

Judge Kollar-Kotelly's laudable approval of the settlement comes next, with a brief commentary on the pointless attempt by Massachusetts to revisit the same issues that had already been examined ad nauseam by three judges, the federal government, and 19 other states. Yet the Massachusetts episode was not the last word, so we take up the final phase of the Microsoft mess: more politicking by Microsoft's rivals and the appalling pronouncement by the European Union.

Judge Jackson's Comeuppance*

Judge Thomas Penfield Jackson and consumers are the big losers in the Microsoft case. There were no winners. Seven judges on the U.S. Court of Appeals for the D.C. Circuit held unanimously that Jackson's appearance of bias "seriously tainted the proceedings . . . and called into question the integrity of the judicial process." Jackson's rubber-stamp acceptance of the Justice Department's proposal to dismember Microsoft—without either an evidentiary hearing or an adequate explanation—is history. Good riddance.

Now the case goes back to the trial court where a new judge— selected randomly from among 10 Clinton appointees and one Reagan appointee—will decide how to remedy Microsoft's transgressions. Because of the "drastically altered scope of liability"—

---

*This section, as revised, was originally published under the title "No Winning Team," *National Review Online*, July 9, 2001, www.nationalreview.com/comment/comment-levy070901.shtml.

about which more below—the appellate judges intimate that divestiture cannot be justified. Moreover, Microsoft is a "unitary" company, not one formed by merging or acquiring separate entities. Thus, dissolution would pose logistical difficulties, said the court. Without a "significant causal connection" between Microsoft's behavior and its maintenance of market power, conduct-related remedies would be more appropriate. In short, breaking up Microsoft is a dead issue.

That's good news. So too is the reversal of Jackson's holding that Microsoft attempted to monopolize the browser market. The government did not properly define the browser market and could not, therefore, show that Microsoft had a dominant share. Nor did the government demonstrate that the browser market is characterized by barriers to entry. Without those proofs, the Justice Department's attempted monopolization charge evaporates.

On the tying question, the Court of Appeals ordered the new trial judge to reconsider Jackson's conclusion that Microsoft broke the law. The court said that requiring customers to take Microsoft's Internet Explorer browser if they want to acquire the Windows operating system is not unlawful, in and of itself. On remand, the lower court will have to apply a "rule of reason" standard—weighing the costs and benefits to consumers of the tie-in. The Justice Department will have to show an actual anti-competitive effect—not just intent—in the browser market. Then Microsoft can proffer a pro-competitive justification, which the government can rebut by proving that the anti-competitive effect is greater.

If the Justice Department renews its claim that Microsoft illegally engaged in "price bundling," it will have to demonstrate that Windows alone—without the browser—would have sold for a lower price. But Microsoft can still prevail by showing that other operating system vendors also bundle an Internet browser, and don't sell the operating system separately for a reduced price. Best bet: Under a "rule of reason" standard, the government will abandon its losing argument that Microsoft's tying arrangement is unlawful.

So far, so good. But the waters get muddier for Microsoft. The appellate court affirmed Jackson's holding that Microsoft is liable for engaging in anti-competitive conduct to maintain its monopoly in operating systems. That anti-competitive conduct purportedly involved the following: preventing PC makers from removing the Internet Explorer browser; crafting exclusionary contracts with

Internet service providers and major online providers like AOL; commingling the browser and operating system program code; threatening Apple with removal of Microsoft's Office Suite if Apple continued to deal with Netscape; extending preferred treatment to selected PC makers in return for restrictive licensing arrangements; pressuring Intel to back Microsoft's version of Sun's Java program; and favoring software vendors who agreed not to support rival platforms. According to Jackson, Microsoft did not demonstrate any efficiency justification for those anti-competitive acts. The Court of Appeals found no basis to overturn that finding.

Those are the charges that will have to be remedied by the trial judge. Meanwhile, the government and Microsoft have until the end of September 2001 to ask the U.S. Supreme Court to review facets of the appellate decision with which they disagree. But the likelihood that the high court will accept the case is slim. The record is voluminous, the case would be enormously time-consuming, at least two of the appellate judges are renowned for their antitrust expertise, the entire appellate court—not just a three-judge panel—ruled on the case, the ruling was unanimous, and it was the unsigned product of multiple judges. Moreover, the Supreme Court might be reluctant to enter the fray if, as expected, the Justice Department and Microsoft open settlement negotiations.

Indeed, many in Congress and others who have followed the case closely recommend a settlement as the best solution. Under its terms, Microsoft would commit to a number of conduct-related remedies— some of which the company has already implemented—for a period of, say, five years. Perhaps an agreement could be structured along the following lines.

First, PC makers would be able to remove the browser from the operating system, delete the Internet Explorer icon, and otherwise have substantial flexibility over the design of the opening screen— short of replacing it entirely—when Windows is initialized. Second, Microsoft would not link its promotion or advertising of Internet access and content providers to their dealings with Microsoft's rivals. Third, all independent software vendors would get timely and complete access to Microsoft's applications programming interfaces, which enable repetitive software functions to be handled by Windows rather than rewritten for each application. Fourth, Microsoft would agree to release key software products (e.g., Office Suite) for non-Microsoft platforms. Fifth, earlier versions of Microsoft's operating systems would remain available to PC makers for a specified period without any change in royalty terms. Finally, Microsoft might be persuaded to cover the attorney fees and other legal costs incurred by the Justice Department and the 19 states that are coplaintiffs in the antitrust action.

There are hints that both Microsoft and the Justice Department would like to put this case behind them. The trick, of course, is to come up with a formula that will appease the state attorneys general, who insist they will keep litigating if a proposed settlement does no more than slap Microsoft on the wrist. That threat may be an empty one if the two principal litigants favor an end to the protracted courtroom battle. Furthermore, the attorneys general surely understand that Microsoft has already been, and will continue to be, punished by this lawsuit in ways quite apart from the remedies that are ultimately put in place.

The cost of the litigation—in time, money, public image, and diversion of executive resources—has been enormous. Microsoft's shareholders, Bill Gates in the lead, lost hundreds of billions of dollars as the price of the company's stock tanked. And Microsoft still faces an onslaught of legal action, both public and private. An increasingly interventionist European Union, raring to establish its independence from the United States, will move forward with its own antitrust probe. Private lawsuits will probably be filed by consumer classes and Microsoft's disgruntled competitors, like AOL-Netscape.

Those private plaintiffs can collect treble damages under U.S. antitrust laws, and they are in a much stronger position as a result of the Justice Department's partial victory. Because the court held that Microsoft has a monopoly in operating systems and behaved anti-competitively, private litigants—without revisiting those issues—can proceed straight to proof of injury. Even consumers, who do not purchase computers directly from Microsoft and are therefore prevented from recovering damages under federal law, can sue in some state courts where the direct purchaser rule doesn't apply.

So whatever conduct remedies might be included in a settlement, Microsoft has a slew of other problems arising from the federal lawsuit. That's regrettable, because the lawsuit was baseless from the beginning. To be fair, the appellate judges on the D.C. Circuit were faced with a triple dilemma. First, they are judges, not legislators. Accordingly, they interpret the law and do not rule on its wisdom or policy implications. Antitrust, as codified in legislation and construed in previous cases, is an amalgam of doctrines that are murky at best. Still, the judges seemed to go out of their way to affirm its vitality in high-tech markets. Down the road, that could be the most destructive aspect of the appellate ruling.

Second, the Court of Appeals commented repeatedly that Microsoft had failed to question the connection between Judge Jackson's findings of fact and his conclusions of law. The judges were disinclined to make those arguments on Microsoft's behalf. Significant conclusions of law were thus affirmed, not because the appellate court necessarily agreed, but because they had not been adequately refuted.

Third, under federal rules of civil procedure, the court had two choices in reviewing Jackson's fact finding: All of his facts could be rejected on account of apparent bias, or all of his facts would have to be scrutinized deferentially—that is, they would be discarded only if "clearly erroneous." There was no middle ground. Because Jackson's misbehavior occurred mostly toward the end of the trial, and related mostly to the remedies phase, the appellate court opted not to dismiss categorically his fact finding. Yet because Microsoft failed to challenge key facts—choosing merely to assert their inaccuracy—they were affirmed, almost by default, and critically affected the outcome of the case.

Microsoft will escape without dismemberment and without permanently disabling conduct-related remedies. Consumers might not be as lucky. They may have to contend with the sterile markets that will result if vigorous antitrust enforcement extinguishes the incentives for new and improved products. In the long term, the solution is to repeal the antitrust laws. They rely on a false ideal of perfect competition, debase property rights, and punish success.

Microsoft's Unsettling Settlement*

Prospects are favorable for settlement of the biggest antitrust case in decades. The good news is that Microsoft's billionaire rivals will

---

*An abbreviated version of this section, with other revisions, was originally published under the title "Soft Settlement," *Los Angeles Daily Journal*, November 26, 2001, p. 6; reprinted in Paul Beckner and Erick R. Gustafson, eds., *Trial and Error: United States v. Microsoft*, 2nd ed. (Washington: Citizens for a Sound Economy Foundation, 2002). See also Robert A. Levy, "Microsoft's Unsettling Settlement," *Washington Times*, December 2, 2001, p. B4.

have failed in their attempt to use government to win in the political arena what they couldn't win in the marketplace. Although Microsoft still faces litigation from competitors, opportunistic trial lawyers, the European Union, and perhaps even state attorneys general who don't agree to the settlement, at least the federal antitrust lawsuit won't be around to drain Microsoft's energies and undermine economic growth so essential to the post-9/11 recovery.

The Microsoft antitrust dispute has been festering in one form or another since the Federal Trade Commission opened its investigation in 1991. Here's a brief chronology of the 10-year debacle.

After a two-year inquiry, the FTC deadlocked in 1993 on whether to file a formal antitrust complaint against Microsoft. A year later, the Justice Department took over and began its own independent probe. That culminated in a 1995 consent decree, which required, in part, that Microsoft no longer compel PC makers who license the Windows operating system to also license other software. But an important provision was added: The decree "shall not be construed to prohibit Microsoft from developing integrated products."

In 1997 the Justice Department sued in U.S. District Court claiming that Microsoft's browser, Internet Explorer, was a product separate from, not integrated with, Windows. Therefore, the government argued, Microsoft violated the consent decree by requiring PC makers to take the browser. In December 1997, federal judge Thomas Penfield Jackson bought the government's argument and ordered Microsoft to offer a version of Windows without the browser. That order was overturned by the U.S. Court of Appeals for the D.C. Circuit in June 1998. The appellate court held that consumers would benefit from the integrated design of Windows with Web browsing functionality. In effect, the court rejected the claim that Windows and Internet Explorer were separate products under the terms of the consent decree.

Without waiting for the appellate court's decision, the Justice Department, the District of Columbia, and 19 state attorneys general (South Carolina later withdrew) filed antitrust suits in U.S. District Court in May 1998. Those suits, separate from any claims under the consent decree, were consolidated and assigned to Judge Jackson. The government charged Microsoft with attempted collusion to divide markets with Netscape, illegal tying arrangements in the sale of Windows to PC makers, and exclusionary contracts with Internet

271

service and content providers. The trial began in October 1998 and ended the following June.

Jackson released his findings of fact in November 1999, once again deciding for the government on virtually every issue. Those fact findings essentially dictated the legal outcome. When Jackson issued his formal conclusions of law in April 2000, he predictably held that Microsoft had violated the antitrust laws. Then came the bombshell. Less than a month later, without a minute of hearings on appropriate remedies, Jackson rubber-stamped the Justice Department's proposal and adopted an array of conduct and structural fixes, including a breakup of Microsoft into two separate companies. Naturally, Microsoft appealed—to the D.C. Circuit Court, which had ruled its way two years earlier. (The appellate court's opinion is discussed in the earlier section of this chapter.)

That brings us to the November 2nd settlement, negotiated by Microsoft and the Justice Department with the help of a court-appointed mediator, Boston University professor Eric Green. In Microsoft's favor, the settlement essentially allows the company to continue bundling whatever products it wishes with the operating system. Otherwise, the settlement addresses and corrects, with a single exception, each and every objection raised by the D.C. Circuit in affirming Judge Jackson's holding of monopoly maintenance.

For example, Microsoft may not retaliate against other companies for supporting competing software; or enter into exclusive agreements with software developers, Internet content providers, or Internet access providers. Nor may Microsoft prevent PC makers and consumers from installing a rival operating system, or removing Microsoft's "middleware" products—described below—and installing rival middleware. Further, Microsoft must disclose and license its applications programming interfaces (APIs) to software developers; and charge uniform, published prices (except for volume discounts) to its 20 top PC-maker clients.

The single Microsoft "transgression" not addressed in the settlement is the commingling of operating system and browser code. Of course, that problem is trivial as long as the consumers and PC makers are not forced to use, and can actually uninstall, Microsoft's browser. Besides, the settlement in two critical respects goes beyond what the appellate court might have instructed. First, the court found that Microsoft had suppressed competition in the middleware market as a means of maintaining its Windows monopoly. Middleware, according to the court, consists of products that expose APIs and thereby compete against traditional operating systems. But the settlement agreement defines middleware more broadly, to include not only browsers but also products like e-mail, instant messaging, and media players. Those products do not expose APIs; they do not compete against Windows; yet Microsoft will be compelled to treat rival "middleware" products as if the court had found—which it did not—that bundling those products somehow constituted an illegal tying arrangement.

Second, the settlement dictates that Microsoft will have to disclose its server protocols so that non-Microsoft servers (like those produced by IBM, Oracle, Sun Microsystems, and Novell) will be able to interoperate with Windows. The allegation, first leveled by Sun in a complaint filed with the European Union in 1998, is that Microsoft is attempting to extend its PC monopoly to the server market by making newer versions of Windows incompatible with servers other than Microsoft's. But the newest version of Windows (XP) has a miniscule share of the operating system market. Quite simply, there is no monopoly to leverage. Older versions (Windows 95 and 98) are perfectly compatible with non-Microsoft servers, which by the way supply about 60% of the server market. Most important, the server issue was never part of the Justice Department's case. On that issue, there was no complaint, no trial, no evidence, and no verdict—just a restriction on Microsoft's behavior.

Taken as a whole, the settlement was good enough for 9 of the 18 states that had joined in the Justice Department's suit. But the remaining 9 states and the District of Columbia have, thus far, demurred. That leaves them with four choices: They can change their mind and sign the settlement. They can try to wring more concessions from Microsoft, which has resisted such entreaties. They can argue before the new trial judge, Colleen Kollar-Kotelly, that the settlement is not in the public interest. Or they can continue to litigate on their own, without help from the Justice Department or the other states.

The major objections by the reluctant states are these: First, they want more teeth in the enforcement process. Presently, a panel of three full-time experts—one appointed by the Department of Justice, one by Microsoft, and a third by both DOJ and Microsoft—will resolve disputes. The panel will have access to all Microsoft books, records, systems, and personnel, including source code. Complaints may be submitted anonymously, then forwarded if necessary to a federal judge for resolution. Evidently, the hold-out states would rather have a special master who reports directly to the court. Second, the attorneys general prefer a 10-year term—double the agreed-upon 5-year period, which is already a lifetime in the software business, and which can be extended for two years if Microsoft violates the decree. Third, they complain of too many escape clauses that might allow Microsoft to exclude rival products, substitute its own products, and avoid disclosing APIs. Fourth, the states insist that Microsoft offer its browser and Office Suite to Linux and every other manufacturer of a competing operating system. Fifth, they demand that Microsoft sell unbundled versions of Windows at lower prices.

Those add-ons were not necessary for the federal government or half of the state attorneys general. Nor will they be accepted by Microsoft. Moreover, if the nonsettling states elect to contest the settlement before Judge Kollar-Kotelly, they will have a tough row to hoe. Under the Tunney Act, the judge must decide whether the settlement serves the public interest. After the settlement is published later this month in the Federal Register, along with the Justice Department's assessment of competitive impact, the public will have 60 days to comment, followed by 30 days for the government and Microsoft to respond, then hearings if the judge thinks they're needed. In rendering her decision, the judge will no doubt be guided by the overriding goal of the Tunney Act: to ensure that the settlement is not a "corrupt bargain." Judge Kollar-Kotelly will want to know whether Microsoft lobbied the Bush White House to pressure the Justice Department. No such contacts have been documented; nor has the Justice Department, Microsoft, or the White House intimated that any took place. Once the judge is comfortable on that ground, she will very likely defer to the Justice Department's characterization of the settlement as a responsible and fair outcome of the lawsuit.

That means the balking states would have to pursue their litigation before the same judge who validated the settlement. Perhaps signaling their intent, some of the attorneys general hired the redoubtable trial lawyer, Brendan Sullivan, of Ollie North fame. He might pick up where the Justice Department left off: evidence gathering now, with a remedies hearing no earlier than March 2002. Leading the charge is California's attorney general, Bill Lockyer, who has accumulated a small war chest for that purpose. Lockyer has been on the receiving end of major political contributions from Microsoft's archrival, Oracle Corporation. He also counts among his influential constituents other Silicon Valley denizens, like Netscape and Sun Microsystems, who have been unalterably opposed to the settlement.

Silicon Valley, supposed bastion of entrepreneurship, has become part of the problem. Multiple governmental entities, responsive to the parochial interests of rival businesses, initially combined to challenge Microsoft. Now, with that challenge resolved to the satisfaction of almost everyone, nine states might dawdle just long enough to foul the country's near-term economic recovery. It's time to shut down this nonsense and let the software industry get back to serving its customers.

Bite No. 2 at the Microsoft Apple*

The Microsoft case continues on two parallel tracks: in a Washington courtroom, where a federal judge ponders whether a long-awaited settlement between Microsoft and the Justice Department serves the public interest; and in that same court, before the same judge, where nine states of the 20 that had originally joined the federal suit demand that Microsoft's conduct be more severely restricted.

Both court proceedings are based on the same trial, the same findings of fact, the same conclusions of law. Both proceedings allege the same injuries to the same people. If that sounds like two bites at the apple for the nine states, double jeopardy for Microsoft, and a waste of taxpayer resources, that's exactly what it is.

Forty-one of 50 states accept the Justice Department's assessment that the settlement advances the public interest. Thirty of those states didn't even sue Microsoft, South Carolina abandoned the suit, New Mexico settled in July 2001, and nine more states signed onto the pending settlement. That leaves the District of Columbia and nine seceding states attempting to substitute themselves as enforcers of the federal antitrust laws.

---

*This section, as revised, combines two previously published articles: "For Nine States, a Second Bite at the Microsoft Apple," *Los Angeles Times*, March 24, 2002; and "The Malign Nine vs. Microsoft," *Washington Times*, April 25, 2002, p. A16.

Attorneys general for the nine states concede that their state and federal claims are the same. They also acknowledge that Microsoft's behavior did not affect their citizens more profoundly than anyone else. Yet they want much broader relief than the settlement affords—to vindicate their singular view of the public interest. But Congress did not intend that states—in a case where the Justice Department has already spoken—could supersede the role of the federal government.

Consider the remarks of respected federal appeals judge Richard Posner, who mediated an abortive Microsoft settlement two years ago. Posner offered these recommendations in a recent issue of the *Antitrust Law Journal*: "I would like to see, first, the states stripped of their authority to bring antitrust suits, federal or state, except . . . where the state is suing firms that are fixing the prices of goods or services that they sell to the state. . . . [States] are too subject to influence by . . . competitors. This is a particular concern when the [competitor] is a major political force in that state. A situation in which the benefits of government action are concentrated in one state and the costs in other states is a recipe for irresponsible state action." Amen to that.

So what is a state to do if it doesn't like the settlement? There is a comprehensive legal process, established by the Tunney Act in 1974 and now under way in this case, for determining whether antitrust decrees are in the public interest and how nonsettling parties can voice their objections. Yet the nine states mostly rejected the formula prescribed by Congress so they could pursue their own strategy to override the federal settlement.

In its motion to dismiss the case, Microsoft argues that the nonsettling states do not have legal standing to bring a separate suit because they did not show injury unique to their residents. When Judge Kollar-Kotelly asked the Justice Department to comment on that argument, the department stated in its brief that no definitive case law *compelled* the case to be dismissed. Nonetheless, Justice offered four powerful reasons why the states' claims, as a matter of equity, should be rejected.

First, "the United States is the sole enforcer of the federal antitrust laws on behalf of the American public." Second, the states' remedies would affect competition and consumers outside of their borders—raising "for the very first time the prospect that a small group of states, with no particularized interests to vindicate, might somehow obtain divergent relief with wide-ranging, national economic implications." Third, many of those remedies "appear unrelated to the theories of illegality advanced by the United States and the plaintiff States at trial and the findings of liability sustained by the Courts." In fact, the remedies extend to "new products, new services [and] new markets." Fourth, the proposed settlement will provide all the relief needed to protect consumers against future antitrust injury. Any doubts in that regard, according to Supreme Court precedent, should be resolved in the federal government's favor.

Essentially, said the Justice Department, "the public interest is best served when federal and state antitrust activity is complementary, not duplicative or conflicting." In this case, however, the nine holdout states "have neither the authority nor the responsibility to act in the broader national interest, and the plaintiff with that authority and responsibility [that is, the United States] has taken a different course." Still worse, the relief sought by the nonsettling states "may harm consumers, retard competition, chill innovation, or confound compliance" with the federal settlement. Echoing the Supreme Court, the Justice Department warned that antitrust redress requires a showing of "harm to competition not competitors." Remedies must be crafted for the benefit of the public, not for the private gain of Microsoft's rivals.

Judge Kollar-Kotelly, having solicited the Justice Department's guidance, would do well to give it great weight. That's the short-term solution. For the longer term, a more permanent approach is necessary. Congress is constitutionally authorized to intervene whenever actual or imminent state practices threaten the free flow of commerce. Congress should use that power and strip the states of their ability to enforce federal antitrust laws. Otherwise, some states will continue to abuse their existing authority—exercising it to impose sovereignty beyond their borders and catering to the parochial interests of politically powerful local constituents.

Would constraints on state antitrust enforcement powers violate time-honored principles of federalism? Not at all. Federalism isn't simply a matter of states' rights. Nor is it exclusively about devolution of power or promoting efficient government. First and foremost, federalism is about checks and balances based on dual sovereignty. Most often, the states are a counterweight to excessive power in the hands of the federal government. Yet antitrust—especially the Microsoft case—is an instance where the federal government must curb excessive power in the hands of the states.

The States' Last Hurrah*

Her opinion was straightforward and hard-hitting: "Harm to 'one or more competitors,' however severe, is not condemned by the Sherman Act in the absence of . . . harm to consumers." With those words, federal judge Colleen Kollar-Kotelly pinpointed the driving force behind the Microsoft antitrust suit—an attempt by Microsoft's unhappy rivals to use government for competitive advantage.

She went on to note that the attorneys general of the nine nonsettling states offered "little, if any, legitimate justification" for the remedies they requested, which, for the most part, were "not supported by any economic analysis." Why, she wondered, would the states ask for relief "at this late stage . . . unrelated to [Microsoft's] monopoly market." Her answer: "Certain of Microsoft's competitors appear to be those who desire these provisions."

Those ringing pronouncements finally garnered acceptance, if not enthusiasm, from everyone—except, that is, Massachusetts Attorney General Tom Reilly. He decided to appeal Judge Kollar-Kotelly's unequivocal rejection of nine states' demands to punish Microsoft more than deemed necessary by the Justice Department, 41 other states, and the large majority of consumers. Thus the Microsoft antitrust case, first investigated by the Federal Trade Commission in 1991, will enter its 13th year. Reilly determined that a dozen years was not enough time to get it right.

Meanwhile, Microsoft shareholders, employees, and customers have suffered mightily at the hands of the regulators. Rather than focus on better ways to serve consumers, Microsoft's most creative executives have been preoccupied warding off legal challenges instigated by competitors like Sun, AOL, RealNetworks, and Palm. Their whining and political jockeying might be just grist for an intriguing tale of corporate cronyism, except that the cost of the litigation

---

*This section, as revised, combines two previously published articles: "Repeal Antitrust Laws, Don't Let States Sue," *Hartford Courant*, November 11, 2002; and "Big Court Wins by Microsoft Haven't Ended States' Suits," *Investor's Business Daily*, December 17, 2002, p. A15.

has been enormous. Microsoft shareholders suffered an erosion of market value measured in hundreds of billions of dollars. Indeed, the company's stock plummeted $80 billion on one day—April 3, 2000, when Judge Thomas Penfield Jackson issued his ill-fated conclusions of law, which were mostly overturned on appeal. Contrast that single-day loss with the mere $60 billion that disappeared from investors' and employees' portfolios in the aftermath of the Enron nightmare.

What, then, still distressed Massachusetts? For starters, there was the question of commingled software. Microsoft has meshed its Windows operating system code with the code of other products, like the Internet Explorer browser. That was one of the few infractions affirmed by the U.S. Court of Appeals when it reviewed Judge Jackson's findings. After unceremoniously dumping Judge Jackson, the appellate court directed Judge Kollar-Kotelly to resolve the commingling issue. She concluded that "forced removal of software code . . . will disrupt the industry, harming both ISVs [independent software vendors] and consumers. . . . [T]he ability to remove end-user access to any commingled functionality would sufficiently address the anti-competitive aspect of the conduct." That solution— the ability to remove end-user access—is precisely the solution embraced in the Justice Department settlement.

Then there was the definition of middleware, which controls many of the restrictions imposed on Microsoft. Judge Jackson defined middleware as products like browsers and Java that interface with software applications and thereby compete against traditional operating systems. The settlement agreement goes further; it defines middleware more broadly to include e-mail, instant messaging, and media players.

That wasn't sufficient for Reilly. He wanted to protect an ever-wider array of competitors from the vagaries of the market. Middleware should include, he insisted, Microsoft Office, digital imaging software, and several other applications. But Judge Kollar-Kotelly cut to the heart of the matter: "Plaintiffs include in their definition of 'middleware' almost any software product, without regard to the potential of the product to evolve into a true platform for other applications . . . technologies which fall outside of the relevant market and which do not pose a threat to Microsoft's monopoly."

Rules are needed to prevent that sort of special interest pleading. Here, for example, are the standards that should govern when states propose to vindicate the private rights of their residents under federal antitrust law: First, states should not be allowed to litigate on behalf of private parties who, on their own, have unhindered access to the courts. Second, injury claims must be those related to residents collectively or to a state's overall economy, not to particular parties. That reduces the likelihood that the litigation will be instigated by special interests. Third, relief should be in the form of money damages only, not conduct-related remedies. The problem with conduct-related remedies is that they invariably affect out-of-state residents. Finally, no state should be permitted to sue if a federal agency is also suing, unless there are state-specific injuries that are not addressed in the federal suit.

The underlying problem is clear-cut: Economic losses from excessive, overlapping regulation often cause immense damage to producers and consumers. The Microsoft litigation is exhibit A. Attorney General Reilly surely could have spent his time and taxpayer dollars more effectively. Enough was enough. In June 2004 the U.S. Court of Appeals for the District of Columbia Circuit unanimously denied the Massachusetts appeal.

Bite No. 3 at the Microsoft Apple*

Triple jeopardy. That's the net effect of the European Union's order imposing additional antitrust sanctions on the world's leading software maker. Microsoft will have to fork over about $610 million in fines, disclose more of its programming code so that rivals' server computers can more easily interact with Windows, and offer dual versions of Windows for sale by PC makers in Europe—one version with Microsoft's Media Player included, and one without.

Bite number one at the Microsoft apple came nearly six years ago when the Justice Department and 20 state attorneys general filed their massive antitrust suit against the company. Federal judge Thomas Penfield Jackson held that Microsoft had misbehaved and recommended, among other things, that it be dismembered. But an appellate court had other ideas. It threw out the dismemberment scheme after finding that Jackson himself had misbehaved. Nevertheless, said the court, Microsoft did illegally maintain its Windows

---

*This section, with minor revisions, was originally published under the title "A Welfare State for Aggrieved Market Losers," *Financial Times*, March 24, 2004, p. 15.

monopoly. A different federal judge, Colleen Kollar-Kotelly was directed to come up with appropriate remedies. The result—three-and-a-half years after the initial filing—was a settlement among Microsoft, the Justice Department, and all but nine of the states.

Before approving the settlement, Judge Kollar-Kotelly took another year to consider more than 30,000 public comments, expert testimony, and lots of advice from Microsoft's supposedly victimized competitors. She decided that the public interest was best served by implementing the settlement, which essentially imposed two unprecedented restrictions on the company's freedom to design and develop its own products. First, Microsoft had to allow PC makers and consumers to hide certain bundled Microsoft products—like its Internet Explorer browser and Media Player—and install competing products. Second, Microsoft had to reveal parts of its software code to companies producing larger-scale server computers that "talk" to Windows-based PCs.

While the settlement approval process unfolded, the nine holdout states opted for bite number two at the Microsoft apple. They asked for broader relief than the federal settlement conferred. But in November 2002, Judge Kollar-Kotelly rejected the remedies proposed by the nine states because they "would require drastic alterations to Microsoft's products, as well as to aspects of its business model which do not involve illegal conduct."

Now comes the EU with bite number three: addressing precisely the same concerns that were first raised by the Justice Department, then later raised and rejected after separate hearings involving the nonsettling states. Still, the EU plows ahead—second-guessing and overriding the judgment of both the judicial and executive branches of the American government, in a matter that concerns management decisions made in the United States by an American company.

What's worse, the entire process has been instigated by U.S.-based competitors that have failed multiple times within the American legal system to accomplish what they have been inept at accomplishing within the global marketplace. Sad to say, the EU has become a sanctuary for disgruntled businessmen who use political influence in an attempt to bring down their rivals.

Indeed, Microsoft tried to placate RealNetworks with a promise to have all PC makers in the European market install three competing media players that the EU would specify. Even that wasn't enough.

EU Commissioner Mario Monti wanted to make history, not settle the case. He conceded that "We made substantial progress towards resolving the problems which have arisen in the past." But he wondered about Microsoft's "future conduct" and concluded that "consumers in Europe ... will be better served with a decision that creates a strong precedent." By contrast, Microsoft's general counsel, Brad Smith, placed the emphasis where it properly belongs: "We have to be sure that the law is not just about competitors' complaints. . . . Consumers must be part of the equation."

Far from promoting consumer interests, the latest EU order, pure and simple, transforms antitrust into a corporate welfare program for market losers. Moreover, the implications will not be confined to the Microsoft case. Without some semblance of regulatory consistency, companies competing globally will not be able to conform their conduct to the dictates of divergent legal regimes. That means special interests pursuing their favorite antitrust forum in an effort to exercise the most political clout. The real costs: fewer jobs, less innovation, inferior products, and higher prices.

Antitrust: The Case for Repeal*

Recall Federal Reserve chairman Alan Greenspan's 1967 characterization of U.S. antitrust laws. He described them as a "jumble of economic irrationality and ignorance." Today, nearly four decades later, Greenspan's assessment is especially applicable to our information-driven, high-tech economy. The conclusion, defended in this chapter and earlier chapters, is that our antitrust laws should be repealed, root and branch. Recapping the lessons of the Microsoft case, here are eight reasons why.

1. Antitrust debases the idea of private property

Too often, when government enforces antitrust laws, it transforms a company's private property into something that effectively belongs to the public, to be designed by government officials and sold on terms congenial to rivals who are bent on the market leader's demise.

---

*This section, with minor revisions, was originally published in *ama-gi, The Journal of the Hayek Society at the London School of Economics*, Michaelmas Term, 2003, pp. 9–10, www.lse.ac.uk/clubs/hayek/amagiM2003.pdf. That article, in turn, was based in part on "The Microsoft Moral: Repeal the Antitrust Laws, for Starters," *American Spectator*, May 2000, p. 56.

Some advocates of the free market endorse that process, despite the destructive implications of stripping private property of its protection against confiscation. If new technology is to be declared public property, future technology will not materialize. If technology is to be proprietary, then it must not be expropriated. Once expropriation becomes the remedy of choice, the goose is unlikely to continue laying golden eggs.

The principles are these: No one other than the owner has a right to the technology he created. Consumers cannot demand that a product be provided at a specified price or with specified features. Competitors are not entitled to share in the product's advantages. By demanding that one company's creation be exploited for the benefit of competitors, or even consumers, government turns a blind eye to core principles of free markets and individual liberty.

2. Antitrust laws are fluid, nonobjective, and often retroactive

Because of murky statutes and conflicting case law, companies never can be quite sure what constitutes permissible behavior. If a company cannot demonstrate that its actions were motivated by efficiency, conduct that is otherwise legal somehow morphs into an antitrust violation. Normal business practices—price discounts, product improvements, exclusive contracting—become violations of law. When they are not accused of monopoly price gouging for charging too much, companies are accused of predatory pricing for charging too little or collusion for charging the same.

3. Antitrust is based on a static view of the market

In real markets, sellers seek to carve out mini-monopolies. Profits from market power are the engine that propels the economy. So what might happen in a utopian, perfectly competitive environment is irrelevant to the question whether government intervention is necessary or appropriate. The proper comparison is with the marketplace that will evolve if the antitrust laws, by punishing success, eliminate incentives for new and improved products. Markets move faster than antitrust bureaucrats could ever move. Consumers rule, not producers. And consumers can unseat any product and any company no matter how powerful and entrenched. Just ask Word-Perfect or Lotus or IBM.

4. Antitrust remedies are designed by lawyers who do not understand how markets work

Economic losses from excessive regulation can do great damage to producers and consumers. But government moves forward in the name of correcting market failure, apparently without considering at all the possibility of government failure.

Proponents of antitrust tell us that government planners know which products should be withdrawn from the market, no matter what consumers actually prefer. The problem with that argument is that it leads directly to paternalism—to the idea than an elite corps of experts knows our interests better than we do, and can regulate our affairs to satisfy those interests better than the market does. The real issue is not whether one product is better than another, but who gets to decide—consumers, declaring their preferences by purchases in the market, or specialists in government rating the merits of various goods and services. When we permit government to make such decisions for us, and we allow those decisions to trump the subjective choices of consumers, we abandon any pretense of a free market. In the process, we reduce consumer choice to a formalistic appraisal centering on technical features alone, notwithstanding that products are also desired for quality, price, service, convenience, and a host of other variables.

5. Antitrust law is wielded most often by rent-seeking businessmen and their political allies

Instead of focusing on new and better products, disgruntled rivals try to exploit the law—consorting with members of the legislature, their staffers, antitrust officials, and the best lobbying and public relations firms that money can buy. Soon enough, the targeted company responds in kind. Once upon a time, Microsoft conspicuously avoided Washington, D.C., politicking. No more. Look at their beefed up Washington offices. Meanwhile, America's entrepreneurial enclave, Silicon Valley, has become the home of billionaire businessmen who use political influence to bring down their competitors.

That agenda will destroy what it sets out to protect. Politicians are mostly order takers. So we will get the kind of government we ask for—including oppressive regulation. Citizens who are troubled by huge corporations dominating private markets should be even more concerned if those same corporations decide that political clout better serves their interest—politicizing competition to advance the private interests of favored competitors.

6. *Barriers to entry are created by government, not private businesses*

Under antitrust law, the proper test for government intervention is whether barriers to entry foreclose meaningful competition. But what is a "barrier"? When a company advertises, lowers prices, improves quality, adds features, or offers better service, it discourages rivals. But it cannot bar them. True barriers arise from government misbehavior, not from private power—special-interest legislation or a misconceived regulatory regimen that protects existing producers from competition. When government grants exclusive licenses to cable, electric, and telephone companies, monopolies are born and nurtured at public expense. When the legislature decrees targeted tax benefits, subsidies, insurance guarantees, and loans; or enacts tariffs and quotas to protect domestic companies from foreign rivals, that creates the same anti-competitive environment that the antitrust laws were meant to foreclose. The obvious answer—which has little to do with antitrust—is for government to stop creating those barriers to begin with.

7. *Antitrust will inevitably be used by unprincipled politicians as a political bludgeon*

The idea is to force conformity by "uncooperative" companies. Remember when President Nixon wanted to browbeat the three major TV networks, he used the threat of an antitrust suit to extort more favorable media coverage. On a tape released a few years ago, Nixon told his aide, Chuck Colson: "Our gain is more important than the economic gain. We do not give a goddamn about the economic gain. Our game here is solely political. . . . As far as screwing the networks, I'm very glad to do it." If Nixon were the only culprit, that would be bad enough. But former *New York Times* reporter David Burnham, in his 1996 book, *Abuse of Power*, shows that U.S. presidents from Kennedy through Clinton routinely demanded that the Justice Department bend the rules in pursuit of political ends. The threat of abusive public power is far greater than the threat of private monopoly.

8. A narrow definition of the "relevant market" can make any firm a "monopolist"

In the Microsoft case, for example, the Justice Department stacked the deck by defining all of Microsoft's rivals out of the market. Microsoft competes, so we were told, only against single-user desktop PCs that run on an Intel chip. Thus, Apple's market share did not count. Nor did the share of Sun Microsystems, many hand-held computers, sub-notebooks, set-top boxes, and other consumer electronics products, which are not Intel-based.

Economist Alan Reynolds estimates that Microsoft's real market share is closer to 65%. If that constitutes a monopoly, the Justice Department had better investigate Quicken, AOL, and Intel—each of which has a larger share than Microsoft. Yet those companies, like Microsoft, acquired market power by relying primarily on human intellect, which economist Julian Simon called the "ultimate resource." No company monopolizes ideas. The history of free enterprise is that better ideas mean better products, and better products win in the market.

More than two centuries ago, in the *Wealth of Nations*, Adam Smith observed that "People of the same trade seldom meet together . . . but the conversation ends in a conspiracy against the public or in some contrivance to raise prices." Coming from the father of laissez-faire capitalism, that warning has been cited repeatedly by antitrust advocates to justify all manner of interventionist mischief. Those same advocates conveniently omit Smith's next sentence: "It is impossible indeed to prevent such meetings, by any law which either could be executed, or would be consistent with liberty and justice."

Antitrust is bad law and bad economics. It deserves an ignominious burial—sooner rather than later.

Notes

Chapter 2

1. Fla. Stat. Ann. § 409.910 (1995).

2. The Florida Supreme Court intervened to ban suits that were already time-barred when the statute was enacted. *Agency for Health Care Admin. v. Associated Inds. of Fla., Inc.*, 678 So. 2d 1239 (Fla. 1996).

3. Ibid., p. 1254.

4. Fla. Exec. Order No. 95-109, March 28, 1995.

5. *Associated Inds. of Fla., Inc. v. Agency for Health Care Admin.*, Case No. 94-3128, Order Denying Defendants' Motion for Summary Judgment (Cir. Ct. for Leon County, May 23, 1995).

6. In order of filing date: Mississippi 5/94, Minnesota 8/94, West Virginia 9/94, Florida 2/95, Massachusetts 12/95, Louisiana 3/96, Texas 3/96, Maryland 5/96, Washington 6/96, Connecticut 7/96, Kansas 8/96, Arizona 8/96, Michigan 8/96, Oklahoma 8/96, New Jersey 9/96, Utah 9/96, Illinois 11/96, Iowa 11/96, New York 1/97, Hawaii 1/97, Wisconsin 2/97, Indiana 2/97, Alaska 4/97, Pennsylvania 4/97, Montana 5/97, Arkansas 5/97, Ohio 5/97, South Carolina 5/97, Missouri 5/97, New Mexico 5/97, Nevada 5/97, Vermont 5/97, New Hampshire 6/97, Colorado 6/97, Oregon 6/97. See http://www.library.ucsf.edu/tobacco/litigation/summary.html.

7. In an 88-page report completed in October 1996, an Alabama task force concluded that the legal arguments advanced by the state's attorney general are "at best weak and at worst bizarre"—an emphatic and perhaps surprising pronouncement coming from a state sometimes characterized as nirvana for tort plaintiffs. In a similar vein, Ohio's attorney general volunteered that "[m]any of the legal theories being used in the lawsuits are untested and unproven." See Bob Van Voris, "AGs' Claims Mere Smoke?" *National Law Journal*, April 28, 1997, p. A1.

8. On March 21, 1997, the attorneys general from 22 states announced a settlement with the Liggett Group, the smallest of the major tobacco companies with about 2% of industry sales. Liggett agreed to label its cigarette packages with a warning that "smoking is addictive"; pay the states and their private attorneys 25% of its pretax profits over the next 25 years; and disgorge documents allegedly showing that the industry knew its products were addictive, designed them to be that way, withheld that knowledge from consumers, and targeted minors with its ads. In return, the states agreed to drop their claims against Liggett (although there is considerable question whether the settlement can bind nonparticipants and future litigants). Cynics noted that the company's profitability is borderline, so the monetary payment could be minimal. Moreover, chief executive officer Bennett LeBow previously testified under oath that tobacco is not addictive. Some analysts think that his willingness to settle is mere posturing in order to attract a merger partner. See Milo Geyelin and Suein L. Hwang, "Liggett to Settle 22 States' Tobacco Suits," *Wall Street Journal*, March 21, 1997, p. A3.

9. See Robert L. Rabin, "A Sociolegal History of the Tobacco Tort Litigation," *Stanford Law Review* 44 (1992): 853.

10. *Carter v. Brown & Williamson Co.*, Case No. 95-934 (Fla. Cir. Ct. 1996).

11. "Tobacco Firm Held Not Liable in Smoker's Death," *Reuters*, May 5, 1997.

12. 15 U.S.C. §§ 1331-40.

13. Public Health Cigarette Smoking Act, 15 U.S.C. §§ 1331-40.

14. *Cipollone v. Liggett Group, Inc.*, 505 U.S. 504 (1992).

15. From 1966 through 1968, federal law required each package of cigarettes sold in the United States to contain a conspicuous label stating: "CAUTION: CIGARETTE SMOKING MAY BE HAZARDOUS TO YOUR HEALTH." Beginning in 1969, the mandatory label was revised to read: "WARNING: THE SURGEON GENERAL HAS DETERMINED THAT CIGARETTE SMOKING IS DANGEROUS TO YOUR HEALTH." With the Comprehensive Smoking Education Act of 1984, 15 U.S.C. § 1333, Congress adopted four still more explicit warning labels to be used on a rotating basis: (1) "Smoking Causes Lung Cancer, Heart Disease, Emphysema, and May Complicate Pregnancy." (2) "Quitting Smoking Now Greatly Reduces Serious Risks to Your Health." (3) "Smoking by Pregnant Women May Result in Fetal Injury, Premature Birth, and Low Birth Weight." (4) "Cigarette Smoke Contains Carbon Monoxide."

16. Suein L. Hwang, "Judge Upholds Law Letting Florida Sue Tobacco Industry," *Wall Street Journal*, June 19, 1995, p. B6.

17. See 42 U.S.C. § 1396; 42 C.F.R. § 430.0.

18. See, for example, *Harmelin v. Michigan*, 501 U.S. 957, 978 n. 9 (1991), in which Justice Scalia admonished that "it makes sense to scrutinize governmental action more closely when the State stands to benefit."

19. *Agency for Health Care Admin.*, 678 So. 2d at 1257.

20. See Edward Felsenthal, "Justices Won't Hear Philip Morris Appeal," *Wall Street Journal*, March 18, 1997, p. B13.

21. "Florida Sees August Trial Start in Tobacco Case," *Reuters*, March 17, 1997.

22. Milo Geyelin, "Tobacco Faces Year of Courtroom Drama," *Wall Street Journal*, February 10, 1997, p. B2.

23. Ibid.

24. John Gonzales, "Most Texans Oppose State's Tobacco Lawsuit, Poll Finds," *Fort Worth Star-Telegram*, June 30, 1996, p. B1.

25. Federalist Society, National Conference on Civil Justice and the Litigation Process, "Do the Merits and the Search for Truth Matter Any More?" September 12, 1996, transcript pp. 200–01.

26. Bryan A. Garner, ed., *Black's Law Dictionary*, abridged 6th ed. (St. Paul, Minn.: West Publishing Co., 1991), p. 38.

27. *Restatement (Second) of Torts* (St. Paul, Minn.: American Law Institute, 1965), § 402A, comment n.

28. See William W. Van Alstyne, "Denying Due Process in the Florida Courts: A Commentary on the 1994 Medicaid Third-Party Liability Act of Florida," *Florida Law Review* 46 (1994): 563, 576.

29. "States did not assume any of the risks of tobacco: they did not inhale." *Associated Inds. of Fla., Inc. v. Agency for Health Care Admin.*, Case No. 96-915, Brief of Respondents in Opposition to Petition for Writ of Certiorari (U.S. Supreme Ct., February 6, 1997), p. 15.

30. Remarks of Richard Scruggs, Federalist Society, National Conference on Civil Justice and the Litigation Process, "Do the Merits and the Search for Truth Matter Any More?" September 12, 1996, transcript p. 188.

31. *Associated Inds. of Fla., Inc. v. Agency for Health Care Admin.*, Case No. 96-915, Brief of Respondents in Opposition to Petition for Writ of Certiorari, pp. 16–17.

32. Ibid.

33. *Cipollone*, 505 U.S. at 513.

34. Milo Geyelin, "How RJR Won Its Latest Tobacco Case," *Wall Street Journal*, May 7, 1997, p. B1.

35. Ibid.

36. See, for example, John E. Calfee, "The Ghost of Cigarette Advertising Past," *Regulation*, November/December 1986, pp. 35–45.

37. See Amy Goldstein, "Experts Uncertain Why Black Youths Shunning Cigarettes," *Detroit News*, August 21, 1995.

38. Roberto Suro, "Clinton Plans Ad Blitz in Domestic Drug War," *Washington Post*, February 13, 1997, p. A1.

39. Michael J. Stewart, "The Effect of Advertising Bans on Tobacco Consumption in OECD Countries," *International Journal of Advertising* 12 (1993): 155–80.

40. Ibid.

41. Calfee.

42. Substance Abuse and Mental Health Services Administration, *Preliminary Estimates from the 1995 National Household Survey on Drug Abuse* (Washington: U.S. Department of Health and Human Services, 1996), p. 68.

43. Ibid., p. 99.

44. See Charley Reese, "No Rational or Legal Basis for States to Sue Tobacco Companies," *Orlando Sentinel*, September 5, 1996, p. A10.

45. John Harwood, "Virginia Voters to Face Historic Election Choice: Gubernatorial Candidate at Odds with Tobacco," *Wall Street Journal*, April 25, 1997, p. A16.

46. *Waugh v. Singletary*, Case No. 95-CVC-J-20, Defendant's Motion to Dismiss (D. Fla., October 4, 1995).

47. Ibid.

48. Richard Kluger, *Ashes to Ashes: America's Hundred-Year Cigarette War, the Public Health, and the Unabashed Triumph of Philip Morris* (New York: Alfred A. Knopf, 1996), p. 760.

49. See *Infusaid Corp. v. Intermedics Infusaid, Inc.*, 739 F.2d 661, 668 (1st Cir. 1984).

50. *Black's Law Dictionary*, p. 1058.

51. See, for example, *Dandridge v. Williams*, 397 U.S. 471 (1970) and *San Antonio Independent School Dist. v. Rodriguez*, 411 U.S. 1 (1973).

52. Kermit L. Hall, ed., *The Oxford Companion to the Supreme Court of the United States* (New York: Oxford University Press, 1992), p. 861.

53. Kluger, p. 15.

54. Ibid., 37–40.

55. *Austin v. State*, 101 Tenn. 562, 566 (1898).

56. Richard Doll and A. Bradford Hill, "Lung Cancer and Other Causes of Death in Relation to Smoking," *British Medical Journal* 2 (1956): 1071.

57. Remarks of Richard Scruggs, p. 188.

58. Milo Geyelin, "Florida Made, Gave Out Prison Cigarettes," *Wall Street Journal*, January 27, 1996.

59. Stephen Rothman, "Tobacco Industry Defense Move Curbed by Fla. Judge," *Reuters*, February 3, 1997.

60. "Third-Party Liability: Lawsuit Against Tobacco Firms Seems Hardly Worth the Effort," *Winter Haven News Chief*, February 24, 1995.

61. See "B.A.T. Plays Down Florida Fund Decision," *Reuters*, May 28, 1997. In late May 1997, for what may have been tactical rather than philosophic reasons, Florida's pension trustees ordered the state's portfolio managers to liquidate tobacco stockholdings.

62. *Associated Inds. of Fla., Inc. v. Agency for Health Care Admin.*, Case No. 96-915, Brief of Respondents in Opposition to Petition for Writ of Certiorari, p. 5.

63. *Congressional Quarterly*, 1996 CQ House Vote 233, Item Key 11734.

64. *Waugh v. Singletary*, Case No. 95-CVC-J-20 (D. Fla., July 11, 1995).

65. Bill McAllister, "Smoking by GIs Raises Liability Issue at the VA," *Washington Post*, April 24, 1997, p. A1.

66. Bruce Ingersoll, "Battle over Federal Aid for Tobacco Heats Up as Lawmakers Debate Issue," *Wall Street Journal*, April 25, 1997, p. A16.

67. McAllister.

68. Laurence Tribe, "Trial by Mathematics: Precision and Ritual in the Legal Process," *Harvard Law Review* 84 (1971): 1329, 1350.

69. W. Page Keeton, et al., *Prosser and Keeton on Torts*, 5th ed., (St. Paul, Minn.: West Publishing Co., 1984), § 41, p. 263. See also *Washington v. Davis*, 426 U.S. 229 (1976), and *Arlington Heights v. Metropolitan Housing Development Corp.*, 429 U.S. 252 (1977), holding that statistical proof, without more, is insufficient to establish discrimination for purposes of a constitutional challenge under the Equal Protection Clause.

70. Glenn G. Lammi, *Suits to Reimburse States for Public Medical Expenses: Creating a Dangerous Precedent for Trial Lawyers* (Washington: Washington Legal Foundation, 1995), p. 13.

71. Fla. Stat. Ann. § 409.910(9)–(9)(a) (1995).

72. *Agency for Health Care Admin. v. Associated Inds. of Fla., Inc.*, 678 So. 2d 1239 (Fla. 1996).

73. Milo Geyelin, "Antitobacco Suit Filed by Florida Is Sharply Limited," *Wall Street Journal*, September 18, 1996.

74. Ibid.

75. Michael Connor, "Tobacco Cos. Win Access to Medicaid Patients," *Reuters*, February 28, 1997.

76. Ibid.

77. According to the tobacco industry, claims fraud is rampant in Florida's Medicaid system. See Scott Gold, "Tobacco Industry Argues Medicaid Fraud in Florida," *South Florida Sun-Sentinel*, May 23, 1997.

78. *City and County of San Francisco v. Philip Morris, Inc.*, Case No. C-96-2090, Order, February 26, 1997, p. 12.

79. Ibid., p. 28.

80. "Around the Nation: Tobacco Industry Wins Round," *Washington Post*, February 15, 1997, p. A10.

81. Brown & Williamson Tobacco Corp., "Maryland Court Dismisses Major Parts of State Lawsuit Against Tobacco Industry," *PRNewswire*, May 21, 1997.

82. Federal Judicial Center, *Reference Manual on Scientific Evidence* (Washington: Government Printing Office, 1994), p. 157 (emphasis added).

83. Charley Reese, "No Rational or Legal Basis for States to Sue Tobacco Companies," *Orlando Sentinel*, September 5, 1996, p. A10.

84. Fla. Stat. Ann. § 409.910(9)(b) (1995).

85. Civil Justice Task Force, *Taxation Through Litigation: A Bad Way to Balance State Budgets* (Washington: American Legislative Exchange Council, 1995), p. 3.

86. Ibid.

87. See *Conley v. Boyle Drug Co.*, 570 So. 2d 275, 285 (Fla. 1990).

88. Ibid., p. 286.

89. Note, "Florida Enacts Market Share Liability for Smoking-Related Medicaid Expenditures," *Harvard Law Review* 108 (1994): 525, 529 n.28.

90. 42 U.S.C. § 1396; 42 C.F.R. § 430.0.

91. Civil Justice Task Force, p. 50.

92. Matt McKinney, "More States Expected to File Tobacco Lawsuits," *Minneapolis Star Tribune*, June 20, 1996, p. 16A.

93. Office of Technology Assessment, *Smoking-Related Deaths and Financial Costs* (Washington: Government Printing Office, 1985).

94. William G. Manning, et al., "The Taxes of Sin: Do Smokers and Drinkers Pay Their Way?" *Journal of the American Medical Association* 261 (March 1989): 1604–1609.

95. Jane G. Gravelle and Dennis Zimmerman, *Cigarette Taxes to Fund Health Care Reform: An Economic Analysis* (Washington: Congressional Research Service, 1994).

96. Manning et al., p. 1604.

97. Although premature death reduces the retirement benefits that the deceased would otherwise have received, it may also reduce the payroll taxes that he would have paid into the various retirement programs. Assuming the deceased would still have been employed had he not died, those lost tax receipts must be counted as a cost attributable to smoking. The same treatment is not appropriate in the case of income taxes, however. Benefits associated with income taxes—contrary to payroll taxes—are presumed to be linked to, and roughly concurrent with, the payment of the tax. Accordingly, any post-death lost income tax receipts would be offset by an equivalent reduction in benefit outlays.

98. Gravelle and Zimmerman.

99. W. Kip Viscusi, "Cigarette Taxation and the Social Consequences of Smoking," in James Poterba, ed., *Tax Policy and the Economy*, vol. 9 (Cambridge, Mass.: MIT Press, 1995), Table 5.

100. Ibid.

101. Ibid., p. 57.

102. Civil Justice Task Force, p. 5.

103. Viscusi, p. 52.

104. Manning et al., p. 1604.

105. See Michael Orey, "Fanning the Flames," *American Lawyer*, April 1996.

106. Carolyn Lochhead, "The Growing Power of Trial Lawyers," *Weekly Standard*, September 23, 1996, p. 21.

107. Ibid.

108. Ibid., p. 22.

109. Ibid., p. 23.

110. *McGraw v. American Tobacco Co.*, Civ. No. 94-C-1707 (Cir. Ct. Kanauha County, November 29, 1995).

111. Jack Deutsch, "McGraw Supporters May Profit from Suit," *Charleston Daily Mail*, August 18, 1994, p. 1B.

112. *McGraw v. American Tobacco Co.*, Civ. No. 94-C-1707, Memorandum in Opposition to Defendants' Joint Motion to Prohibit Prosecution of Action Due to Plaintiff's Unlawful Retention of Counsel (Cir. Ct. Kanauha County).

113. *Berger v. United States*, 295 U.S. 78, 88 (1935).

114. See Myron Levin and Henry Weinstein, "Legions of Lawyers Lead Charge in Tobacco War," *Los Angeles Times*, March 18, 1997; Saundra Torry and John Schwartz, "While Adversaries Negotiate, Legal Attacks on Cigarette Makers Step Up," *Washington Post*, June 1, 1997, p. A7.

115. Ibid.

116. Andrew Popper, "Tobacco's Black April," *Legal Times*, May 5, 1997, p. 23.

117. Milo Geyelin, "RJR's Tobacco Unit Wins a Big Victory: Jury Clears It of Blame in Smoker's Death," *Wall Street Journal*, May 6, 1997, p. A3.

118. Milo Geyelin, "How RJR Won Its Latest Tobacco Case."

119. Law offices of Stanley M. Rosenblatt, "Statewide Class Action Seeks Compensation for Florida Smokers Suffering from Medical Conditions Caused by Cigarette Smoking," *PRNewswire*, February 5, 1997.

120. Goodkind Labaton Rudoff & Sucharow LLP, "Early Trial Date Set for Lawsuits Against Tobacco Companies," *PRNewswire*, April 4, 1997.

121. See, for example, Fed. R. Civ. P. 23(a); Fla. R. Civ. P. 1.220(a).

122. See John C. Coffee Jr., "The Corruption of the Class Action," *Wall Street Journal*, September 7, 1994, p. A1.

123. In October 1996, the Supreme Court agreed to decide whether class participants can sue on their own if they are unhappy with the outcome of the class action and they were not permitted to opt out. See *Adams v. Robertson*, Case No. 95-1873. [Author's note: Subsequent to publication of the paper in which this chapter originally appeared, the Supreme Court changed its mind and decided not to review the case. The Court determined that the opt-out question had not been, and must first be, properly presented to the state's highest court. See *Adams v. Robertson*, 520 U.S. 83 (1997).]

124. At the federal level, the *Castano* case seems to have minimized any chance for a nationwide class of smoker-plaintiffs. Among the more difficult problems that a national class action would encounter is the potential for conflict among the laws of numerous jurisdictions. The *Castano* court indicated that it would make more sense to allow state courts to develop and apply their own law on a case-by-case basis. *Castano v. American Tobacco Co.*, 84 F.3d 734 (5th Cir. 1996).

125. Alix M. Freedman and Suein L. Hwang, "Philip Morris, RJR and Tobacco Plaintiffs Discuss a Settlement," *Wall Street Journal*, April 16, 1997, p. A1.

126. Alix M. Freedman and Suein L. Hwang, "Tobacco Firms Seek Curbs on Lawsuits," *Wall Street Journal*, May 7, 1997, p. A3.

127. *Coyne Beahm, Inc. v. United States Food & Drug Admin.*, Civ. No. 2:95CV00591 (M.D.N.C. April 25, 1997).

128. On May 28, 1997, the Federal Trade Commission, voting three-to-two, re-enlisted in the war against tobacco. In an upcoming hearing before an administrative law judge, the commission will seek an order barring R. J. Reynolds from using "Joe Camel" in ads accessible to children. See "FTC Votes to Bar RJR from Using Joe Camel Ads," *Reuters*, May 28, 1997. If the Commission prevails at the administrative level, its actions will undoubtedly be challenged in court on both statutory and constitutional grounds.

129. *Central Hudson Gas & Electric Corp. v. Public Service Comm'n*, 447 U.S. 557 (1980).

130. *Bolger v. Youngs Drug Prods. Corp.*, 463 U.S. 60, 73-74 (1983) ("level of discourse . . . cannot be limited to that which would be suitable for a sandbox").

131. *44 Liquormart, Inc. v. Rhode Island*, 116 S. Ct. 1495 (1996).

132. Edward Felsenthal and Yumiko Ono, "Outdoor Ads for Tobacco Can Be Curbed," *Wall Street Journal*, April 29, 1997, p. B1.

133. Judge Osteen's holding rests on the controversial *Chevron* doctrine that commands courts to be deferential when reviewing an administrative agency's interpretation of an ambiguous statute that Congress has entrusted to its overview. *Chevron U.S.A. Inc. v. Natural Resources Defense Council Inc.*, 467 U.S. 837 (1984). In this instance, the industry argued without success that the FDA itself had disclaimed jurisdiction over tobacco until recently, that various statutes requiring warning labels on cigarettes preempted the Food, Drug and Cosmetic Act, and that the question whether the FDA should regulate tobacco was to be resolved by Congress and not by the agency. See Saundra Torry, "Tobacco, FDA Count Down to Appeals Court Face-Off," *Washington Post*, May 5, 1997, p. 7. [Author's note: Subsequent to publication of the paper in which this chapter originally appeared, the Supreme Court affirmed the U.S. Court of Appeals for the Fourth Circuit, which had overruled Judge Osteen, holding that Congress had not granted the FDA jurisdiction to regulate tobacco products. See *Food and Drug Administration v. Brown & Williamson Tobacco Corp.*, 529 U.S. 120 (2000).]

134. Andrew Popper, "Tobacco's Black April," *Legal Times*, May 5, 1997, p. 23.

135. Letter from David A. Kessler to Scott D. Ballin, February 25, 1994.

136. Kelly D. Brownell, "A 'Sin-Tax' on High-Fat Foods May Be Needed," *Journal American*, December 17, 1994.

137. Robert Bolt, *A Man for All Seasons* (New York: Vintage Books, 1990), pp. 65–66.

Chapter 3

1. Paul M. Barrett, "HUD May Join Assault on Gun Makers," *Wall Street Journal*, July 28, 1999, p. A3.

2. See Robert A. Levy, "Tobacco Medicaid Litigation: Snuffing Out the Rule of Law," Cato Institute Policy Analysis no. 275, June 20, 1997.

3. Quoted in Fox Butterfield, "New Orleans Takes on Gun Manufacturers in Lawsuit," *NY Times of the Web*, November 4, 1998.

4. Gail Appleson, "Two More Cities Sue Gun Makers," *Washington Post*, January 28, 1999, p. A6.

5. Butterfield.

6. "Remarks of Mayor Richard M. Daley—Gun Lawsuit Press Conference," November 12, 1998, available at www.ci.chi.il.us/Mayor/Speeches/GunLawSuit.html.

7. See, for example, Susan Kimmelman, "Stick 'Em Up; Suing Gunmakers for the Cost of Urban Violence," *In These Times*, July 26, 1998, p. 13.

8. See Carolyn Lochhead, "The Growing Power of Trial Lawyers," *Weekly Standard*, September 23, 1996, p. 21.

9. *Berger v. United States*, 295 U.S. 78, 88 (1935).

10. The Clinton administration supported the tobacco bill introduced by Sen. John McCain (R-AZ). See S. 1414, 105th Cong. (1997) (A bill to reform and restructure the processes by which tobacco products are manufactured, marketed, and distributed, to prevent the use of tobacco products by minors, to redress the adverse health effects of tobacco use, and for other purposes).

11. See Eugene Volokh, Testimony on the Second Amendment before the Senate Judiciary Committee, Subcommittee on the Constitution, Federalism and Property Rights, September 23, 1998.

12. Robert L. Cottrol, "Gun Control Is Racist, Sexist & Classist," *American Enterprise*, September-October 1999, p. 58, at 60.

13. *United States v. Miller*, 307 U.S. 174 (1939).

14. Ibid. at 179.

15. Nelson Lund, "The Ends of Second Amendment Jurisprudence: Firearms Disabilities and Domestic Violence Restraining Orders," *Texas Review of Law & Politics* 4, no. 1 (Fall 1999): 157, at 171.

16. Sanford Levinson, "The Embarrassing Second Amendment," *Yale Law Journal* 99 (December 1989): 637.

17. Laurence H. Tribe and Akhil Reed Amar, "Well-Regulated Militias and More," *New York Times*, October 28, 1999, p. A31.

18. See *United States v. Emerson*, 46 F. Supp. 2d 598 (N.D. Tex. Apr. 7, 1999). [Author's note: Subsequent to publication of the paper in which this chapter originally appeared, the U.S. Court of Appeals for the Fifth Circuit affirmed that the Second Amendment secures an individual right to keep and bear arms. Nonetheless, said the appellate court, that right is not absolute and the restriction imposed on Emerson was reasonable in light of the possible threat to his estranged wife. See *United States v. Emerson*, 270 F.3d 203 (5th Cir. 2001), *cert. denied*, 536 U.S. 907 (2002).]

19. Ibid., 601.

20. David B. Kopel and Richard E. Gardiner, "The Sullivan Principles: Protecting the Second Amendment from Civil Abuse," *Seton Hall Legislative Journal* 19 (1995): 739.

21. Ibid.

22. *Emerson* at 601.

23. See Volokh.

24. See Lund, p. 176.

25. Quoted in Raymond N. Haynes, "Second Amendment at Stake in Appellate Case," *Los Angeles Metropolitan News-Enterprise*, June 27, 2000, p. 9.

26. See Lund, p. 175.

27. Ibid.

28. *United States v. Emerson*, U.S. Court of Appeals for the Fifth Circuit, Case No. 99-10331 (1999), amicus brief, Academics for the Second Amendment.

29. Paul M. Barrett, "HUD May Join Assault on Gun Makers," *Wall Street Journal*, July 28, 1999, p. A3.

30. Ibid.

31. Quoted in Anne Gearan, "White House Preparing Gun Suit," *Associated Press*, December 8, 1999.

32. Ibid.

33. Quoted in Howard Blum, "Reluctant Don," *Vanity Fair*, September 1999, p. 148, at 165.

34. See Richard A. Epstein, "Lawsuits Aimed at Guns Probably Won't Hit Crime," *Wall Street Journal*, December 9, 1999, p. A26.

35. See Andrew Stern, "Judge Dismisses Chicago Suit against Gun Industry," *Reuters*, September 15, 2000.

36. *City of Bloomington v. Westinghouse Electric Corp.*, 891 F.2d 611 (7th Cir. 1989).

37. See, for example, *New York Eskimo Pie Corp. v. Rataj*, 73 F.2d 184, 185 (3d Cir. 1934) (general test for liability in Pennsylvania is whether person of ordinary intelligence would have foreseen injury as natural and probable outcome of conduct).

38. John R. Lott Jr., "Suits Targeting Gun Makers Are Off the Mark," *Wall Street Journal*, March 2, 1999, p. A18.

39. Devon Spurgeon and Paul M. Barrett, "Operation Gunsmoke, Touted as a Big Deal, Makes a Small Mark," *Wall Street Journal*, April 6, 2000, p. A1.

40. Kopel and Gardiner, pp. 762–63.

41. John R. Lott Jr., "Gun Laws Can Be Dangerous, Too," *Wall Street Journal*, May 12, 1999, p. A22.

42. Peter J. Boyer, "Big Guns," *New Yorker*, May 17, 1999, p. 54, at 62.

43. Cited in Edward Walsh, "Clinton Plans Gun Initiative," *Washington Post*, January 18, 2000, p. A2.

44. Fox Butterfield, "Limits on Power and Zeal Hamper Firearms Agency," *New York Times*, July 22, 1999, p. A1.

45. Quoted in ibid.

46. Cited in "Treasury Makes Case for Gun Show Clampdown," *Reuters*, June 21, 2000.

47. Boyer, p. 62.

48. Saundra Torry, "Federal-Local Gun Control Venture Stymied by Success," *Washington Post*, September 11, 1999, p. A1.

49. Ibid.

50. I thank George Mason University law professor Dan Polsby for this insight.

51. "Guns in Court," Editorial, *Washington Post*, October 12, 1999, p. A18.

52. *Wasylow v. Glock, Inc.*, No. 94-11073-DPW, slip op. (D. Mass. April 4, 1996).

53. *Hamilton v. Accu-Tek*, 935 F. Supp. 1307, 1323 (E.D.N.Y. August 12, 1996).

54. Matt Labash, "Lawyers, Guns, and Money," *Weekly Standard*, February 1, 1999, pp. 25–29.

55. Jake Tapper, "City Slickers," *Salon News*, July 13, 1999.

56. Ibid. See also Vanessa O'Connell and Paul M. Barrett, "Unloading Old Police Guns: More Cities Ban Trade-Ins and Resales," *Wall Street Journal*, November 10, 1999, p. B1.

57. Vanessa O'Connell and Paul M. Barrett, "Cities Suing Gun Firms Have a Weak Spot: They're Suppliers Too," *Wall Street Journal*, August 16, 1999, p. A1.

58. Other suits have been allowed to proceed in part, but none has prevailed on final judgment. In 1999, Atlanta survived a motion to dismiss its design defect claim. The following year, New Orleans also survived full dismissal, as did Cleveland, Wayne County (Michigan), and San Diego. In April 2001, however, the Louisiana Supreme Court threw out the New Orleans claim, citing state law that bans litigation by cities against the gun industry. See "Supreme Court: State Can Block New Orleans from Suing Gun Makers," *Associated Press*, April 3, 2001.

59. Quoted in "Court Rejects Cincinnati Suit Against Gun Industry," *Reuters*, October 7, 1999.

60. Quoted in Paul M. Barrett, "Judge Dismisses Cincinnati's Gun-Industry Suit," *Wall Street Journal*, October 8, 1999, p. B11.

61. Paul M. Barrett, "Florida Judge Dismisses Suit Against Gun Makers," *Wall Street Journal*, December 14, 1999, p. B15.

62. Quoted in "Florida Appeals Court Rejects Gun Suit," *Reuters*, February 23, 2001.

63. Andrew Stern, "Judge Dismisses Chicago Suit against Gun Industry," Reuters, September 15, 2000.

64. Quoted in Shannon P. Duffy, "Philly Loses Its Gun Maker Suit," *National Law Journal*, January 8, 2001, p. A4.

65. "Colt Exiting Consumer Handgun Business," *Reuters*, October 11, 1999.

66. Paul M. Barrett and Alexei Barrionuevo, "Handgun Makers Recoil as Industry Shakes Out," *Wall Street Journal*, September 20, 1999, p. B1.

67. Gary Fields, "For Smith & Wesson, Blanks Instead of a Magic Bullet," *Wall Street Journal*, August 24, 2000, p. A24.

68. See Edward Walsh and David A. Vise, "U.S., Gunmaker Strike a Deal," *Washington Post*, March 18, 2000, p. A1; Paul M. Barrett, "Smith & Wesson Rivals Face Antitrust Probe," *Wall Street Journal*, March 31, 2000, p. B18. New York, Chicago, and Boston stated that they would not dismiss their litigation against Smith & Wesson. See Sharon Walsh, "Gun Industry Views Pact as Threat to Its Unity," *Washington Post*, March 18, 2000, p. A10. Subsequently, Boston announced that its lawsuit had been settled. See "Boston, Smith & Wesson Settle Suit," *Associated Press*, December 12, 2000.

69. Walsh and Vise. On April 13, 2000, Smith & Wesson issued a clarification—disputed by lawyers for the settling cities—regarding the scope of background checks. Smith & Wesson insisted that checks were required only for its weapons, not for those of other manufacturers, and that checks at gun shows applied only to licensed dealers, not to private citizens. See "Smith & Wesson, Government Reaffirm Settlement," *Washington Post*, April 14, 2000, p. A7.

70. Alice Ann Love, "Smith & Wesson OKs Safety Locks," *Associated Press*, March 17, 2000.

71. Walsh and Vise.

72. Love.

73. Ibid.

74. "Agreement Between Smith & Wesson and the Departments of Treasury and Housing and Urban Development, Local Governments and States," March 18, 2000, available at www.hud.gov/pressrel/gunagree.html.

75. Love.

76. Sharon Walsh.

77. Edward Walsh and Helen Dewar, "Government Coalition to Try to Pressure Gunmakers," *Washington Post*, March 23, 2000, p. A8.

78. Alan Fram, "House Votes Affect Gun Agreement," *Associated Press*, June 21, 2000.

79. Fields.

80. "Gun Maker to Suspend Factory Lines," *Associated Press*, June 13, 2000.

81. Lisa Richwine, "Gunmakers File Suit against U.S., States, Mayors," *Reuters*, April 26, 2000.

82. Fields.

83. Walsh and Dewar.

84. "Gunmakers Drop Suit against HUD," *Washington Post*, January 6, 2001, p. A12.

85. Barrett, "Smith & Wesson Rivals Face Antitrust Probe."

86. Quoted in Peter Slevin and Sharon Walsh, "Conn. Subpoenas Firms in Gun Antitrust Probe," *Washington Post*, March 31, 2000, p. A2.

87. H. Sterling Burnett, "Making Guns Safe for Lawyers," *Washington Times*, January 25, 1999, p. A19.

88. John R. Lott Jr., "Will Suing Gunmakers Endanger Lives?" *Chicago Tribune*, November 17, 1998, p. 19.

89. Kathleen Maguire and Ann L. Pastore, eds., *Sourcebook of Criminal Justice Statistics* (Washington, D.C.: Bureau of Justice Statistics, 1997). Cited in H. Sterling Burnett, "Suing Gun Manufacturers: Hazardous to Our Health," National Center for Policy Analysis Policy Report No. 223, March 1999, p. 7.

90. "Concealed Weapons," *Las Vegas Review-Journal*, June 6, 1997, p. B16.

91. Lott, "Will Suing Gunmakers Endanger Lives?"

92. Jonathan Rauch, "And Don't Forget Your Gun," *National Journal*, March 19, 1999.

93. Ibid.

94. Gun Owners Foundation, "Firearms Fact-Sheet (1999)," available at www.gunowners.org/fs9901.htm.

95. Rauch.

96. John R. Lott Jr., *More Guns, Less Crime: Understanding Crime and Gun Control Laws* (Chicago: University of Chicago Press, 1998), p. 51.

97. Quoted in Elizabeth A. Palmer, "House Votes to Expand Federal Judges' Gun Rights, Use of Cameras in Court," *CQ Weekly*, May 27, 2000, p. 1277.

98. "Gun Control: Less Protection, More Crime," *Florida Times Union*, April 7, 1999, p. B6. See also David B. Kopel, *The Samurai, the Mountie, and the Cowboy* (Buffalo, N.Y.: Prometheus Books, 1992), pp. 193–232.

99. John R. Lott Jr., "Gun Control Advocates Purvey Deadly Myths," *Wall Street Journal*, November 11, 1998, p. A22. See also Kopel, *The Samurai, the Mountie, and the Cowboy*, pp. 233–56, 278–302.

100. Lott, "Gun Control Advocates Purvey Deadly Myths."

101. Massad Ayoob, "Arm Teachers to Stop School Shootings," *Wall Street Journal*, May 21, 1999, A12.

102. Ann Coulter, "The Other Side of the Gun Issue," *Universal Press Syndicate*, August 20, 1999.

103. Ibid.

104. Paul M. Barrett, "In Gun Debate, Both Sides Simplify Data to Make a Case," *Wall Street Journal*, May 27, 1999, p. B1.

105. Dan Polsby, *Firearms and Crime* (Oakland, CA: Independent Institute, 1997).

106. Barrett, "In Gun Debate, Both Sides Simplify Data to Make a Case."

107. Cited in David B. Kopel, "Guns, Germs, and Science: Public Health Approaches to Gun Control," *Journal of the Medical Association of Georgia* 84 (June 1995): 271.

108. Kopel and Gardiner, pp. 747–48.

109. John R. Lott Jr., draft of an open letter to members of Congress, June 3, 1999.

110. Quoted in ibid.

111. Ibid.

112. Robert L. Cottrol, "Gun Control Is Racist, Sexist & Classist," pp. 58–60.

113. Gregory P. Kane, "NAACP Gets Good, Bad Marks," *Richmond Times-Dispatch*, August 15, 1999, p. F3.

114. Quoted in ibid.

115. John R. Lott Jr., "More Gun Controls? They Haven't Worked in the Past," *Wall Street Journal*, June 17, 1999, p. A26.

116. Ibid.

117. Cited in Gary Fields, "Gun Conundrum: More on Streets, Fewer Incidents," *Wall Street Journal*, December 11, 2000, p. B1.

118. Jeff Jacoby, "Would We Care About Buford Furrow If He Hadn't Used a Gun?" *Boston Globe*, August 23, 1999.

119. "Nation in Brief," *Washington Post*, April 7, 2000, p. A23.

120. Cited in Vanessa O'Connell and Paul M. Barrett, "Bill to Ban Police from Gun Trade-Ins for Discounts Is Introduced in Congress," *Wall Street Journal*, November 19, 1999, p. A10.

121. "Gun-Related Death Rate Plummets," *Associated Press*, November 19, 1999.

122. Cited in June Kronholz, "School Firearm Expulsions Dropped in '97–'98," *Wall Street Journal*, August 11, 1999, p. A4.

123. Cited in "Some Frequently Overlooked Facts in Gun Policy Discussions," Independence Institute, Issue Backgrounder no. 99-V, November 9, 1999.

124. "The President's Shift on Guns," Editorial, *Washington Post*, January 31, 2000, p. A18.

125. George Will, "Handguns and Hired Guns," *Washington Post*, January 24, 1999, p. B7.

126. Quoted in Barrett, "Judge Dismisses Cincinnati's Gun-Industry Suit."

127. Kopel and Gardiner, p. 763.

128. Ibid.

129. Paul M. Barrett, "'Smart' Guns Trigger a Debate," *Wall Street Journal*, January 27, 2000, p. B1.

130. Quoted in ibid.

131. Quoted in John F. Harris, "Clinton and Hollywood: A Double Bill," *Washington Post*, May 17, 1999, p. C1.

132. Harris.

133. Quoted in Joe Carroll, "Six Children Shot in Zoo Gunfight," *Irish Times*, April 25, 2000, p. 11.

134. Paul M. Barrett and Vanessa O'Connell, "White House and Gun Industry May Discover Some Talking Points to Reach Deal on Lawsuit," *Wall Street Journal*, December 13, 1999, p. A36.

135. Caroline E. Mayer, "Safety Standards Sought after Gun Locks Fail Test," *Washington Post*, February 7, 2001, p. A1.

136. Josh Sugarmann, "Loaded Logic: Making Guns Smart Won't Stop Killings like the One in Michigan," *Washington Post*, March 5, 2000, p. B2. In December 1999, Colt announced that its iColt smart gun project was "on hold." Concurrently, SIG Swiss Industrial Company Holding announced the introduction of its smart gun, equipped with a personal locking system, which was expected to sell for about $950. See Vanessa O'Connell, "Swiss Company Is Set to Market a 'Smart Gun,'" *Wall Street Journal*, December 13, 1999, p. A36.

137. The National Center for Health Statistics reports 17,566 suicides, 13,522 homicides, and 981 accidents out of 32,436 firearms deaths in 1997. Cited in "Some Frequently Overlooked Facts in Gun Policy Discussions."

138. Sugarmann.

139. Barbara Vobejda and Sharon Walsh, "In Many Crimes, Trail Leads to a Tiny Fraction of Stores," *Washington Post*, June 8, 1999, p. A1.

140. Morgan O. Reynolds, "Off Target with Gun Controls," National Center for Policy Analysis, Brief Analysis no. 294, June 11, 1999.

141. Lott, "Gun Laws Can Be Dangerous, Too."

142. Edward Walsh, "At Shows, Firepower with No Questions Asked," *Washington Post*, May 18, 1999, p. A1.

143. Quoted in ibid.

144. Lott, "Gun Laws Can Be Dangerous, Too."

145. Cited in Reynolds.

146. Cited in "Treasury Makes Case for Gun Show Clampdown," *Reuters*, June 21, 2000.

147. Jo Becker, "Md. Activists Seek Tight Restrictions on Gun Shows," *Washington Post*, February 18, 2001, p. C1. Meanwhile, a federal appeals court ruled in 1997 that Santa Clara's ban on sales at a county fairground was an unconstitutional suppression of truthful speech about a legal product. Prohibiting sales at shows but not elsewhere would do nothing to curb overall availability, said the court. Ibid.

148. Quoted in ibid.

149. "Gun Vote May Haunt Republicans," *Morning Call*, June 24, 1999, p. A16.

150. Eric Pianin and Juliet Eilperin, "House Defeats Gun Control Bill; Angry Democrats, Republicans Blame Each Other for Stalemate," *Washington Post*, June 19, 1999, p. A1.

151. Declan McCullagh, "FBI's Gun Check Full of Bugs," *Wired News*, June 21, 2000.

152. Lott, "Gun Laws Can Be Dangerous, Too."

153. Quoted in Guy Gugliotta, "Brady Law's Effect Is Discounted," *Washington Post*, August 2, 2000, p. A1.

154. Ibid.

155. William Claiborne, "Rampage Suspect Bought Guns from Street Dealer," *Washington Post*, July 7, 1999, p. A3.

156. David B. Ottaway and Barbara Vobejda, "Gun Control's Limited Aim," *Washington Post*, September 19, 1999, p. A1.

157. "The Senate Misfires," Editorial, *Orange County Register*, May 23, 1999, p. G2.

158. "Dreams Destroyed: Adults Must End the Gun Violence That Is Killing Our Children," Ethnic Newswatch, *Emerge* 11, no. 8 (June 30, 2000): 56.

159. "ATF Traces Guns Used in Shooting," *Associated Press*, February 6, 2001.

160. Michael A. Fletcher and Sharon Waxman, "Boasts to Friends Went Unbelieved," *Washington Post*, March 6, 2001, p. A1.

161. See John J. Miller and Ramesh Ponnuru, "California's Tragedy," *Washington Bulletin: National Review's Internet Update*, March 6, 2000, available at www.national review.com. See also "No Easy Fixes," Editorial, *Wall Street Journal*, March 7, 2001, p. A22.

162. See Jeff Jacobs, "The Jock as a Target," *Hartford Courant*, April 26, 1999, p. C1.

163. Remarks of J. Harvie Wilkinson, chief judge, U.S. Court of Appeals, 4th Circuit, at the Federalist Society conference, "Did the Law Cause Columbine?" October 1999, Washington, D.C.

164. Quoted in Charles Babington, "President Backs Gun Registration," *Washington Post*, June 5, 1999, p. A1.

165. Quoted in David B. Kopel and James Winchester, "Unfair and Unconstitutional: The New Federal Juvenile Crime and Gun Control Proposals," Independence Institute, No. 3-99, June 3, 1999, available at http://i2i.org/suptdocs/crime/unfair.htm.

166. Robert B. Reich, "Smoking Guns," *American Prospect*, January 17, 2000, p. 64.

Chapter 4

1. See David Segal, "After Tobacco Success, Lawyers Pick Gun Fight," *Washington Post*, January 5, 1999, p. A1.

2. Bob Van Voris, "Gun Cases Use Tobacco Know-How: The Sequel," *National Law Journal*, December 7, 1998, p. A1.

3. Saundra Torry, "Lead Paint Could Be Next Big Legal Target," *Washington Post*, June 10, 1999, p. A1.

4. See Milo Geyelin, "Former Makers of Lead Paint Are Sued by Rhode Island for Child Health Care Costs," *Wall Street Journal*, October 13, 1999, p. A3.

5. Mary Flood, "State Looming as Key Ground in Legal Fight over Lead Paint," *Houston Chronicle*, May 8, 2001.

6. Editorial, "Lead Paint and Lawsuits," *Washington Post*, April 11, 2001, p. A26.

7. Wayne Slater, "AG's Office Says Donor Not an Issue; Cornyn Still Reviewing Rhode Island Suit against Lead-Paint Manufacturers," *Dallas Morning News*, April 17, 2001, p. 17A.

8. Flood.

9. Rachell Zoll, "Judge Allows State to Sue Lead Paint Industry," *Associated Press*, April 2, 2001.

10. Geyelin.

11. See *Skipworth v. Lead Indus. Ass'n*, 690 A.2d 169, 171–73 (Pa. 1997); *Brenner v. American Cyanamid*, 699 N.Y.S.2d 848, 849 (N.Y. App. Div. 1999); *Santiago v. Sherwin Williams Co.*, 3 F.3d 546, 550–51 (1st Cir. 1993); *Philadelphia v. Lead Indus. Ass'n*, 994 F.2d 112, 123–27 (3rd Cir. 1993); *Jefferson v. Lead Indus. Ass'n*, 106 F.3d 1245 (5th Cir. 1997).

12. Editorial, "Suing the Wrong People," *Providence Journal-Bulletin*, June 21, 1999, p. 4B.

13. *Sindell v. Abbott Laboratories*, 607 P.2d 924 (Cal. 1980).

14. *Brenner v. American Cyanamid*, 699 N.Y.S.2d at 854.

Chapter 5

1. Martin F. Connor, "Taming the Mass Tort Monster," BRIEFLY . . . Perspectives on Legislation, Regulation, and Litigation 4, no. 10 (October 2000): 4.

2. See Tresa Baldas, "Verdicts Swelling from Big to Bigger," *National Law Journal*, November 25, 2002, pp. A1, A6.

3. David Hechler, "Study Sees Rise in Cost of Tort System. Is It Right?" *National Law Journal*, December 22, 2003, p. 12.

4. Center for Legal Policy, *Trial Lawyers Inc.* (New York: Manhattan Institute, 2003), p. 2.

5. Hechler, "Study Sees Rise in Cost of Tort System," p. 12.

6. *Trial Lawyers Inc.*, p. 5.

7. See, for example, Walter K. Olson, *The Rule of Lawyers: How the New Litigation Elite Threatens America's Rule of Law* (New York: St. Martin's, 2003); Catherine Crier, *The Case against Lawyers* (New York: Broadway Books, 2002); and Philip K. Howard, *The Death of Common Sense: How Law Is Suffocating America* (New York: Warner Books, 1994).

8. *Gibbons v. Ogden*, 9 Wheat. 1, 224 (1824) (Johnson, J., concurring in the judgment).

9. Ibid. at 231.

10. 123 S. Ct. 1513 (2003).

11. Class action reform is a third procedural change that we would support at the federal level. We exclude that important topic from this paper only because Cato Institute senior fellow Mark Moller will soon be publishing a Policy Analysis devoted exclusively to that subject.

12. Help Efficient, Accessible, Low-cost, Timely Healthcare (HEALTH) Act of 2003, H.R. 5, 108th Cong., 1st sess., March 13, 2003.

13. Juliet Eilperin, "House Struggles to Find Its Place on Hill; Feeling Ignored, Members Say Most High-Profile Issues Are Decided in Senate," *Washington Post*, April 4, 2003, p. A4.

14. Air Transportation Safety and System Stabilization Act of 2001, Pub. L. No. 107-42 (2001), codified at 49 U.S.C. § 40101 (2003).

15. Bipartisan Patient Protection Act, H.R. 2563, 107th Cong., 1st sess., August 2, 2001; S. 1052, 107th Cong., 1st sess., June 29, 2001.

16. See *United States v. Lopez*, 514 U.S. 549 (1995).

17. Betsy J. Grey, "The New Federalism Jurisprudence and National Tort Reform," *Washington and Lee Law Review* 59 (2002): 477 and accompanying footnotes.

18. Ibid. Currently, under 28 U.S.C. § 1332 (2002), federal courts can exercise "diversity jurisdiction" over litigation even if state legal questions are at issue, but only when each and every plaintiff is from a different state than each and every defendant, and more than $75,000 per plaintiff is in dispute.

19. Grey, p. 477.

20. Ibid.

21. U.S. Const. Art. I, § 8, cl. 3.

22. See Ronald D. Rotunda and John E. Nowak, *Treatise on Constitutional Law: Substance and Procedure,* vol. 1, 3rd ed. (St. Paul: West Group, 1999), § 4.8.

23. *Lopez* at 562–63.

24. *United States v. Morrison,* 529 U.S. 598, 614 (2000).

25. See Gene Healy and Robert A. Levy, "Federalism under the Gun," *Human Rights* 29 (Fall 2002): 24.

26. According to a Department of Justice study, 31.9% of all state tort trials in the nation's 75 largest counties involved automobile accidents. Carol J. DeFrances and Marika F. X. Litras, *Civil Trial Cases and Verdicts in Large Counties* (Washington: Bureau of Justice Statistics, 1999), p. 2.

27. Public choice problems often arise when money is transferred from "the many" to "the few." Those transfers provoke more intense support from the few who reap the benefits than they do opposition from the many who bear the burden. As a result, inefficient transfers from the many to the few typify public policy in mass democracies. See James M. Buchanan and Gordon Tullock, *The Calculus of Consent: Logical Foundations of Constitutional Democracy* (Ann Arbor: University of Michigan Press, 1965), pp. 31–39.

28. *Batson v. Kentucky,* 476 U.S. 79, 88 (1986) (racial bias in jury selection violates Equal Protection Clause).

29. *Respondeat superior* holds an employer vicariously liable for negligent behavior by an employee while on the job. *Hern v. Nichols,* 91 Eng. Rep. 256 (Ex. 1708).

30. See Neal Miller, "An Empirical Study of Forum Choices in Removal Cases under Diversity and Federal Question Jurisdiction," *American University Law Review* 41 (1992): 369, 408–9 (attorneys responding to a survey indicated that out-of-state status was more frequently the cause of jury bias than corporate status or type of business); and Alexander Tabarrok and Eric Helland, "Court Politics: The Political Economy of Tort Awards," *Journal of Law and Economics* 42 (1999): 157, 161–64.

31. For a summary of state tort reform laws, see American Tort Reform Association, "Tort Reform Record," December 2003, www.atra.org/files.cgi/7668_Record12-03.pdf.

32. Ibid.

33. Ibid.

34. See, for example, *Osborne v. McMasters*, 41 N.W. 543 (Minn. 1889) (early product liability suit against a local apothecary, who had mislabeled a drug, resulting in poisoning of the victim). See also Michael I. Krauss, "Product Liability and Game Theory: One More Trip to the Choice-of-Law Well," *Brigham Young University Law Review* (2002): 759, 772–84 and accompanying footnotes.

35. See Thomas J. Kuhn, *The Structure of Scientific Revolutions* (Chicago: University of Chicago Press, 1970).

36. See Theodore Eisenberg, "Judicial Decisionmaking in Federal Products Liability Cases, 1978–1997," *DePaul Law Review* 49 (1999): 323, 326. ("Plaintiffs, their lawyers, and most other observers of the legal system believe the jury to be more sympathetic to plaintiffs, on average, than the judge. Plaintiffs therefore route a weaker set of cases to juries.")

37. The retailer may also be sued, but recovery is typically against the manufacturer. Because the retailer is usually local, its inclusion as a codefendant may be designed to foreclose federal court jurisdiction, which requires that all plaintiffs reside in a different state than all defendants. See, for example, *Guerrero v. Gen. Motors Corp.*, 892 F. Supp. 165, 166 (S.D. Tex. 1995).

38. This is true even for automobiles; most driving almost certainly takes place near one's home and in one's state of residence.

39. Commonsense Consumption Act of 2003, S. 1428, 108th Cong, 1st sess., July 17, 2003.

40. H.R. 339, 108th Cong., 1st sess., January 27, 2003.

41. See Michael I. Krauss, "Suits against 'Big Fat' Tread on Basic Tort Liability Principles," *Washington Legal Foundation Legal Backgrounder* 18, no. 6 (March 14, 2003).

42. *Pelman v. McDonald's Corp.*, 2003 WL22052778, Slip Op. (S.D.N.Y. 2003).

43. Emily Johns, "Living XX-Large: Pending Bill Fights Suits Filed against the Food Industry," *Minneapolis Star Tribune*, February 9, 2004, p. A6. Ironically, the Big Daddy settlement allowed customers with receipts to receive a refund for ice cream they had purchased—or two free cups of Big Daddy ice cream.

44. Krauss, "Suits against 'Big Fat' Tread on Basic Tort Liability Principles."

45. One settlement did arise when a group of vegetarian and Hindu students sued McDonald's for not publicizing the beef flavoring in its French fries. See Sandra Guy, "24 Groups to Share $10 Mil. McD's Vegetarian Award," *Chicago Sun-Times*, May 20, 2003, p. 49. Allegedly, McDonald's misrepresented that the fries were cooked in 100% vegetable oil. The plaintiffs received a whopping $10 million, with another $2.5 million going to their lawyers. That litigation had nothing to do, however, with the obesity claims that have been the central focus of the suits that the McConnell and Keller bills would ban.

46. The American Tort Reform Association has characterized 13 jurisdictions as "judicial hellholes." See www.sickoflawsuits.org/news/03_11_06.cfm; and American Tort Reform Association, "Bringing Justice to Judicial Hellholes," www.atra.org/reports/hellholes/report.pdf.

47. Lawsuits involving a manufacturing defect (e.g., a gun explodes when fired and injures its user) are traditional tort actions that do not raise novel or bizarre legal theories.

48. See Michael I. Krauss, *Fire and Smoke: Government Lawsuits and the Rule of Law* (Oakland, CA: Independent Institute, 2000), for a detailed refutation of these suits.

49. See, for example, *Moore v. R.G. Indus.*, 789 F.2d 1326 (9th Cir. 1986); *Perkins v. F.I.E. Corp.*, 762 F.2d 1250 (5th Cir. 1985); *Martin v. Harrington & Richardson*, 743 F.2d

1200 (7th Cir. 1984); *Hamilton v. Accu-tek*, 935 F. Supp. 1307 (E.D.N.Y. 1996); *Delahanty v. Hinkley*, 564 A.2d 758 (D.C. 1989); *Rhodes v. R.G. Indus.*, 325 S.E.2d 469 (Ga. 1985); *Forni v. Ferguson*, No. 132994/94, slip op. (N.Y. Sup. Ct. August 2, 1995), aff'd, 648 N.Y.S.2d 73 (N.Y. App. Div. 1996); and *Burkett v. Freedom Arms, Inc.*, 704 P.2d 118 (Or. 1985).

50. A few trial court rulings, declining to dismiss firearms suits and ordering a full trial, are still in litigation.

51. Pub. L. No. 103-322, 103 Stat. 1796 (September 13, 1994).

52. See *Nat'l Rifle Ass'n v. Magaw*, 132 F.3d 272 (6th Cir. 1997).

53. The 33 states are Alabama, Alaska, Arizona, Arkansas, Colorado, Florida, Georgia, Idaho, Indiana, Kansas, Kentucky, Louisiana, Maine, Maryland, Michigan, Mississippi, Missouri, Montana, Nevada, New Hampshire, North Carolina, North Dakota, Ohio, Oklahoma, Pennsylvania, South Carolina, South Dakota, Tennessee, Texas, Utah, Virginia, West Virginia, and Wyoming.

54. *Cincinnati v. Beretta U.S.A. Corp.*, 1999 WL 809838 (Ohio C.P. October 7, 1999), aff'd, 2000 WL 1133078 (Ohio Ct. App. August 11, 2000), appeal allowed, 740 N.E.2d 1111 (Ohio 2001), rev'd, 768 N.E.2d 1136 (Ohio 2002).

55. *Ganim v. Smith & Wesson Corp.*, 26 Conn. L. Rptr. 39 (Conn. Super. Ct. 1999), aff'd, 258 Conn. 313 (Conn. 2001).

56. *Penelas v. Arms Tech., Inc.*, 1999 WL 1204353 (Fla. Cir. Ct. December 13, 1999), aff'd, 778 So. 2d 1042 (Fla. Dist. Ct. App. 2001).

57. *Morial v. New Orleans*, 785 So.2d 1 (La.), cert. denied, 534 U.S. 951 (2001).

58. *Merrill v. Navegar, Inc.*, 26 Cal. 4th 465 (Cal. 2001).

59. *Ganim v. Smith & Wesson Corp.*, 258 Conn. 313 (Conn. 2001), aff'd 26 Conn. L. Rptr. 39 (Conn. Super. Ct. 1999).

60. "Bridgeport Mayor: Appeal of Gun Lawsuit Decision Unlikely," *Associated Press Newswires*, October 9, 2001.

61. Protection of Lawful Commerce in Arms Act, H.R. 2037, 107th Cong., 1st sess., May 25, 2001.

62. Protection of Lawful Commerce in Arms Act, S. 659, 108th Cong., 1st sess., March 19, 2003.

63. Ibid. at § 2(a)(5) (emphasis added).

64. See Edward Epstein, "Gun Liability Bill Shot Down in Senate; Defeat Comes after Assault-Ban Proposal Passes," *San Francisco Chronicle*, March 3, 2004.

65. White House, "President Proposes Major Reforms to Address Medical Liability Crisis," news release, July 25, 2002, www.whitehouse.gov/news/releases/2002/07/20020725-1.html.

66. Allison H. Eid, "Tort Reform and Federalism: The Supreme Court Talks, Bush Listens," *Human Rights* 29 (Fall 2002): 10, 11.

67. Technically, there is no "spending power" in the Constitution. Some authorities believe that the spending power is implicit in the power to tax; see U.S. Const. Art. I, § 8, cl. 1. Other authorities, myself included, believe that spending is authorized only if it is necessary and proper; see U.S. Const. Art. I, § 8, cl. 18, for executing powers enumerated elsewhere in the Constitution. We need not resolve that controversy here; the constitutionality of federal spending for medical care in the context of malpractice reform has not been challenged. The dispute here is not whether federal medical spending is itself legitimate but whether malpractice reform can be and has been legitimately imposed as a condition on state recipients of the spending.

68. White House.

69. See, for example, *South Dakota v. Dole*, 483 U.S. 203 (1987).

70. Eid, p. 11.

71. White House.

72. See Laura-Mae Baldwin et al., "Defensive Medicine and Obstetrics," *Journal of the American Medical Association* 274 (1995): 1606–10; and Daniel Kessler and Mark McClellan, "Do Doctors Practice Defensive Medicine?" *Quarterly Journal of Economics* 111 (1996): 359.

73. See Lisa Dubay et al., "The Impact of Malpractice Fears on Cesarean Section Rates," *Journal of Health Economics* 18 (1999): 491–522.

74. See Gary M. Fournier and Melayne Morgan McInnes, "The Case for Experience Rating in Medical Malpractice Insurance: An Empirical Evaluation," *Journal of Risk and Insurance* 68 (2001): 274 (physicians, especially rural obstetricians, are choosing to limit practice or self-insure rather than pay soaring premiums unrelated to their own claims experience); "Echo Malpractice Mess," editorial, *Charleston Gazette and Daily Mail*, January 3, 2002, p. 4A (physicians are leaving West Virginia because lawsuits are increasing the cost of insurance coverage); Ovetta Wiggins, "Doctors to Protest Premium Increases," *Philadelphia Inquirer*, April 23, 2001, p. B1 (Pennsylvania Medical Society asserts that 11% of Pennsylvania physicians "have either moved out of state, retired [prematurely], or scaled back their practices [due to] 'skyrocketing' malpractice insurance rates"); and Patricia Poist-Reilly, "Malpractice Maelstrom: Skyrocketing Malpractice Insurance Premiums Have Doctors and Healthcare Professionals Here—and Around the State—Clamoring for Reform," *Lancaster New Era/Intelligencer Journal/Sunday News*, December 17, 2001, p. 1 (high jury awards pushing up insurance rates and forcing physicians to retire early, move to more rate-friendly states, or limit patient access to medical care).

75. See, for example, David M. Studdert et al., "Can the United States Afford a 'No-Fault' System of Compensation for Medical Injury?" *Law and Contemporary Problems* 60 (1997): 33–34; Paul C. Weiler, "Fixing the Tail: The Place of Malpractice in Health Care Reform," *Rutgers Law Review* 47 (1995): 1165; Richard L. Abel, "The Real Tort Crisis—Too Few Claims," *Ohio State Law Journal* 48 (1987): 448; Paul C. Weiler et al., *A Measure of Malpractice: Medical Injury, Malpractice Litigation, and Patient Compensation* (Cambridge, MA: Harvard University Press, 1993): pp. 61–76; and Philip Slayton and Michael J. Trebilcock, eds., *The Professions and Public Policy* (Toronto: University of Toronto Press, 1978).

76. See, generally, Nancy K. Bannon, *AMA Tort Reform Compendium* (Chicago: American Medical Association, 1989) (detailing tort reforms then in effect); and American Tort Reform Association, "Tort Reform Record," June 30, 2002, www.atra.org/wrap/files.cgi/7469_record602.htm.

77. See American Tort Reform Association, "Tort Reform Record," December 2003, www.atra.org/files.cgi/7668_Record12-03.pdf, for a summary of state reforms enacted since 1986.

78. H.R. 5, 108th Cong., 1st sess., February 5, 2003; and S. 607, 108th Cong., 1st sess., March 13, 2003.

79. Rebecca Adams, "Democrats Argue Federalism Case As Committee Approves Malpractice Bill," *Congressional Quarterly Daily Monitor*, March 5, 2003.

80. *State Farm Mutual Automobile Insurance Co. v. Campbell*, 123 S. Ct. 1513 (2003). This section of the chapter and the following sections through "Reconciling Tort Reform and Federalism" are extracted in major part from Robert A. Levy, "The

Conservative Split on Punitive Damages: *State Farm Mutual Automobile Insurance Co. v. Campbell,"* Cato Supreme Court Review 2 (2003): 159–86.

81. *BMW of North America, Inc. v. Gore*, 517 U.S. 559 (1996).

82. *Cooper Industries, Inc. v. Leatherman Tool Group, Inc.*, 532 U.S. 424, 432 (2001).

83. In *State Farm*, for example, the Utah Supreme Court relied on trial testimony indicating that "State Farm's actions, because of their clandestine nature, will be punished at most in one out of every 50,000 cases as a matter of statistical probability." Quoted in *State Farm*, 123 S. Ct. at 1519.

84. See *Liggett Group v. Engle*, 2003 Fla. App. LEXIS 7500 (Fla. Dist. Ct. App. May 21, 2003).

85. For further commentary on the *Engle* case, see Robert A. Levy, "Tobacco Class Decertified in Florida: Sanity Restored," *The Hill*, June 11, 2003, www.thehill.com/news/061103/ss_tobacco.aspx.

86. David Hechler, "Tenfold Rise in Punitives," *National Law Journal*, February 3, 2003, p. C3.

87. *Gore* at 575.

88. *State Farm*, 123 S. Ct. at 1518.

89. Ibid.

90. *Campbell v. State Farm Mutual Automobile Insurance Co.*, 65 P.3d 1134 (2001).

91. *State Farm*, 123 S. Ct. at 1521.

92. Ibid. at 1526.

93. Ibid. (citation omitted).

94. Ibid. at 1521.

95. Ibid. at 1522.

96. Ibid.

97. Ibid. at 1523.

98. Ibid. (quoting *Gore* at 582).

99. Ibid. at 1524–25.

100. Ibid. at 1520 (quoting *Honda Motor Co. v. Oberg*, 512 U.S. 415, 432 (1994)).

101. Ibid. at 1525.

102. Ibid. at 1527 (Ginsburg, J., dissenting).

103. Ibid. at 1531.

104. George F. Will, "License to Legislate," *Washington Post*, April 17, 2003, p. A23.

105. *State Farm*, 123 S. Ct. at 1531 (Ginsburg, J., dissenting). Notably, Justice Ginsburg has been willing to invoke substantive due process in other contexts. See, for example, *Lawrence v. Texas*, 123 S. Ct. 2472 (2003), which she joined, holding that substantive due process protects an unenumerated right to private acts as a component of liberty.

106. Ibid. at 1526 (Thomas, J., dissenting) (quoting *Cooper Inds.*, 532 U.S. at 443 (Thomas, J., concurring) (citing *Gore*, 517 U.S. at 599 (Scalia, J., joined by Thomas, J., dissenting))).

107. Ibid. at 1526 (Scalia, J., dissenting).

108. *TXO Production Corp. v. Alliance Resources Corp.*, 509 U.S. 443 (1993).

109. Ibid. at 458 n. 24 (internal references omitted).

110. Ibid.

111. Ibid. at 466–67 (Kennedy, J., concurring in part and concurring in the judgment).

112. Ibid. at 467.

113. *State Farm*, 123 S. Ct. at 1519–20 (citing *Cooper Inds* at 433; *Gore* at 562).

114. *Seaboard Air Line R. Co. v. Seegers*, 207 U.S. 73, 78 (1907) (cited by *State Farm*, 123 S. Ct. at 454).

115. *Southwestern Telegraph & Telephone Co. v. Danaher*, 238 U.S. 482 (1915) (cited in *State Farm*, 123 S. Ct. at 454).

116. *State Farm*, 123 S. Ct. at 1520 (quoting *Gore* at 574).

117. *Saenz v. Roe*, 526 U.S. 489 (1999) (Thomas, J., dissenting, joined by Rehnquist, CJ).

118. Robert Bork, *The Tempting of America: The Political Seduction of the Law* (New York: Free Press, 1990), p. 180.

119. *Slaughter-House Cases*, 16 Wall. (83 U.S.) 36 (1873).

120. Kimberly C. Shankman and Roger Pilon, "Reviving the Privileges or Immunities Clause to Redress the Balance among States, Individuals, and the Federal Government," Cato Institute Policy Analysis no. 326, November 23, 1998, p. 1.

121. Theodore Olson, "Some Thoughts on Punitive Damages," Manhattan Institute Civil Justice Memo no. 15, June 1989, www.manhattan-institute.org/html/cjm_15.htm.

122. Mark A. Klugheit, "Where the Rubber Meets the Road: Theoretical Justifications vs. Practical Outcomes in Punitive Damages Litigation," *Syracuse Law Review* 52 (2002): 806 (footnotes omitted).

123. See, for example, *Darcars Motors of Silver Spring v. Borzym*, 818 A.2d 1159, 1164 (2003).

124. *State Farm*, 123 S. Ct. at 1520.

125. Connor, p. 21.

126. *State Farm*, 123 S. Ct. at 1523.

127. Connor, p. 23.

128. See *Browning-Ferris Industries of Vermont, Inc. v. Kelco Disposal, Inc.*, 492 U.S. 257 (1989).

129. Ibid. at 282 (O'Connor, J., concurring in part and dissenting in part).

130. See, for example, Roy C. McCormick, "Punitive Damages Defined and Reviewed for Questions and Changes Ahead," *Rough Notes*, November 1995, p. 68.

131. Olson.

132. Quoted in Fox Butterfield, "New Orleans Takes on Gun Manufacturers in Lawsuit," *New York Times*, November 4, 1998, online edition.

133. Carolyn Lochhead, "The Growing Power of Trial Lawyers," *Weekly Standard*, September 23, 1996, p. 21.

134. *Berger v. United States*, 295 U.S. 78, 88 (1935).

135. Michael Horowitz, "Can Tort Law Be Ethical?" *Weekly Standard*, March 19, 2001, p. 16.

136. See Robert A. Levy, "Twisted Tobacco Logic," *Washington Times*, April 11, 2001, p. A12.

137. Kristin Armshaw, ed., "Disorder in the Court: A Guide for State Legislators," American Legislative Exchange Council, June 2003, especially pp. 7–14.

138. Fla. Stat. Ann. § 409.910 (1995).

139. Sheila R. Cherry, "Litigation Lotto," *Insight on the News*, April 3, 2000, p. 10.

140. Paul H. Rubin, John Calfee, and Mark Grady, "BMW v. Gore: Mitigating the Punitive Economics of Punitive Damages," *Supreme Court Economic Review* 5 (1997): 179, 203–4.

141. *International Shoe Co. v. Washington*, 326 U.S. 310 (1945).

142. *World-Wide Volkswagen Corp. v. Woodson*, 444 U.S. 286 (1980).

143. *Asahi Metal Industry Co., Ltd. v. Superior Court of California*, 480 U.S. 102 (1987).

144. Ibid. at 112.

145. Rubin, Calfee, and Grady, p. 210.

146. See Krauss, "Product Liability and Game Theory," pp. 759, 761.

147. See, for example, Michael McConnell, "A Choice-of-Law Approach to Products-Liability Reform," in Walter Olson, ed., *New Directions in Liability Law* (New York: Academy of Political Science, 1988), p. 90.

148. See 28 U.S.C. § 1332 (2002).

149. See *Erie Railroad Co. v. Tompkins*, 304 U.S. 64 (1938).

150. See Krauss, "Product Liability and Game Theory," pp. 775, 826. The Supreme Court has limited the availability of federal diversity jurisdiction by interpreting federal statutes to require "complete diversity"—that is, that each plaintiff be from a different state than each defendant. See *Strawbridge v. Curtis*, 7 U.S. (3 Cranch) 267, 267–68 (1806). As a result, plaintiffs have been able to guarantee a state court forum by including an in-state defendant—typically a retailer in a product liability suit—in the litigation. To get around that problem, the Court's holding in *Strawbridge* would have to be reversed, or Congress would have to provide that "minimal diversity"—that is, when any plaintiff is from a state different than any defendant—is sufficient to trigger federal jurisdiction in specified tort suits. (At this writing, Congress is considering a minimal diversity provision in connection with a federal class action reform package.)

151. See Michael Greve, "Eulogy for a Lost Clause," *National Law Journal*, May 26, 2003, p. 27.

152. See William Niskanen, "Do Not Federalize Tort Law," *Regulation* 18, no. 4 (1995): 18.

153. One problem, not addressed here, is the inequity that could arise if an innocent bystander is injured by a defective product purchased in a jurisdiction with a defendant-friendly tort regime. The bystander could neither decline to purchase the product, nor pay less, to offset the prospect of uncompensated injury. See Krauss, "Product Liability and Game Theory," p. 824, for a suggested solution to this problem.

154. Michael S. Greve, "Torts, Federalism, and the Constitution," American Enterprise Institute, undated, www.federalismproject.org/masterpages/tort/torts,fed,cnt.html.

155. Ibid.

Chapter 7

1. For persuasive arguments against the very premises of antitrust law, see D. T. Armentano, *Antitrust and Monopoly* (Oakland, Calif.: Independent Institute, 1990); D. T. Armentano, "Time to Repeal Antitrust Regulation?" *Antitrust Bulletin* 35 (Summer 1990): 311–28; Fred S. McChesney, "Law's Honour Lost: The Plight of Antitrust," *Antitrust Bulletin* 31 (Summer 1986): 359–83; William J. Baumol and Janusz A. Ordover, "Use of Antitrust to Subvert Competition," *Journal of Law and Economics* 28 (1985): 247–65; Thomas J. DiLorenzo, "The Origins of Antitrust: An Interest-Group Perspective," *International Review of Law and Economics* 5 (1985): 73–90; and Thomas J. DiLorenzo and Jack C. High, "Antitrust and Competition, Historically Considered," *Economic Inquiry* 26 (July 1988): 423–34. For arguments against antitrust based largely on efficiency or utilitarian grounds, see Robert H. Bork, *The Antitrust Paradox: A Policy at War with Itself* (New York: Basic Books, 1978). For a critique of the "robber-baron"

thesis, which led to antitrust in the first place, see Burton W. Folsom Jr., *The Myth of the Robber Barons* (Herndon, Va.: Young America's Foundation, 1996).

2. See Alan Murray, "Antitrust Isn't Obsolete in an Era of High-Tech," *Wall Street Journal*, November 10, 1997, p. A1.

3. Quoted in John R. Wilke, "Senate Internet Panel to Probe Microsoft's Power," *Wall Street Journal*, November 3, 1997, p. B2.

4. Alan Greenspan, "Antitrust," in Ayn Rand, ed., *Capitalism: The Unknown Ideal* (New York: New American Library, 1967), p. 70.

5. See Janusz A. Ordover, "Bingaman's Antitrust Era," *Regulation* 20, no. 2 (Summer 1997): 21.

6. See Don Clark, "How Microsoft Lost Cloak of Invincibility While Getting On-Line," *Wall Street Journal*, November 5, 1997, p. A1.

7. Rajiv Chandrasekaran, "Microsoft Calls Browser Vital to Windows 95," *Washington Post*, December 5, 1997, p. A16.

8. Ibid.

9. *United States v. Microsoft Corp.*, Civil Action 94-1564 (D.D.C. December 11, 1997). On a related matter, Judge Jackson upheld Microsoft's right to require contractually that computer makers notify Microsoft when disclosing information to the government about the company's products or practices. The judge found no evidence that Microsoft used the contractual provision to prevent businesses from complaining to government regulators.

10. David Lawsky, "Government Seeks to Hold Microsoft in 'Civil Contempt,'" *Reuters*, December 7, 1997.

11. Quoted in Michael Schroeder, "Microsoft Says Older Software Follows Order," *Wall Street Journal*, December 24, 1997, p. B8.

12. David Lawsky, "Microsoft Must Explain Browser Position," *Reuters*, December 20, 1997. Microsoft has filed a formal objection to Judge Jackson's out-of-court uninstall demonstration, claiming that it occurred "without prior notice to counsel and without participation by the parties." See David Lawsky, "Microsoft Attacks on Judge 'Risky,' Experts Say," *Reuters*, December 24, 1997.

13. Rajiv Chandrasekaran, "Microsoft to Allow Browser Blocking," *Washington Post*, January 23, 1998, p. G1.

14. See Russ Mitchell, "From Two Different Planets: The Culture Clash between Microsoft and the Justice Department," *U.S. News & World Report*, January 12, 1998, p. 44.

15. "Microsoft Appeals Preliminary Injunction," *PRNewswire*, December 15, 1997.

16. David Bank and Michael Schroeder, "Microsoft Corp. Seeks to Oust 'Special Master,'" *Wall Street Journal*, January 6, 1998, p. B4. Bank and Schroeder report that, in a series of e-mails to a Netscape attorney, Lessig complained about the difficulty of installing Internet Explorer. He wrote, "OK, this is making me really angry, and Charlie Nesson [also a Harvard law school professor] thinks we should file a lawsuit." Lessig also used the phrase "sold my soul" in describing his decision to install a Microsoft product so that he would qualify to enter a contest.

17. Rajiv Chandrasekaran, "Microsoft Appeals Judge's Decision," *Washington Post*, January 17, 1998, p. D2.

18. Rajiv Chandrasekaran and Elizabeth Corcoran, "Ruling Halts 'Master' in Microsoft Case," *Washington Post*, February 3, 1998, p. D1.

19. Elizabeth Corcoran and Rajiv Chandrasekaran, "For Microsoft, Separation Anxiety?" *Washington Post*, December 13, 1997, p. F1, quoting Joe Sims, a former DOJ official who is now a lawyer in private practice.

20. David Bank and John R. Wilke, "Microsoft and Justice End a Skirmish, Yet War Could Escalate," *Wall Street Journal*, January 23, 1998, p. A1.

21. Ibid.

22. Ibid.

23. Oral argument on Microsoft's appeal of the preliminary injunction will be held on April 21, 1998, in the U.S. Court of Appeals for the District of Columbia Circuit.

24. See Walter S. Mossberg, "Knowing the ABCs of the Antitrust Case against Microsoft," *Wall Street Journal*, October 30, 1997, p. B1.

25. Peter Huber, "Reno Rewrites Your Operating System," *Forbes*, December 1, 1997.

26. Rajiv Chandrasekaran, "Justice Counters Microsoft Claims," *Washington Post*, November 21, 1997, p. G4.

27. John R. Wilke, "Microsoft Internal E-Mail Bolsters Case against Software Maker, U.S. Contends," *Wall Street Journal*, November 21, 1997, p. B20.

28. John R. Wilke, "Microsoft, Justice Department Square Off in Court," *Wall Street Journal*, December 8, 1997, p. B6.

29. See *Jefferson Parish Hospital District No. 2 v. Hyde*, 466 U.S. 2, 21–22 (1984).

30. See D. T. Armentano, "Curb Law, Not Microsoft," *Journal of Commerce*, November 19, 1997.

31. Corcoran and Chandrasekaran.

32. Don Clark, "Microsoft Is Unlikely to Be Hurt by Ruling," *Wall Street Journal*, December 15, 1997, p. B8.

33. Quoted in "Microsoft under Attack, but Who Is It Hurting?" *USA Today*, October 23, 1997.

34. See Elizabeth Corcoran, "Speaking Out on Microsoft, Monopolies," *Washington Post*, October 26, 1997, p. H1.

35. Bill Gates, "Why the Justice Department Is Wrong," *Wall Street Journal*, November 10, 1997, p. A22.

36. Ibid.

37. Bank and Wilke.

38. "Microsoft under Attack, but Who Is It Hurting?"

39. "Netscape Communications Sees Losses for 4th Quarter, Full Year," Nasdaq, January 5, 1998. Excluding nonrecurring charges, Netscape expects to report profits for 1997, but at a lower level than in 1996. Revenues for 1997 are expected to increase by 54%, however.

40. On January 22, 1998, Netscape announced that it would resume making its browser available free of charge. Moreover, the company plans to release the program "source code" to encourage product improvements by third-party software developers. See Don Clark, "Netscape to Share Browser Program Code," *Wall Street Journal*, January 23, 1998, p. B6.

41. "Network computers" have been touted as the ultimate replacement for PCs. In a network computing environment, software applications reside on, and are accessible from, the Internet, which substitutes for the PC's hard disk. To those who contend that technological progress will come from making PCs easier to use and less costly, advocates of network computers respond that the complexity and cost of a PC is not necessary when the objective is simply to communicate. They cite the telephone as an example of a system in which the bulk of the complexity and cost is in the infrastructure, not in the telephone itself.

42. See Elizabeth Corcoran, "Rivals Unite to Combat Microsoft," *Washington Post,* November 16, 1997, p. A1.

43. Dean Takahashi, "Intel, Confronting New Market, Develops Own Design for Low-Cost PC Alternative," *Wall Street Journal,* December 3, 1997, p. B4.

44. Elizabeth Corcoran, "Is Intel's Partnership with Microsoft Waning?" *Washington Post,* December 4, 1997, p. E1.

45. See Microsoft's "Open Letter to Ralph Nader Appraising the Nader Conference," *PRNewswire,* November 13, 1997.

46. Colleen Frye, "What a Web Year," *Software Magazine,* July 1997.

47. *Worldwide Software Review and Forecast* (Framingham, Mass.: International Data Corp., 1997).

48. *United States v. E.I. du Pont de Nemours & Co.,* 351 U.S. 377, 404 (1956).

49. *Worldwide Software Review and Forecast.*

50. "Microsoft Rivals Say Browser War Is Really about Windows," CNN Interactive, October 20, 1997.

51. Prices are deemed to be "predatory" only if they are fixed (a) at a level below marginal cost, (b) in the realistic expectation of driving competitors out of the market, and (c) with the goal of raising prices afterward to recoup prior losses. Microsoft contends that what appears to be a zero price for its browser is not predatory. First, according to the company, the marginal cost of Internet Explorer is nearly zero. Second, the price of the combined product more than covers aggregate costs. Third, Netscape is the market leader, strongly allied with companies like Sun and Oracle; it is therefore implausible that Netscape could be ousted from the browser business even if Explorer were given away. Fourth, Netscape also prices below cost by allowing computer users to run Navigator without charge. To date, DOJ has not accused Microsoft of predatory pricing.

52. David Bank, "Why Software and Antitrust Law Make an Uneasy Mix," *Wall Street Journal,* October 22, 1997, p. B1.

53. Stephen C. Littlechild, "Misleading Calculations of the Social Cost of Monopoly Power," *Economic Journal* 91 (June 1981): 358 (emphasis in original).

54. F. A. Hayek, "The Meaning of Competition," in Friedrich A. Von Hayek, ed., *Individualism and Economic Order* (Chicago: University of Chicago Press, 1948), pp. 94–106.

55. Israel M. Kirzner, "The Market as a Discovery Process," in *Discovery, Capitalism, and Distributive Justice* (Oxford: Basil Blackwell, 1989), pp. 72–96.

56. See, for example, *United States v. Grinnell Corp.,* 384 U.S. 563, 570–71 (1966) ("The offense of monopoly under § 2 of the Sherman Act has two elements: (1) the possession of monopoly power in the relevant market and (2) the willful acquisition or maintenance of that power as distinguished from growth or development as a consequence of a superior product, business acumen, or historic accident").

57. *Northern Pacific Railway v. United States,* 356 U.S. 1, 5 (1958).

58. Sherman Act of 1890, 15 U.S.C. § 1.

59. Clayton Act of 1914, 15 U.S.C. § 14.

60. *United Shoe Machinery Corp. v. United States,* 247 U.S. 32 (1918).

61. *Chicago Board of Trade v. United States,* 246 U.S. 231, 238 (1918).

62. *International Salt Co. v. United States,* 332 U.S. 392 (1947).

63. *Northern Pacific Railway* at 5.

64. *Jefferson Parish* at 21–22.

65. *Times-Picayune Publishing Co. v. United States,* 345 U.S. 594 (1953).

66. *Heatransfer Corp. v. Volkswagenwerk, A.G.*, 553 F.2d 964 (5th Cir. 1977), cert. denied, 434 U.S. 1087 (1978).

67. *Digidyne Corp. v. Data General Corp.*, 734 F.2d 1336 (9th Cir. 1984), cert. denied, 105 S. Ct. 3534 (1985).

68. *Eastman Kodak Co. v. Image Technical Services, Inc.*, 504 U.S. 451 (1992).

69. Ibid. at 497 (Scalia, J., dissenting).

70. See, for example, Roger D. Blair and Jeffrey Finci, "The Individual Coercion Doctrine and Tying Arrangements: An Economic Analysis," *Florida State University Law Review* 10 (1983): 531–68.

71. See, for example, Philip Areeda, *Antitrust Analysis*, 3rd ed. (New York: Aspen Law & Business, 1981), p. 735; Richard N. Pearson, "Tying Arrangements and Antitrust Policy," *Northwestern University Law Review* 60 (1976): 632–34; D. T. Armentano, *The Myths of Antitrust* (New Rochelle, N.J.: Arlington House, 1972), pp. 199–203; and Richard S. Markovits, "Tie-Ins, Reciprocity and the Leverage Theory Part II: Tie-Ins, Leverage, and the American Antitrust Laws," *Yale Law Journal* 80 (1970): 292–93.

72. *Jefferson Parish* at 26.

73. See Henry N. Butler et al., "The Futility of Antitrust Attacks on Tie-In Sales: An Economic and Legal Analysis," *Hastings Law Journal* 36 (1984): 181.

74. See Bork, p. 310.

75. Defenders of the antitrust laws argue that collusion among firms operating on the same level of the product distribution chain (e.g., two or more competing manufacturers) is a third source of barriers to entry. Those so-called horizontal restraints are, of course, already prohibited by antitrust law, and the underlying collusive agreements are not enforceable. Because horizontal collusion is a subject that is beyond the scope of this paper, I note only that such arrangements cannot endure in a free market. One would be hard-pressed to identify a single monopoly of more than fleeting significance that arose from collusive conduct. Experience teaches that cartels do not hold; once prices exceed market levels, the temptation to break the agreement becomes all but irresistible. In that rare case in which collusion is surreptitious, and camouflaged by public pronouncements to the contrary, which consumers rely upon, government action might conceivably be justified—but the justification is closer to anti-fraud than to antitrust.

76. For an analysis of targeted government largesse, see Stephen Moore and Dean Stansel, "How Corporate Welfare Won: Clinton and Congress Retreat from Cutting Business Subsidies," Cato Institute Policy Analysis no. 254, May 15, 1996.

77. Competition would be further intensified if patent laws, like copyright laws, permitted an otherwise infringing product to be marketed without infringement, provided the product was independently created.

78. See *IBM v. United States*, 298 U.S. 131, 139 (1936) (use of punch cards not meeting IBM specifications "causes inaccuracies in the functioning of the [collators], serious in their consequences and difficult to trace to their source, with consequent injury to the reputation of the machines").

79. See David Friedman, *Hidden Order: The Economics of Everyday Life* (New York: HarperCollins, 1996), pp. 263–64.

80. Some forms of price discrimination—not those addressed herein—are prohibited by the 1936 Robinson-Patman Act, 15 U.S.C. § 13. Broadly speaking, the intent of the act was to protect small retailers from "unfair" competition by the larger chain stores that paid less at wholesale for the same merchandise. The act prohibits price

discrimination that might have an anti-competitive effect—unless justified by cost differentials or undertaken to match prices offered by competing producers.

81. Many companies meter usage by installing copy counters or similar gadgets. One author has remarked that it is "bizarre to attack price discrimination when the firm uses tying but not when it employs revolution counters or the endless variety of alternative devices." William F. Baxter, "The Viability of Vertical Restraints Doctrine," *California Law Review* 75 (1987): 938.

82. Keith K. Wollenberg, "An Economic Analysis of Tie-In Sales: Re-Examining the Leverage Theory," *Stanford Law Review* 39 (1987): 755–56.

83. Ibid., pp. 751–52.

84. See W. Brian Arthur, *Increasing Returns and Path Dependence in the Economy* (Ann Arbor: University of Michigan Press, 1994); and Paul Krugman, "The Economics of QWERTY," in *Peddling Prosperity: Economic Sense and Nonsense in the Age of Diminished Expectations* (New York: W. W. Norton, 1994).

85. See Stan Liebowitz and Stephen E. Margolis, "Don't Handcuff Technology," *Upside*, September 1995, pp. 64–73. "[E]arlier versions of Windows were quite unsuccessful. Microsoft was able to wean customers away from DOS only when Windows 3.0 was able to demonstrate a clear superiority" (p. 72).

86. See Stan Liebowitz and Stephen E. Margolis, "Policy and Path Dependence from QWERTY to Windows 95," *Regulation* 18, no. 3 (1995): 33–41.

87. James M. Buchanan and Gordon Tullock, *The Calculus of Consent* (Ann Arbor: University of Michigan Press, 1962).

88. Quoted in Walter Pincus and George Lardner Jr., "Nixon Hoped Antitrust Threat Would Sway Network Coverage," *Washington Post*, December 1, 1997, p. A1.

89. Quoted in Declan McCullagh, "In God We Antitrust," *Netly News*, January 9, 1998.

90. David Burnham, *Above the Law: Secret Deals, Political Fixes, and Other Misadventures of the U.S. Department of Justice* (New York: Scribner, 1996).

91. "Competition in the Software Industry," Microsoft white paper, January 1998, p. 7.

92. Julian L. Simon, *The Ultimate Resource 2* (Princeton, N.J.: Princeton University Press, 1996).

93. See F. A. Hayek, *The Fatal Conceit: The Errors of Socialism*, in *The Collected Works of F. A. Hayek*, vol. 1 (Chicago: University of Chicago Press, 1989).

94. Kenneth J. Arrow, Declaration in support of Microsoft Consent Decree, January 17, 1995.

95. James F. Moore, "U.S. v. Microsoft: The Bigger Question," *New York Times*, January 25, 1998, p. 12-BU.

96. Greenspan, p. 71 (emphasis in original).

97. See Microsoft's "Open Letter to Ralph Nader Appraising the Nader Conference."

98. Ibid.

99. Virginia I. Postrel, "Creative Insecurity: The Complicated Truth behind the Rise of Microsoft," *Reason* (January 1998): 6.

100. See Moore.

Chapter 8

1. Originally, 20 state attorneys general filed suit against Microsoft, but South Carolina attorney general Charles Condon subsequently withdrew from the litigation.

2. See, for example, Robert Bork, "What Antitrust Is All About," *New York Times*, May 4, 1998, p. A19.

3. Stan Liebowitz, "A Defective Product: Consumer Groups' Study of Microsoft in Need of Recall," *On Point*, Competitive Enterprise Institute, February 9, 1999, p. 3.

4. Peter Huber, "Reno Rewrites Your Operating System," *Forbes*, December 1, 1997.

5. See, for example, Bernard J. Reddy, et al., "Why Does Microsoft Charge So Little for Windows?" Press Release, National Economic Research Associates, January 7, 1999.

6. Stan Liebowitz, "Bill Gates' Secret? Better Products," *Wall Street Journal*, October 20, 1998, p. A22.

7. Stan Liebowitz, "A Defective Product: Consumer Groups' Study of Microsoft in Need of Recall," pp. 4–5.

8. Annual reseller training and services survey, *Computer Reseller News*, April 6, 1998.

9. Bernard J. Reddy, et al., p. 1.

10. Alan Reynolds, "The Monopoly Myth," *Wall Street Journal*, April 9, 1999, p. A12.

11. Jim Carlton, "Apple's Profit Tops Forecasts as iMac Sales Soar," *Wall Street Journal*, October 15, 1998, p. B6.

12. David Beckman and David Hirsch, "The Line on Linux," *ABA Journal*, October 1998, p. 81.

13. Data as of September 9, 1999, from www.linux.org/vendors/systems.html.

14. Holman Jenkins, "Microsoft's Season of FUD," *Wall Street Journal*, March 31, 1999, p. A23.

15. Jon G. Auerbach, "IBM to Use Linux Operating System on Several Servers, Workstations, PCs," *Wall Street Journal*, February 8, 1999, p. B8.

16. Eric Auchard, "Dell Boosts Windows Rival Linux," *Reuters*, April 6, 1999.

17. Rajiv Chandrasekaran, "Judge Sets Sept. Trial for Microsoft," *Washington Post*, May 23, 1998, p. D1.

18. Steve Lohr, "Microsoft Has Seen the Enemy," *New York Times*, July 5, 1998, sec. 4, p. 6.

19. Alan Reynolds, "The Monopoly Myth."

20. Don Clark, "Software Becomes an Online Service, Rattling Industry," *Wall Street Journal Interactive*, July 21, 1999.

21. Quoted in ibid.

22. David P. Hamilton, "Sun to Challenge Microsoft 'Office' Suite," *Wall Street Journal*, August 31, 1999, p. A3.

23. Scott McNealy, "Why We Don't Want You to Buy Our Software," *Wall Street Journal*, September 1, 1999, p. A26.

24. As reported in David Ignatius, "Microsoft's Next Monopoly," *Washington Post*, June 13, 1999, p. B7.

25. Statement of Scott G. McNealy before the Joint Economic Committee June 16, 1999, National Summit on High Technology, reported in *Federal Document Clearing House Congressional Testimony*, June 17, 1999.

26. Lee Gomes, "You Just Can't Beat This Price: Beyond Linux, Free Systems Help Build the Web," *Wall Street Journal*, September 10, 1999, p. B1.

27. John R. Wilke and Keith Perine, "Microsoft Trial Looks at AOL-Netscape," *Wall Street Journal*, December 17, 1998, p. A3.

28. Alan Reynolds, "A Deal That's Good for the Internet . . . But Bad for the Justice Department," *Wall Street Journal*, November 25, 1998, p. A18.

29. Ibid.

30. August 19, 1999, www.news.com/News/Item/0,4,0-38605,00.html?st.ne.lh.ni.

31. See *United States v. Microsoft*, Civil Action 98-1232, Defendant's Proposed Findings of Fact, Summary Document (D.D.C. Aug. 10, 1999).

32. For a more complete treatment of this topic, see Robert A. Levy, "Microsoft and the Browser Wars: Fit to Be Tied," reprinted herein.

33. *United States v. Microsoft*, Civil Action 98-1232, Plaintiffs' Joint Proposed Findings of Fact, Overview (D.D.C. Aug. 10, 1999).

34. Steve Lohr, "Issue du Jour at Microsoft Trial: Are Consumers Harmed?" *New York Times*, January 13, 1999, p. C5.

35. See *United States v. Microsoft*, Civil Action 98-1232, Defendant's Proposed Findings of Fact, Summary Document.

36. Kara Swisher and Nick Wingfield, "Netscape to Expand Internet Service, Boosting Its Rivalry with Other Firms," *Wall Street Journal*, March 13, 1998, p. A3.

37. Charles F. Rule, "The Last Gasp of a Case That Deserves to Die: The Desperate State of the Government's Case against Microsoft," speech delivered to the National Press Club, September 2, 1998.

38. Rajiv Chandrasekaran and Elizabeth Corcoran, "Microsoft's Web Browser Overtakes Netscape's," *Washington Post*, October 1, 1998, p. C2.

39. See Don Clark, "How Microsoft Lost Cloak of Invincibility While Getting On-Line," *Wall Street Journal*, November 5, 1997, p. A1.

40. David Bank and John R. Wilke, "Microsoft and Justice End a Skirmish, Yet War Could Escalate," *Wall Street Journal*, January 23, 1998, p. A1.

41. Stan Liebowitz, "Bill Gates' Secret? Better Products."

42. See Stan Liebowitz, "A Defective Product: Consumer Groups' Study of Microsoft in Need of Recall," p. 5.

43. David B. Yoffie and Michael Cusumano, "A Deal That's Good for the Internet," *Wall Street Journal*, November 25, 1998, p. A18.

44. See Benjamin Klein, "Microsoft's Use of Zero Price Bundling to Fight the Browser Wars," Progress and Freedom Foundation, Washington, D.C. February 5, 1998.

45. *United States v. Microsoft Corp.*, 147 F.3d 935, 948, 950 (1998).

46. Clyde Wayne Crews Jr., "Micro-Managing Bill Gates," *Washington Times*, March 2, 1998, p. A19.

47. Rajiv Chandrasekaran, "Microsoft Bullied IBM, Court Told," *Washington Post*, June 8, 1999, p. A1.

48. John R. Wilke, "Remedies Are Studied in Microsoft Case," *Wall Street Journal*, March 1, 1999, p. A3.

49. Microsoft Corporation, Summary of Written Testimony of John Rose in *United States v. Microsoft*, Civil Action 98-1232.

50. John R. Wilke and Keith Perine, "Compaq Discloses It Feared Microsoft Retaliation," *Wall Street Journal*, February 19, 1999, p. A3.

51. Microsoft Corporation, Summary of Written Testimony of Cameron Myhrvold in *United States v. Microsoft*, Civil Action 98-1232.

52. *United States v. Microsoft*, Civil Action 98-1232, Direct Testimony of Richard L. Schmalansee, January 3, 1999, p. 228.

53. Microsoft Corporation, "Setting the Record Straight: Microsoft Statement on Government Lawsuit," October 1998, p. 21.

54. See Rajiv Chandrasekaran, "Microsoft's Courting of AOL Is Exhibit A," *Washington Post*, October 8, 1998, p. A1.

55. *Lorain Journal Co. v. United States*, 343 U.S. 143 (1951).

56. Bork.

57. David P. Hamilton, "Sun Suffers Setback in Battle over Java," *Wall Street Journal*, August 24, 1999, p. B8.

58. See Dean Takahashi, "Intel and Microsoft Remain Allied Despite Squabbles," *Wall Street Journal*, September 25, 1998, p. B5.

59. Rule.

60. Microsoft Corporation, Summary of Written Testimony of Eric Engstrom in *United States v. Microsoft*, Civil Action 98-1232 ("independent third parties have confirmed [that] Apple, not Microsoft is the cause of the problem").

61. Microsoft Corporation, *Microsoft Trial News*, Volume 1, Issue 3, November 6, 1998.

62. John R. Wilke, "Netscape Secretly Offered Microsoft a Stake," *Wall Street Journal*, October 22, 1998, p. B7.

63. John R. Wilke, "In New Twist, Microsoft Says It Was 'Set Up,'" *Wall Street Journal*, October 27, 1998, p. A3.

64. Alan Reynolds, "A Deal That's Good for the Internet . . . But Bad for the Justice Department."

65. John R. Wilke and Don Clark, "U.S. Adds to Case vs. Microsoft and Gates," *Wall Street Journal*, September 2, 1998, p. A3.

66. See, for example, *Ocean State Physicians Health Plan v. Blue Cross & Blue Shield*, 883 F.2d 1101, 1113 (1st Cir. 1989) (a "desire to crush a competitor, standing alone, is insufficient to make out a violation of the antitrust laws").

67. *Ball Memorial Hospital, Inc. v. Mutual Hospital Insurance*, 784 F.2d 1325, 1339 (1986).

68. This section of the chapter was previously published in somewhat modified form. See Robert A. Levy, "Dismember Microsoft? Consumers Will Foot the Bill for Antitrust Remedies," *Legal Times*, April 5, 1999, p. 22.

69. Amy Cortese et al., "What to Do About Microsoft?" *Business Week*, April 20, 1998, p. 120.

70. Joel Brinkley, "If Microsoft Loses Suit, 19 States Plan to Seek a Radical Overhaul," *New York Times*, March 16, 1999, p. C1.

71. Rajiv Chandrasekaran, "Microsoft Lawyers Ridicule U.S. Case," *Washington Post*, October 21, 1998, p. A1.

72. Microsoft Corporation, "Clinton/Gore Administration Proposes Huge Increase for Antitrust Campaign," February 3, 1999.

73. "The Federal Assault on High Tech: Is the Government Wired or Just Unplugged?" Citizens Against Government Waste, February 9, 1999, pp. 14–15.

74. Kara Swisher, "Netscape Seems to Have Mixed Feelings About Starring Role in Microsoft Probe," *Wall Street Journal*, May 20, 1998, p. B6.

75. *Berger v. United States*, 295 U.S. 78, 88 (1935).

76. Thomas Sowell, "Microsoft Debate Hindered by Bad Attack of Mushy Thinking," *Sun-Sentinel*, Fort Lauderdale, June 2, 1998, p. 11A.

77. "One State Drops Out of Microsoft Suit," *Reuters*, December 7, 1998.

Chapter 9

1. *United States v. Microsoft Corp.*, 147 F.3d 935 (1998).

2. *United States v. Microsoft Corp.*, Civil Action 98-1232 (D.D.C. 1998).

3. Thomas J. DiLorenzo, "MS-Nationalization," Ludwig von Mises Institute, June 8, 2000, available at www.mises.org/fullstory.asp?control=442.

4. See *Sun Microsystems, Inc. v. Microsoft Corp.*, Civil Action C-97-20884-RMW (N.D. Cal. 1997).

5. *United States v. Microsoft Corp.*, Civil Action 98-1232, Transcript (September 17, 1998), p. 7.

6. *United States v. Microsoft Corp.*, Civil Action 98-1232, Transcript (April 4, 2000), p. 8–9.

7. Ibid. at 11.

8. *United States v. Microsoft Corp.*, Civil Action 98-1232, Memorandum and Order (June 7, 2000), p. 4.

9. Quoted in James V. Grimaldi, "Reluctant Ruling for Judge," *Washington Post*, June 8, 2000, p. A1.

10. *United States v. Microsoft Corp.*, Civil Action 98-1232, Memorandum and Order (June 7, 2000), p. 5 (footnote omitted).

11. See Fred S. McChesney and William F. Shughart II, eds., *The Causes and Consequences of Antitrust: The Public Choice Perspective* (Chicago: University of Chicago Press, 1995).

12. Quoted in John R. Wilke, "For Antitrust Judge, Trust, or Lack of It, Really Was the Issue," *Wall Street Journal*, June 8, 2000, p. A1.

13. Quoted in Joel Brinkley and Steve Lohr, "Retracing the Missteps in the Microsoft Defense," *New York Times*, June 9, 2000, p. C8.

14. See John R. Wilke and Rebecca Buckman, "U.S. Judge Calls Abrupt End to Microsoft Trial," *Wall Street Journal*, May 25, 2000, p. A3.

15. *United States v. Microsoft Corp.*, Civil Action 98-1232, Memorandum and Order (June 7, 2000), p. 3.

16. See *United States v. E.I. du Pont de Nemours & Co.*, 366 U.S. 316, 326 (1961).

17. Quoted in James V. Grimaldi, "Microsoft Judge Says Ruling at Risk; Every Trial Decision Called 'Vulnerable,'" *Washington Post*, September 29, 2000, p. E1.

18. Ibid.

19. See Leonard Orland, "Jackson's Unethical Press Talks," *National Law Journal*, August 14, 2000, p. A17.

20. As adopted by the U.S. Judicial Conference, reprinted in 175 F.R.D. 363 (1998).

21. James V. Grimaldi, "Hearsay," *Washington Post*, June 12, 2000, p. F31. Despite finding that Judge Jackson had been lax in his observance of judicial ethics, the appellate panel concluded that his infraction was not sufficient to justify his removal from the case.

22. *United States v. Microsoft Corp.*, Civil Action No. 98-1232, Findings of Fact (November 1999), para. 412.

23. *United States v. Microsoft Corp.*, Civil Action No. 98-1232, Conclusions of Law (April 2000), p. 20.

24. *United States v. Microsoft Corp.*, Civil Action No. 98-1232, Findings of Fact (November 1999), para. 23.

25. IDC, for example, predicts that by 2002, there will be more than 55 million handheld and notebook-style information appliance devices and that by 2005, shipments of those appliances will exceed shipments of PCs. Cited in a Red Hat, Inc. press release, "Red Hat and North Carolina State University Partner to Establish First Open Source-Based University," Business Wire, October 18, 2000.

26. *United States v. Microsoft Corp.*, Civil Action No. 98-1232, Conclusions of Law (April 2000), pp. 21–23.

27. *United States v. Microsoft Corp.*, Civil Action No. 98-1232, Findings of Fact (November 1999), para. 12.

28. Ibid., para. 35.

29. Richard B. McKenzie, *Trust on Trial: How the Microsoft Case Is Reframing the Rules of Competition* (Cambridge, MA: Perseus Publishing, 2000), pp. 64–66 and table 2.1, p. 33.

30. International Data Corporation, "Computer Operating Environments Co-evolve," *IT Forecaster*, August 8, 2000, available at www.idc.com/itforecaster/itf20000808.stm.

31. Lee Gomes and Rebecca Buckman, "Unintended Consequences?" *Wall Street Journal*, June 2, 2000, p. B1.

32. See *United States v. Microsoft Corp.*, Civil Action 98-1232, Plaintiffs' Joint Reply to Microsoft's Proposed Conclusions of Law (January 2000), p. 3 ("Apple products ... [were] carefully examined and found not to be in the same market").

33. See Bill Howard, "Thin Is Back," *PC Magazine*, April 4, 2000, p. 168. IBM's network computers use BSD Unix, Sun's use Solaris, and Compaq offers Linux or Windows CE. Sun Ray and Neoware have their own proprietary operating systems.

34. Gartner Group, "Gartner's Dataquest Says Worldwide Server and Workstation Markets Experience Double-Digit Growth in Second Quarter 2000," Press Release, available at gartner11.gartnerweb.com/public/static/aboutgg/press rel/pr20000802a.html. In the second quarter of 1999, Sun was number one with 22.9% of global workstation shipments, but that slipped to 19.3% a year later as Dell captured the low end of the market.

35. See chart accompanying Ariana Eunjung Cha, "Ruling Threatens New Product," *Washington Post*, June 8, 2000, p. A21. The data from the chart seem to be drawn from PC Data (one of several sources listed), which collects sales figures from 17 major software retailers.

36. *United States v. Microsoft Corp.*, Civil Action No. 98-1232, Testimony of Frederick R. Warren-Boulton (November 18, 1998), p. 20. Warren-Boulton added naked computers to Microsoft's share, but that is inappropriate. Naked computers must use some sort of operating system but it is unlikely to be a new version of Windows. If some naked computers use old versions of Windows that would show that Microsoft has to compete against itself when trying to sell new or upgraded software.

37. *United States v. Microsoft Corp.*, Civil Action No. 98-1232, Findings of Fact (November 1999), para. 47.

38. Richard McKenzie, "Microsoft's 'Applications Barrier to Entry': The Missing 70,000 Programs," Cato Institute Policy Analysis no. 380, August 31, 2000.

39. *United States v. Microsoft Corp.*, 147 F.3d 935, 950 (1998) (citation omitted).

40. *Jefferson Parish Hosp. Dist. No. 2 v. Hyde*, 466 U.S. 2 (1984).

41. *United States v. Microsoft Corp.*, 147 F.3d 935, 948 (1998).

42. Ibid. at 953.

43. *United States v. Microsoft Corp.*, Civil Action 98-1232, Brief of Lawrence Lessig (1999), p. 17.

44. *United States v. Microsoft Corp.*, Civil Action 98-1232, Findings of Fact (November 1999) para. 140.

45. Ibid., para. 408.

46. Ibid., para. 217.

47. See *WGN Continental Broadcasting Co. v. United Video, Inc.*, 693 F.2d 622, 625 (7th Cir. 1982).

48. *United States v. Microsoft Corp.*, Civil Action 98-1232, Conclusions of Law (April 2000), p. 39.

49. United States v. Microsoft Corp., Civil Action 98-1232, Conclusions of Law (April 2000), p. 9.

50. *United States v. Microsoft Corp.*, Civil Action 98-1232, Final Judgment (June 7, 2000), sec. 3.a.iii.

51. Ibid., sec. 3.b.

52. Ibid., sec. 3.g.

53. See ibid., sec. 7.g, where Judge Jackson's bizarre definition of middleware somehow encompasses even Microsoft Office.

54. See Gary Robbins and Aldonna Robbins, "The Real Economic Costs of the Microsoft Decision," Institute for Policy Innovation, October 3, 2000, available at www.ipi.org.

55. See Gary Rivlin, *The Plot to Get Bill Gates* (New York: Times Books, 1999).

56. *United States v. Microsoft Corp.*, Civil Action 98-1232, Testimony of Paul Maritz (January 22, 1999), para. 155.

57. Karen Foerstel, "GOP Deplores Microsoft Ruling, Urges Gates to Support Party," CQ Weekly, April 8, 2000, pp. 833–34.

58. Ibid.

Index

About the Author

Robert A. Levy is a senior fellow in constitutional studies at the Cato Institute, which he joined in 1997 after 25 years in business. He is also an adjunct professor at the Georgetown University Law Center, a director of the Institute for Justice, and a member of the board of visitors of the Federalist Society. Levy received his Ph.D. in business from the American University in 1966. That year he founded CDA Investment Technologies, a major provider of financial information and software. Levy was chief executive officer of CDA until 1991. He then earned his J.D. in 1994 from George Mason University, where he was chief articles editor of the law review. During the next two years he clerked for Judge Royce C. Lamberth on the U.S. District Court in Washington, D.C., and for Judge Douglas H. Ginsburg on the U.S. Court of Appeals for the D.C. Circuit. Levy has written numerous articles on investments, law, and public policy. His writing has appeared in the *New York Times, Wall Street Journal, USA Today, Washington Post, National Review, Weekly Standard, Journal of the American Medical Association*, and many other publications. He has also discussed public policy on national radio and TV programs, including ABC's *Nightline*, CNN's *Crossfire*, Fox's *The O'Reilly Factor*, MSNBC's *Hardball*, and NBC's *Today Show*.

Cato Institute

Founded in 1977, the Cato Institute is a public policy research foundation dedicated to broadening the parameters of policy debate to allow consideration of more options that are consistent with the traditional American principles of limited government, individual liberty, and peace. To that end, the Institute strives to achieve greater involvement of the intelligent, concerned lay public in questions of policy and the proper role of government.

The Institute is named for *Cato's Letters*, libertarian pamphlets that were widely read in the American Colonies in the early 18th century and played a major role in laying the philosophical foundation for the American Revolution.

Despite the achievement of the nation's Founders, today virtually no aspect of life is free from government encroachment. A pervasive intolerance for individual rights is shown by government's arbitrary intrusions into private economic transactions and its disregard for civil liberties.

To counter that trend, the Cato Institute undertakes an extensive publications program that addresses the complete spectrum of policy issues. Books, monographs, and shorter studies are commissioned to examine the federal budget, Social Security, regulation, military spending, international trade, and myriad other issues. Major policy conferences are held throughout the year, from which papers are published thrice yearly in the *Cato Journal*. The Institute also publishes the quarterly magazine *Regulation*.

In order to maintain its independence, the Cato Institute accepts no government funding. Contributions are received from foundations, corporations, and individuals, and other revenue is generated from the sale of publications. The Institute is a nonprofit, tax-exempt, educational foundation under Section 501(c)3 of the Internal Revenue Code.

CATO INSTITUTE
1000 Massachusetts Ave., N.W.
Washington, D.C. 20001
www.cato.org